The Governors of Arkansas

The Governors of Arkansas

ESSAYS IN POLITICAL BIOGRAPHY

SECOND EDITION

Edited by
Timothy P. Donovan,
Willard B. Gatewood Jr.
Jeannie M. Whayne

THE UNIVERSITY OF ARKANSAS PRESS
FAYETTEVILLE 1995

99 98 97 96 95   5 4 3 2 1

Designed by Ellen Beeler

⊛ The paper used in this publication meets the minimum requirements of the
American National Standard for Permanence of Paper for Printed Library Materials
Z39.48-1984.

LIBRARY OF CONGRESS CATALOGING-IN-PUBLICATION DATA

The governors of Arkansas : essays in political biography / edited by Timothy P.
    Donovan, Willard B. Gatewood, Jr., and Jeannie M. Whayne. — 2nd ed.
        p. cm.
    Includes bibliographical references (p. 311) and index.
    ISBN 1-55728-331-1 (c: alk. paper)
        1. Governors—Arkansas—Biography. 2. Arkansas—Politics and government.
    I. Donovan, Timothy Paul. II. Gatewood, Willard B. III. Whayne, Jeannie M.
    F410.G6 1995
    976.7'0099—dc20
        [B]   94-45806
                                                                              CIP

*This book was supported in part by the Arkansas Humanities Council and the National
Endowment for the Humanities.*

In memory of
Timothy P. Donovan,
friend and colleague

CONTENTS

CONTRIBUTORS

RAYMOND O. ARSENAULT, Professor of History at the University of South Florida and an authority on the American South, is the author of *The Wild Ass of the Ozarks: Jeff Davis and the Social Bases of Southern Politics.*

W. DAVID BAIRD, the author of *The Quapaw Indians* and other books on American Indians, is Professor of History at Pepperdine University.

WILLIAM MCDOWELL BAKER died prior to the publication of the original edition of this work.

DIANE D. BLAIR is Professor of Political Science at the University of Arkansas, Fayetteville, and the author of *Arkansas Politics and Government: Do the People Rule?*

WILLIAM H. BURNSIDE, formerly Professor of History at John Brown University, is the author of *The Honorable Powell Clayton.*

TOM W. DILLARD, the Director of Archives and Special Collections of the University of Central Arkansas, is the coauthor of *Researching Arkansas History* and other studies related to Arkansas history.

TIMOTHY P. DONOVAN, formerly University Professor of History at the University of Arkansas, Fayetteville, and coeditor of the first edition of this volume, is deceased.

MICHAEL B. DOUGAN, Professor of History at Arkansas State University, is the author of *Confederate Arkansas* and other works on Arkansas history.

DAN DURNING is a member of the political science faculty at the University of Georgia and the author of numerous studies including a contribution to *Gubernatorial Leadership and State Policy.*

F. CLARK ELKINS is Emeritus Professor of History at Arkansas State University and the author of studies on the agricultural history of Arkansas.

TOM FORGEY is a member of the history faculty at Southern
Arkansas University whose publications have appeared in the
Journal of Southern History and *New York History*.

WILLARD B. GATEWOOD JR., Alumni Distinguished Professor of
History at the University of Arkansas, Fayetteville, is the
coeditor of *The Arkansas Delta: Land of Paradox*.

DONALD HOLLEY, Professor of History at the University of
Arkansas, Monticello, is the author of *Uncle Sam's Farmers: The
New Deal Communities in the Lower Mississippi Valley* and other
works.

JAMES E. LESTER, who teaches at Denver Academy in Denver,
Colorado, is the author of numerous works on Arkansas topics,
including *A Man for Arkansas: Sid McMath and the Southern
Reform Tradition*.

FOY LISENBY, Professor of History at the University of Central
Arkansas, has published articles in the *Arkansas Historical
Quarterly, American Journalism,* and *Mid-South Folklore*.

LEON C. MILLER, Manuscript Librarian at Tulane University, has
published various articles on Arkansas history.

WADDY W. MOORE, Emeritus Professor of History at the University
of Central Arkansas, has published extensively in the field of
Arkansas history.

RICHARD L. NISWONGER, Professor of History at John Brown
University, is the author of *Arkansas Democratic Politics,
1896–1920* and various other historical works.

HARRY W. READNOUR, Professor of History at the University of
Central Arkansas, is a specialist in the American South and
was a contributor to *The Governors of Virginia* (1981).

BOBBY ROBERTS is the Director of the Central Arkansas Library
System and the author of various aspects of Arkansas history,
including a volume in the *Portraits of Conflict* series of which he
is coeditor.

PAMELA WEBB SALAMO, who resides in Fayetteville, Arkansas, has
published articles in the *Arkansas Historical Quarterly*.

JOE SEGRAVES is a member of the history faculty at Harding
University and an authority on Arkansas history.

WILLIAM L. SHEA, Professor of History at the University of
Arkansas at Monticello, is the author of many studies in
Arkansas history and coauthor of *Pea Ridge: Civil War
Campaign in the West*.

C. CALVIN SMITH, a member of the history faculty at Arkansas State University who has published extensively in the field of Arkansas history, is the author of *War and Wartime Changes: The Transformation of Arkansas, 1940–1945*.

JERRY J. VERVACK teaches history at Northwest Arkansas Community College and is the author of articles in the *Arkansas Historical Quarterly*.

DAVID WALLACE is a member of the history faculty of Indiana University Southeast, New Albany, Indiana.

BEVERLY WATKINS, archivist with the National Archives, the Great Lakes Region, Chicago, has published articles on Arkansas history.

JEANNIE M. WHAYNE, a member of the history faculty at the University of Arkansas, Fayetteville, and editor of the *Arkansas Historical Quarterly*, edited *Shadows Over Sunnyside: An Arkansas Plantation in Transition, 1830–1945* and coedited *Arkansas Delta: Land of Paradox*.

C. FRED WILLIAMS, Professor of History at the University of Arkansas, Little Rock, is the author and editor of numerous works on Arkansas history, including *A Documentary History of Arkansas*.

WILLIAM B. WORTHEN, Director of Arkansas Territorial Restoration in Little Rock, is the coauthor of *Arkansas Made: A Survey of the Decorative, Mechanical and Fine Arts Produced in Arkansas, 1819–1870*.

PREFACE TO THE SECOND EDITION

In 1981 the University of Arkansas Press published the first edition of *The Governors of Arkansas: Essays in Political Biography.* In order to bring the work up to date, the Press authorized a second edition in 1993 to include the administrations of Governors William Jefferson Clinton, Frank Durwood White, and James Guy Tucker. While this new edition has not involved a rewriting of each essay, the authors of the original essays have had an opportunity to review their contributions with a view toward correcting errors of both omission and commission. Such errors were extraordinarily few in number and, with one or two exceptions, were of minor significance. The appendix providing brief sketches of acting governors includes those individuals who have served in that capacity since 1981 as well as two from years prior to that date which were omitted from the original edition. The bibliography reflects the changes and additions made herein.

As with the first edition, it is our hope that this work will make data easily accessible about diverse aspects of Arkansas politics and history, especially about issues confronted by governors since 1836 and the ways in which the state's chief executives responded to them.

In expanding and revising this study of Arkansas's political leadership, we have incurred numerous debts. In addition to the original contributors and those who contributed essays to the new edition, we are especially indebted to the following individuals: Andrea Cantrell, Michael Dabrishus, Diane Gleason, David Malone, Brent Aucoin, Michael Strickland, Todd Lewis, Lori Bogle, and Jerri Shaw and others on the staff of Attorney General Winston Bryant. We owe a special debt to William J. Smith for generously sharing his wide-ranging knowledge of Arkansas government and politics with us.

We gratefully acknowledge the role Timothy P. Donovan played in the preparation of the original edition of this work and have greatly missed his scholarship, editorial expertise, and good humor in the production of the new edition. We would like to take this opportunity to honor the memory of a fine scholar and a cherished colleague by dedicating this volume to Timothy P. Donovan.

November 1994
W. B. G. and J. M. W.
Fayetteville, Arkansas

PREFACE TO THE FIRST EDITION

In Arkansas the popular election of the governor has been a feature of all five constitutions under which the state has operated since its admission to the Union in 1836. The constitution of 1836, adopted at the high tide of Jacksonian Democracy, reflected the political trends of the era, especially in regard to the restraints and powers that defined the role of the state's chief executive. The creation of three other executive offices—secretary of state, treasurer, and auditor—also popularly elected to "share executive power with the governor" was the Jacksonian method of restraining and balancing gubernatorial power. Nevertheless, the governor was the commander in chief of the militia and was responsible for the execution of laws, was granted veto and pardoning powers, and was authorized to recommend legislation to the general assembly. The term of office was four years, but no governor could serve more than eight years out of any twelve. Whenever a vacancy occurred by reason of the governor's "death, resignation, removal or otherwise," the president of the senate, and after him the speaker of the house, was to succeed to the office as acting governor.

The second constitution, adopted in 1861 when Arkansas seceded from the Union and joined the Confederacy, was with certain exceptions a duplicate of the 1836 document with the phrase "Confederate States of America" substituted for "United States of America." Among the most significant changes included in the 1861 constitution was a provision that was interpreted to mean a reduction of the gubernatorial term from four to two years.

A third constitution, drafted and ratified three years later during the phase of Reconstruction known as presidential Reconstruction, made several changes in provisions concerning the executive branch. One of these was the creation of the office of lieutenant governor to be filled at the same time and in the same manner as the governorship. Both the governor and the lieutenant governor were to be elected for two-year terms.

The inauguration of congressional or Radical Reconstruction in 1867 led to the adoption of Arkansas's fourth constitution in the following year. This document, which differed in many respects from its predecessors, retained the office of lieutenant governor but again extended the term of office for both governor and lieutenant governor to four years. Among the significant changes instituted by the 1868 constitution was a vast extension in the appointive powers of the governor who was now authorized to select tax assessors and virtually all judicial officials. The individual whose name has been most often associated with the constitution of 1868 and with Radical Reconstruction was Powell Clayton. He not only served as governor and U.S. senator but also functioned for many years as the Republican boss of Arkansas. Not until almost a century later when the South was in the throes of what has been called the "second Reconstruction" did the state elect another Republican governor, Winthrop Rockefeller, who served two terms.

Arkansas's fifth constitution, adopted in 1874, was largely the handiwork of Democrats intent on reestablishing their control of state government and on correcting what they considered the abuses of Reconstruction. Determined to curb the power of the governor, the delegates to the constitutional convention drafted a document that reestablished a two-year gubernatorial term and substantially reduced both the governor's powers of appointment and his authority over the militia. But following the example of the Confederacy, the Arkansas constitution of 1874 did expand the governor's veto power to include the item veto. Despite numerous amendments and several unsuccessful attempts to secure its replacement, the constitution of 1874 has remained for a century the fundamental law of Arkansas.

The thirty-nine individuals from James Sevier Conway through David Hampton Pryor, who have been elected governor of Arkansas under one of the state's five constitutions, are the subjects of the essays in this volume. The essays have been written by people with special knowledge of and interest in appropriate areas of Arkansas history and politics. Although the editors prescribed guidelines for each essay's format and for the types of factual data to be included in it, the contributors were allowed wide latitude in the matter of interpretation. In allocating the amount of space to be devoted to each governor, the editors considered a number of factors, including the long-term significance of his activities and contributions, his length of tenure in office, and unusual circumstances confronting him as chief executive. Powell Clayton and Orval Eugene Faubus, therefore, receive considerably more attention than William Read Miller and John Sebastian Little. While each essay attempts to be as comprehensive as possible, the focus is on the performance of an individual as governor. Less emphasis has been placed on other offices that a governor may have held. For example, Joseph Taylor Robinson, who had a long and important career in the U.S. Senate but whose tenure as governor was brief, has not been treated in as lengthy an essay as some other individuals whose overall historical significance was substantially less than his. Those individuals who served as acting governor but who were never elected to the office are the subjects of short biographical sketches included in an appendix.

Each essay attempts to provide an accurate summary of a particular governor's life so that the reader can obtain an overview of his career and can easily locate specific facts and dates. In almost all cases the essays contain information regarding the governors' origins, family, education, and occupation that may be useful to those interested in collective biography. Since some readers may desire additional information, a brief annotated bibliography appears at the end of the book.

It is our hope that this volume will make information easily accessible on diverse aspects of Arkansas history and politics during the first 143 years of statehood. Since the contents focus on the issues confronted by governors and on their responses to them, the work will, we also hope, constitute something of a composite portrait of political leadership in Arkansas and will provide insight into the social and cultural values exemplified by those elected by Arkansas voters to serve as chief executives of their state. From this volume one will be able to ascertain much about the evolution and development of the office of governor in one trans-Mississippi state.

We owe a large debt of gratitude to numerous institutions and individuals for assisting us in the preparation of this work. In particular we are indebted to the Arkansas Endowment for the Humanities and the University of Arkansas, Fayetteville, which jointly sponsored and funded the project. To Margaret Ross of the Arkansas Gazette Foundation, Boyce Drummond of Henderson State University, and Walter Brown of the University of Arkansas, who served as members of the project's advisory editorial committee, we are grateful for their wise counsel and willingness to share with us their knowledge of Arkansas and its past. Contributors to the volume responded graciously to our requests and were remarkably prompt in meeting deadlines. From scores of individuals throughout the state of Arkansas and elsewhere we solicited and received valuable aid. Among those to whom we are especially indebted are Russell Baker of the Arkansas History Commission, Little Rock; Ethel Simpson of Mullins Library,

University of Arkansas, Fayetteville; Robert L. Gatewood of the Bradley County Historical Society; Wanda Rankin of Nogales, Arizona; Tom E. Tappan of Helena; Dan Dennington of the Lafayette County Historical Society; J. B. Lemley of the Pope County Historical Society; Rebecca DeArmand of the Drew County History Project; J. E. Griner of Arkansas State University; Robert Walz of Southern State University; Elizabeth Jacoway of the University of Arkansas, Little Rock; James Morgan of the Jackson County Historical Society; Mrs. Jack Hughey of the Marianna Branch of the Lee-Phillips-Monroe County Regional Library and Denyse Killgore of Fayetteville. Throughout this project we have been assisted by Jamie Freeman Lax whose efficiency, discerning eye, and expert typing have contributed much to the completion of this volume.

September 1980
T. P. D. and W. B. G. Jr.
Fayetteville, Arkansas

The Governors of Arkansas

JAMES SEVIER CONWAY

1836–1840

JAMES SEVIER CONWAY (4 December 1796–3 March 1855), surveyor and planter, was born in Greene County, Tennessee, the son of Thomas Conway and Anne (Rector) Conway. The Conway family, quite wealthy by frontier standards, grew corn and cotton and raised livestock on their Tennessee plantation. Conway's father placed a premium on education and employed private tutors to teach his seven sons and three daughters. In 1818, for undetermined reasons, the family moved to St. Louis, Missouri, where Conway learned the art of land surveying from his uncle Elias Rector. Rector was also deeply involved in politics and secured appointments for Conway and his older brother Henry as public-land surveyors for the newly formed territory of Arkansas. In 1820 the brothers were placed in charge of a contingent of survey teams and were assigned to the southwestern corner of the territory.

Entering Arkansas by way of the Red River, they settled in Lafayette County some fifteen miles west of the present town of Bradley. Conway named this strip along the river the Long Prairie and established a base there to supervise the survey teams in the field. Henry remained with the survey for only a short time before choosing a career in politics. He served as Arkansas's territorial delegate to the U.S. Congress from 1823 until his death in 1827. In the meantime Conway, in addition to his duties as a surveyor, began to purchase land, acquire slaves, and grow corn and cotton. In time his landholdings reached more than two thousand acres and required the labor of some eighty slaves. He also built a summer cottage at Magnet Cove and, in partnership with Samuel W. Reyburn, opened a bathhouse at Hot Springs. In 1826 he married Mary Jane Bradley, daughter of a pioneer family in the Red River area. The couple had ten children, five of whom died in infancy or early childhood.

Following the death of his brother, Conway, as the next oldest son, assumed the mantle of political leadership. In 1828 he was defeated in an attempt to represent Lafayette and Union Counties in the territorial legislature. Undeterred, he campaigned successfully in 1831 to fill an unexpired term from the same district. His political fortunes were further enhanced when Pres. Andrew Jackson appointed him commissioner of Arkansas. This position involved working with a similar official in Louisiana to survey the boundary between the two regions. In 1825 Conway had been selected to survey the boundary separating Arkansas from the Choctaw Indian nation. This survey became the center of a protracted controversy between the Choctaw and the state of Arkansas. Although instructed to survey a "true south line" beginning one hundred paces west of Fort Smith and running to the Red River, Conway deviated slightly to the southwest. As later surveys demonstrated, this variation allowed the state to gain more than 130,000 acres of land at the Choctaw's expense. The dispute was not settled until 1875, when the U.S. Congress enacted special legislation accepting Conway's survey as the true written boundary of Arkansas. In 1832 President Jackson appointed Conway as surveyor general for the territory. He was serving in that capacity in 1836 when he accepted the Democratic party's nomination to run for governor of the new state of Arkansas.

The 1836 gubernatorial campaign set the tone for state politics in the antebellum period. As the nominee for the Democratic party, Conway represented a combination of national politics, regional issues, and family connections. He refused to canvass the state as the other candidates did, arguing that his responsibilities as surveyor general kept him too busy to campaign. However, he did issue a circular in which he emphasized his support for Jackson and his public-land policy. Conway also reminded the voters that Arkansas's statehood bill had been pushed through Congress by members of the Democratic party and that he was a friend and relative by marriage of Ambrose H. Sevier, territorial delegate to the U.S. Congress.

There was little subtlety in Conway's message. In addition to being responsible for Arkansas becoming a state, his party's national connections also promised the best hope for the state's future. Arkansans were apparently persuaded by these arguments. Conway won the support of more than 61 percent of the voters and defeated his Whig opponent, Absalom Fowler, and the independent candidate, Alexander Walker, by almost two thousand votes.

As the state's first chief executive, Conway placed a major emphasis on internal improvements and public education. In his inaugural address, he asked the general assembly to create a board to oversee construction of roads, canals, and other internal improvements and to establish a special commission to supervise the sale of pubic lands. The income from such sales was to be used for financing a state university. Unfortunately, the assembly refused to enact legislation on either proposal. Conway supported the legislature's attempts to create a state banking system and spearheaded efforts to obtain federal assistance for protection against potential Indian attacks on the frontier and for locating a federal arsenal in Little Rock.

Much of Conway's administration was marred by controversy. During the campaign he was forced to deny charges that he had used his office as surveyor general to locate and purchase land-donation and preemption claims. Within weeks after his inauguration, he was embroiled in a dispute involving the state militia. The dispute erupted during the summer of 1836 with reports that Indians were gathering in force on the state's western border and were threatening to attack. To meet this threat, Conway authorized the assignment of a militia unit of battalion strength to federal officials at Fort Towson. Strong disagreement arose over the choice of a commander for the volunteers. In an early election, Fowler, the Whig candidate for governor and a captain in the Pulaski County unit, was chosen commander. Several weeks later, however, the troops reversed their decision and chose Leban C. Howell, captain of the Pope County militia, to lead the unit. To complicate matters, Fowler refused to yield. He ordered Howell arrested for inciting a mutiny and appealed to the governor for support. When Conway refused to accept his political opponent's arguments, Fowler demanded a court of inquiry to investigate the governor's conduct. When the court's findings proved less than definitive, Fowler boasted that his position had been justified. Angered by this response, Conway released the court's findings to the newspapers along with a letter in which Fowler had been highly critical of Conway. The effect of the so-called Fowler affair was to further polarize political opinion between Whig and Democratic voters in the state.

Perhaps the most controversial issue during Conway's administration was the state's banking system. As its first two official acts, the general assembly passed legislation creating a state bank and a real-estate bank. The governor signed both bills without hesitation. The state bank was to serve as a general depository for state funds, and the real-estate bank was designed to promote the interest of agriculture in the state. Both institutions were authorized to raise sufficient revenue to begin operations by selling bonds. Unfortunately a combination of mismanagement, a depressed national economy, and an overextension of credit forced both banks to cease operations and to default on interest payments on the bonds. Critics not only blamed Conway for a lack of leadership but also charged that Sevier had converted a portion of the bond sales to his personal use. Sevier was later reprimanded by the general assembly but not charged with wrongdoing. Even so, the banking crisis left a cloud of suspicion over the Conway administration.

Another issue involved a boundary dispute between Arkansas and the Republic of Texas. Both governments claimed the territory organized as Miller County. Soon after taking office, Conway informed residents of the county that they should make assessments and pay taxes to the state of Arkansas. When his instructions were ignored, the governor threatened to use military force to assist the local sheriff in collecting the taxes. His threat was never implemented, primarily because he was unable to find an individual to do the collection. Despite arguments from various citizens and a few political leaders that the state should enforce its laws in the region, Conway decided not to contest the matter. Instead he referred it to federal officials in Washington and agreed to abide by their decision. Representatives from the United States and Texas finally reached agreement in 1840: Texas, now a state, received all the disputed area in Miller County.

In November 1837 Conway called the legislature into special session, primarily to revise the tax structure. The state constitution constrained the legislature from levying taxes in excess of the revenue required to run state government. However, federal legislation in 1837 provided for the redistribution to the states of surplus funds from land sales. Under the formula, Arkansas's share came to almost $50,000. To accommodate this excess in revenues, Conway recommended that tax schedules be lowered and the treasury surplus used to underwrite state expenses. Legislators agreed and set the new rates at ⅙ of 1 percent rather than the ¼ of 1 percent originally enacted. Conway also urged the general assembly to establish a state university and a state library, but neither measure was approved.

During the summer of 1838 Conway became ill and seriously considered resigning as governor. He was forced to take leave from office, and the president of the senate, Samuel Calhoun Roane, became acting governor from May until September. Only strong encouragement from friends persuaded Conway to remain in office, and he was adamant in refusing to seek a second term. Some historians have suggested that an almost certain challenge from Archibald Yell, the popular, energetic congressman from northwest Arkansas, and a rapidly deteriorating state economy were more important factors than health in Conway's decision.

In his second message to the legislature, Conway again called attention to the need to keep the state militia ready for use against possible Indian attacks. He also urged legislators to establish a state penitentiary and reiterated his recommendation for a state university and a board to oversee internal improvements. The second session of the legislature proved to be more receptive to Conway's proposals than the first had been. It appropriated $20,000 to begin construction on the state prison, authorized the governor to sell seminary lands at public auction to raise revenue for funding the university, and passed a bill chartering the University of Arkansas. Ironically, even though both houses approved the bill, no evidence has been discovered that the governor either signed or vetoed the measure. Some historians have speculated that the bill was overlooked by the printers and never engrossed. Legislators, however, ignored Conway's suggestions about the militia and the board for internal improvements.

As Conway prepared to leave office, he pointed with pride to the economic growth of the state. Population had increased from 52,240 when he took office to 97,574 in 1840, the federal government had completed construction of the arsenal in Little Rock and had reconditioned the fortification at Fort Smith, and the state's combined wealth had reached $20 million. But the outgoing governor also left some rather ominous legacies. The surplus that had been in the treasury only two years earlier had been depleted, redistribution of surplus funds from the federal government had ceased, and the banking systems, chartered with such enthusiasm by the first general assembly, had accumulated an indebtedness of almost $3 million.

Upon the expiration of his term, Conway returned to his plantation in Lafayette County. In 1837 he completed construction of a new house a short distance from his original homesite on Long Prairie. Walnut Hill, as the plantation was known, provided him with an opportunity to retire to private life in relative comfort. He maintained his political ties in the Democratic party and was quite active in civic affairs. Never satisfied with the legislature's support for education, he led efforts to establish Lafayette Academy in his home county; the institution was chartered by the general assembly in 1842. Early in 1855 he became ill with pneumonia and never regained his health. He died on 3 March 1855 and was buried in the family cemetery at Walnut Hill.

ARCHIBALD YELL

1840–1844

ARCHIBALD YELL (1799?–23 February 1847), attorney and war hero, is the subject of some controversy in regard to the date and place of his birth. No month or day was ever recorded, and the year is variously given as 1797 or 1799. The place of his birth is even more in dispute. One contemporary source reported Kentucky, while North Carolina is given by numerous authorities and is on his gravestone. However, Tennessee is actually the most likely location. Yell himself wrote in 1835: "I was bornd [*sic*] in the year 1799 in Jefferson County: East Tennisse [*sic*] and raised in the State" (*Territorial Papers*, 21:1025). Records show that his father, Moss Yell, lived in Rockingham County, North Carolina, in 1790 with his wife, a daughter, two sons, and five slaves. His property consisted of 113 acres and was located on Troublesome Creek. On 20 November 1795 the elder Yell sold this property and moved to East Tennessee where Archibald, if he was not born there, at least grew up, first in Jefferson County and then at Shelbyville in Bedford County. After receiving a limited education, he volunteered for military service during the War of 1812. He eventually rose to the rank of sergeant in the Second Regiment of Tennessee Mounted Volunteer Gunmen. Yell took part in the battle of New Orleans where he attracted the favorable notice of the victorious commander, Gen. Andrew Jackson. On returning from the service, Yell was made captain of the Forty-seventh Tennessee Militia and in 1818 served as a first lieutenant in the Seminole War.

At the end of his military career, he returned to Shelbyville where he studied law under William Gilchrist, who later became his law partner. On 8 November 1821 he married Mary Scott, a local planter's daughter, only to lose her in childbirth along with one of her twin children in January 1823. The surviving child, Mary Scott Yell, was raised by her maternal grandparents.

In 1827 Yell was elected to the Tennessee legislature, defeating an anti-Masonic incumbent. He played a major role in Masonry in Tennessee, serving as state grand master in 1830. (He later helped to organize a Masonic chapter at Fayetteville, Arkansas.) Also in 1827 he married Ann Jordan Moore, by whom he had three daughters—Artemesia, Jane Rochester, and Elizabeth Lawson—and a son, DeWitt Clinton. After the death of the second Mrs. Yell, he married a widow, Mary Ficklin. Yell's political career in Tennessee began as a follower of Andrew Jackson. However, his best political and personal friend was James Knox Polk, later called "Young Hickory." Yell supported Jacksonian measures, especially those favoring economy in government. In 1830 he was one of four participants in a brawl growing out of political and personal charges. The unfavorable publicity led him to retire from Tennessee politics and to accept the appointment from President Jackson as receiver of public moneys at Little Rock in Arkansas Territory.

Yell's first visit to Arkansas was not propitious. Struck by fever in the disease-ridden territory, he abandoned his post and returned to Tennessee to recover his health. But he retained an interest in Arkansas's affairs, and in 1835, when his health improved, he applied for and was appointed to the territorial bench as a circuit judge. His district encompassed northern Arkansas (the healthier part), and Yell settled at Fayetteville, erecting Waxhaws, a fine example of Greek revival architecture. His house was painted white at a time when the town contained mostly log or unpainted structures. Although Yell did not demonstrate extraordinary legal talent, his personal qualities made him a success throughout his wide circuit. He acquired a popularity among the common people that neither Robert Crittenden, the territorial secretary of earlier days and Whig leader, nor Ambrose H. Sevier, the leader of the Sevier-Conway political dynasty, could match.

In January 1836 Arkansas began drafting a constitution with the intent of obtaining statehood in time to vote for Martin Van Buren for president. Although Yell was not a delegate to the constitutional convention, his views on the emerging document were important. One hotly debated issue was representation. Those counties with large slave populations desired the adoption of a formula similar to the federal "three-fifths rule" in determining representation. Yell, on the other hand, was firmly committed to equal white suffrage, a stand that made him popular in the northern counties. Although the convention did not adopt the three-fifths rule, it did impose a residency requirement for gubernatorial candidates that Yell, who had privately expressed a wish to run for governor, could not meet.

Once Arkansas was admitted to the Union, Yell announced as the Democratic candidate for the new state's sole congressional seat. The Whigs nominated William Cummins, a Little Rock lawyer. Despite the efforts of the Whigs, who mounted an active campaign against the Democrats, Yell won the election. When President Van Buren called a special session of Congress to deal with the panic of 1837, there was some legal question as to whether Yell won unopposed. In 1837 he again sought election to Congress. His Whig opponent was Batesville banker and speculator John Ringgold. The major issue of the campaign was Ringgold's charge that Yell was not defending Southern rights because of his absence from the House during debates over anti-slavery petitions. Yell, however, carried the northern counties and swamped Ringgold, although by a smaller margin than he had defeated Cummins. Yell did not seek reelection in 1838. As a Jacksonian politician, he opposed the Bank of the United States, land speculators, extravagance in government, and special favors. However, his consistent Democratic record was marred by his continued support for internal improvements in Arkansas.

In 1840 Yell fulfilled his original ambition and ran for governor. He was virtually unopposed. Once in office, his major task was to deal with the complete collapse of the state banking system. Upon entering the Union, Arkansas had chartered two banks, the publicly owned State Bank and the privately owned but state-supported Real-Estate Bank. Both banks were created and run by politicians and speculators to their own advantage without adequate fiscal safeguards. Beginning their operation just as President Jackson's specie circular called a halt to freewheeling state banking, both institutions closed their doors amid charges of fraud. Yell, apprised of the banks' conditions, called for financial investigation and legislative action. The legislature, however, proved uncooperative at first, while the Real-Estate Bank turned over its affairs to a group of trustees over whom the state had no control. Yell fought this action in the courts, and when a divided state supreme court decided to uphold the transfer, he vowed to have the two probank judges, Townsend Dickinson and Thomas Lacy, removed. The judges submitted the legal questions to Joseph Story and Chancellor Kent, perhaps the greatest lawyers in America at that time, who upheld their decisions. Yell was unimpressed. Yell's clash with the general assembly over its desire to have legislators paid their per diem in specie rather than in Arkansas paper money, his veto of a law granting property rights to married women on the grounds that it would destroy the family, and his refusal to appoint a state geologist to carry out a geological survey also sparked considerable controversy during his administration. Yell did support aid for public schools and the abolition of imprisonment debt.

In 1844, for political reasons, he resigned before his term of office expired to reclaim his congressional seat. Nationally, the Whigs were benefiting from the hard economic times, which they blamed on the Democrats. In Arkansas the Whigs made a major effort to gain the state's congressional seat by nominating David Walker of Fayetteville. Walker, a respected attorney who had been a leading member of the 1836 constitutional convention, was also Yell's legal and business associate in a number of ventures, most notably the development of the town of Ozark in Franklin County. The campaign issues included national economic policy, Yell's onetime ownership of fifty-one shares of stock in the Real-Estate Bank, and his alleged statement that "every man left his honesty and every woman her chastity on the other side of the Mississippi, on moving to Arkansas." But for the voters the real issues were the personalities of the candidates, and in this, as Walker ruefully reported, Yell was all things to all men. John Hallum's account, written from sources who remembered the campaign, is worthy of quotation.

> When on the way to Yellville to fill an appointment they stopped on the wayside at a shooting match in progress for beef. Judge Walker's conscientious convictions cut him off from either shooting for beef or indulging in a drink. Yell after shaking the hands of every man and boy on the ground, bought a chance in the match for beef, and fortuitously made the best shot and won first choice. The crowd yelled and hazzaed for Yell, whilst Judge Walker looked on in calm and cold stoicism and some degree of disgust. Governor Yell then inquired for the most necissitous [*sic*] widow in the vicinity, and sent his beef to her. These attainments and achievements filled the estimate of congressional qualifications in the opinion of the sovereign electors. (Hallum, *Biographical and Pictorial History of Arkansas*, p 117)

Victorious over Walker, Yell returned to Congress, becoming a powerful figure because of his close personal friendship with President Polk, with whom he also had financial ties in Red River valley lands.

With the coming of the Mexican War, which Yell supported, he left Washington without resigning his seat in Congress and returned to Arkansas to enroll as a private in Capt. Solon Borland's volunteers. When the regiment assembled to elect its commanding officers, Yell was a candidate for colonel. With Polk's help he was able to defeat Albert Pike. When the regiment left to join Gen. Zachary Taylor's army in Mexico, Yell was having difficulties with other Arkansas Democrats. It was reported that he wanted to be chosen U.S. senator and that his delay in resigning from the House was a part of that plan. The Arkansas legislature finally forced his resignation, in part by expelling Lawrence County state senator J. S. Ficklin, an in-law of Yell's wife, for joining the army and leaving the state. Yell's senatorial ambitions also conflicted with those of Chester Ashley, whose close ally, William E. Woodruff, now the editor of the *Arkansas Democrat,* found a number of grounds for criticizing Yell. Yell, unable to secure the senate post, which went to Ashley, also had plenty of problems as a military commander. He quarreled with his officers, including Borland, a previous political ally, and with the commanding general, John E. Wool. His command was noted for being poorly disciplined and was referred to as "Col. Yell's Mounted Devils" in reference to the men's exuberant conduct. Various correspondents from the army kept Arkansas readers informed of these problems.

The American army in northern Mexico saw action at the battle of Buena Vista on 23 February 1847. The Arkansas regiment was routed in an attack by Mexican lancers. Yell, in a desperate attempt to stem the retreat, led a countercharge. By one account his reins broke and he lost control of his horse. Mexican lances pierced his face and chest, killing him instantly. After the battle, his body was recovered and buried at Saltillo; it was reinterred at a family plot in Fayetteville and was later moved to Evergreen Cemetery in that town.

As a Jacksonian politician in the age of acquisitive speculators, Yell was something of an enigma. His leadership characteristics and prepossessing personal appearance, "full of pleasant humor and sunshine, and magnetic in every presence," his auburn hair and piercing blue eyes, appealed to the common man around whose support Yell built his career. Yet while Yell lectured small farmers on the dangers of land speculators, he was involved in the speculative purchase of Mississippi River land with Benjamin Johnson and Walker, dealt in Red River lands with Polk, and personally helped to sell lots at Ozark. His Washington County holdings of eight hundred acres and eight slaves, his predilection for Greek revival architecture, and his personal ambitions contrasted sharply with his public image. In the end, perhaps only in his grammar and spelling did Yell remain on a level with the common man.

THOMAS STEVENSON DREW

1844–1849

THOMAS STEVENSON DREW (25? August 1802–? January 1879), planter and attorney, was born in Wilson County, Tennessee. He was the son of Newit Drew, a gunsmith. Drew's mother's name is unknown, but she may have been from the Mansker family of early Tennessee settlers. There is little accurate information about Drew's youth, but he appears to have received a rudimentary education. His family ultimately moved to Claiborne Parish, Louisiana, where his father purchased a small farm and acquired a few slaves.

In 1817 Drew left Louisiana and moved to Clark County in the southern part of Arkansas Territory. For the next few years he worked as an itinerant peddler and schoolteacher, and by the 1820s he had begun to play a minor role in territorial politics. In October 1824 he was appointed clerk of the Clark County Court, and three months later he assumed the office of justice of the peace of Caddo township. In September 1825 he became the postmaster of the Clark County courthouse and also contracted to carry the mail. However, when a federal law enacted the following year barred postmasters from acquiring mail contracts, Drew resigned the postmastership in order to continue the more lucrative contracting business. By the fall of 1826 he had established a number of routes in southern Arkansas and northern Louisiana.

On 2 February 1827 Drew married Cinderella, the daughter of Ransom Bettis, a prosperous landowner in Greenwood, Missouri. The Drews eventually had five children: James, Sally, Thomas, Emma, and Joe(?). Bettis also owned land in northeastern Arkansas and offered the couple eight hundred acres near present-day Biggers. Since Drew's effectiveness as a mail carrier was being seriously questioned by the postmaster general, he immediately took advantage of the gift and relocated in northeastern Arkansas. For the next few years he primarily devoted his attention to developing his farming operation and to establishing himself as a member of the landed aristocracy. By 1832 he was not only a successful planter who owned more than twenty slaves but also a power in local politics. In that year he was elected judge of the Lawrence County Court. He held that position until 1835 when the territorial governor created Randolph County, which included the Drew plantation.

The establishment of Randolph County coincided with the election of delegates to the 1836 constitutional convention to prepare Arkansas for statehood. Drew was chosen as a delegate. When the convention met in January 1836, one of its tasks was the apportionment of representatives to the future general assembly. This issue was divisive because of the conflict between the counties dominated by slaveholding planters and those controlled by yeoman farmers. Drew served on the convention's judiciary committee and introduced one of several proposals designed to resolve the issue. Although the delegates did not vote on Drew's proposal, it probably served as a model for the later compromise.

Between 1836 and 1844 Drew became an influential figure in the Democratic party, but he showed no inclination to run for statewide office. Clearly he preferred to remain in the background and to use his influence within the party structure. His political connections are illusive, but he seems to have been accepted by the dominant party faction, the Johnson-Conway-Sevier political dynasty, and by those independent Democrats who hoped to establish their power outside of the faction's political influence. Apparently Drew had few enemies in the party, and he received his share of political patronage. For example, James Sevier Conway, Arkansas's first governor and a leading member of the Family, appointed him to the directorship of the Batesville branch of the State Bank. In 1843, when a more independent politician, Gov. Archibald Yell, persuaded the legislature to liquidate the defunct State Bank, Drew became the financial receiver of the Batesville branch.

Since statehood, the powerful Johnson-Conway-Sevier family had dominated Arkansas politics, but it had not ruled unchallenged. Independent Democrats and Whigs often mounted substantial threats, and by 1844 several developments had seriously eroded the Family's power and the Democratic party's unity. The most disruptive event, the failure of the banking system, had left the state with a huge debt and bitter political divisions over the whole banking system. The Family and the party also suffered when Congress began investigating Sen. Ambrose H. Sevier's handling of the State Bank's bond transactions. These problems, as well as the temporary absence in 1843 of a statewide Democratic newspaper, the animosity between the supporters of John C. Calhoun and Martin Van Buren, and the ambitions of politicians who yearned to increase their own power, seriously divided the party and jeopardized the Family's control.

Faced with these problems, the Democratic party held its first statewide nominating convention in December 1843, but only sixteen of forty-six counties sent delegates. Drew, who saw himself as a party harmonizer, served as the chairman of the committee to nominate delegates to the forthcoming presidential convention; he helped to ensure that the Arkansas delegation remained uncommitted to any national candidate.

For state offices, the convention nominated state auditor Elias Nelson Conway for governor and David Chapman for Congress. Neither candidate contributed to party unity. Conway, a senior member of the Family, alienated many independent Democrats, and Chapman was politically unknown. Opposition emerged when state senator Richard C. Byrd, an independent Democrat, announced as a candidate for governor. Tension increased when a longtime enemy of the Family, Chester Ashley, openly attacked the convention as a "rump" gathering unrepresentative of the party's rank and file. When the Whigs nominated the popular David Walker of Fayetteville for Congress, it became obvious that the Democratic party was in trouble. Fearing the growing power of the Whigs and the independents, Democratic leaders not only persuaded Conway to support a second convention but also approached Governor Yell about replacing Chapman in the race against Walker. Yell agreed, and a hastily called convention nominated him for Congress. Apparently Chapman decided to cooperate if he received the nomination for governor. Conway, realizing the seriousness of the party's plight, agreed to withdraw his candidacy to make way for Chapman. The new ticket strengthened the congressional race, but it did not improve Democratic chances to retain the governorship. When Chapman emerged as a weak campaigner, it became apparent to most party leaders that he had to be replaced. Having no active party support, Chapman pleaded ill health and in July 1844 withdrew from the race. Such abrupt changes further divided the Democratic party and threatened to throw the election into the hands of the Whigs.

To prevent a Whig victory, the Democrats needed to find a suitable candidate. At a caucus in Little Rock, they agreed to support Drew because he was acceptable to all factions. Even though Drew owned slaves, he was on the geographic fringes of the Black Belt. Thus, he would appear to be above both faction and section, and he might keep the party vote together. Certainly Drew believed that his sole purpose was to keep the party united.

During the campaign the Whigs attacked Drew as a nullifier and as a candidate picked by a clique of powerful men. Drew's supporters ignored such attacks and presented their nominee as a man who would be acceptable to all factions. In a close three-way election, Drew won 47 percent of the vote, thereby becoming Arkansas's first governor to be elected by a plurality.

As governor, Drew supported a moderately progressive program for the state. He urged the general assembly to use the proceeds from the sale of recently acquired federal lands to create a board of internal improvement with powers to clear rivers and improve the state's abysmal roads. He supported the right of preemption on these federal lands, and he requested the legislature to establish a state college. Although the general assembly never acted on these proposals, Drew continued to support them until his resignation in January 1849.

On national issues Drew was in the mainstream of Southern political thought. He endorsed Pres. John Tyler's plans to annex Texas, and in 1846 he actively supported the war with Mexico. After the conflict, he staunchly opposed any effort to ban slavery from the newly acquired territories.

The major problem that Drew faced throughout his administration was the pressing need to restore the state's financial solvency that had been wrecked by the panic of 1837, the banking fiasco, and hopelessly inadequate state revenues. Like most of his contemporaries, Drew had no real solution for the perplexing banking issues or for the problem of increasing state revenues, and in the absence of any constructive program, the financial situation continued to deteriorate. By 1846 an empty treasury and ruined credit threatened to bring state government to a complete halt. Under such conditions, Drew, who had been reluctant to increase taxes in the past, urged the general assembly to take some action to augment revenues. The legislature responded by raising both the base and the rate of taxable property. The new revenue allowed Arkansas to pay most of its immediate expenses, but it did nothing to restore the state's credit. That would require more taxation than either Drew would support or the citizens could pay. Consequently, Arkansas continued to teeter on the verge of bankruptcy.

In political affairs Drew professed neutrality toward intraparty struggles, but given the extreme partisanship of Arkansas politics, such a posture was difficult to maintain. There is substantial evidence that he did play an active role in the strife within the Democratic party. In 1846 he strongly opposed Ashley and supported Yell for the Senate. Even though Drew's opposition did not prevent Ashley's election, it did strengthen Drew's position with the Johnson-Conway-Sevier family, which had been embarrassed by Yell's defeat. In the Family-dominated convention of 1848, Drew easily won nomination for a second term.

Shortly after his renomination, however, he broke with the Family over the appointment of a replacement for Senator Sevier, who had resigned his seat to become a peace commissioner in Mexico. The resignation, though carefully calculated to avoid a later political fight, ultimately hurt the Family because it opened the way to power for one of Arkansas's most ambitious politicians, Solon Borland. An ex-supporter of the Family, Borland made no secret of his ambition to replace Sevier in the Senate. Drew was expected to support Sevier's request that the vacant Senate seat be given to a Family intimate, Samuel H. Hempstead. Instead, Drew ignored the request and appointed Borland. Why he decided to disregard Sevier's wishes is unclear. According to contemporaries, Borland and Drew had reached an agreement whereby the governor would grant Borland the appointment in exchange for a future political favor. Borland may have agreed not to oppose Drew on a fusion ticket with the Whigs, a proposal that had been discussed in some quarters. However, it is also possible that he offered to help Drew to gather legislative support to raise the governor's salary. In any case, it was too late for Drew's action to have any effect on the gubernatorial election. With no formal opposition, he received 15,962 votes out of a total of 16,455.

Drew appeared to be at the height of his political power, but he began his second term in November 1848 in personal economic trouble. The decade-long economic stagnation had seriously eroded his financial resources, and apparently Drew's investment in the railroad-construction schemes popular in Arkansas during the mid-1840s exacerbated those difficulties. Because of these financial problems, Drew had been reluctant to run for a second term and probably consented only with the explicit understanding that his supporters would work to get the governor's salary increased. When they failed to carry through their promise, Drew felt betrayed, and on 10 January 1849, after publicly declaring that his friends had failed to increase his salary, he resigned.

Drew's activities during the next three years are obscure, but he probably spent most of his time trying to recover his financial losses. He had little success until 17 April 1853, when he secured an appointment as the superintendent of Indian affairs for the southern superintendency headquartered in Van Buren. He remained there until March 1855, when the Bureau of Indian Affairs summarily removed him. Drew then began practicing law in Fort Smith, and by 1860 he had reestablished his solvency. While in Fort Smith, Drew deserted the regular Democrats. In 1855 he briefly joined the Know-Nothing party, and three years later he waged a halfhearted campaign as an independent Democrat for the newly created Second Congressional District. After little more than a month, he withdrew from the race. He never ran for public office again.

Although his activities during the Civil War are practically unknown, he probably remained in Fort Smith until the Union army occupied the town in September 1863. There is some evidence that he then moved to Dardanelle, but near the end of the war, he probably returned to his old home in northeastern Arkansas. In 1866 he was employed as a bookkeeper in a store in Pocahontas. He soon resumed the practice of law, but he never recovered from the financial losses suffered during the war. He remained in Randolph County until after his wife's death on 19 November 1872. Shortly afterward he left Arkansas and eventually joined his daughter in Lapin, Hood County, Texas, where he died in January 1879. Forty years later a delegation of Arkansans exhumed his body, and on 30 May 1923 he was reinterred at Pocahontas.

JOHN SELDEN ROANE

1849–1852

JOHN SELDEN ROANE (8 January 1817–7 April 1867), attorney, the son of Hugh Roane, a storekeeper, and Mattie (Selden) Roane, was born near Lebanon, Wilson County, Tennessee. The family was influential in Tennessee politics, and Roane's uncle, Archibald Roane, served as governor of that state from 1801 to 1803. Roane attended school in Wilson County and later enrolled in Cumberland College at Princeton, Kentucky, but it is not certain that he graduated from that institution.

In 1837 Roane moved to Arkansas and settled in Pine Bluff. There he studied law under his brother, Samuel Calhoun Roane (27 February 1793–8 December 1852). Sam Roane had come to Arkansas Territory in 1818 as an ambitious young lawyer. By 1837 he was Arkansas's leading jurist and owner of one of the state's largest plantations. By that date, he had served as U.S. district attorney, judge of the First Territorial Circuit Court, representative from Clark County to the territorial legislative council, and state senator from Arkansas and Jefferson Counties. Backed by his elder brother's influence and patronage, John Roane moved easily and comfortably among the leaders of Jefferson County.

Roane remained in Jefferson County until 1840 when he moved to Van Buren, Crawford County, to begin his duties as the first prosecuting attorney of the newly created Second Judicial District. Undoubtedly Sam Roane's influence helped to secure the post for his twenty-three-year-old brother. John Roane served as prosecuting attorney until 19 September 1842. Returning to Pine Bluff, he was elected in October as representative from Jefferson County to the Fourth Arkansas General Assembly (4 November 1842–4 February 1843). After serving one term, he returned to Van Buren, and in 1844 the citizens of Crawford County chose him as their representative to the Fifth Arkansas General Assembly (4 November 1844–10 January 1845). By a vote of thirty-six to thirty-two, the house elected him speaker. The principal problem facing the new administration and the general assembly was how to restore the state's financial solvency. The panic of 1837 and the failure of the banking systems, coupled with the government's inadequate fiscal policies, had left Arkansas in a state of virtual bankruptcy. Unfortunately neither Gov. Thomas Stevenson Drew nor the general assembly did much to rectify the situation, and few important bills passed the fifth session.

Roane might have run for another term except for the Mexican War. Immediately after the declaration of war, he raised a company called the Van Buren Avengers, and, as their elected captain, he led them to Washington, Hempstead County, Arkansas, where other Arkansas volunteers gathered to organize a regiment. The men elected as the field officers of the regiment on 4 July 1846 were three ambitious Democrats. Archibald Yell, a former governor, received the colonelcy. The men chose twenty-nine-year-old Roane as lieutenant colonel, and Solon Borland, a staunch Democrat and editor of the *Arkansas Banner,* as major. Neither Borland nor Roane had one whit of military experience, though Yell had seen some action in the War of 1812. The officers' major opponent had been Capt. Albert Pike of the Little Rock Guards, a powerful Whig who wished to lead the regiment and who understood the need for proper military leadership. He may have accepted defeat by the popular Yell, but losing to Roane and Borland was too much for his ego. Through the war, Pike harbored bitter personal resentment against all three men and openly questioned their military abilities. Clearly the regiment was a political tool controlled by ambitious politicians, and, not surprisingly, serious military problems immediately developed. The field officers failed to properly train the men, and by the time the regiment reached San Antonio in August 1846, dissension had emerged within the ranks. Many company-grade officers were openly critical of Yell because, as one stated, he was "totally and profoundly ignorant of tactics" and neglected even the basic techniques of military discipline and hygiene. Roane was described as a "clever, jovial companion" but "too dull and indolent to succeed" as a soldier.

Under such questionable leadership, it was inevitable that the regiment would perform badly. In the battle at Buena Vista (22–23 February 1847), the Mexicans completely routed the four companies under Roane's command, and four others under Yell's leadership scarcely did better. In the midst of battle, Mexican lancers killed Yell, and Roane succeeded to the command of the badly shaken troops. Only Pike's soldiers, who had been on detached duty but had arrived in time to participate in some of the most bitter fighting, acquitted themselves honorably. Fortunately, the regiment saw no more action in the war, and by July 1847 it was back in Arkansas.

The regiment's performance at Buena Vista soon became the subject of heated controversy. Pike, who had taken the time to train and discipline his men, was harshly critical of the performance of the regiment. In a letter to the *Arkansas Gazette,* he attacked the election of incompetent officers who had been chosen for political rather than military considerations. With Yell dead and Borland captured, Roane bore the brunt of Pike's attacks. Although a court of inquiry attempted to settle the dispute, relations between Pike and Roane continued to deteriorate. Finally, when Roane publicly rebuked Pike and claimed that Pike's company did not even participate in the battle, the Whig captain challenged his Democratic lieutenant colonel to a duel. Roane gladly accepted, and on 29 July 1847 the two men met on a sandbar in the Arkansas River near Fort Smith. Roane and Pike fired two shots without causing bloodshed. While they prepared themselves for a third exchange, the duelists' surgeons successfully imposed an armistice. With their honor intact, the antagonists shook hands and adjourned to the house of Elias Rector for a celebration.

After the Mexican War, Roane returned to Pine Bluff to await his next political opportunity. He occupied himself with overseeing a newly acquired plantation and with establishing his legal practice. He remained in private life until 1849, when Drew's resignation suddenly made the governorship available.

Drew had suffered serious financial reverses during his first administration (1844–1848), and he had been reluctant to seek a second term. Only a promise from his friends of legislative support for a salary increase induced him to run. But the legislature refused to even consider such a measure, and Drew announced in mid-November that he would resign at the end of the legislative session.

On 8 December 1848, the Democratic members of the legislature caucused to select a candidate to run for governor if Drew carried out his threat to resign. Since a special election would be called quickly after the governor's resignation, it was important to have a viable person ready to campaign. Three strong candidates emerged: James Yell, the nephew of the late war hero; George W. Clarke, editor of the Van Buren *Intelligencer*; and Roane, former speaker of the house and a somewhat tarnished war hero. Initially the caucus favored Yell, but he was unable to get the necessary majority on the first ballot. By the fifth ballot, enough votes had shifted to Roane to give him the nomination by a vote of forty-four to twenty-four. Roane, like Governor Drew, was a compromise candidate. The Democratic leadership could agree on him because he was not identified with either the influential Johnson-Conway-Sevier faction or with those groups that opposed it. Roane's principal political asset was that party leaders had no strong objections to or preferences for him.

Outside the caucus, Roane was not particularly popular among Democrats, but the opposition failed to coalesce on an alternative candidate. Thus, at various times several dissatisfied Democrats announced for office, but none survived to the 14 March 1849 special election. The Whigs nominated state senator Cyrus W. Wilson of Pulaski County to oppose Roane, but neither party showed much interest in the election. Roane presented a program that included a state college, internal improvements, and financial retrenchment, but he made no effort to campaign across the state. Most Whig newspapers contented themselves with attacking Roane as a "caucus candidate." They also questioned the legality of his holding the governorship since an 1837 act required that the oath of office include a statement that the incumbent had not dueled since 1 January 1838. Voting in the special election was light, and Roane with 3,290 votes barely outpolled Wilson with 3,228 votes.

As governor, Roane proposed programs similar to those of both his recent Whig opponent and Governor Drew. He presented plans to the Eighth Arkansas General Assembly (4 November 1850–13 January 1851) for making statewide internal improvements and for establishing several educational institutions. He hoped to finance these programs by using the proceeds from the sale of federal lands that had previously been given to the states for such purposes. Unfortunately, in Arkansas the earlier legislature had dispersed the funds by passing a series of distribution bills that gave the proceeds to the counties. Instead of benefiting education or improving transportation, the monies were squandered on political patronage. Roane urged the general assembly to repeal these distribution laws. He also asked the legislature to support a constitutional amendment to make all state and county offices elective, and he wanted a bankruptcy law that would protect the debtor's home.

Like Drew, Governor Roane's most pressing issue was the need to reestablish the state's financial solvency. The central problems were how to pay the debts created by the collapse of state banking and how to increase revenues so that needed programs could be introduced.

Roane clearly saw the dilemma that the banking issue created. He asked a friend: "Should I recommend the legislature to pay the bonds, or repudiate the debt? The one we cannot do and the other would disgrace us. What should we do?" Roane's question went unanswered, and in his 4 November 1850 message to the legislature, the governor frankly admitted that he had no real policy for dealing with the Real-Estate Bank. Since that "mystic monument of modern banking" continued to obstruct any effort to have its books inspected publicly, Roane suggested that a thorough investigation by the state might prove fruitful. Roane also attacked the mismanagement of the State Bank, but he opposed repudiation and urged that an individual be given the power to collect the bank's debts forthwith.

In regard to state revenues, he praised the previous legislature's courage in increasing the tax rate and base. That decision at least enabled the state to meet its daily needs, but it did not provide adequate financing for any new programs. Since Roane wanted to increase revenues but felt that the people could not be further taxed, he proposed that the state undertake a program to advertise Arkansas's natural resources to attract a larger population. The governor believed that his programs for internal improvements and education, if supplemented with a geological survey to advertise the state's mineral wealth, would attract labor and capital. This population increase would solve the financial crisis by multiplying the number of taxpayers without raising either the base or the rate of taxation.

The general assembly responded to Roane's proposals by lowering the tax base; by refusing to force the payment of debts to the State Bank; and by failing to act on the suggested constitutional amendment, bankruptcy law, or geological survey. Since the political cronies of the legislators were the main patronage beneficiaries of the county distribution acts, the legislature refused to repeal those laws. Angered by this intransigency, Roane, in his message to the Ninth Arkansas General Assembly (1 November 1852–12 January 1853), vigorously attacked the obstructionist attitudes of the past membership and reiterated substantially the same proposals that he had made two years earlier. Again the legislature refused to act in any substantive way.

On national issues, Roane clearly sympathized with the Southern radicals. He believed that the states were sovereign bodies and had the right to leave the Union and that slaves were property and could only be regulated by the states. Roane felt that the South could not remain in the Union if the federal government tampered with slavery.

After a disappointing administration, Roane chose not to seek reelection in 1852 and returned to his plantation and his law practice in Pine Bluff. On 5 July 1855, he married Mary Kimbrough Smith, the daughter of Gen. Nat G. Smith of Tulip, Arkansas. The couple lived on Roane's Pine Bluff plantation where they reared five children: Sallie Kimbrough, Mary Selden, Bethuna, Martha, and Hugh.

Roane was in Pine Bluff at the beginning of the Civil War, and on 20 March 1862 he received a commission as brigadier general in the Confederate Army. After commanding a brigade at the battle of Prairie Grove (7 December 1862), he served principally on garrison and detached duties in Arkansas, Louisiana, and Texas. On 11 July 1865, Roane was paroled at Shreveport, Louisiana. He returned to Pine Bluff, where he died suddenly on 8 April 1867. He was buried in Oakland Cemetery, Little Rock.

ELIAS NELSON CONWAY

1852–1860

ELIAS NELSON CONWAY (17 May 1812–28 February 1892), attorney and land agent, was born at Greeneville in Greene County, Tennessee. He was the youngest of seven sons and the ninth of ten children born to Thomas and Ann (Rector) Conway. His grandfather, Henry Conway, served as an officer from Virginia in the Revolutionary War. During the war, his father moved with the family to what is now Tennessee; his grandfather followed and became speaker of the senate of the short-lived state of Franklin in 1786. When Conway was six years old, his family moved to St. Louis and later to Saline County, Missouri. After attending the school of Alonzo Pearson in Howard County, he received further education at Bonne Femme Academy in Boone County, Missouri.

In 1820 Henry Wharton Conway, Elias's eldest brother, moved to Arkansas Post, having been appointed receiver of public monies for the Arkansas Land District. Ambrose H. Sevier, first cousin to the Conway brothers, arrived later in 1820, immediately becoming temporary clerk of the house in the territorial legislature. In 1823 Henry Conway was elected delegate to Congress from Arkansas Territory. In the same year, James Sevier Conway, another brother, moved to Arkansas permanently, having fulfilled a surveying contract in the territory in 1820; he became surveyor general of the territory in 1832.

In 1833 Elias Conway moved to Little Rock. On 12 February 1834, he was appointed U.S. deputy surveyor, with a contract in northwestern Arkansas. On 25 July 1835, Gov. William Savin Fulton appointed him territorial auditor to fill the unexpired term of William Pelham, and the territorial legislature elected Conway to that position on 12 October 1835.

The First Arkansas General Assembly elected him first auditor of the state, and he served from 1 October 1836 to 3 January 1849, except for a short period from 17 May until 5 July 1841, when A. Boileau was acting auditor. Elias's brother James was elected the first governor of the state in 1836.

In his 1840 audit report to the governor, Elias Conway advised the general assembly to donate lands forfeited to the state to actual settlers so the lands would at least generate tax revenue. Passed by the general assembly, this act undoubtedly contributed to Arkansas's pre–Civil War growth. Historian John Hallum charged that Andrew Johnson appropriated this idea and presented it to Congress where it became national policy in the Homestead Act.

Conway early became involved in Democratic party politics, and in 1843 the opposition newspaper quoted hearsay evidence that he had been "governor in fact" when his brother James held office. While this was probably an exaggeration, Elias Conway did aspire to the office. Conway had celebrated his thirtieth birthday in May 1842, thus reaching the minimum age required by the constitution for holding the office of governor. But unfortunately for Conway, when the *Arkansas Gazette* shifted its allegiance to the Whig party, he and the Democrats lost their journalistic mouthpiece. After their attempt to purchase the *Gazette* from William E. Woodruff failed, Conway and the members of the Democratic central committee launched the *Arkansas Banner.*

On 5 December 1843 the Democratic party convention nominated Conway for governor, and the next day he accepted this "unsolicited and distinguished honor." The nomination received widespread criticism because only sixteen of forty-six counties were represented at the convention and because Conway was young, had done little beyond government work, and was "one of a long line of office-seeking relations." These office-seeking relations, known by such names as the "Family," "royal family," and "the reigning dynasty," consisted of the Johnson-Conway-Sevier families and friends, who dominated politics in Arkansas before the Civil War. (Hallum totals 188 years of public service by these cousins in nineteenth-century Arkansas.)

Because of the criticism, on 6 January 1844 Conway agreed to another convention that met in April and nominated Daniel Chapman for governor, since Conway had withdrawn to "harmonize and unite the whole of the party." When Chapman withdrew, party leaders nominated Thomas Stevenson Drew, who was ultimately elected governor.

Conway continued as state auditor until 1848 when C. C. Danley, a Mexican War veteran, defeated him by two votes in his bid for renomination. Conway returned to private life as an "attorney at law and general land agent," but he remained active in the councils of the

Democratic party. He and Danley clashed again in 1850 in another bid for the auditorship. This time Danley won by a single vote.

Drew remained governor until personal financial troubles forced him to withdraw in favor of John Selden Roane. In 1852, Conway was nominated for governor by the Democratic party convention. Roane later claimed that he was "set aside" by the Family to make room for one of its own.

Bryan H. Smithson became Conway's independent Democratic opponent in 1852. Instead of nominating a candidate, the Whigs endorsed Smithson, who campaigned as supporter of internal improvements. The *Arkansas Gazette* labeled Conway the "dirt roads candidate" because of his unenthusiastic support for railroads and his advocacy of good dirt roads for the state.

Always a politician but never a strong speaker, Conway believed that a proper candidate for governor should be well enough known to gain election without having to actively seek votes. By this definition, he was a "proper candidate." In the election on 2 August 1852, Conway defeated Smithson by a vote of 15,442 to 12,414. Four years later, Conway outpolled James Yell, the American (Know-Nothing) party candidate, by an even greater margin, 27,612 to 15,249. First inaugurated as governor on 15 November 1852, Conway served for exactly eight years, the constitutionally defined limit at the time; he was in office longer than any other governor of Arkansas except Orval Eugene Faubus and William Jefferson Clinton.

In his message to the legislature on 27 November 1852, Conway addressed most of the issues that he would have to grapple with during his tenure. The first item on his agenda concerned internal improvements that included railroads, dirt roads, and the handling of swamp and saline lands. He also discussed the seminary fund and the needs of the penitentiary. Finally, he criticized the banks, especially the State Bank and the Real-Estate Bank.

In its ninth regular session (Conway's first as governor), the general assembly chartered five railroad companies. Shortly after the legislature adjourned in 1853, Congress granted lands to the state for the development of railroads. Before these lands could be transferred to various companies, conditions for their dispersal needed to be set by the legislature. When Conway hesitated to call a special session to take action on the matter, he received strong criticism, especially from the *Arkansas Gazette*, which in March 1853 had been sold to Danley, who was still auditor. A bitter newspaper battle raged between Danley and Richard H. Johnson, the editor of the *True Democrat* (formerly the

Banner). As Johnson was also Conway's private secretary, there is little doubt that the *True Democrat* spoke for Conway.

Johnson expressed fear of "hasty and ill-natured legislation," feeling that "we have no men or companies in our midst who are able to take these lands and give that security for their proper application that ought to be demanded." Conway was waiting for surveyors representing a group of New York capitalists who were to work with the Cairo and Fulton Railroad Company. The president of the Cairo and Fulton was Roswell Beebe, a good friend of Governor Conway. Later, Johnson was elected to the company's board of directors.

Conway felt that a special session would have been a waste of money and, to buttress that contention, requested from Danley the quarterly reports legally required of the auditor. Danley, however, refused to submit the requested documents. He claimed that he followed the precedent set by Conway when, as auditor, he had completed the quarterly statements shortly before the convening of the legislature. On 20 June 1854 Conway turned the matter over to the courts. Ten days later, Danley filed the reports and resigned shortly thereafter.

Another consideration that lay behind Conway's desire to postpone the convening of the general assembly had more to do with politics than with railroads. In April 1853, Solon Borland resigned from the U.S. Senate to become minister to Central America, providing Conway with an opportunity to appoint his successor until the legislature convened. Rep. Robert Ward Johnson, the brother of Conway's private secretary and another member of the Family, received the appointment. Because the special session was never called, Robert Johnson had almost a year and a half to establish himself as senator before the regular session convened.

While the 1850s exuded enthusiasm for the railroad and the marvelous benefits it might bring, only the Memphis and Little Rock Railroad Company fulfilled any of this promise in Arkansas before the Civil War. Conway never had a personal commitment to the Memphis line, having close ties with the organization of the Cairo and Fulton, which, it was argued, would connect Arkansas more directly to the industrial North; "Why go to Memphis?" the *True Democrat* asked.

After the tenth session of the general assembly acted on the federal grant for the railroads, the *True Democrat* criticized the Memphis and Little Rock Railroad Company for spending the "enormous sum" of $25,000 per mile to build the road and for allowing citizens of Memphis to dominate its board of directors. The newspaper also warned Little Rock and Pulaski County of the enormous burdens placed on them by subscriptions to the Memphis and Little Rock.

Nevertheless, by July 1857 several miles of track had been laid from Hopefield, opposite Memphis, toward Little Rock, and in September reporters, railroad officials, and other dignitaries were treated to an excursion on the locomotive "Little Rock," which was described as the first railroad ride in Arkansas. The second station on the road was named Conway, in honor of the governor. On 11 November 1858, the Memphis and Little Rock was opened for passenger and freight service from Hopefield to Madison on the St. Francis River. Progress continued until the Civil War.

While railroads proved to be the most immediate issue that Conway had to deal with, less dramatic internal improvements meant as much to the state. During his administration, the general assembly placed the management of swampland reclamation in the governor's office due to earlier questionable practices. At the end of his term of office, Conway could point to over six million cubic yards of reclaimed swampland and to the almost four million cubic yards of levee work completed during his administration. Following his advice, the general assembly created the office of state geologist; Conway appointed Dr. David Dale Owen, who undertook a geological survey for the state. Conway also oversaw major physical improvements in the state penitentiary.

The most chronic internal issue facing state government in the nineteenth century proved to be the complex problem of the state's credit, which had serious ramifications for the reputation and economic future of Arkansas. Created by the administration of James Sevier Conway, the State Bank and the Real-Estate Bank promised a strong financial footing for land-rich, money-poor Arkansas, but questionable management ended that promise. In January 1843 the State Bank went into receivership, with liabilities of $1,910,023 and assets of only $1,176,810.

The Real-Estate Bank, unlike the State Bank, was not a government entity, though the faith of the state was pledged for the payment of the bonds issued by it. When the central board of the bank placed its affairs in liquidation, it did so by the assignment of all assets to appointed trustees. The trustees, as it turned out, were all board members of the bank. The state, therefore, was excluded from the entire liquidation process but was saddled with the debt.

Succeeding governors attempted to resolve the situation and failed, but Conway finally prevailed. In 1855, following his advice, the general assembly acted "to aid in bringing to light the true condition of the Real Estate Bank" and to create a new court of chancery in Pulaski County. One act would clarify the financial picture of the bank, while the other would overcome chronic delays in transferring the bank's assets to a receiver.

In Conway himself rested the authority to appoint the chancellor. To blunt any potential partisan criticism, he named Hulbert F. Fairchild, a Whig from Batesville, to that position. On 20 April 1855, the Real-Estate Bank went into receivership, and Conway gained his greatest triumph.

Unfortunately, the battle proved easier to win than the war. The report of William M. Gouge and William Read Miller, the accountants charged with analyzing the state of the Real-Estate Bank, affirmed what everyone feared regarding poor management. The state remained burdened with the debts from two ill-fated financial institutions.

Conway's policy toward the Real-Estate Bank consisted of accounting for and collecting its assets, and then applying that money toward paying the bank's debts. Such funds would not go too far. At the end of his eight years in office, Conway proudly pointed to $2,341,996.17 paid on the state's debt. But debts of $1,098,717.50 remained from the State Bank and of $1,922,230.99 from the Real-Estate Bank, including principal and interest on the so-called Holford bonds, the most controversial of the Real-Estate Bank's liabilities. Because Conway could never bring himself to support the use of tax monies to relieve the state of these debts, the problem remained unsettled.

Otherwise, the state enjoyed unprecedented prosperity, having an increase of almost $100 million in taxable property during the Conway administration. Conway left $304,106.98 in specie in the state treasury, and he strengthened the state's monetary system by persuading the legislature to prohibit the circulation of low-denomination paper money "in the form of bill, bank note, check, or ticket." His concern for the financial soundness of state government also prompted him to pocket veto a tax reduction passed by the twelfth general assembly.

The prosperity of the 1850s saw the plantation system of the Old South established in Arkansas. In one decade, the number of slaves increased from 47,100 to 111,115, and anxieties related to the presence of blacks increased to the point that in 1858 Conway recommended to the general assembly that "free men of color" be prohibited from living in Arkansas. Although the law had been proposed before, the mounting crisis and Conway's support ensured its passage. Free blacks not leaving the state after 1860 were to be enslaved for a year; their earnings from that period were to be used for their removal.

The general assembly incorporated the School for the Blind during Conway's administration, and on his recommendation the state assumed control of it on 4 February 1859. Conway promoted other educational improvements, but little else was actually accomplished.

No chief executive gets everything he wants from the legislative branch, but Conway proved to be remarkably successful. No doubt some of this success stemmed from the waning but still potent influence of the Family, but much was due to his commitment to his duties. The general assembly never really challenged him, but Conway had an opportunity to become the first governor to adjourn that body, when in January 1859 the house and senate deadlocked on the issue of adjournment.

Late in his term of office, Conway toyed with the idea of seeking a seat in the U.S. Senate, but he decided against it. It was a wise decision, based on the imminence of war and Conway's own analysis of the national situation. In a message to Arkansas militiamen on 27 August 1860, he blamed the British for their "unceasing efforts" to overthrow the U.S. government by stirring up and intensifying the conflict between the free and slave states. He urged the states to set aside their sectional rivalries and to form a united front against their foreign enemy.

In June 1860 Albert Rust, a former ally of the Family, said of Conway: "He has administered the government of Arkansas for the last eight years as though it were a private estate out of which he had a right to manufacture political capital for himself and his friends." The last clause of that statement reflects the partisan attitude of an opponent of the Family, but even Conway's supporters agreed with the rest of the statement. Conway spent his adult life through 1860 in public service. He felt obligated to serve his family and his state. He survived as the last of the dynasty that led and dominated the territory and the state. As if tending a private estate, he concerned himself with the soundness of the state's operation, occasionally overlooking the convenience of the people. Opponents tried to make scandals out of many of his activities as governor, but nothing came of such criticism. The last member of the dynasty helped to create an Arkansas in which such a dynasty could not exist: the state's population soared from 209,897 to 435,450 in the 1850s, and its unprecedented prosperity eroded the foundations on which the political fortunes of his family had been built.

There were two institutions to which Conway would not submit—a religious denomination and marriage. He attended several churches, including at one time during the height of the Know-Nothing era a Roman Catholic one, and he contributed money on occasion to the denomination of his parents, the Methodist church, but he never became a member. He never married.

Conway retired from public office in 1860 and spent the next three decades managing his private affairs in a state of near-seclusion. His death occurred when he fell head first into the fireplace. He was buried in the Mount Holly Cemetery in Little Rock.

HENRY MASSIE RECTOR

1860–1862

HENRY MASSIE RECTOR (1 May 1816–12 August 1899), planter and attorney, was born at Fountain Ferry near Louisville, Kentucky, the only child surviving to maturity of Elias and Fannie Bardella (Thurston) Rector. Rector's father was a land surveyor, speculator, and postmaster of St. Louis, Missouri, who acquired considerable land including claims to large tracts in Arkansas. Following Elias's death in 1822, Fannie Rector married Stephen Trigg, who operated a salt works in northwestern Missouri. Rector worked for his stepfather and was provided the rudiments of education by his mother. For two years beginning in 1833 he attended a school in Louisville, Kentucky, directed by Francis Goddard. In October 1838 he married Jane Elizabeth Field of Louisville. They had four sons—Frank N., William, Henry M., Jr., and Elias W.—and four daughters—Ann Baylor, Julia Sevier, Fanny Thurston, and Ada E. His wife died in 1857, and he married Ernestine Flora Linke three years later. They had one child, a daughter named Ernestine Flora.

In 1835 Rector settled in Arkansas and assumed the management of the substantial landholdings that he had inherited from his father. He vigorously pressed his claims to the famous Hot Springs, but after lengthy litigation the government eventually confirmed individual claims to land around the springs but reserved the springs themselves for public use. Appointed teller in the State Bank at Little Rock in 1839, Rector left that position less than two years later when he moved to a plantation near Collegeville in Saline County where he farmed and read law.

In 1842 Pres. John Tyler appointed him U.S. marshal for the district of Arkansas, a post that he had not solicited. At the expiration of Tyler's administration, Rector was succeeded in that office by a cousin who had been appointed by Pres. James Polk. In 1848 Rector was elected to the first of two terms in the state senate representing the district composed of Perry and Saline Counties. In the senate he devoted considerable attention to questions relating to the state penitentiary and acquired a wide reputation as a skilled debater. In 1852 he was chosen a Democratic presidential elector.

In 1854 Rector moved to Little Rock and opened a law office there while he carried on extensive farming operations along the Arkansas River. In the same year he was elected on the Democratic ticket to represent Pulaski County in the lower house of the general assembly. After a single term, he returned to private life and devoted his energies to the practice of criminal law. He also served as U.S. surveyor general for Arkansas (1853–1857). In 1859 the general assembly elected him to the state supreme court.

The Democratic faction known as the Johnson-Conway-Sevier dynasty dominated antebellum politics in Arkansas. This group was commonly called the Family because most of its leaders were related either by blood or marriage. In 1860 the Democratic state convention nominated one of the pillars of the Family, Richard H. Johnson, for governor. Rep. Thomas Carmichael Hindman of Phillips County, who had launched an anti-Family movement two years earlier, urged Rector to oppose Johnson as an independent Democrat. Even though Rector was related to the Conways, he agreed to challenge Johnson. The key issues in this exciting race were Johnson's close ties to the banks and his place in the state political machine. The result was a victory for Rector. He polled 31,518 votes to Johnson's 28,662 and became the sixth governor of Arkansas.

The Republican victory in the presidential election of 1860 set in motion the secession of the Deep South. Rector's inaugural address, presented to the general assembly on 15 December 1860, stated his conviction that the crisis was reducible to the questions, "Was it to be the Union without slavery, or slavery without the Union?" He cited personal-liberty laws of the Northern states as proof of their rejection of the Constitution, but he stopped short of calling for immediate secession.

He approved the general assembly's provision for a special election on 15 February 1861 to permit the people of Arkansas to decide whether or not they desired to secede. When the delegates chosen in that special election met on 4 March 1861, the antisecessionists succeeded in electing David Walker as chairman of the convention. Walker rejected immediate secession but approved the calling of an election on 5 August, at which time the voters could decide whether they wanted to cooperate with the Union or to secede from it.

Meanwhile, on 8 February 1861 Governor Rector, supported by secessionists from eastern Arkansas, seized the federal arsenal in Little Rock and sent Solon Borland with troops of the state militia to seize the Fort Smith arsenal. After the fall of Fort Sumter, Pres. Abraham Lincoln called for volunteers, and Rector's dramatic rejection of the call set the stage for Walker's reconvening of the secession convention in Little Rock on 6 May 1861. After withdrawing from the Union and joining the Confederacy, the convention rewrote the state constitution. In the process the Family got its revenge on Rector by securing a constitutional provision that shortened his term to two years. After making an unsuccessful attempt to have the supreme court set the provision aside, Rector ran for reelection in the 6 October 1862 election. He lost to Harris Flanagin, the Family candidate, who received 18,187 votes to Rector's 7,419; a third candidate, John S. Rainey, polled 708 votes. On 3 November 1862 the new general assembly met. Rector reported on conditions in the state and then resigned, eleven days before his term officially ended.

As Arkansas's first war governor, Rector presided over the mobilization of the state. He was commander in chief of the state militia and chairman of the state war board. The secession convention, dominated by the Family, played a key role in the mobilization and by the end of 1861 Arkansas had 21,500 men enrolled for military service. When wartime inflation and profiteering ran unchecked, Hindman, who had become a general commanding the Confederate army in Arkansas, blamed Rector and tried to circumvent him by declaring martial law. The clash resulted in Hindman's replacement.

After Rector's reelection bid failed in 1862 and his application for a commission in the Confederate army was rejected, he volunteered in the state reserve corps as a private for the duration of the war. Two of his sons were killed in action. After Appomattox, Rector returned to farming and hauled cotton in wagons from his plantations in Hempstead, Garland, and Pulaski Counties to Little Rock. He waged many court battles over his Hot Springs claims. He was a delegate to the constitutional convention in 1874 from Garland County. He lived in Little Rock until his death on 12 August 1899 and was buried in Mount Holly Cemetery. Three days before his death he had joined the Methodist church.

HARRIS FLANAGIN

1862–1864

HARRIS FLANAGIN (3 November 1817–23 October 1874), attorney and land speculator, was born in Roadstown, Cumberland County, New Jersey, the son of James and Mary (Harris) Flanagin. His grandfather, James Flanagin, had emigrated from Ireland to America in 1765; his father was a cabinetmaker and merchant by trade. Flanagin first attended a Quaker school in New Jersey where his educational advance was marked. At the age of eighteen he was made professor of mathematics at Clermont Seminary in Frankfort, Pennsylvania. The next year he moved west and opened his own school at Paoli, Illinois. While in Illinois he studied law and after two years was admitted to the bar. In 1839 the young lawyer moved to Arkansas, settling first in Greenville, Clark County, and later moving to Arkadelphia when that town was chosen county seat in 1842. He lived in Arkadelphia the rest of his life; the law office he built still stands on the town square. On 3 July 1851, when he was thirty-four years old, he married Martha Elizabeth Nash from Hempstead County. They had three children: two sons—Nash and Duncan—and a daughter, Laura.

By 1845 the formerly impecunious lawyer owned 120 acres and no slaves; eight years later his holdings had increased to 2,720 acres, thirteen town lots, six slaves, $1,500 worth of furniture, four cows, and a carriage. This success was partly due to his business association with Benjamin Duncan, a friend Flanagin had known at Clermont Seminary and after whom he named his second son. A Whig, Flanagin was elected in 1842 to the lower house of the fourth general assembly for one term. During the Mexican War, his name appeared on a list of volunteers for a company of soldiers, but apparently the group was never organized. He was elected captain of a company of militia in 1847, but no record of any service has been found. The following year Flanagin was again a candidate for public office, this time running against a prominent Clark County Democrat, Hawes H. Coleman, for the state senate. Flanagin won this spirited contest and served one term.

During the 1850s, when the Whig party in Arkansas collapsed, Flanagin is reported to have limited his political activity to serving as an Arkadelphia alderman. However, when the election of Abraham Lincoln in 1860 precipitated Southern secession and led the Arkansas legislature to authorize the summoning of a convention on 18 February, Flanagin, who supported Arkansas's withdrawal from the Union, was elected to represent Clark County in the secession convention. Although he voted with the secessionists, many of his former political friends remained unionists until after the firing on Fort Sumter in April, and Flanagin kept their goodwill. His support for secession was recorded as being based on the inevitability of the event rather than on its desirability. After the ordinance of secession was passed on 6 May 1861, Arkansas began arming for war. Flanagin left the convention to accept the command with the rank of the captain of Company E of the Second Arkansas Mounted Rifles. He participated in the action at Wilson's Creek (Oak Hills) and at Pea Ridge (Elk Horn Tavern). In the latter battle, regimental colonel James McIntosh was killed, and in the reorganization of the regiment Flanagin was elected colonel without serious opposition. After Pea Ridge, his regiment was transferred across the Mississippi River to the Army of Tennessee. His military career was uneventful during the summer and fall of 1862.

In addition to passing a secession ordinance, the secession convention had drafted an entirely new constitution for Arkansas. Convinced that incumbent Gov. Henry Massie Rector was incompetent or worse, the convention delegates had scheduled the next gubernatorial election for the fall of 1862, thus cutting two years from Rector's term. Rector opposed this action, but in the summer of 1862 the state supreme court ordered the election held, and Rector agreed to comply. A caucus of state political leaders of all shades of prewar opinion met and selected Flanagin as a suitable compromise candidate. Two historians, David Y. Thomas and Farrar Newberry, have reported that Flanagin learned of his nomination the day before the election. Flanagin's diary sheds no light on this matter, recording only the news of the actual election. But a letter from a soldier in the Army of Tennessee indicates that Flanagin's men were aware of the impending election and were anxious for their commander to win. Rector found it difficult to fight the absentee soldier. A pro-Rector newspaper attempted to stir up xenophobic reactions by describing Flanagin as a Yankee Irishman whose real name was O'Flanagin. But such tactics were unsuccessful. The complete wreck of state government left by Rector and the united front that all forces threw against him led to Flanagin's polling 18,187 votes to Rector's 7,419.

On 14 November 1862 Flanagin was inaugurated in Little Rock as Arkansas's seventh governor. He called attention to wartime problems of rising prices, shortages of salt and every kind of manufactured article, the soldiers' hungry families, and the continued wartime distillation of liquor. The legislature responded with new laws, but the problems continued to mount because Arkansas had financed the war effort with paper bonds while suspending tax collections and thus had no money to implement the policies. Growing lawlessness, especially in the region north of the Arkansas River, compounded the situation. Widespread guerrilla and bushwhacker activities made the laws unenforceable and forced thousands to flee to Texas. In this situation Flanagin, a strict constitutionalist and legalist, refused to take any initiative. It was rumored that the governor "loves whiskey too well to get him to stop still houses." It can be argued that the state of Arkansas, for whatever reasons, made the poorest showing of any state in the Confederacy in attending to human needs. Most of the blame rested with Rector, but Flanagin did little to reverse the course of events.

Militarily Flanagin inherited a state that had been fought over by both sides but had been mostly left in Confederate control. Gen. Thomas Carmichael Hindman had tried to use military authority to make Arkansas a useful contributor to the war effort, but his methods had aroused such discontent that the Confederate government in Richmond sent Gen. Theophilus H. Holmes to Arkansas to quiet the state. In most instances the actions undertaken by Hindman—martial law, price control, cotton seizures, and conscription—were abandoned or modified. Flanagin generally cooperated with the military authorities and did not oppose conscription, unlike some other Southern wartime governors, notably Georgia's Joseph Brown. However, when the conscript officers attempted to draft the clerk of the state supreme court, Flanagin was furious. He also insisted on a vigorous defense of Arkansas, accompanying the army to Helena during June and July 1863 for an unsuccessful assault on that town. When Confederate authorities began removing machinery and supplies to Texas after the battle, Flanagin vigorously protested the action.

With threatened invasion, Flanagin reassumed a military role. In January 1863 the federals captured Arkansas Post and appeared ready to march up the river to Little Rock. Flanagin called for the state volunteers to assemble for sixty days. As evidence of the condition of state government, the men were told to bring their own arms. When the federals did make their move in August 1863, Flanagin called for older men to turn out to fight under his personal leadership. Some men actually did assemble, but the unit did not function well, he reported, "for want of skill or experience." Little Rock fell on 10 September 1863, and the Confederate state government went into exile.

After the fall of Little Rock, Flanagin went to Arkadelphia and remained there about a month. Finally he moved to Washington in Hempstead County and reassembled the shattered remnants of state government. While many secessionists were calling for total guerrilla war, Flanagin did little besides pardoning soldiers convicted of various offenses. In correspondence with Sen. Robert Ward Johnson, the head of the powerful Johnson-Conway-Sevier dynasty in Arkansas politics, Flanagin defended his actions as constitutionally correct and promised to behave like Louisiana's energetic Gov. Henry Watkins Allen. Flanagin did support the removal of General Holmes, whose premature senility and incompetence were manifest, but he was represented by proxy when the Trans-Mississippi commander, E. Kirby Smith, held a governors' conference at Marshall, Texas. Flanagin's exact sentiments are not recorded, but the letters received from former unionist friends were defeatist if not treasonous.

In the summer of 1864 an effort was made to revive the state government. A series of state supreme court rulings paved the way for a session of the legislature in the fall. When that body convened, Flanagin painted a dismal picture. Law and order had ceased to exist unless enforced by the military. Slaves had fled, fields were abandoned, and families were homeless, while the state, with no money, was providing no services. However, the legislature voted more nonexistent monies in aid and altered a number of laws to adjust for a government-in-exile. New elections for the legislature were held in the Confederate-controlled southwest in 1865, but the end of the war came before the next session of the legislature could assemble.

Militarily, the Trans-Mississippi defended itself. The major Union attack was a two-pronged effort in the spring of 1864. As Gen. Nathaniel Banks moved up the Red River, Gen. Frederick J. Steele moved south toward Washington before veering off to Camden. Flanagin briefly abandoned Washington, staying at Rondo until the crisis passed. In the end Banks was defeated and Steele's army was almost cut off.

Gen. Robert E. Lee's surrender in the east in April 1865 led to a crisis in the Trans-Mississippi theater. Another governors' conference assembled at Marshall, this time with Flanagin attending. The civil leaders wanted some kind of terms. Flanagin, on his return to Arkansas, proposed to the federal authorities that he be allowed to summon the legislature, repeal all acts of secession and war, and then resign. In addition, he wanted Union recognition of county officials in the Confederate-controlled portion of the state. The federals refused to negotiate; Flanagin was permitted only to return the state archives to Little Rock and then to retire unmolested to Arkadelphia.

In Arkadelphia Flanagin attempted to rebuild his law practice. His overwork in this regard was considered a factor in his early death. Politically he remained in touch with the ex-Whigs and conservative Democrats who led the opposition to the Republican party from 1868 to 1874. His advice was usually conservative and moralistic, opposing violent methods and political trickery. In 1872 he was selected as a delegate to the Democratic National Convention. With the impending demise of Reconstruction after the Brooks-Baxter War, he was even mentioned as a possible candidate for governor. Elected to the constitutional convention of 1874, he served as chairman of its judiciary committee. The claim has been made that he was the ablest man at the convention. He died on 23 October 1874, before the final ratification of the constitution, although he signed a draft previous to his death.

Flanagin had been raised a Baptist but had never joined a Baptist church in Arkansas. His wife was a Presbyterian, and he attended that church regularly in her company. He was "a large man, thin faced, and had the appearance of a man of sorrow." His friends and family were devoted to him, and his slaves remained with the family after the war. He was buried at Rose Hill Cemetery at Arkadelphia.

ISAAC MURPHY

1864–1868

ISAAC MURPHY (16 October 1799–8 September 1882), teacher and attorney, the son of Hugh and Jane (Williams) Murphy, was born and raised just outside Pittsburgh, Pennsylvania, in fairly comfortable circumstances. Little is known of his early years except that he attended nearby Washington College and was admitted to the bar of Allegheny County on 29 April 1825. Five years later he moved to Clarksville, Tennessee, where he taught school and practiced law, his two lifelong vocations. He married Angelina Lockhart of Clarksville on 31 July 1830; the couple eventually produced six daughters. The Murphys joined the swelling westward migration in 1834 and moved to the raw frontier settlement of Fayetteville in Arkansas Territory.

Murphy resided in or near Fayetteville for twenty years and held a number of local public offices including that of Washington County treasurer. He operated a school and in 1843 was a founder and member of the board of visitors of Far West Seminary, which some claim to be the first college in the state. In 1846 and again in 1848 Murphy was Washington County's representative to the Arkansas General Assembly. At the age of fifty he set out for the newly discovered California goldfields. Like many other forty-niners, he failed to strike it rich and returned home two or three years later in considerably reduced circumstances. In 1854 Murphy moved twenty miles east to Huntsville in Madison County where he and his oldest daughters established the Female Seminary of Huntsville and other schools. He continued to practice law as well. Two years after his arrival in Huntsville, the citizens of Madison and Benton Counties elected him to the state senate.

By this time Murphy and most other Arkansans were becoming embroiled in the national controversy over the expansion of slavery into the western territories. When Republican Abraham Lincoln was elected president in 1860, seven Southern states seceded from the

Union and formed the Confederate States of America. The eight remaining slave states, Arkansas among them, waffled uncertainly. The people of Arkansas were divided over secession. Well into 1861 many Arkansans—especially those in the northwestern counties— wished to remain a part of the United States. When the general assembly called for a special convention to decide the issue, Murphy was one of two men elected by Madison County residents to represent their unionist feelings at Little Rock. Murphy was in the majority during the first weeks of the convention, but secessionist sentiment swelled after Fort Sumter. On 6 May 1861 the convention passed a secession resolution sixty-five votes to five. The five unionist delegates were asked to change their votes so that the resolution might be approved unanimously. Four did so, but Murphy reportedly declared: "I have cast the vote after mature reflection, and have duly considered the consequences, and I cannot conscientiously change it. I therefore vote 'No.'" He remained in the convention until it adjourned and then returned home.

Murphy attempted to resume the quiet life of a schoolmaster in Madison County, but partisan feelings intensified when a federal army under Gen. Samuel R. Curtis entered the northwestern corner of the state early in 1862. In April, several weeks after the battle of Pea Ridge, Murphy was forced to flee to the protection of the federal forces. He was made a civilian member of Curtis's staff and spent much of the next eighteen months campaigning in the northern half of Arkansas from Fayetteville to Helena. His daughters remained behind in Huntsville for a time (his wife had died in 1860) and were severely harassed by hostile neighbors and Confederate irregulars.

Little Rock fell to federal forces in September 1863, and the Confederate state government fled to Washington in the southwest corner of the state. Arkansas was the third Confederate state to come under some degree of federal control. These developments led President Lincoln to issue his Proclamation of Amnesty and Reconstruction on 8 December 1863. The proclamation stated that as soon as 10 percent of the people in a rebel state who had voted in 1860 took an oath of allegiance to the United States of America, those men could then begin to establish a new, loyal, unionist government in their state. This mild policy lasted four years and was the cornerstone of what is known as presidential Reconstruction. It reflected Lincoln's desire to restore the shattered Union as quickly and as painlessly as possible, and it was the legal basis of the Murphy administration.

As Lincoln had hoped, there was considerable desire in the northern and central parts of Arkansas for a unionist government, and a constitutional convention was called. Delegate selection was highly irregular—only twenty-four of fifty-seven counties were represented—but probably nothing better could have been accomplished under the circumstances. The convention met in Little Rock on 4 January 1864 and adopted the 1836 constitution with only a few changes. The convention chose Murphy as provisional governor and Calvin C. Bliss as provisional lieutenant governor by acclamation. They were sworn in on 20 January; the convention adjourned three days later.

Murphy was aware of the tenuous legal status of the convention and later stated that he "assumed no power, and felt unwilling to perform any executive act until the constitution and ordinances were ratified by the people." The constitution was ratified in a special election on 14–16 March 1864 in which only twelve thousand people voted. Murphy was elected governor without opposition in that same election. He was inaugurated on 18 April at the statehouse, the scene of his determined stand for the Union three years earlier. Murphy's inaugural address was bland and conciliatory. He called for a return to the Union, made a lengthy plea on behalf of expanded public education, and asked Arkansans to work together to help the state recover from the ravages of war.

The Murphy administration faced enormous problems. Half of the state was under Confederate control, and Confederate irregulars roamed the other half almost at will. The treasury was empty and the only currency in circulation was worthless Confederate money. Finally, the unionist government depended for its very existence on the federal forces in Arkansas commanded by Gen. Frederick J. Steele. The importance of this last factor was underscored only a few weeks after Murphy's inauguration with the failure of Steele's Camden expedition. The defeat was a serious blow to Arkansas unionists. Confederate military activity increased, and for most of the rest of the war, the Murphy administration was isolated in Little Rock.

Under these circumstances, relatively little was accomplished. The rump legislature, which was elected along with Murphy, disenfranchised Arkansans who remained in Confederate service after the establishment of the unionist government, and on 13 April 1865 it unanimously approved the Thirteenth Amendment to the Constitution, which prohibited slavery in the United States. Murphy supported both actions.

By the war's end in 1865 Arkansas was close to being officially restored to its former status in the Union. Lincoln and his successor,

Andrew Johnson, recognized the legitimacy of the Murphy administration despite its clouded beginnings and later problems. The final authority in such matters, however, was the Congress, and before that body could act, the Arkansas Supreme Court nullified the recent law disenfranchising ex-Confederates. The result was predictable. In the 1866 legislative elections, the unionists were overwhelmed; not one member of Murphy's first legislature was returned to office. The general assembly that convened in November 1866 was composed entirely of conservatives, mostly Democrats, who had supported the Confederacy. Now began the second and most troublesome phase of Murphy's administration.

Murphy treated former Confederates with extraordinary fairness considering his family's wartime hardships. He urged President Johnson to pardon 125 high-ranking Arkansas Confederates who had not been included in Lincoln's amnesty proclamation. In this same generous, forward-looking vein, Murphy urged the members of the new general assembly to put the war behind them and to go along with federal policies so that Arkansas might be speedily restored to its place in the Union. The legislators ignored his advice. They defiantly rejected the Fourteenth Amendment, which guaranteed equal rights for blacks and whites, and passed a series of laws that distressed Murphy and infuriated the Congress: financial transactions made during the Confederate period were legitimized; a pension plan for Confederate veterans and their survivors was established; and freedmen (former slaves) were forbidden to vote, to serve on juries, to marry whites, or to attend public schools. Murphy's vetoes of these acts were overridden with little difficulty. On the other hand, at Murphy's urging, the legislators did establish the first statewide public school system (albeit for whites only) and accepted the provisions of the 1862 Morrill Act, which eventually led to the establishment of the University of Arkansas.

In March 1867 Congress passed the Reconstruction Acts, a sharp departure from the more generous Lincoln-Johnson policy. These laws were a response to the recalcitrance of the Arkansas legislators and of other political leaders across the defeated Confederacy. Southern states were placed under military control, ex-Confederates were disenfranchised, and voter registration of freedmen was begun. Arkansas and Mississippi composed the Fourth Military District commanded by General E. O. C. Ord. Murphy worked closely with Ord for the remaining fifteen months of his term. The general dissolved the conservative-dominated assembly and restricted the activity of the state judiciary, but otherwise allowed Arkansas's government to function in a normal manner because of Murphy's cooperative attitude and unionist reputation. During this period, Murphy supervised administrative operations, particularly those of a fiscal nature, but did nothing that might have been construed as an attempt to challenge or to usurp the authority of the military.

In accordance with the provisions of the Reconstruction Acts, elections were held in early 1868 for a new constitutional convention, a new legislature, and a new governor. Most of those elected were Radical Republicans, a mixture of unionists, carpetbaggers, and freedmen. Murphy did not run for reelection. During the spring the lame-duck governor addressed his third general assembly. He again appealed for moderation and harmony and urged the legislators to support the public school system so that every Arkansas child could obtain "a thorough American education." On 22 June 1868 Congress finally readmitted Arkansas to the Union. Twelve days later, on 2 July, Powell Clayton was inaugurated as governor. Murphy, now sixty-nine, returned to Huntsville where he farmed, practiced law, and occasionally served as a judge. He lived there quietly and in very modest circumstances until his death at the age of eighty-two.

Murphy was governor during the most difficult period in Arkansas history. Throughout the uneasy transition from war to peace, his administration was buffeted by powerful outside forces over which he had no control. His wartime election was questionable; he had no political following; nearly all of his term was served in a kind of legal limbo; and at one time or another he had to work with radicals, exrebels, and generals. His greatest achievement as governor was not legislation but the creation of a viable state government out of the chaos of the times. Murphy was not a dynamic or charismatic leader; he was a quiet, conservative, country schoolmaster who strove to heal the wounds of war and to ease Arkansas and its people back into the Union. Ridiculed and vilified at first by extremists on both sides, he eventually gained the respect of his opponents. According to historian David Y. Thomas, he was "a man of sound common sense, of good intentions, and of scrupulous honesty."

POWELL CLAYTON

1868–1871

POWELL CLAYTON (7 August 1833–25 August 1914), engineer, business-man, and diplomat, was born in Bethel County, Pennsylvania, the son of John and Ann (Clarke) Clayton. Politics and public service were traditional in Clayton's family. One ancestor, William Clayton, had come to America with William Penn in the late seventeenth century. One relative served as a U.S. senator from Delaware, and another, Thomas H. Clayton, was a judge in Pennsylvania. Powell Clayton's mother was the daughter of a British army officer; his father, a car-penter, was active in Whig politics but did not hold public office him-self. As a delegate to the Baltimore convention in 1840, John Clayton had nominated William Henry Harrison for president.

Powell Clayton attended Partridge Military Academy at Bristol, Pennsylvania; studied civil engineering at Wilmington, Delaware; and in 1855 moved west to Leavenworth, Kansas, where, as a Democrat, he was elected city engineer and surveyor in 1859 and voted for Stephen A. Douglas in the presidential election of 1860. At the outbreak of the Civil War, Clayton joined the Union army, serving first as captain of the First Kansas Infantry, and later as colonel of the Fifth Kansas Cavalry.

When Clayton arrived in Arkansas in 1863 to participate in the Union army's occupation of Little Rock, he was a young cavalry officer with a receding hairline and a rather unkempt mustache and goatee. His weather-beaten face made him appear older than his thirty years. Clayton's army photograph revealed alert, dark eyes and a tight-lipped, determined expression. Of medium height with light-colored hair and a "graceful, haughty bearing," Colonel Clayton was well known for his "personal dash and courage" and, despite his "fiery temperament," was "possessed of a suave manner." A capable soldier, Clayton was decisive, hard-hitting, and aggressive. He repulsed a Confederate attack on Pine Bluff and shortly before the end of the war was promoted to brigadier general "for continuous meritorious service." Gen. John Marmaduke and other Confederate cavalrymen considered him the "ablest Federal commander of cavalry west of the Mississippi."

While still the commanding colonel at Pine Bluff, Clayton made "judicious investments" in cotton and acquired sufficient capital to purchase a Pine Bluff plantation where he settled after the war. He married Adaline McGraw of Helena, the orphaned daughter of a steamboat captain, on 14 December 1865. The Claytons had five children: Lucy, Powell, Charlotte, Kathleen, and Glover (who died in infancy). Two of Clayton's three daughters married diplomats from Belgium and from England. Powell Clayton Jr. followed a military career, including a tour of duty as military attaché to the U.S. embassy in Mexico City while his father was ambassador.

Clayton had gone to Arkansas as a Democrat and found in the state a strange mixture of Democrats, Whigs, unionists, and conservatives. Union sentiment was strong in parts of Arkansas before and during the war, especially in the northwest, but no state Republican party existed. On 2 April 1867, 139 men assembled in convention at Little Rock and proclaimed themselves the Union State Convention. At this convention Clayton served on the committee on resolutions. The convention launched the official party newspaper, the *Daily Republican,* and created the Republican State Central Committee, which included Clayton as a member from the Second Congressional District.

Democrats captured the state legislature in 1866, but the two U.S. senators chosen by that body were refused seats in the Republican-controlled Congress, which enacted a measure in March 1867 declaring the governments of Arkansas and nine other former Confederate states illegal. Congressional Reconstruction established military rule throughout the South in 1867. Gen. E. O. C. Ord, who was appointed military governor of the Fourth Military District, which included Mississippi and Arkansas, disbanded the Arkansas legislature and called for a constitutional convention.

Due to the scarcity of Democrats who could take the "ironclad oath" that they had neither served in the Confederacy nor given "aid or comfort" to the enemy, most of the delegates to the 1868 constitutional convention were Republicans. Clayton was not a delegate to the constitutional convention, but he did participate in the Republican state nominating convention in 1868, which was meeting at the same time. That convention selected Clayton as the Republican gubernatorial nominee and James M. Johnson, a native Arkansan and a "consistent

Union man," as its candidate for lieutenant governor. From that time Clayton emerged as a political figure of statewide prominence.

Though vitriolic political campaigns are rather common in Arkansas history, the contest over ratification of the constitution of 1868 was more violent than most. Union leagues, Republican clubs, Democratic clubs, and the Ku Klux Klan "supplemented the usual campaign activities," as one historian expressed it. Clayton, like other leading Republicans, stumped the state charging the Democrats with intimidation and terrorism and proclaiming "doctrines of loyalty, freedom, Negro rights, economic development, and free public education for both races alike." The Democrats responded with slander, ridicule, innuendo, and inflammable rhetoric, calling Republicans "you damnable curs," and other similar epithets. On 1 April 1868 the state board of election commissioners announced ratification of the constitution and Clayton's election as governor of Arkansas. Congress accepted the Arkansas constitution of 1868 as legal. Pres. Andrew Johnson promptly vetoed it, but the Republican-dominated Congress quickly overrode his veto.

The Arkansas legislature met in April, and the state was readmitted to representation in Congress when Clayton was inaugurated as governor of Arkansas on 2 July 1868. The new legislature unanimously accepted the Fourteenth Amendment and Congress now declared Arkansas "reconstructed."

Political power in Arkansas was clearly in the hands of the Republican party, identified now as the "Reconstruction party." Clayton dominated Arkansas Republican politics—as much as he was able—in an authoritarian style that was consistent with his background, military training, political philosophy, and personality. A conscientious and competent administrator, Clayton saw both the power and political limitations of his office. He also realized the value of patronage in maintaining political control of the state and personal control of the party. A letter sent by Clayton to all state tax assessors whom he had appointed illustrated this point. After urging the assessors to personally see that "a fair and correct assessment" was made, he added:

> The Governor hopes too that you will look after the interest of the party and keep him informed from time to time in reference to the political situation in your County. He trusts that you will do all you can for the Party. He would be pleased if you would make out at your leisure and send to him a list of the prominent Republicans in your County

names and Post Office addresses together with a list of moderate Democrats who may be led to work with us by means of Documents sent to them—as also the names of those who are likely to be candidates for Election to the Legislature.

With the Republicans in control of both the legislative and the executive branches, the governor was the key figure in the Arkansas political structure. His powers included final authority in granting state credit to railroads and patronage appointments, especially of assessors and registrars. He could fill vacancies in state, county, and local elections and could appoint county officials. The governor's power to designate the official newspaper in each county in which legal notices were to appear helped to counterbalance a hostile political opposition.

The legislative program under the new constitution established a system of fees and commissions for collection of taxes that was conducive to corruption. Tax assessors were given 3 percent of the collections made on their assessments; sheriffs received 5 percent of theirs. The solicitor general received a fee of 10 percent on the collections he made of old bank debts, using the power of the state. The Arkansas secretary of state received fees for issuing commissions to county officials.

Much constructive legislation was passed by the 1868 legislature, including the building of levees along rivers, reclamation of swamplands, the establishment of free public schools, and the creation of state institutions for the physically handicapped. A bill of 14 July 1868 gave blacks the same social, economic, and political rights as whites. Racial discrimination was prohibited in public transportation, housing, restaurants, and businesses.

Governor Clayton's first nine months in office were a time of great violence in Arkansas, engendered in part by the organization of the Ku Klux Klan in April 1868. When murders and intimidation became commonplace, the governor proclaimed martial law in eleven counties and organized the state militia to restore order. The number of murders and outbreaks of violence was enormous; specific instances included the killing of a congressman and the wounding of a state representative while en route to a Republican meeting. One of Clayton's militia captains and a former Confederate general were also murdered. Intimidation was so widespread that it was difficult to find people willing to serve as voting registrars.

Many Arkansans viewed the situation differently, of course, believing that Clayton had declared martial law in order to give himself greater direct power and had used black troops to intimidate white Arkansans. Frustrated by a lack of political power, Arkansans resorted to extralegal and illegal means of political expression. Political justifications for their actions often appeared in the testimony of former Klansmen.

An influential historian, Thomas S. Staples, thought Clayton "exaggerated every local disturbance into an indisputable evidence of the diabolical KKK. The end which some of Clayton's secret agents or corps of imported detectives met was enough to convince a man of Clayton's type that nothing short of the strong arm of martial law could save the state from anarchy."

The national government was well aware of what was happening in Arkansas, but when Clayton requested arms, he got none. President Johnson was unsympathetic and Gideon Welles, secretary of the navy, was openly hostile. The Radicals were not strong enough in Congress to legislate aid, and Gen. John M. Schofield, secretary of war, refused Clayton's request to use government arms in the federal arsenal at Little Rock without congressional appropriation. Welles regarded the problem as one of partisan politics, not as criminal or insurrectionary. At a cabinet meeting on 23 October 1868, he wondered "if the Governor of Arkansas was afraid of the people of Arkansas?" He opposed letting Clayton have arms "for his party" to permit "the black and ignorant element" to control "the intelligent white population." Welles called Clayton's alarm "The unreasonable apprehension of a party leader who feared the people he professed to govern."

Clayton sought unsuccessfully to borrow arms from the governors of other states. He finally sent state agents to purchase arms but could find no steamship company willing to handle the cargo. Ever resourceful, Clayton chartered a steamer, the *Hesper,* but it was run aground by another boat, boarded, and the arms confiscated. Federal authorities could have been expected to respond to such piracy on an interstate waterway (the Mississippi River near Memphis), but they did not.

Eventually order was restored, sometimes by the militia and sometimes by local posses. Many Klansmen were repelled by the Klan's activities and left the organization. Clayton revoked martial law in January 1869; two months later the Klan in Arkansas disbanded.

Throughout these harrowing months, Governor Clayton displayed firmness, decisiveness, and personal courage though his life was often endangered, particularly since his political opponents would have much preferred to have Lieutenant Governor Johnson in power instead of Clayton. One example of Clayton's courage was his appeal for order at a public meeting at Lewisburg in Conway County without taking any troops for his own protection.

By 1869 there was a visible lack of Republican party unity. Opposition to the regular party organization centered more on personalities than on ideological differences. Governor Clayton apparently did not make a sharp distinction between loyalty to the party and loyalty to himself. As party leader, he sought to run his organization as he had commanded his battalion. Resentment resulted, especially when Clayton, following his motto, "men that do the work shall have the rewards," distributed patronage primarily to those who had shown personal loyalty to him.

Intraparty strife surfaced on 8 April 1869 when Lieutenant Governor Johnson and seventeen state legislators met to organize a new party in opposition to Clayton. This group charged Clayton with criminal abuse of his power as commander in chief of the state militia, criminal and corrupt mismanagement of railroad interests through his "unfair distribution of state aid," and extravagant appropriations for the state government.

The new organization sought to attract the old Whigs of Arkansas who, though unionists, had never been nationalists, believing as they did in state and sectional autonomy within the federal Union. They established the *Liberal* as a party newspaper and formally organized the Liberal Republican party of Arkansas on 14 October 1869 with Joseph Brooks as one of the principal leaders. The new party called for greater economy in government, a reduction of gubernatorial powers, and universal manhood suffrage.

A rather startling incident involving this party split occurred in the summer of 1869 when Clayton went to New York on state funding matters. He did not notify Lieutenant Governor Johnson that he was going to be out of the state, but some of Clayton's political enemies learned of his absence and requested the lieutenant governor, who was at home in northern Arkansas, to go immediately to Little Rock to assume the office of governor that Clayton had allegedly "vacated" by leaving the state. Clayton hastened back to Little Rock to occupy "the governor's office" as well as "the office of governor" and beat Johnson to Little Rock, thus averting a virtual coup within the state government. Rumors suggested that Lieutenant Governor Johnson might even have had Clayton arrested and impeached by the legislature.

Johnson charged Clayton and some of his associates with corruption in awarding state aid to railroads and in handling the state debt.

Clayton responded by initiating quo warranto proceedings against Johnson, forcing him to show legally how he held his office. This charge was no more than legal harassment, and the matter was later dropped.

The schism between the governor and lieutenant governor complicated Governor Clayton's ambition to become Senator Clayton. Clayton was elected to the U.S. Senate by the Arkansas legislature on 10 January 1871 by a rather large margin, much of it apparently motivated by the prospect of removing Clayton from the state government and replacing him with Lieutenant Governor Johnson. The legislature elected in 1870 had a larger number of Democrats than its predecessor, so each of the three political factions—regular Republicans, Liberal Republicans, and Democrats—were more evenly divided.

But Clayton was not to be eliminated so easily. He wanted to go to the Senate, but not until the governor's office was protected from Johnson. Quo warranto proceedings were again initiated against Johnson in the legislature but failed by one vote. Finally Clayton demonstrated either a sense of humor (which he seemed to lack) or his influence in Washington even in those early years by offering Johnson the federal office of minister to the Sandwich Islands, a post that Johnson declined.

At this juncture, the anti-Clayton forces, comprised of Liberal Republicans and Democrats, seized the initiative and brought impeachment proceedings against Clayton, charging him with conspiracy to unlawfully deprive Lieutenant Governor Johnson of his office, with unlawfully removing public officials from office, with directing election frauds, and with misusing his powers to issue railroad bonds. However, two legislative inquiries failed to find evidence against Clayton, and the legislature dropped the prosecution.

Arrangements were then made (specifically by whom is not clear) for Arkansas Secretary of State Robert J. T. White to resign; Clayton offered to appoint Johnson as his successor. Johnson, "now battered and beaten," accepted. According to historian Orval T. Driggs Jr., White later testified (at an unspecified time and unspecified place) that he had been paid $5,000 in cash and $25,000 in bonds for agreeing to the deal. However, in the 1872 special congressional investigation of "Allegations against Senator Powell Clayton," the official report stated that White "swears that months afterward he received some money through Senator Clayton, but he explains what it was for, and states positively that it was not in consideration of his vacating the office of Secretary of State." White claimed that he resigned simply in the interest of party harmony. The legislature again elected Clayton to the Senate and the pro-Clayton president of the Arkansas senate, Ozro A. Hadley, became governor in March 1871.

Clayton's three-year "reign" as governor was a turbulent period. Attacks on him were virulent and scurrilous; hostility and character assassinations characterize much of what has been written about him. He was charged with all sorts of infamous deeds, from being a dictator motivated by a desire to "humiliate the Southern people," to murdering Gov. Jeff Davis's aunt. He was impeached by the Arkansas legislature and investigated by the U.S. Congress, but both times the motivation seemed clearly political and the charges were dropped. Clayton's enemies were more than anxious to find him criminally guilty of something; that they were never able to do so is an indication of either his astuteness or his honesty. Comments from his enemies on the question of corruption or integrity are revealing. Margaret Rose, wife of distinguished Arkansas jurist U. M. Rose, wrote many years later: "I do not think Clayton enriched himself as did those under him—perhaps he had a kind of pride that kept him from it."

The *Arkansas Gazette* reported as late as August 1896 that the state auditor had not found Clayton connected to the fraudulent issuance of bonds. Staples, in his study, *Reconstruction in Arkansas, 1862–1874,* reported a damaging rumor that "a carpetbagger" had negotiated for aid for an unspecified railroad company on the condition that Clayton received $300,000 in railroad bonds. But, in Staple's words, "there is no conclusive evidence that Clayton ever received railroad bonds for granting state aid bonds." Staples then added the gratuitous comment: "Neither is it clear that he and the commissioners received no rewards in other forms."

Two persistent issues of Clayton's administration plagued him occasionally throughout his political career. One was the question of the governor's handling of state aid to railroads and the other was the issue of which part of the state debt should be funded, the "Holford bonds" controversy.

George H. Thompson, in his *Arkansas and Reconstruction,* saw Arkansas's Reconstruction history as a legitimate but too optimistic effort to restore state credit and to help develop natural resources by encouraging and aiding railroad construction in key areas of the state. Unsubstantiated allegations were made from time to time that Clayton had received kickbacks in exchange for approving state aid to specific railroads, but the available evidence indicated the contrary. Clayton wrote in 1914:

I was frequently criticized for my actions in connection with the issuance of bonds to aid in the construction of the various railroads and while I was never openly charged with appropriating any of them for my own use, it was strongly hinted that I had been well paid for the aid I had given to the railroads.

I will state positively that until the year 1892 when ten of them came into my possession, I had never owned nor held a single bond that had been issued to aid in the construction of railroads.

It should be noted, however, that in 1873, not long after his term as governor ended, Clayton assumed the presidency of the newly consolidated Little Rock, Mississippi River, and Texas Railroad Company. Clayton said he accepted the position "very reluctantly" but finally did so because the line ran through his Pine Bluff plantation on ground that he had donated to the railroads.

There seemed little reason to doubt Thompson's conclusion that Reconstruction was a "period of exaggerated expectations arising from the use of state credit to finance the development of natural resources." Add to this "the hostility felt toward a de facto government" and it is easy to understand charges of graft and corruption. Thompson asked the provocative question, "If the establishment of credit had been successful, would the deeds of the political villains appear so dark?"

Clayton was the best-known so-called political villain in Arkansas during Reconstruction. He had scarcely arrived in Washington to begin his single term as senator when he was indicted by an Arkansas grand jury (15 May 1871) for issuing a false certificate of election in the 1870 election. Clayton had disallowed votes in several townships in the Third Congressional District for alleged fraud. Everett Swinney, who studied the case in detail, concluded that the "*United States v. Powell Clayton* was a political prosecution from beginning to end."

By 1871 the regular Republicans, led by Clayton, were known as "Minstrels," and the opposing reform Republican faction, led by Joseph Brooks, was called "Brindletails." The Brindletails had "broken with Clayton over patronage matters" and now sought to break his hold over Arkansas Republican politics. Both the district attorney and the marshal involved in the case were Brindletails and the grand jury that framed the indictment was dominated by anti-Clayton men. Swinney did admit, however, that "it is difficult, if not impossible, to know what the truth may have been. Clayton was certainly quite capable of dissimulation." The case backfired on the Brindletails. Clayton persuaded President Grant to remove W. G. Whipple, the district attorney, and Marshal R. F. Catterson from office; he replaced them with Minstrels—regular Republicans.

Clayton's political enemies next attempted to secure his removal from the Senate or his censure by it, as a "joint select committee" investigated whether Clayton had "corruptly used his executive power as Governor of Arkansas" to gain his Senate seat. The majority conclusion was that he did not.

Clayton profited politically from this congressional investigation. He later wrote that it had the "effect of making me solid with the administration and with the Republican United States Senators, and put me in complete control of the situation at home. I was made the referee for Arkansas for all Federal appointments in every department of the Government." This also led to his appointment as the Republican national committeeman from Arkansas in 1872.

The 1872 election saw continued intraparty squabbles between the Minstrels and Brindletails, which eventually gave Arkansas Democrats the opportunity to regain dominance in state politics. On 3 March 1873, in an election with a surprisingly small turnout, Arkansas voters accepted the removal of constitutional restrictions on the franchise. The way was open for the Democratic party to gain control of the legislature in 1874. Party strategy was a cautious policy of maintaining good relations with Republican Gov. Elisha Baxter. Baxter's eventual replacement of certain key Republican officeholders with Democrats led to an intraparty power struggle between Minstrel and Brindletail Republicans, known as the Brooks-Baxter War. In an effort to prevent the Democratic party from regaining control of the Arkansas government, Clayton sponsored the Senate resolution that created the Poland committee on 27 May 1874 to inquire into affairs in Arkansas. The committee conducted hearings in Washington twice, and members of the committee went to Little Rock twice. After prolonged debate, the Poland committee concluded that it was improper for the federal government to interfere with the existing government in Arkansas.

After again unsuccessfully seeking intervention by a sympathetic but cautious President Grant, Clayton finally capitulated and advised his followers: "The action of Congress on Arkansas affairs is conclusive. The validity of the new constitution and the government established thereunder ought no longer to be questioned. It is the duty of Republicans to accept the verdict and render the same acquiescence which we would have demanded had the case been reversed."

Clayton did, of course, blame Baxter for the Republican loss of power in Arkansas; in 1914 he wrote: "from the moment Elisha Baxter surrendered the State Government to the Democrats that party became and has remained supreme in the state."

More fundamentally, the national Republican party, still firmly in control of the Congress, was no longer interested in imposing its rule on the South. Clayton must have realized this because he finally gave up his legal and political maneuvers to try to maintain political domination over a hostile state.

These events showed Clayton's basic orientation toward Washington. With the Republican party permanently unseated from power at the state level, he sought to establish Republican influence in scattered local enclaves within Arkansas (particularly in the northwest) and to secure Republican control of federal patronage positions within the state. With the exception of the administrations of Pres. Grover Cleveland, Republicans controlled the presidency from 1868 to 1913 and, therefore, Clayton, as leader of the Arkansas Republican party, controlled all federal appointments in the state of Arkansas.

Since Clayton's political influence depended particularly on his control of patronage, and since the availability of federal patronage depended on the election of Republican presidents, he took an active role in all presidential elections in the late nineteenth century. He influenced the nomination process as well as the election itself. For nearly forty years, he was a member of the Republican National Committee. Although Arkansas remained his power base, his political influence was not limited to that state. Since delegates to national conventions were apportioned on the basis of state population rather than on party strength within the state, Arkansas had a sizable delegation to national conventions and, occasionally, could exert significant influence on the nominating process. During the election itself, Clayton campaigned nationally.

By 1896 the state was set for the most significant presidential election in decades. Republicans were anxious to return to power; Democrats were determined to use their power to stay there; and militant Populists clamored that neither major party was coming to grips with the growing problems of the new industrialism and the plight of the American farmer.

As a member of the Republican National Committee and boss of one of the reliable Southern state organizations, Clayton was an important part of William McKinley's strategy for winning the Republican nomination. Clayton delivered the entire Arkansas delegation to McKinley and in each case of contested delegates he voted for the "regular" McKinley delegates.

In the election campaign of 1896, Clayton was in charge of the Republican speakers' bureau for the East Coast. He was not really needed in Arkansas during the campaign since Republicans did not expect to capture Arkansas's eight electoral votes. Whatever the victory of McKinley and the Republicans might mean to the nation as a whole, it certainly meant that an enormous number of federal offices would be occupied by Republicans instead of by Democrats. Clayton was not first in line for patronage, but he had amassed a lifetime of political indebtedness by his faithful and productive service for the Republican party. Clayton now considered the time right to seek appointive office for himself. McKinley even considered him for a cabinet-level position, but Clayton sometime earlier had decided that he wanted to be minister to Mexico, a rather quiet, pleasant post that not only paid $17,500 a year plus a $5,000 contingency fund but also would allow him enough leisure time to continue his involvement in Arkansas Republican politics through his longtime friend and assistant in state politics, Harmon L. Remmel, a Little Rock insurance executive.

Clayton served as ambassador from 1897 to 1905, a quiescent period in Mexican-American relations. From Mexico City Clayton controlled Republican politics and patronage in Arkansas and took frequent leaves of absence from his embassy post to travel to Arkansas or Washington in order to maintain that control. Clayton's political viewpoints, his style, and personality suited him quite well for the position of ambassador to Mexico during the Porfirio Diaz era. He acted in accordance with the expectations of both the American and Mexican governments.

When Ambassador Clayton resigned his diplomatic post in 1905, he returned to Washington, D.C., rather than to Arkansas. He remained a member of the Republican National Committee and continued to control federal patronage in Arkansas. The state central committee of the Republican party consistently obtained his advice and consent before presenting its recommendations for appointments to the national administration. As late as 1912, Pres. William Howard Taft still wrote this sort of message to Clayton: "Whom do you wish appointed as postmaster at Pine Bluff?"

Not long after Woodrow Wilson's election as president in 1912 and the return of a Democratic national administration for the first time in sixteen years, Clayton resigned as Republican national committeeman from Arkansas and retired from politics. He spent the remaining months of life in Washington and died there on 25 August 1914 at the age of eighty-one. Following private funeral services, he was buried in Arlington National Cemetery with military honors.

ELISHA BAXTER

1873–1874

ELISHA BAXTER (1 September 1827–31 May 1899), merchant, farmer, and attorney, was born in Rutherford County, North Carolina. His father, William Baxter, had emigrated from Ireland in 1789 and had settled in western North Carolina; Elisha was the sixth son of William and his second wife, Catherine Lee Baxter. Elisha's formal education was limited. He sought and received an appointment to the military academy at West Point but gave it up at his father's insistence. At the age of twenty, he entered the mercantile business at Rutherfordton in partnership with his brother-in-law Spencer Eaves. In 1849 he married Harriet Patton of Rutherford County, by whom he had six children: Millard P., Edward A., Catherine M., George E., Hattie O., and Fannie E. Edward became a well-known physician in northwestern Arkansas.

In 1852 Baxter moved to Batesville, Arkansas, continuing in business with his brother Taylor A. Baxter. Elected mayor of the town in 1853, he was chosen as state representative from Independence County in 1854 to the tenth general assembly. In the following year, his firm failed, and Baxter went to work in the office of the Batesville *Independent Balance* as a typographer for twenty dollars a month. At the same time he studied law under Hulbert F. Fairchild (associate justice, Arkansas State Supreme Court, 1860-1864). In 1856 he was admitted to the bar. He regained his seat in the legislature two years later, serving in the twelfth general assembly. In the congressional elections of 1858 and 1860, he was a political ally of Rep. Thomas Carmichael Hindman, a noted Southern extremist; prior to that time Baxter is reported to have been a Whig. In 1861 he was elected prosecuting attorney for the Seventh Judicial Circuit. Although he was purported to have been a slaveholder, the evidence offered by the Independence County slave schedule for 1860 is inconclusive. His brother owned a single slave, and an illegible entry in the schedule might have been Baxter's.

Baxter apparently played little if any role in the political events preceding secession in Arkansas. In his autobiography he said he believed secession to be "unjust to the Federal Government" and "disastrous to the people of the South." In May 1862 the Union army of Gen. Samuel Curtis arrived in Batesville and began recruiting Arkansas Union regiments. The command of one of these regiments was offered to Baxter. He declined it, saying "I did not feel that it was my *duty* to make War upon the people of the South." After the federals left the area, the Confederacy reasserted control, and Baxter fled to Missouri. In 1863 he was captured there while teaching school. Arrested and brought to Little Rock to be tried for treason, Baxter escaped and, surviving on green corn and berries, reached Union lines at Springfield, Missouri. Now seeing a duty to fight, he recruited the Fourth Arkansas Mounted Infantry of which he was elected colonel.

Baxter's military service was of short duration. The Union army had occupied Little Rock and had installed Isaac Murphy as governor, and Murphy appointed Baxter to the state supreme court. Again his tenure was brief, for the new unionist legislature elected Baxter and William Meade "Fishy" Fishback as U.S. senators. The two men journeyed to Washington in a futile effort to convince the Radicals to seat them. The debate over the admission of the Arkansas senators was of key importance to the Radicals in formulating a response to Pres. Abraham Lincoln's plans for presidential Reconstruction, and it set the stage for the bitterly partisan struggles over Radical Reconstruction that followed. On the floor of the Senate, the career of Fishback, who had been a member of the secession convention and who had voted for secession, was explored in merciless detail, while Baxter's credentials were hardly discussed. On returning to Arkansas, Baxter played a minor role in the establishment of Republican hegemony under the constitution of 1868. On 25 July 1868 he was appointed by Gov. Powell Clayton as judge of the Third Judicial Circuit, and the following year he became registrar in bankruptcy for the First Congressional District, holding both positions simultaneously.

Baxter's return to political prominence was a result of splits within the Republican party. By 1872 there were two major factions. The regulars or "Minstrels," so called because of the former occupation of one of their leaders, supported Clayton and his policies of law and order, education, and economic development. The opposition consisted of Republicans associated with the national Liberal Republican movement, who opposed the corruption of the Grant administration and advocated a policy of amnesty for ex-Confederates. Locally the

Liberals tended to include a number of native white Republican leaders (scalawags) who felt they had been passed over in the distribution of patronage in favor of outsiders (carpetbaggers). They made opposition to Clayton's dictatorial ways the central feature of their platform. Their popular name, "Brindletails," was derived from a description of their 1872 gubernatorial candidate, Joseph Brooks, an Iowan and thus a carpetbagger who appealed primarily to scalawags. To counter this threat, the faction composed primarily of carpetbaggers nominated a scalawag, Elisha Baxter. The contest was solely between Brooks and Baxter, as the Democratic-Conservatives after some deliberation and a number of false starts, decided to let the Republicans fight it out among themselves.

In the campaign, both men offered future amnesty to ex-Confederates and promised clean government and retrenchment. The real battle occurred after the votes were cast: it took the Minstrel election officials two months to work their way through the ballots and declare a winner. The most recent historian of the period, George H. Thompson, declares that in reality Brooks polled more votes than Baxter, but the "official" returns show that Baxter received 41,681 votes to Brooks's 38,415. Ballots from four counties that, according to Brooks's supporters, gave their candidate a majority were declared invalid, and the returns reveal that Baxter lost in the southwest and northwest but won in the delta. Besides electing Baxter governor, the voters also gave control of the legislature to the Minstrels. However, when the Minstrel-elected congressmen presented their credentials in the House, they were challenged, and W. W. Wilshire was ousted in favor of Brooks supporter T. M. Gunter. Brooks immediately began collecting evidence of election fraud, but under the constitution of 1868 he would have to take his appeal to the state legislature where his friends were few.

Baxter's inauguration took place on 6 January 1873. Besides making some general conciliatory remarks, he promised to work for the enfranchisement of ex-Confederates before the next general election. With his blessing, the legislature submitted a franchise amendment to the voters in March, and it was overwhelmingly passed. As Baxter grew in popularity with the Democratic-Conservatives, he declined in the estimation of the Republicans, principally Chief Justice John "Poker Jack" McClure, editor of the *Daily Republican*. The first crisis of the new administration was what the *Gazette* called the "McClure-Baxter War." First, newspaper criticism of Baxter appeared. Then McClure allegedly made a deal with Brooks to revive the issue of the legitimacy

of Baxter's election. However, the attempt to get Brooks's case introduced before the legislature was defeated, and though Baxter skir-
mished with McClure, he remained on friendly terms with Sens.
Powell Clayton and Stephen Dorsey.

McClure made his next move in the summer of 1873. A quo warranto was requested by T. D. W. Yonley, the attorney general, from the
state supreme court. According to the *Gazette,* if the writ was granted,
Baxter would be removed and Lt. Gov. Volney Voltaire Smith, a
Republican, would be made acting governor until the trial could take
place. Since, according to this theory, McClure did not want to dispose
of Baxter simply to install Brooks, the legal proceedings would have
been made to last until the next election. But the plan failed because
McClure could not secure the support of his colleagues on the state
supreme court. The rumor that the old militia officers were in
McClure's camp led Baxter to make another overture to the
Democratic-Conservatives: he appointed Col. Robert C. Newton, who
had arrested him in Missouri in 1863, to command the state militia.
Through the governor's extensive appointive power, newspapers holding public printing contracts and appointed officials were brought
around to Baxter's position.

The following year presented Baxter with new challenges. Although
the governor had signed $400,000 in railroad bonds, he decided on
16 March 1874 not to issue any more, even though the company
requesting the bonds, the Arkansas Central Railroad, was politically
associated with Senator Dorsey. Baxter not only declined to issue any
new bonds but, in an elaborate opinion eventually sustained by the
state supreme court, held that all the bonds issued were without constitutional sanction. Thus the entire economic program of the
Republicans and the state's good faith and credit were placed in jeopardy. The crisis united Republicans of every interest as the McClure,
Dorsey, and Clayton forces were compelled to rally around Brooks as
the only way to save Reconstruction in Arkansas.

The Brooks-Baxter War began as Pulaski Circuit Judge John
Whytock called up from his docket the case of *Brooks v. Baxter,* and,
in the absence of Baxter's attorney, declared Brooks the de jure governor of Arkansas. McClure, who had sworn in Baxter, now swore in
Brooks, and Brooks and about a dozen armed men then hurried to
the governor's office in the statehouse and physically expelled Baxter.
Baxter retired to a nearby hotel, the famous Anthony House, as both
sides armed for war. In the following month four bloody skirmishes
occurred in Little Rock, near Pine Bluff, and on the Arkansas River

with perhaps fifty men killed or wounded. The crisis sharply divided the state. Ex-Confederates could be found on both sides, although slightly more of them supported Baxter than Brooks; blacks could also be found on both sides, perhaps about equally divided.

More important than any development in the state was what action President Grant would take in Washington. Since Baxter had been the recognized governor for over a year, the burden of proof was on Brooks to show cause why Baxter should not be sustained. Brooks benefited from the support of Clayton and Dorsey but was opposed by the astute Democratic-Conservative leaders, notably Augustus Hill Garland. In the end Grant sustained Baxter. Brooks's forces were disbanded after 15 May 1874 as a jubilant Baxter returned in triumph to the barricaded and stinking statehouse. The legislature rejected Brooks's final pleas and paved the way for a constitutional convention to complete the dismantling of Reconstruction. Brooks was pensioned off with a patronage appointment as Little Rock postmaster. When the House of Representatives sent a congressional investigating committee (the Poland committee) to Arkansas to take testimony, all was quiet in the state. Congressional acceptance of the committee's majority report, which concluded that things in Arkansas were best left alone, formally brought to a close the Reconstruction phase of Arkansas history.

During the summer of 1874 the new constitutional convention met and drafted a replacement for the 1868 constitution. The new document emasculated the powers of the governor, limited the taxing power, and returned government to the hands of the ex-Confederates. Baxter acquiesced in their actions, including the loss of two years from his four-year term of office as governor. After some discussion, the Democratic-Conservative party convention in September tendered the gubernatorial nomination to Baxter only to have him refuse it. The convention then made the request unanimous but again Baxter refused. However, in 1878 he sought elevation to the U.S. Senate only to be rejected by the Democratically controlled legislature. The private opinion of some Democrats was that Baxter had to be offered the gubernatorial nomination out of gratitude for his sacrifice but that the demands of the Senate were beyond his capacity. In addition, the pro-Brooks forces felt that Baxter's past participation in frauds was too great to warrant supporting him. Thereafter he lived on a small farm near Batesville, practicing law until his death in 1899. He was buried in Oak Lawn Cemetery beside his wife who had died the preceding year.

The vacillation that characterized Baxter's political career in Arkansas contrasted sharply with the posture of his brother John Baxter an able and consistent unionist from North Carolina and Tennessee. Elisha Baxter seemed to waver between being a spokesman of the hill country yeomanry and the envious emulator of the rich planters. His troubles as governor began when he turned his back on Senator Clayton and called into question the central element of the policy of the Republican party—railroad construction. This betrayal made him a hero to men anxious to overthrow Republicanism and all its works. At his death the *Arkansas Gazette* suggested that the white Democrats of Arkansas should build a monument to mark the grave of the man who overthrew Reconstruction in Arkansas. That no such monument was erected does not deny the significance of Baxter's contribution to the restoration of Democratic rule in the state.

AUGUSTUS HILL GARLAND

1874–1877

AUGUSTUS HILL GARLAND (11 June 1832–26 January 1899), attorney, was born in Tipton County, Tennessee, the son of Rufus and Barbara (Hill) Garland. Early in 1833 his family moved to Lost Prairie on the Red River where his father had a store. After his father's death later the same year, his mother moved the family to nearby Spring Hill. In 1836 she married Thomas Hubbard, and the family settled in Washington, Arkansas, where Garland began his education at a private school. He later attended St. Mary's College in Lebanon, Kentucky, and graduated from St. Joseph's College in Bardstown, Kentucky, in 1849. Returning to Arkansas, he taught school in 1850 in the Mine Creek community, Sevier County, before beginning the study of law under Simon P. Sanders, clerk of Hempstead County. In 1853 Garland was admitted to the bar, formed a law firm with his stepfather, and married Sarah Virginia Sanders, his mentor's daughter. He became active in conservative politics, and his contacts with former Whigs led to a partnership with Ebenezer Cummins of Little Rock, once a law partner of Albert Pike. Cummin's death less than a year later left Garland with a thriving law office, and he was admitted to the bar of the U.S. Supreme Court in 1860. In the election of that year, Garland worked for the Constitutional Union party, supporting John Bell for president and his stepfather for governor. Garland himself was chosen for presidential elector in 1860.

Garland was elected to the secession convention in 1861 as a representative of Pulaski County. A unionist, he opposed secession during the first session of the convention, but following President Lincoln's call for troops, he joined the majority in voting for the ordinance of secession. He was chosen as one of five delegates to the provisional congress where he was the youngest member of that body. In 1861 in an election contested by Jilson P. Johnson, Garland was elected to represent Arkansas's Third Congressional District in the House of

Representatives of the Confederate Congress. He remained in the House until 1864 when he was appointed to the Confederate Senate after the death of Charles B. Mitchell. A conservative constitutionalist, Garland worked to establish a supreme court and generally supported the Jefferson Davis administration, except for his opposition to the laws suspending the writ of habeas corpus. In May 1865 Garland and E. C. Boudinot went to Little Rock at the request of Gov. Harris Flanagin and arranged to turn over the state's records to Gov. Isaac Murphy.

On 15 July 1865 Garland received a pardon from President Johnson and returned to his law practice. His cases included *Mississippi v. Johnson,* which sought to enjoin the president from enforcing the Reconstruction Acts, and *Osborn v. Nicholson,* which established the validity of contracts for the sale of slaves. His most important case was Ex parte *Garland* in which he defended his right to appear before the U.S. Supreme Court. His name had stayed on the roll of attorneys, and his cases had been continued, but when Garland returned to the Court in 1865, the rules of practice had been changed to require lawyers to take the ironclad oath that they had never borne arms against the United States nor held office in a government hostile to it. In his brief, Garland argued that this requirement was an ex post facto law and therefore unconstitutional, and that it abridged the presidential pardoning powers defined in the Constitution. In a five-to-four decision, the Court agreed.

Although the Arkansas legislature elected Garland to the U.S. Senate in 1867, he was not allowed to take his seat since the state had not been readmitted to the Union. Garland then withdrew from active politics to attend to his law practice, but he remained an important figure in the Democratic-Conservative party. His name was mentioned for governor in 1872, and he was considered for the Senate in 1873. A newly formed county was named for him. In the Brooks-Baxter War in 1874, Garland was a leader of the Baxter forces and served as deputy secretary of state. He actively supported the calling of the 1874 constitutional convention and, as the Democratic nominee for governor, led the drive to get the new constitution approved by the voters.

On 12 November 1874 Garland was inaugurated as governor in a quiet ceremony. He was faced with an unusual situation. A congressional committee was investigating political affairs in Arkansas as a result of the Brooks-Baxter War. Garland was called to testify about his inauguration and about whether the state was peaceful. The committee's report was not issued until March 1875, so until that time

Garland's administration was hampered by the possibility that the committee would declare that the 1874 election and the new constitution were invalid.

The most serious problem facing Garland was the state's finances. The state debt had risen to over $17 million; more than $13 million of this debt had been acquired during Reconstruction, mostly from the issuing of state scrip and railroad and levee bonds. Garland tackled this problem through the use of a sinking fund and through a board of finance with powers to negotiate loans for current expenses. As a result of these and other measures, the debt had been substantially reduced by the time he left office.

Although organizing the state government under the new constitution and solving the state's financial problems occupied most of his term, Governor Garland was also involved with other issues. A new lease for operating the state penitentiary was bringing money into the treasury, but he worried that the buildings and grounds were too small and that the system of working convicts encouraged escapes. In education he was an enthusiastic supporter of the Arkansas Industrial University in Fayetteville, and he implemented the legislation establishing the Branch Normal College in Pine Bluff to train black teachers. He also sought financial support from the legislature for the schools for the blind and deaf.

Convinced that a growing population would bring prosperity to the state, Garland made several efforts to improve the state's image and to encourage immigration. He urged the legislature to establish a bureau of statistics and a bureau of agriculture, mining, and manufacturing. He named James Smithee as the commissioner of immigration and attended regional meetings on the subject. The most impressive part of his campaign to improve the state's image was the Arkansas Building at the Centennial Exposition in Philadelphia in 1876. An octagon eighty-two feet in diameter, topped with a fifty-foot dome, the building, filled with exhibits of the state's natural resources and agricultural products, won an award for its unique features. The state seal and the fountain from that building are now at Arkansas's first state capitol in Little Rock.

Garland did not run for reelection in 1876. In early 1877 he was once again elected to the U.S. Senate. While there he earned respect for his committee work and gained a reputation as an authority on the Constitution. Although his brother was a leader of the Greenback party in Arkansas, Garland supported sound money measures and tariff reform and opposed the movement in the Arkansas legislature to repudiate certain bonds. He also supported internal improvements and other issues that would help his state, including civil-service reform and the Blair bill to give federal aid to schools. Concerned about flooding along the Mississippi River, he sponsored a bill giving the new Mississippi River Commission the power to construct and repair levees. The death of his wife on Christmas Eve of 1877 left him responsible for his four surviving children, so his mother joined the family to manage his Washington household.

On 9 March 1885 Garland resigned his Senate seat to become attorney general under Pres. Grover Cleveland. He was chosen because of the ability he had demonstrated as a lawyer and as a member of the Senate Judiciary Committee, as well as to help balance the cabinet by providing a Southern and Western point of view. During his term of office, he was involved in cases on the exclusion of Chinese immigrants, the limitations on foreign investors, and the abuse of railroad land grants. He urged President Cleveland to support legislation to regulate interstate commerce and pressed Congress to establish a federal prison system. Much of his work as attorney general suffered from a scandal involving the patent for the telephone. Garland owned stock in the Pan-Electric Telephone Company, which was challenging the patent held by Bell. Without Garland's knowledge, a member of his department began a suit to test the validity of the Bell patent, which would have made Garland's stock very valuable if the suit had been successful. Garland declared he had not used his influence on behalf of Pan-Electric, and the suit was dropped, but a congressional investigation kept the situation before the public for almost a year.

When his term as attorney general ended, Garland refused offers to be nominated again to the Senate and, remaining in Washington, resumed his law practice. He also tried his hand at writing, publishing a pamphlet, *Third Term Presidential,* in 1896, and a book, *Experience in the Supreme Court of the United States,* in 1898. He was a coauthor of *A Treatise on the Constitution and Jurisdiction of the United States Courts,* a two-volume work also published in 1898. On 26 January 1899 Garland collapsed while arguing a case before the Supreme Court; he died a few minutes later. A service was held in Washington before his body was returned to Little Rock where he was buried in Mount Holly Cemetery. The *Arkansas Gazette,* feeling that the modest headstone placed at his grave by the family was not enough, conducted a public subscription drive and erected a memorial.

Garland was most often described as a modest man, full of humor, kindness, and thoughtfulness. He served his state in critical times, restoring its credit and bringing about a period of peace after the uncertainties of Reconstruction. He went on to serve his nation and, as of 1994, was one of two Arkansans appointed to a cabinet position.

WILLIAM READ MILLER

1877–1881

WILLIAM READ MILLER (23 November 1823–29 November 1887), attorney and the first native Arkansan elected governor of the state, was born and reared on a farm near Batesville, Arkansas Territory, one of three sons and seven children of John and Clara (Moore) Miller. In 1814 his grandfather, Simon Miller, who probably migrated from Virginia, settled in an area that later became Randolph County. His father, John Miller, settled eventually at Batesville, where he was register of the U.S. Land Office and was active in Democratic politics, serving as a presidential elector in 1836 and 1840. Described by an acquaintance as "a charitable, public-spirited, plain, unassuming gentleman," Governor Miller stood almost six feet tall and possessed "a business rather than a professional manner."

Educated in local schools, Miller early stated a preference for politics and law. Two historians, Josiah H. Shinn and Dallas T. Herndon, recount an incident from Miller's youth when, in the course of the 1836 presidential campaign, he exchanged shouted remarks with the Whig notable C. F. M. Noland, but their interpretations of this altercation differ. Herndon offers it as an instance of political precocity, but Shinn sees it as evidence that Miller was "a holy terror as a boy." There seems, however, to be no reason to think of Miller as anything other than an ambitious and studious youth. Although his father questioned his decision to study law, Miller was ultimately admitted to the Arkansas bar in 1868. In the meantime, he served from 1848 to 1854 as clerk of Independence County, leaving to accept Gov. Elias Nelson Conway's appointment to fill the unexpired term of state auditor C. C. Danley, who had resigned. The legislature named the Know-Nothing candidate, A. S. Huey, to the auditor's office in 1855, and Miller was appointed by Conway to be accountant of the State Real-Estate Bank, in which capacity he and William M. Gouge prepared a 192-page *Report of the Accountants . . . to Investigate the Affairs of the Real*

Estate Bank of Arkansas (Little Rock, 1856). In 1856 the legislature returned him to the auditor's office.

On 27 January 1849 Miller married Susan Elizabeth Bevens, the daughter of Judge William C. Bevens. The couple had seven children, four of whom grew to maturity: Louisa, born at Batesville in 1850; Effie; William R.; and Hugh, all born at Little Rock. Two other daughters, Haddie and Alice, died before their father and were buried at Little Rock.

Reelected state auditor in 1858, 1860, and 1862, Miller served until 18 April 1864 when he was succeeded by J. R. Berry. Two years later, he again became auditor after defeating Berry but was removed during Reconstruction in 1868. Admitted to the bar in that year, he returned to Batesville where he apparently practiced law. Family tradition had it that his home was sold for nonpayment of the direct tax levied on officials of the Confederate state governments. With the victory of the conservative Democrats, he was returned to the auditor's office in the election of 1874, and it was during this term that he published a seventy-three-page *Digest of the Revenue Laws of the State of Arkansas* (Little Rock, 1875).

In anticipation of Gov. Augustus Hill Garland's elevation to the U.S. Senate, several newspapers in early 1876 proposed Miller as a successor likely to continue Garland's policies as governor. He was nominated by the Democratic convention in June, winning over a distinguished field that included Simon P. Hughes, Thomas Fletcher, and Grandison Royston. Miller campaigned on a reconciliation platform and offered assurances to black voters, winning by a substantial margin in September over a divided Republican opposition. He seems to have earned a reputation for personal probity and sound financial management. Because he was reluctant to grant pardons to individuals convicted by jury trials and given death sentences, he was sometimes referred to as "the hanging governor." Notwithstanding outbreaks of violence in some counties, his tenure in office was marked by general good feeling, by a continuing commitment to public education and the state university, and above all by a constant effort to redress and establish the state's credit. A movement was afoot to repudiate much of the state's indebtedness by submitting the so-called Fishback Amendment to a popular vote. Miller, Garland, and U. M. Rose led the opposition to debt repudiation but were only temporarily successful in forestalling eventual passage of the amendment. Despite rising Greenback sentiment, however, Miller was easily renominated and reelected in 1878 without Republican opposition. Another bid for renomination failed in 1880, when he encountered resistance to the idea of a third term.

Miller had served on the governing board of the University of Arkansas and had received that institution's honorary doctorate. He was named president of the Kansas City and New Orleans Railroad Company in 1880 and was associated with other railroad enterprises, but he does not seem to have become a wealthy man. After serving as deputy treasurer of the state in 1881–1882, he was returned to his old office of state auditor in the election of 1886, defeating the incumbent for renomination in what was described as an exciting contest. There seems to have been a general feeling "that he needed the position." He died the following year in Little Rock and was buried in Mount Holly Cemetery in a grave that remained unmarked until after his widow's death in 1905.

THOMAS JAMES CHURCHILL
1881–1883

THOMAS JAMES CHURCHILL (10 March 1824–14 May 1905), attorney and planter, was born on his father's farm near Louisville, Jefferson County, Kentucky. He was one of seven children—five boys and two girls—born to Samuel and Abby (Oldham) Churchill. His sister Julia was married to Dr. Luke P. Blackburn, governor of Kentucky. His earliest American ancestors were great-great-grandparents William and Elizabeth (Armistead) Churchill of Middlesex County, Virginia. Great-grandparents were Armistead and Lucy (Harrison) Churchill; their son Armistead was Churchill's grandfather. Churchill was educated in the public schools of Kentucky and was graduated from St. Mary's College at Bardstown in 1844. He received his training in law at Transylvania University in Lexington.

With the outbreak of the Mexican War in 1846, Churchill enlisted as a lieutenant in the First Kentucky Mounted Riflemen commanded by Col. Humphrey Marshall. En route to Mexico, Marshall's command stopped briefly in Little Rock where Lieutenant Churchill was entertained in the home of Judge Benjamin Johnson and there met his future wife, Ann Sevier, the daughter of Sen. Ambrose H. Sevier and the judge's granddaughter. In January 1847 he was with a scouting party of seventeen men in the vicinity of Encarnación when they were captured by the Mexican cavalry. Lieutenant Churchill was held prisoner in Mexico City and then granted the freedom of the city on parole. When American armies under Gen. Winfield Scott advanced on Mexico City, Churchill was moved to Toluca and later released in an exchange of prisoners. By then the war was virtually over.

In 1848 he settled in Little Rock where, on 31 July 1849, he and Ann Sevier were married in Judge Johnson's home. They were the parents of six children: Abbie (or Abby), born 25 March 1854; Samuel J., born 17 March 1856; Ambrose S., born 2 December 1858; Juliet (or Juliette), born 20 January 1861; Emily, born 29 August 1865; and

Matilda (Mathilde), born 15 January 1868. Churchill pursued farming interests on a large plantation near Little Rock. In 1857 Pres. James Buchanan appointed him postmaster at Little Rock, a position he held until 1861.

With the beginning of the Civil War, Churchill raised a regiment of cavalry that was mustered into Confederate service under his command as the First Arkansas Mounted Riflemen. He served with distinction in the battle of Wilson's Creek (or Oak Hills) and the battle of Pea Ridge and on 4 March 1862 was promoted to brigadier general from his original rank of colonel. Churchill's brigade joined E. Kirby Smith and contributed to the victory at Richmond, Kentucky. He was assigned to the Trans-Mississippi Department on 10 December 1862, and on reporting to Gen. Theophilus H. Holmes in Little Rock was given command of the Arkansas-Texas troops defending Arkansas Post. These Confederate forces had the important assignment of blocking Union troop movements up the river. They also threatened the command that was trying to capture Vicksburg. In early January 1863 superior Union forces (50,000 to 60,000 men according to Churchill and other Confederate leaders, 32,000 as reported in federal records) under the command of Gen. John A. McClernand and Admiral Porter launched an attack on Arkansas Post. According to Churchill, only three thousand of the five or six thousand men at his disposal were effective to defend the installation. Inadequate weapons, ineffective gunpowder, and insufficient forces did not prevent Confederate troops from repeatedly repulsing the Union troops during the first two days of fighting. General Holmes ordered Churchill "to hold out until help arrives or all dead." But several unauthorized white flags unexpectedly displayed by some of the Texas troops during the third day of attacks forced the Confederates to surrender on 11 January 1863. The men were paroled and later exchanged. General Churchill was imprisoned for three months at Camp Chase, Ohio, before he was exchanged. He reported to General Bragg in Tennessee and was again assigned to the Trans-Mississippi Department. Major General Churchill—he was promoted 17 March 1863—commanded a division of Arkansas infantrymen and participated in the battles of Pleasant Hill and Jenkins's Ferry and in other lesser engagements before following Smith into Texas where he finally surrendered.

In the so-called Brooks-Baxter War of 1874, Churchill actively supported Baxter and helped to enroll volunteers in his militia. When the Democrats regained control of the state he was elected state treasurer, reelected in 1876 and again in 1878. After twenty-four ballots at the

Democratic state convention, he was nominated for governor in 1880 and defeated his Greenback opponent, W. P. Parker, by a vote of 84,088 to 21,284 in the general election.

A proposed constitutional amendment repudiating the state debt had not been an issue between the candidates. However, failure to approve the amendment resulted in legislation that provided that the auditor and treasurer would not be required "to report the Railroad Aid and Levee Bonds, and what is known as the Holford Bonds, as part of the indebtedness of the State of Arkansas in their biennial reports." Governor Churchill permitted this act to become a law without his signature. Other significant legislative enactments during his term as governor included an act levying a one-mill tax for two years to fund an appropriation of $150,000 for the establishment of a facility for the insane; an appropriation of $10,000 to establish a branch normal school of the Arkansas Industrial University in Pine Bluff; regulations governing the practice of medicine; authorization for the establishment of a medical department of the Arkansas Industrial University in Little Rock; an act to create a state board of health; freight- and passenger-rate regulations on railroads of fifty miles or less in Arkansas; provisions for the collection of overdue taxes; a joint resolution supporting a farmers' congress in St. Louis; and a resolution stating that Arkansas "should be pronounced in three syllables, with the final 's' silent, the 'a' in each syllable with the Italian sound, and accent on the first and last syllables."

Allegations of discrepancies in the treasurer's account for 1874–1880 emerged during the legislative session of 1881. Churchill and his friends were somewhat inept in defending his record as treasurer, while antiadministration Democrats, Republicans, and Greenbackers took advantage of the shortage charges to attempt to discredit the Democratic party and/or Governor Churchill. Committees that examined the treasurer's records encountered pressures and much parliamentary maneuvering by pro- and anti-Churchill groups. The many months of investigation by the committees irritated the governor's critics, especially the editor of the *Arkansas Democrat* who appeared determined to humiliate him. Committee reports fixed the shortage at figures ranging from approximately $14,000 to $233,616. The latter amount was cited in the final committee report presented to Governor Churchill and forwarded by Churchill to Atty. Gen. Charles B. Moore for action. Nothing further was accomplished until Churchill's successor, James Henderson Berry, was in office. On 30 May 1883 a suit against the former treasurer and his bondsmen was filed in Pulaski

Chancery Court. The case was referred to Thomas H. Simms, a special master in chancery from Washington, Hempstead County. During extended hearings before Simms the defendants continued to assert that the alleged shortages were attributable to bookkeeping errors, failures to record proper credits, and the inadvertent burning of the scrip by the state debt board. They were able to establish numerous credits against the amounts found in the committee's report and to satisfactorily explain some of the discrepancies. Simms finally reported a deficit of $23,973 in currency, $56,438 in state scrip, and $110 in swampland scrip. These were the amounts affirmed in the chancellor's decree. The case was appealed to the state supreme court where the decree of the chancellor was upheld. The amount of the currency deficit was paid by the defendants. Since the scrip in question was never presented for payment or cancellation, Churchill's contention that it had been burned by mistake without crediting his accounts would appear to have been validated. The entire episode is difficult to follow. Based on limited evidence the court decision appears just in terms of the records available to Simms. At the same time, Churchill's explanation of the alleged shortages was probably true.

The second major problem Governor Churchill encountered also occurred during his first year in office. In July 1881 factional differences in Perry County caused the county judge to report to the governor that extensive lawlessness in the county prevented him from performing his duties. As a specific example of lawlessness the judge cited the burning of the office of the *Fourche Valley Times* at Perryville. Gen. Robert C. Newton investigated the situation for Churchill and reported that many people disapproved of the judge and his policies and believed that J. L. W. Matthews, the editor of the burned Perryville newspaper, had inspired these policies. General Newton recommended that the circuit judge convene a special session for the trial of those suspected of destroying property. While Governor Churchill was attempting to implement this recommendation, Matthews was assassinated and the sheriff requested state aid in apprehending and prosecuting the guilty parties. The governor complied with the request and sent General Newton and the Quapaw Guards to Perryville. He also employed W. L. Terry as special counsel to assist the prosecuting attorney. Warrants were issued and the suspects were examined and bound over to the court. After about three weeks, civil authorities felt capable of maintaining law and order and the militia returned to Little Rock. The necessary but unfortunate and distasteful presence of the militia in Perry County further weakened Churchill politically. Disastrous floods in 1881 and 1882, severe drought in 1881, mounting agrarian discontent, the Perry County incident, the merciless treatment of the governor's record as treasurer, and the political aspirations of other Democrats combined to limit Churchill to one term as governor.

After retiring as governor in 1883, Churchill did not seek public office again. He devoted his attention primarily to his farming interests. Active in the affairs of the United Confederate Veterans, he served as commanding major general of the Confederate Veterans of Arkansas. Following an illness of several months, he died at his daughter's home in Little Rock shortly after his eighty-first birthday and was buried with military honors in Mount Holly Cemetery.

JAMES HENDERSON BERRY
1883–1885

JAMES HENDERSON BERRY (15 May 1841–30 January 1913), attorney, was born in Jackson County, Alabama, the son of James M. and Isabelle (Orr) Berry. In 1848 the Berry family sold their Alabama farm and moved to Carrollton in Carroll County, Arkansas. There Berry's father bought a farm and later opened a store. In this small community Berry grew up in circumstances that were not unusual for the Ozark frontier. Surrounded by nine brothers and sisters, he worked on the family farm, attended the local school in Carrollton for a few winter terms, and at age seventeen, enrolled in a private academy at Berryville only a few miles from his home. Expenses related to the illness and death of his mother forced him to leave the academy after only one year, which ended his formal schooling. He found employment as a clerk in a Yellville store owned by his father's cousin, also named James H. Berry.

On 19 September 1861 twenty-year-old Berry enlisted in the Confederate army. He was elected second lieutenant of the newly organized Company E of the Sixteenth Arkansas Infantry. Berry participated in the battle of Pea Ridge, March 1862, and later the same year in the battles of Iuka and Corinth in Mississippi. In the latter engagement, he suffered a serious leg wound and was captured. Because of the wound, his right leg was amputated above the knee. After spending two months recuperating in a Union hospital at Iuka, he was paroled to return home to Arkansas sometime in 1863. In the closing months of the war he went to Texas where he remained until the conflict ended.

On his return to Arkansas, Berry was employed for a few months as a teacher at Ozark. There, on 31 October 1865, he married Lizzie Quaile, the daughter of a prominent Ozark businessman, James F. Quaile. The couple settled in Carrollton where Berry found another teaching position and prepared for a new career by reading law in his spare time. In 1866 he was elected to the Arkansas House of Representatives on the Democratic-Conservative ticket. He was admitted to the bar just before he took his seat as the youngest member of the legislature. At the conclusion of the legislative session in 1867, Berry returned to Carrollton to begin a law practice. Two years later he moved to Bentonville, the county seat of Benton County, and formed a law partnership with his brother-in-law, Col. Sam W. Peel. The two men maintained their practice for five years and both later served together in Washington, with Peel in the House and Berry in the Senate.

In September 1872 Berry was again elected to the Arkansas legislature, this time as a representative of Benton and Washington Counties. By the end of the session in 1873 he was considered one of the party leaders in the house, and in the extraordinary session of the legislature that Gov. Elisha Baxter convened in May 1874 to deal with the Brooks-Baxter affair, Berry was chosen speaker of the house. Throughout both the 1873 and 1874 sessions he loyally supported the Democratic efforts to end Reconstruction. He did not seek any elective office in 1874. Instead, he returned to Bentonville and formed a law practice with R. W. Ellis.

Ending a two-year respite from active politics, Berry was chosen chairman of the Democratic state convention in 1876. Two years later he was elected judge of the Fourth Judicial Circuit. The competence he showed in this position won him respect throughout the district. Although he enjoyed his work on the bench and later regretted leaving it, he resigned his judgeship in 1882 to run for governor.

Berry's prospects of winning the nomination and election as governor appeared promising. Through his work as legislator, party leader, and circuit judge, he had gained wide recognition and had established valuable political ties throughout the state. His Civil War service, particularly the loss of his leg, enhanced his appeal. Furthermore, the incumbent governor, Gen. Thomas James Churchill, was unlikely to seek reelection because of charges that there had been shortages in his accounts during his term as state treasurer. An aggressive preconvention canvass lined up so many delegates behind Berry that the other Democratic gubernatorial candidates withdrew before the state convention opened, permitting Berry to win the nomination unopposed.

The general election that followed pitted Berry against the Republican hopeful, W. D. Slack, and the Greenback nominee, Rufus K. Garland. Slack was widely respected, but his personal qualities could not compensate for his party affiliation. Berry and the Democrats portrayed Slack as a puppet of Powell Clayton and reminded voters that Republicans had been responsible for Radical Reconstruction. Berry carried all but eleven counties and won a total vote of 87,675 to 49,352 for Slack and 10,142 for Garland.

In his inaugural address on 13 January 1883, Berry outlined a program for legislative action. He pointed to the need for increased taxation on railroads. Railroad property was generally underassessed, and some railroad companies claimed complete tax exemption under their charters. To correct tax inequity, Berry asked for a revenue law requiring assessment of all property at its actual value. He urged the legislature to resubmit the so-called Fishback Amendment to the voters in the next general election. This proposed constitutional amendment, designed to repudiate most of the state's bonded indebtedness carried over from the Reconstruction period, had been narrowly defeated in 1880. To reduce election expenses and to minimize the time lost by voters, he requested that state and federal elections be held on the same day. He encouraged efforts to promote the flow of capital and population into the state and asked for increased support for education. Finally, he asked that there be no unnecessary delay in determining the extent of shortages in the accounts of some state officials.

Governor Berry had mixed success with the general assembly. The body did make provision for placing the Fishback Amendment on the ballot in 1884. The lawmakers created a railroad commission composed of the governor, secretary of state, and auditor to assess railroads, but the law made a major concession to the railroad lobby in exempting several classes of railway property from taxation. Berry was authorized to employ attorneys to assist the attorney general in prosecuting state officers accused of mishandling their accounts. A token appropriation was made to finance an Arkansas promotional exhibit in major expositions at Louisville and New Orleans. The general assembly rejected the governor's proposal to consolidate state and federal elections because of strong opposition from some counties where Democrats used illegal methods to carry local elections.

When Governor Berry and the railroad commission attempted to increase assessments on railroad property, the companies sought an injunction, claiming that any increase would violate their charters. The commission's stand was upheld first in Arkansas courts and finally in the U.S. Supreme Court. The Berry administration thereby made good its pledge to increase railroad taxes, but since the legislature had excluded several classes of railroad property from assessment, the increase in revenue was modest.

The state's efforts to collect claims against former state officials was only partially successful. Legal action forced John Crawford, former auditor, to reimburse the state for almost $10,000 missing in his account. The effort to collect a much larger judgment against Churchill and his bondsmen was still in court when Berry's term ended. Eventually, in 1887, the state supreme court found Churchill and his bondsmen liable for only $30,000 of the $130,000 shortage.

Berry promised equal justice and protection for all citizens regardless of their class or race. Actually, his attitude toward the black citizens of his state was rather paternalistic. Although he insisted that blacks be allowed to exercise their rights, he believed that their progress would come through education and economic advances rather than through political activities. His stand for equal justice was severely tested in the summer of 1883 when a group of Howard County blacks killed a white farmer whom they accused of assaulting a black woman. A white posse quickly reacted, killing at least two blacks and jailing more than forty others. A race war appeared imminent. Berry visited Howard County and warned local authorities that he would tolerate no mob action against the prisoners. Their fate must be determined by a court, not by a lynch mob. Three of the prisoners were sentenced to hang and most of the others received prison sentences. Berry pardoned five of the latter group and granted stays to the three condemned men so that their cases could be reviewed by the state supreme court. All three were eventually executed. There may not have been equal justice in the Howard County affair, but Berry's firmness defused a dangerous situation so that the courts were at least allowed to function.

The prison system inherited by the Berry administration can only be described as barbaric. Arkansans of that era assumed that the penal system should be self-supporting and perhaps even profitable to the state. Since penitentiary facilities were inadequate for profitably working all the prisoners, many were leased to private contractors who paid the state for the right to work them. Taxpayers were thus freed of the expense of supervising and maintaining many of the prisoners, but the convicts were often brutally treated. When Berry found abuse, he threatened to cancel contracts of lessees unless they improved conditions. In his final message to the general assembly he denounced the whole convict-lease system as "uncivilized, inhumane, and wrong." While legislatures could hardly disagree with his assessment, they rejected his recommendation for appropriations to buy necessary equipment to work all convicts under direct state supervision within the penitentiary walls. Berry's efforts to reform the penal system fell victim to the economy-minded legislature.

In reality, Berry shared the legislature's commitment to economy in government. When the state superintendent of public instruction proposed that the revenue from liquor licenses and the proceeds from the sale of forfeited lands be reserved for the public schools, Berry strongly protested. Such a policy, he warned, would force Arkansas to resume deficit spending and would make it impossible to reduce the state tax rate. He was pleased with the fact that during his administration the state was able to reduce its indebtedness. Most of the outstanding scrip was redeemed, short-term loans were repaid, and some bonds were retired. Ratification of the Fishback Amendment in 1884 formally voided most of the Reconstruction debt.

Although Berry could almost certainly have won reelection, he refused to run for a second term. Expenses of office had exceeded his salary and had forced him to spend his savings. He simply could not afford another term as governor. Besides, he had already made the decision to seek the seat in the U.S. Senate that was to be filled in 1885. As the incumbent governor, he was in a strong position for a Senate race; however, he faced two formidable opponents, Rep. Poindexter Dunn and James K. Jones. After a deadlock developed in the legislature among supporters of the three strong contenders, Berry, who was trailing the other two, withdrew, which allowed Jones to be elected.

A second opportunity for a Senate seat was presented to Berry shortly after he left the governorship when Sen. Augustus Hill Garland resigned his seat to take a post in the cabinet of Pres. Grover Cleveland. In this contest the legislature selected Berry over Dunn and several other candidates. The choice of Berry was generally praised by Arkansans, but some even among his own party doubted his ability to succeed the distinguished Garland. In any case, on 25 March 1885 Berry took his seat in the Senate, a post that he occupied for the next twenty-two years.

As a senator, Berry was diligent but not prominent or dynamic. He quietly supported his party and tried to promote the interests of his state. Major committee assignments included membership on the Rivers and Harbors, Public Lands, Commerce, and Appropriations committees. His voting record was neither consistently conservative nor progressive. On the one hand, he favored tariff reductions, more effective regulation of railroads and trusts, a graduated income tax, increased coinage of silver, expansion of the money supply, and the direct election of U.S. senators. On the other hand, he opposed extension of the civil service, a law to prevent adulteration of food, a constitutional amendment giving women the vote, and some other progressive measures. He opposed the annexation of Hawaii and was especially critical of American acquisition and control of the Philippines, though he favored building the Panama Canal. Overall, his Senate record was not particularly distinguished, but he received warm praise from his supporters in Arkansas for his faithful service. Consequently, he was repeatedly reelected by the legislature until he was challenged by Gov. Jeff Davis in 1906.

Berry was no match for the energetic, colorful, and popular Davis. Through his years in the governor's office, Davis had built a powerful political organization that he used effectively in his campaign against Berry. Although supported by most of the leading newspapers and most of the conservative interests of the state, Berry still lost to Davis in the senatorial primary. The defeat of the aged senator marked the passing of the old order, for he was the last Confederate veteran to represent Arkansas in the U.S. Senate.

At the expiration of his term in March 1907 Berry returned to his home in Bentonville. Since he had been away from the practice of law so long, he felt unable to resume his profession and anticipated a quiet retirement. He seemed to have neither the strength nor the desire to run for another elective office, but he remained active in the Arkansas chapter of the United Confederate Veterans and served briefly as a member of the Arkansas History Commission. In 1910 the secretary of war appointed him commissioner to mark the graves of Confederate soldiers who had died in Union prisons. This assignment, completed in December 1912, was his last public service. He died the following January at his home in Bentonville and was buried in City Cemetery. He was survived by his wife, two sons, and two daughters.

For over half of his adult life Berry served his state and its people in various public offices. Whatever the office, he worked hard to fulfill its responsibilities. Yet his record of achievement was neither brilliant nor remarkable. He launched few new programs and championed few reforms. Consequently, neither the nation nor the state was perceptibly altered by his long public career. Those who knew him respected him less for his accomplishments than for his loyalty, honesty, and faithful service.

SIMON P. HUGHES

1885–1889

SIMON P. HUGHES (14 April 1830–29 June 1906), attorney, was born near Carthage, Smith County, Tennessee, the third son and seventh child of Simon P. and Mary (Hubbard) Hughes. His father was a native of Prince Edward County, Virginia, who emigrated to Tennessee where in 1818 he met and married Mary Hubbard, a native of Oglethorpe County, Georgia. A prosperous farmer, Hughes's father was also active in politics. He believed that his sons should be exposed to all aspects of agriculture and allowed them to go to the primitive schools of the area only during the fall and winter when they could best be spared from the farm. He also served as sheriff and was a member of the Tennessee legislature in 1842–1843. When Hughes's mother died in 1842, his distraught father moved to Bowie County, Texas, where he died in 1844. Thus, at the age of fourteen, the future governor of Arkansas was orphaned and thrown primarily on his own resources.

In 1844 Hughes accompanied some relatives to Pulaski County, Arkansas, where he worked on a farm for wages. In 1846 he returned to Tennessee and entered Sylvan Academy in Sumner County, studying Latin and mathematics under the supervision of Prof. Peter Hubbard, his maternal uncle. Since he was determined to be a lawyer, in 1848 he became a student at Clinton College in his native county where he paid his expenses by rendering manual labor. Although he advanced rapidly in his studies, he was financially unable to complete his formal education even though he taught in the local public school. In late 1849 he decided to return to Arkansas where he established residence in Monroe County on the White River near Clarendon. He worked on various farms and became the friend and patron of the sheriff, J. A. Harvick, who endorsed him as his successor in 1853. This initial campaign was one of the most difficult Hughes ever faced, but the twenty-four-year-old farmer convinced the voters that his courage, integrity, and nerve warranted his election. During his tenure from 1854 to 1856, Hughes began to study law and gained admission to the bar on his retirement from the sheriff's office. In 1857 he established a law practice in Clarendon with W. W. Smith, who afterwards became associate justice of the Arkansas Supreme Court (1882–1888). The partnership endured until 1874 and was Hughes's principal source of income during these years, although he did acquire some farmland that provided him with supplementary funds.

Shortly after the establishment of his law firm, on 2 June 1857, Hughes married Ann E. Blakemore, a native of Clarendon. She was the only child of George W. Blakemore, a prominent planter of Monroe County and native of Tennessee, and had been educated at the Young Ladies Model School, Somerville, Tennessee. Her attractive demeanor and balanced judgment made her an asset throughout her husband's political career. Nine children were born to this couple, beginning with William B. on 30 December 1859; five others reached maturity: Sarah (Sallie), Robert, Lillian, George, and John. One of the infants who did not survive, Simon P., died in Cherokee County, Texas, in 1864 at the age of three. Hughes had removed his family to Texas to get them away from the dangers of war. This unpleasant sojourn in Texas was one of the few events to mar the otherwise happy personal life of the Hughes family.

The sectional crisis that resulted in the Civil War profoundly affected Hughes and his family. In political philosophy, he professed to be a Whig as long as that party could be said to be in existence. During the presidential campaign of 1860 he championed the cause of John Bell of Tennessee, the nominee of the Constitutional Unionists, and then made several speeches against secession following the election of Lincoln. However, when war began, he enlisted in the Confederate army and became the captain of Company F in Col. Charles W. Adams' Twenty-third Arkansas Infantry Regiment. He rose to be lieutenant colonel of the regiment. When the regiment was reorganized following the battle of Shiloh, he joined Morgan's Texas Battalion of Cavalry as a private and served with that unit until the cessation of hostilities.

During the war, he became a proponent of the Democratic party and in 1866 he was elected to the Arkansas House of Representatives by the citizens of Monroe County. He was chosen as one of four commissioners sent to Pres. Andrew Johnson in an effort to avoid the ordeal of a harsh reconstruction program for Arkansas. The mission was a failure, and the state would experience the so-called Radical

Reconstruction after 1867. Hughes, a prewar officeholder who had joined the Confederate army, was disenfranchised from 1867 to 1874. During that time, he practiced law and devoted considerable energies to enhancing his agricultural interests, especially his fine stock of horses.

In 1874 he returned to politics when the conservatives called for a new constitution, and he ably served at the constitutional convention as the delegate from Monroe County. His work at the convention sufficiently impressed his associates to give him a statewide political base. On 9 September, at the Democratic convention that nominated Augustus Hill Garland for governor, Hughes was chosen as the party's candidate for attorney general. The election for both state officials and for ratification of the proposed constitution was held on 13 October 1874. Garland, Hughes, and the constitution all received overwhelming mandates.

Hughes was sworn in as attorney general on 12 November 1874 and served until the end of 1876. He cooperated strongly with Governor Garland and the other newly elected officials in putting the new government created by the constitution of 1874 into successful operation. He was also diligent in the performance of his official duties and rendered invaluable service to the state in its efforts to collect taxes from certain railroads. He sent a written opinion to the general assembly that lands granted by Congress to aid in the construction of railroads in Arkansas were subject to taxation. When the legislature levied such taxes, they were eventually ruled valid by the state and federal supreme courts. Hughes personally appeared as counsel for the state before the Arkansas Supreme Court in the case of the St. Louis, Iron Mountain, and Southern Railway in 1875. Following the court decision the railroads paid taxes on those lands, which they had never done previously.

With this commendable record, Hughes sought the gubernatorial nomination in 1876. Prior to the Democratic state convention in June, the officers for the meeting had been selected in a caucus. Since many of these men were friends of state auditor William Read Miller, the leading candidate, Hughes and the other nine candidates charged that a "State House ring" was steamrolling the convention. Miller was nominated on the third ballot nonetheless and scored a notable victory in the general election. Hughes spent the next eight years practicing law in Little Rock, his residence for the remainder of his life, and pursuing his agricultural interests.

In 1884 Hughes emerged once more as a candidate for the Democratic gubernatorial nomination. When the incumbent, Gov. James

Henderson Berry, announced that he would not seek reelection since the salary was inadequate, aspirants for the nomination made their formal announcements and began campaigning much earlier than in previous years. The campaign for the party nomination was further complicated by the rise of the Agricultural Wheel, a farmers' organization that was increasingly interested in committing the state's Democratic party to numerous agrarian relief measures. Hughes's leading opponent was a Little Rock merchant, Col. John G. Fletcher, who had considerable support among farmers. Both candidates canvassed the state thoroughly and were about equal in strength when the convention convened on 25 June. On the first fourteen ballots, Fletcher led by about ten votes but could not secure a majority and, on the thirty-third ballot, Hughes finally emerged triumphant. He then stumped the state in the campaign against Thomas Boles, his Republican opponent, and on 1 September won a landslide victory of 100,875 votes to 55,388.

Hughes was inaugurated as governor on 17 January 1885. In his inaugural address to the general assembly, he made several suggestions and requests in the process of outlining his program. He stressed the need to make adequate provision for such state institutions as the insane asylum, Arkansas Industrial University, the Institute for the Blind, the Deaf Mute Institute, and the penitentiary. He further noted that the capitol needed extensive repairs. His most significant concern was that the legislature provide a sound basis for repayment of the undisputed or "just" portion of the state debt. This matter related to the recent passage of the so-called Fishback Amendment, which had provided for repudiation of most of the Reconstruction-era debts.

Since the new governor kept in close and sympathetic touch with the legislators during the session, several significant measures were enacted and implemented during his first administration. Although the state government was committed to economy and retrenchment and had ceased to borrow money, the governor could point with pride at the end of his term to some notable achievements: several buildings had been erected at the state's penal and charitable institutions; the capitol had been repaired; state support for public schools had been increased; the treasury enjoyed a surplus. Part of the reason for this achievement was the handling of the state debt, most of which had been repudiated by the Fishback Amendment. The undisputed or just portion of the debt was made the responsibility of the state debt board (composed of the governor, auditor, treasurer, and attorney general) that was created on 2 April 1885. The board labored assiduously and successfully at the task of reducing the state's outstanding indebtedness without impairing its current obligations.

Hughes's success in office assured the support of most elements of the party for his renomination, especially after some disgruntled farmers decided to back the Agricultural Wheel in its attempt to create a new political party. The Wheel nominated Colonel Fletcher, Hughes's opponent for the 1884 Democratic nomination, but selected Charles E. Cunningham, a former Greenbacker, after Fletcher declined to head the new group's ticket. The Republicans chose Lafayette Gregg, who had been an associate justice of the state supreme court during Reconstruction, as their standard-bearer. On 6 September 1886 Hughes polled 90,649 votes to Gregg's 54,064 and Cunningham's 19,069. The results of the election guaranteed the state an extraordinary stability in personnel. Along with Hughes, the following Democrats were reelected: Secretary of State E. B. Moore, State Treasurer William E. Woodruff, Atty. Gen. Daniel Webster Jones, Commissioner of State Lands Paul M. Cobbs, and Superintendent of Public Instruction Wood E. Thompson Jr., while ex-Governor Miller was elected auditor for the fifth time. One-party dominance of state government seemed to be complete.

Governor Hughes appeared before the general assembly without elaborate ceremony and took the oath of office for his second term on 15 January 1887. He reviewed the actions of his first term and stressed that the expenditures for public facilities had been made without the necessity of borrowing. He offered few specific recommendations to the legislators this time, although he did restate his desire to see that the railroads bore their fair share of taxes. In one specific instance, this desire was met by legislative agreement with his recommendation to accept the sum of $250,000 from the St. Louis, Iron Mountain, and Southern Railway Company in settlement of all claims for back taxes due, a dispute that went back to the 1875 case when he was attorney general. The twenty-sixth general assembly also created the office of state geologist, provided for a geological survey of the state, reorganized the Arkansas Industrial University, abolished public executions, imposed several limitations on the sale of intoxicating beverages, and made provision to pay the state's indebtedness in a manner prescribed by the state debt board. In the only conflict with the chief executive, the legislature failed to override his vigorous veto of a bill allowing butcher shops and bakeries to remain open until 10:00 A.M. on Sundays.

During his second term Governor Hughes asserted that the state had not only escaped many calamities but was enjoying a fair degree of progress and prosperity. In deciding to seek a third term in 1888, he cited several evidences of progress that had occurred during his tenure: a large growth in population (the total reached almost one million) and in wealth (taxable values had risen to $140 million); an improved physical plant at most state institutions; the stable condition of state finances; and increases in the total of cultivated land, in the means of transportation, and in public school facilities. He delayed in announcing his intention, however, and several other candidates emerged. Moreover, discontent was increasing among some farmers owing to their economic distress. Consequently, when Hughes began to canvass the state in the spring of 1888, he found the Democratic party badly divided regarding its gubernatorial choice.

When the state Democratic convention assembled on 31 May in Little Rock, one of its hardest-fought intraparty battles commenced. Hughes, the candidate of most officeholders and others who were impressed with his record, found himself facing three other major candidates, each of whom had significant elements of strength. Fletcher, his opponent for the nomination in 1884, was backed by many businessmen and, paradoxically, by some sympathizers of the Agricultural Wheel that had offered the Little Rock merchant its nomination in 1886. James Philip Eagle, a planter from Lonoke County and speaker of the house during Hughes's first term, appealed to farmers and others by stressing economy and retrenchment. The fourth candidate, William Meade Fishback of Fort Smith, aroused support by stressing his long advocacy of repudiating the unjust debt that had culminated in the adoption in 1885 of the first amendment of the constitution. As the front-runner, Hughes found himself under severe attack from these and other aspirants for the office. Many felt that Hughes had been the beneficiary of convention manipulations in 1884, and Fletcher's followers were especially determined to see that their choice was not deprived of the prize again.

On the first ballot the vote for major candidates was Hughes, 122; Fletcher, 113; Eagle, 97; and Fishback, 25. For five days, the Democrats remained deadlocked in the struggle. When Fishback withdrew on the one hundred seventeenth ballot, the next one gave Hughes 180, Fletcher 139, and Eagle 107. On the one hundred twenty-sixth ballot Fletcher's weary supporters began to desert, and most of his agrarian adherents joined Eagle with the final result being 248 votes for Eagle and 205 for Hughes. In his acceptance speech, the nominee heartily endorsed the achievements of Governor Hughes and thereby partially restored party harmony. The convention also unanimously chose Hughes to be the Democratic national committeeman from Arkansas.

During the subsequent campaign, which again resulted in Democratic success, Hughes stumped the state in behalf of his party. When he left office on 17 January 1889, his popularity was considerable and numerous friends welcomed his resumption of his profitable law practice in Little Rock. That same year, however, the number of supreme court justices was increased from three to five, and Hughes was chosen an associate justice of the Arkansas Supreme Court. He was elected to his initial eight-year term on 2 April and was reelected in 1896. In this latter part of his public career, he labored diligently in discharging his duties and received praise for his zeal for even-handed justice. Fears that his long political career might color his judgments proved groundless. The brevity and clarity of his written opinions were lauded by lawyers and laymen and further contributed to the high esteem in which he was held. His announcement that he would not seek another term after nearly sixteen years of service on the high court elicited regrets from people throughout the state.

Following his retirement on 1 November 1904, Justice Hughes suffered from increasingly poor health and was confined for several months to his magnificent residence at Twelfth and Cumberland streets in Little Rock. It was there that the widely respected public servant died in the early morning hours of 29 June 1906. His funeral services were conducted at the First Methodist Episcopal Church South, of which he was a member and a trustee, and he was interred at Mount Holly Cemetery.

JAMES PHILIP EAGLE

1889–1893

JAMES PHILIP EAGLE (10 August 1837–20 December 1904), planter and minister, was born in Maury County, Tennessee, the son of James and Charity (Swain) Eagle. The family of the state's sixteenth governor was of German descent and emigrated to the United States from Switzerland. After first settling in Pennsylvania in 1743, later generations moved to North Carolina, then to Tennessee. In November 1839 Eagle's father, a farmer, brought his family to Arkansas and purchased a farm in Pulaski County, approximately twenty-three miles northeast of Little Rock. In 1857 the Eagle family moved to the Richwoods community, some ten miles northeast of the present city of Lonoke, at the time located in Prairie County. When the legislature created Lonoke County in 1877, the Eagle farm became a part of that county.

Eagle apparently received only the most rudimentary education in the county schools and devoted himself almost exclusively to assisting his father on the family farm. In 1859 he was appointed deputy sheriff of Prairie County, a position that he held until the outbreak of the Civil War. In June 1861 he enlisted as a member of the Fifth Arkansas Mounted Regiment and was assigned to Indian Territory. He saw action at the battle of Hominy Creek in December 1861 and at Pea Ridge in March 1862. Enlisting as a private, within a year he rose to the rank of lieutenant.

His rifle regiment was disbanded after the Confederate defeat at Pea Ridge but was reorganized at Corinth, Mississippi, a few months later. Eagle was elected a captain in the new unit and saw action in Richmond, Kentucky, and Murfreesboro, Tennessee. At Murfreesboro he was taken prisoner and confined at Camp Chase, Ohio. Later he was transferred to Fort Delaware, then to City Point, Virginia, where in May 1863 he was part of a prisoner exchange. Rejoining his regiment at Chattanooga, Tennessee, he participated in battles at Jackson, Mississippi; Chickamauga, Georgia; and Atlanta, Georgia. He received a severe abdominal wound at Atlanta, the ball emerging just above his left hip. However, he was only incapacitated for two months and rejoined his unit in north Georgia in September 1864. For the remaining months of the war, Eagle participated in campaigns in Tennessee and North Carolina. During that time he rose in rank from major to lieutenant colonel. He surrendered with his unit, which had been reorganized into the First Arkansas Regiment, at Greensboro, North Carolina.

After the surrender, Eagle returned to the family farm in Arkansas. The war had two profound effects on the direction of his career. Soon after the war broke out, his family moved to Texas where his father died, leaving Eagle most of his estate. He was able to build on the family's original holdings in Arkansas and became one of the most prosperous farmers in the central Arkansas area. Another equally important influence on his career came as a result of his wartime conversion to Christianity. He joined the New Hope Baptist Church shortly after returning home and was licensed to the ministry in 1868. Two years later he was ordained by the Lonoke Baptist Church.

Eagle's new role as a Baptist minister convinced him that he needed more education. He attended day school in Lonoke for a few months in 1869 and 1870, then enrolled at Mississippi College in 1871. Unfortunately, illness forced him to discontinue his studies before he completed the first year. For the next several years he devoted much of his time to the work of the Baptist church in the state. He was a leading figure in organizing the Arkansas Baptist Printing and Publishing Company, which published the state's official *Baptist News* magazine. He also spent a great deal of time in ministerial work, preferring to work with small, rural churches that could not financially support a full-time minister.

Eagle also became involved in politics. In 1872, without his knowledge, friends placed his name in nomination for representative from the Twelfth District, which included Arkansas, Prairie, and Lincoln Counties. He was elected and began his political career at the time when the entire state became involved in the Brooks-Baxter dispute over the governor's office. Eagle actively supported Elisha Baxter and organized six companies of volunteer troops when Baxter issued a call for protection of the governor's office. Eagle later served as one of three commissioners appointed by the legislature to investigate claims growing out of the Brooks-Baxter War and served in the special session called by Baxter in May 1874. He also served as a delegate from his legislative district to the 1874 constitutional convention. He was an ardent supporter of Augustus Hill Garland for governor and U.S. senator.

As a legislator, Eagle introduced a bill to create Lonoke County, then served as representative from that county in the twenty-second session of the general assembly (1877–1879) and in the twenty-fifth session (1885–1887). In the latter assembly he was chosen speaker of the house. As speaker he was known for his impartiality, and even though some legislators became impatient with his slow, deliberate style in reaching a decision, none questioned his integrity. Eagle interrupted his political career in 1882 to wed Mary Kavanaugh Oldham, daughter of William K. and Katie Oldham, of Richmond, Kentucky. The couple had met during the Civil War and had carried on a long-distance courtship before their marriage on 3 January. By the time of his marriage Eagle had become one of the largest landowners in central Arkansas. From his father's original homestead he had increased his holdings to some twenty-four hundred acres of farmland in Lonoke County and fourteen lots in the city of Little Rock. But the Baptist minister was never far from Democratic party politics. His political involvement coupled with his statewide connections in religious circles made him a favorite among Bourbon Democrats. Although he resisted efforts by friends who encouraged him to enter the 1880 gubernatorial race, he did consent to seek the party's nomination to that office in 1888.

The Democratic convention in 1888 was the longest and one of the most heated in the state's history. Five major candidates, including the incumbent governor, sought the party's endorsement. It took three days of speeches and 126 ballots before Eagle won the nomination. The campaign that followed was also one of the most hotly contested in the state's history. Eagle narrowly defeated his Union-Labor opponent, C. M. Norwood, by a fifteen-thousand-vote margin. His victory was marred, however, by Union-Labor charges of fraud. Within weeks after the election, Norwood began preparing a petition to protest the results. He claimed to have been defrauded of several thousand votes in twenty counties and to have lost another thousand votes in Pulaski County where the poll books had been stolen.

On that basis Norwood petitioned the general assembly to have a special committee investigate the charges. The senate received the petition and voted to begin the investigation if Norwood would post bond to cover the cost of a new election should his charges prove valid. When Norwood refused, the legislators allowed him to withdraw the petition.

The assembly's action angered Eagle, and he vetoed the legislators' resolution. In his words, withdrawing the petition did not resolve the charges of fraud and left a cloud of doubt over his administration. Instead, he urged the legislators to reconsider their action and to give him an opportunity to clear his name. The assembly refused, and the matter was never settled. Ironically, most historians now agree that Eagle, the Baptist minister, had won by fraudulent means due to the many election irregularities committed by his colleagues.

During his first term as governor, Eagle made a determined effort to reduce discontent against the Democratic party. He urged the legislature to create an equalization board that would provide a more equitable distribution of the tax burden. He also called for the creation of a railroad commission with power to establish passenger and freight rates and for an improved system for maintaining public roads. He advocated liberal support for education, reform in the state penitentiary system, and a liberal policy on immigration.

The legislature only partially supported the governor's recommendations. Conspicuously absent in the legislative package was any reference to a railroad commission or an equalization board. However, the legislators did provide for some railroad regulation and tax reform, at least on a local level. These measures, plus their compromise proposal with Governor Eagle on prison reform and public roads, added a degree of harmony to the party and improved the Democrats' credibility with the voters. In the 1890 election, Eagle increased his margin of victory by some twenty-two thousand votes; Democratic candidates in general ran stronger races, and there were fewer charges of election irregularities.

In his second term Eagle again called for a railroad commission and an equalization board as well as for election reform and for administrative reorganization of the state prison. He was particularly concerned with the convict-lease system and recommended that the state "take control of and work its own convicts." Under the existing system, the state accepted bids from contractors to "lease" prisoners for private use. Eagle urged the legislators to appropriate money for a new penitentiary building and to furnish "machinery suitable for industrial work, to make use of the state's raw materials." As he envisioned the program, prisoners would cut the granite and marble for the building, then would make furniture, wagons, and other vehicles as well as hats, shoes, and other clothing to be used at the penal institution. He also suggested that prisoners with special skills be used within the prison, while the unskilled could be assigned to work on farms, roads, and other outside projects controlled by the state. The legislators, however, were reluctant to take such major steps toward regulation or overall reform and opted instead for more specific legislation.

The fifty-first session of the general assembly was perhaps best remembered for its action on segregation. One act, the "separate coach law," required transportation companies to provide separate travel accommodations for white and black citizens. Although Governor Eagle refused to include such a request in his legislative program, he did not actively oppose the law. Legislators also submitted a proposed constitutional amendment to establish a poll tax. The amendment was approved after Eagle left office.

After retiring from the governor's office, Eagle remained in Little Rock and continued his active work with the Southern Baptist churches. He was elected president of the Arkansas Baptist Convention in 1880 and served in that capacity until 1904; he declined the nomination for reelection. He was also elected president of the Southern Baptist Convention in 1902 and was twice reelected before refusing to accept a fourth term.

As one of his last acts of public service, Eagle sat on the second capitol commission appointed by Gov. Jeff Davis to oversee construction of the new state capitol building. He was fired from the commission in April 1902 when Davis charged him with campaigning for one of the governor's opponents.

Eagle died of heart failure and a "general weakened condition" in his home at 219 East Seventh Street in Little Rock. He was buried in Mount Holly Cemetery, Little Rock. His wife had died the previous year, and the couple had no children. As a result, Eagle's estate was divided among his family, including his younger brother, W. H. Eagle, and his four sisters, Roberta C. Long, Mary L. Jones, Martha A. Boyd, and Sally A. Mewer.

WILLIAM MEADE FISHBACK

1893–1895

WILLIAM MEADE FISHBACK (5 November 1831–9 February 1903), attorney and newspaper editor, was born in Jeffersonton, Culpeper County, Virginia, the oldest son and first child of Frederick and Sophia Ann (Yates) Fishback. One ancestor, John Fishback, had come to America from Germany in 1714 with twelve other families and had settled at Germana, Virginia. Four governors of Arkansas (James Sevier Conway, Elias Nelson Conway, William Meade Fishback, and Henry Massie Rector) would be among the descendants of this notable German colony of 1714. Frederick Fishback, the governor's great-grandfather, moved to Maryland where the settlement of Frederickstown was established. The family eventually moved back to Virginia, where the governor's father, Frederick, married a member of a locally prominent family, the Stiths. In addition to the future governor, eight other children were born who survived to adulthood: Frederick, Sally, Harrison, Lucy, Fanny, Benjamin, Henry Ward, and Yates.

As the son of a prosperous farmer in Culpeper County, Fishback received the rudiments of a classical education in his native county and was then sent to the University of Virginia in nearby Charlottesville. At that institution he was influenced by the nationally known educator, William Holmes McGuffey. After graduating in 1855, he taught school and studied law in the Richmond office of Luther Spellman. In 1857 he moved westward to Springfield, Illinois, and was admitted to the bar there. As an attorney practicing in the state capital, he came in contact with several Illinois politicians including Abraham Lincoln. He had some business relations with Lincoln's firm but was apparently unimpressed with Springfield as a suitable location to practice law. In November 1858 the adventuresome young lawyer moved further west to Fort Smith, Arkansas. Within a month he decided to move to nearby Greenwood where he entered into a flourishing partnership with Judge Solomon F. Clark.

The coming of the Civil War disrupted the young attorney's law practice and propelled him into public life. His expression of unionist views led to his election as a Sebastian County delegate to the special convention called to determine Arkansas's course in the secession crisis. Fishback voted against secession in the first ballot and the proposed ordinance failed thirty-five to thirty-nine. But when the convention reconvened after the firing on Fort Sumter, he joined the majority in first passing the ordinance sixty-five to five. (In a subsequent revote, Isaac Murphy cast the lone vote against secession.) His rationale was his opposition to Lincoln's policy of coercion and his hope that when the North saw the withdrawal of the Southern states, it might be forced into accepting the Crittenden compromise, thereby restoring harmony within the Union. When the opening of hostilities dashed his hopes of a peaceful solution to the sectional crisis, he and David Walker, the president of the convention, went to Missouri where they took the oath of allegiance to the Union. Fishback moved to St. Louis where he served as an editor for the *St. Louis Democrat*.

After the capture of Little Rock by Union forces in 1863, Gen. J. M. Schofield designated him to form the Third Infantry Regiment there, but instead he established a unionist newspaper, *The Unconditional Union,* and the infantry regiment was forgotten. Fishback subsequently engaged in recruiting about nine hundred men for the Fourth Arkansas Cavalry, but he returned to politics rather than taking the field with that Union unit. He advised the loyal state government that was organized in 1864 with Isaac Murphy as governor and was instrumental in writing the Union constitution of 1864, sometimes referred to as the "Fishback constitution." Its most controversial provision restricted the suffrage to whites and was probably a factor in enhancing his subsequent political career as a unionist sympathizer who successfully affiliated with the Democratic party after the war. On 5 May 1864 he and Elisha Baxter were elected by the Murphy or loyal legislature to the U.S. Senate but their seating was delayed in part because of the "white" qualification for the electoral franchise. In February 1865 their admission was denied along with that of several other representatives from ex-Confederate states.

After the war he served in Little Rock as a federal treasury agent for Arkansas and contributed to his future popularity throughout the state by using his discretionary powers to protect many impoverished ex-Confederates from property seizures. However, he soon returned to Sebastian County where he resumed his law practice from his offices in Fort Smith. For most of the next decade, he remained aloof from politics and concentrated on building his legal firm into one of the most notable in western Arkansas.

On 4 April 1867 he married Adelaide Miller of Fort Smith, the orphaned daughter of Joseph Miller, a prominent merchant of that city who had been robbed and murdered on a Mississippi River steamboat in 1850. The Fishbacks established their home in a lovely residence in suburban Fort Smith. Mrs. Fishback was an active communicant in the Episcopal church as had been both of Fishback's parents. Although he never formally associated with the church, he was a member of several civic organizations including the Commercial League of Fort Smith, the Masons, and the Elks. During the fifteen-year marriage, six children were born, five of whom reached maturity: Louis, William, Mary, Bertha, and Herbert. Adelaide Fishback died on 6 December 1882, and Fishback never remarried.

Having spurned Republican overtures to be the party's candidate for the legislature in 1867, Fishback professed membership in the Democratic party and voiced his displeasure with Reconstruction developments. However, he did not return to public office until 1874 when he was elected as a delegate from Sebastian County to the constitutional convention. After the adoption of the constitution, he was selected as a Democratic nominee for the legislature and in 1876 was elected to the twenty-first general assembly. He was reelected in 1878.

During his service in the constitutional convention and in the legislature, he became more concerned with the matter with which his name is usually linked—the question of the Arkansas debt. While a member of the constitutional convention, he had expressed his distaste for the state's assumption of all classes of debts accumulated by previous Arkansas governments. On the grounds that some of the state debt had been contracted fraudulently and that other portions of it were unjustly imposed by the Reconstruction regime, Fishback had unsuccessfully attempted to include a rejection of certain categories of the debt in the proposed constitution. In subsequent years he reiterated his stand that only the "just" debt should be paid and that the remainder could be, and ought to be, legally repudiated. His theme became increasingly popular in the late 1870s and early 1880s as stagnant state revenues made the cost of indebtedness increasingly burdensome. In time, he would wear the label "The Great Repudiator" with pride.

There were three categories of debt that Fishback felt had been incurred without value received by the state: the "Holford bonds," the railroad aid bonds, and the levee bonds. The so-called Holford bonds were partially a legacy of the prewar credit problems of a developing state. The bonds had been issued to the Real-Estate Bank, chartered in 1836, and some had been sold in bad faith to a London banker, James Holford, after the bank began to default on its obligations. Holford had been unable to settle his claim for payment at par prior to the war, but in 1869 the Republican government had issued new bonds funding the bonds at the principal and interest then due. This effort at restoring the state's credit failed, however, and added to the dissatisfaction with Republican fiscal policies. The railroad and levee bonds were challenged on the grounds that the monies had produced little tangible results. Moreover, these latter bonds had been issued improperly, and litigation before the Arkansas Supreme Court resulted in the invalidation of most of them by 1877. It was not until 2 April 1879 that the legislature approved the Fishback Amendment to the constitution, which prohibited the legislature from levying any tax or from making any appropriation to pay either principal or interest on the three categories of bonds.

Certain conservatives in the state, especially former Gov. Augustus Hill Garland, opposed repudiation and defeated the proposal in 1880, but Fishback and his allies continued to champion the measure. In 1884, the proposal was favored 119,806 to 15,492 by voters in the general election. It was declared adopted as the first amendment to the constitution on 14 January 1885, and Fishback was hailed as the leader of those who had erased as much as $14 million of the state's indebtedness. While some of this debt was questionable, it should be remembered that the state and its citizens had benefited to some degree from the expenditures. Consequently, total repudiation was not ethically justifiable although the voters of the state overwhelmingly endorsed that action.

Fishback was not as successful in gaining office as he was in securing the adoption of his constitutional proposal. His candidacy for the Democratic gubernatorial nomination in 1880 floundered as did his quest for a seat in the U.S. Senate in 1884. However, he was again elected to the legislature from Sebastian County in 1884, and in 1888 he made another fairly strong but unsuccessful effort to capture the gubernatorial nomination. His persistent efforts culminated in an overwhelming endorsement by the Democrats on 14 June 1892, when he received the gubernatorial nomination on the first ballot.

His victory at the convention was matched by the one in the general election. The newly formed People's party nominated Jacob P. Carnahan, a manufacturer of wood products and formerly a professor of mathematics at Cane Hill College, while the Republicans chose William G. Whipple, a former mayor of Little Rock. The Democratic advantages in the campaign were significant. The election law of 1891 and the proposed poll-tax amendment hampered the Republican appeal to black Arkansans while the Populists were dismissed as tools of the Republicans. Moreover, unlike his two opponents, Fishback was a veteran statewide campaigner. The race was conducted on a higher plane than in previous years. Each candidate chose his own issues to stress, and there was much less demagoguery. Fishback responded to Carnahan's advocacy of free silver by claiming that Arkansas was hurt most by the Republican's high tariff policy that Whipple so warmly praised. On 5 September the Democratic candidate carried all but seven of the state's seventy-five counties. The popular vote was almost as one-sided: Fishback, 90,115; Whipple, 33,644; and Carnahan, 31,117.

The mandate that Fishback received from the voters did not translate into effective control of the state government after his inauguration in January 1893. Owing to his personal proclivities, he declined to dictate to the legislature and usually adhered to his view that governments should be a limited force in society. Moreover, although he could not be denied the nomination in 1892, he was not especially popular with much of the Democratic establishment. In particular, certain officeholders such as E. B. Kinsworthy, president of the senate, and James Paul Clarke, attorney general, jealously guarded their prerogatives when dealing with the chief executive. When Fishback made an abortive attempt to take the senatorial nomination from the incumbent, James Henderson Berry, instead of concentrating on the gubernatorial prize in 1894, Clarke easily secured the governorship while Kinsworthy became attorney general.

In his 1892 acceptance speech, Fishback had commented on his interest in the upcoming Columbian Exposition or World's Fair of 1893 in Chicago. It is ironic that his principal contribution as governor was enhancing the national image of Arkansas at a time when agrarian distress was rising and the full impact of the panic of 1893 was striking the state's economy. Since the governor felt he could exercise little political power over the legislature, he concentrated his energies on the Arkansas exhibition and on similar public-relations activities. He felt that the exposition was an opportunity for the South and especially for Arkansas to demonstrate the region's progress and to attract desirable immigrants and industries. The state exhibition did win several awards and helped to dispel the notion that Arkansas was still a wilderness inhabited by ignorant, indolent squatters. Other achievements of the Fishback administration included the negotiations with federal authorities that resulted in the establishment of Fort Logan H. Roots at Big Rock. In addition, the governor and the general assembly cooperated in organizing the St. Francis Levee District, which encompassed over 1,500 square miles between Crowley's Ridge and the Mississippi River. Within twenty years, over one million acres were reclaimed and brought under cultivation through the operations of the levee district.

After his departure from the governor's office in January 1895, Fishback never again held public office. He did continue to participate in politics, however, and rendered yeoman service to the Democratic party in the 1896 election when he stumped the state on behalf of William Jennings Bryan. By that time he had joined other prominent state Democratic party leaders in becoming fervent silverites and in endorsing an inflated currency as a solution to agrarian distress. Such actions contributed to party unity and fended off Populist efforts to gain hegemony within the state.

The ex-governor continued to practice law in Fort Smith until he suffered a stroke in early February 1903. He died peacefully in his sleep and was buried in Oak Cemetery as Fort Smith's most honored citizen.

JAMES PAUL CLARKE

1895–1897

JAMES PAUL CLARKE (19 August 1854–1 October 1916), attorney, was born in Yazoo County, Mississippi. His father, Walter Clarke, a civil engineer and architect, died in Mississippi in 1861 leaving his wife Ellen (White) Clarke, the daughter of a prominent Mississippi planter, to raise her young son. After attending the public schools in Yazoo City and Professor Tutwilder's Academy at Greenbrier, Alabama, Clarke returned to his hometown to edit a newspaper. In 1878 he was graduated by the University of Virginia with the LL.B. degree. One of his fellow law students recalled him later as being "a strong, able, self-willed, determined man."

He moved to Arkansas in 1879, settling first at Ozark but within the year moving to Helena in Phillips County where he began a successful law practice. He married Sallie (Moore) Wooten of Moon Lake, Mississippi, on 10 November 1883; they produced a son, James P., Jr., and two daughters, Julia and Marion. In 1886, Clarke won election to a two-year term as the Phillips County representative to Arkansas's lower house. The next election (1888) saw Clarke elevated to the state senate where he served two successive terms, holding the position of president of the senate during his second term (1891), an office that also made him ex officio lieutenant governor for two years. In 1892 he easily won election to the office of attorney general but chose to serve only one term in order to seek the governor's chair. He later followed a similar pattern when he turned down almost certain reelection as governor to launch an ill-fated campaign for the U.S. Senate.

At their state convention in July 1894, Arkansas Democrats chose Clarke as their nominee by acclamation. Rumors suggested that Col. Elias W. Rector had agreed to step aside in return for Clarke's promise to back Rector for governor in 1896. In the same month the Populist party chose David Edward Barker and the Republicans selected Harmon L. Remmel to do battle with Clarke for the governor's office.

On the last day of July the gubernatorial campaign officially opened with the three candidates speaking at Conway. The Democrat received one hour to open the debate and one half-hour to close; the other two candidates received only one hour. Because a platform had not been constructed, Clarke made his Conway speech "flat on the ground." He also faced an unusually large group of Populist party supporters who had come to cheer Barker on. Opposition seldom deterred Clarke but rather seemed to whet his appetite for battle. Before beginning a tirade against Barker that continued undiminished during the campaign, he made several complimentary remarks about his Republican opponent. Remmel was "a very acceptable gentleman, so far as personal and business considerations" were concerned. He would not use the epithet "carpetbagger" to describe Remmel because he had come to the state to make an honest living and not to exploit the "ignorance and superstition" of the people. Remmel's chief error was to associate himself with the party of the hated Powell Clayton, Reconstruction governor.

Clarke attacked Barker as unrepresentative of the farming classes that the Populist party claimed to serve. He was not really a farmer but a landlord who controlled large areas of farmland. No one in Drew County had ever seen him with a hoe. Clarke accused Barker of having virtually advocated a return to slavery conditions when he proposed to the 1879 legislature the "Whipping Post bill." The proposed legislation, which failed to pass, provided for ten to seventy-eight lashes for minor offenses. Barker had claimed that whipping without imprisonment was more humane than being kept in a penitentiary where beatings sometimes led to death.

The three candidates continued their joint campaign with thirty-two speeches, ending finally at Glenwood on 1 September. During the campaign Clarke defended the Democratic party's record as a friend of silver despite Grover Cleveland's successful crusade to repeal the Sherman Silver Purchase Act. Clarke's espousal of the silver cause demonstrated a tendency among Democrats to shift to the left in order to undercut the rising strength of agrarian agitators like Barker and the Populist party. The Democratic candidate also struck at both the Populist and Republican threats by upholding white supremacy as a keystone of the Democratic party. "The people of the South," he said in his closing speech of the canvass, "looked to the Democratic party to preserve the white standards of civilization." Clarke easily defeated Barker, Remmel, and a weak Prohibitionist candidate in the state election on 3 September.

In his inaugural address in January 1895, Governor Clarke advised the general assembly to call a constitutional convention to revise the 1874 Reconstruction constitution. The request was denied to Clarke but granted later to Gov. Charles Hillman Brough (1917–1921), although the product of Brough's convention was rejected at the polls. The holding of state elections on a date different from that of federal elections seemed wasteful to Clarke. During Reconstruction Southerners feared that consolidation would mean a loss of control over their state elections, but Clarke thought the danger had subsided. Consolidation, however, was not effected until the administration of George Washington Hays (1913–1917). Clarke's proposals for a four-year term for state and county offices, quadrennial instead of biennial sessions of the general assembly, and a constitutional provision for a tax on franchises (the privilege to operate a business) all fell on deaf ears. The franchise tax would have eased the tax burden on landowners during a time of severe depression (1893–1897). Although the legislature did pass a weak bill that would establish machinery to prepare for a convention, it left the final decision on whether to hold such a convention with the general assembly. Clarke vetoed this convention bill and with its defeat many of the proposals made in his inaugural address also failed.

With Clarke's and Daniel Webster Jones's administrations, the post-Reconstruction conservative bias of the Democratic party began to show signs of weakening before the attack of agrarian and Populist reformers. Clarke and Jones made concessions to the farmers' protest movement that foreshadowed the more blatantly populistic tendencies of Gov. Jeff Davis (1901–1907). Clarke's proposal for consolidated elections elicited warm response from Populists, but the *Arkansas Gazette* accurately forecast the defeat of the proposal. State legislators viewed consolidation as a Populist wedge to bring about federal interference in local elections. Clarke's concern for election reform seemed less intense when in his farewell message to the state legislature he opposed the new governor's call for a secret ballot and fairer election laws. In this case Clarke was not as willing as Jones to concede a point to the Populists. Clarke had campaigned on a platform advocating free coinage of silver at the inflationary ratio of sixteen to one, a favorite rallying cry of the debtor farmer. The platform also supported creation of a graduated income tax. Both of these were national issues, beyond the control of an Arkansas governor, but Clarke did use his power to sign into law a tax on treasury notes and national bank notes, two forms of currency in circulation at that time.

One of the most dramatic and popular agrarian reforms debated in Clarke's administration concerned regulation of the railroad corporations. Joseph Taylor Robinson, later a governor and U.S. senator, introduced in the Arkansas House of Representatives a bill creating a railroad commission. Joining Robinson in the struggle to secure passage was the representative from Clarke's own Phillips County, George W. Yancey, and the governor himself. Yancey claimed to have gone "into the detective business," with Clarke's knowledge and encouragement, in order to smoke out corrupt lobbyists. More than once, the Iron Mountain Railroad representative, Thomas L. Cox, fell into the trap when he offered bribes to Yancey for his vote against the commission bill. On 5 March 1895 in an interview with a reporter from the Memphis *Commercial Appeal,* Governor Clarke charged that the Iron Mountain Railroad had "purchased the defeat of the Railroad Commission Bill." Clarke's statements cast suspicion on those who had voted against the bill. W. R. Jones, representative from Marion County, publisher of the Yellville *Mountain Echo,* and chairman of the House Ways and Means Committee, led the opposition to the commission bill and took heated exception to Clarke's insinuations of bribery and "boodling." Jones later accused Clarke of having given no clear signal to the house of representatives about his position on the bill.

In April 1895 the two sides exchanged verbal assaults. Jones, in a speech before the lower house, accused Clarke of putting "spies on the backs of the people's representatives." In his reluctance to take a clear stand on the railroad bill he had behaved like an "assassin in the dark, with a knife up his sleeve." Governor Clarke's famous temper flared to a white heat on Sunday morning, 7 April 1895. He went to the capitol building in search of Representative Jones, but he was not among those who were writing letters at their desks. At 2:00 in the afternoon, finding Jones at Gleason's Hotel, Clarke asked him to step into a side room and in Clarke's words took him "by the ear." Jones refused to budge and after an exchange of angry words the governor spit in Jones's face. When Clarke pulled a pistol from his pocket, his intended victim threw a poorly aimed blow, but bystanders were able to restrain the combatants. In later years Senator Robinson remembered Clarke as a man whose "physical courage was primitive, at times almost savage." He never avoided conflict and would pursue an enemy relentlessly.

Governor Clarke achieved a tentative agreement with the Grover Cleveland administration concerning the precise amount of debts owed by the state to the federal government. The general assembly did not approve Clarke's compromise until after his term expired in the 1897 session. As part of the compromise Arkansas would surrender property claims to 273,000 acres that had been granted to railroads by Congress. Clarke also won public attention by his crusade to prevent prizefighting in Arkansas. When the James Fitzsimmons–James J. Corbett fight was scheduled for Hot Springs, the governor made a personal visit to the resort to prevent the match. He threatened to use the state militia, if necessary, to enforce his decision.

Rather than seek the second term Arkansas traditionally granted its governor, Clarke chose to oppose Sen. James K. Jones in the 1896 primary elections. Most politicians and newspapers backed Jones and expected "old cotton top," as Clarke was called, to go down in defeat. Pointing to Jones's record as a moderate prosilverite, Clarke sought to establish his own reputation as a more fervent silver advocate. After defeat in a series of county primaries, however, he withdrew from the race. Before returning to active politics Clarke practiced law in Little Rock. In 1902 Governor Davis and Clarke formed a political alliance that gave the Davis machine new strength in the delta region and gained Clarke a powerful advocate in his second attempt to unseat Jones. Since Jones had been chairman of the Democratic National Committee, a close associate of William Jennings Bryan, and an influential figure in state politics, the challenge proved divisive to the Arkansas Democratic party. Both Clarke and Jones had agreed that the state legislature should choose the primary winner as senator, but after losing in a stormy campaign, Jones began to hedge on his promise. The general assembly upheld the primary decision and sent Clarke to the Senate in January 1903. The new senator supported Davis's successful 1906 bid for the seat of James Henderson Berry, the senior Arkansas senator. A long-standing enmity with Berry partly explains Clarke's support of Davis. Clarke won reelection to the Senate in 1909 and again in 1914. In the 1914 Democratic primary election William F. Kirby, an agrarian radical Democrat, gathered the remnants of the Davis political machine behind him and almost unseated Clarke. Kirby might have won if voting irregularities in Poinsett County had not turned the tide for "old cotton top."

In Clarke the Senate gained an independent-minded and volatile personality. The *Gazette* characterized him as having "a tongue like a scythe blade that can cut and carve." The Democrats could not count on the obstreperous Clarke to toe the party line. Republican Pres. Theodore Roosevelt praised him for supporting the Panama Canal treaty when the Democratic leadership had taken an opposing stance.

Clarke's rebelliousness did not deter his party from selecting him as president pro tempore of the Senate in 1913 and 1915. He also served as chairman of the Commerce Committee.

During his tenure in the Senate, he frequently supported progressive legislation. He voted for the Hepburn bill strengthening the rate-setting powers of the Interstate Commerce Commission. He also accepted the more radical views of Robert La Follette on rate setting based on physical valuation of railroad property. Clarke supported the creation of a children's bureau in the Labor Department, the direct election of senators, and the Clayton Anti-Injunction Act. He unsuccessfully proposed a measure to grant independence to the Philippines. Clarke locked horns with his own Democratic president when he organized opposition to Woodrow Wilson's ship-purchase bill. The plan would have created a federal corporation to purchase merchant vessels to carry American goods during the First World War. Republicans enjoyed Clarke's help in defeating the program. In his firm opposition to the Adamson Act, a bill limiting railroad workers to an eight-hour day, Clarke exhibited both his willingness to defy Wilson's leadership as well as the limits of his own progressivism.

During the last year of his life Clarke's health declined, but he did not slacken his pace. After a four-day illness he died at his home in Little Rock on 1 October 1916; he was buried in Oakland Cemetery.

DANIEL WEBSTER JONES

1897–1901

DANIEL WEBSTER JONES (15 December 1839–25 December 1918), attorney, was born in Bowie County, Texas, during the era when Texas was an independent republic. His father, Dr. Isaac N. Jones, served as a member of the Texas Republic Congress and was a practicing physician. Jones's mother was the former Elizabeth W. Littlejohn. In 1840 the family purchased a large plantation in Lafayette County and moved to Washington, Arkansas, in Hempstead County. James Black, creator of the famed Bowie knife, came to live with the Jones family in 1842 vainly hoping that Jones's father might restore his eyesight. In later years Jones claimed that Black had promised to reveal the complex processes of producing the "genuine Arkansas toothpicks," but that Black's memory failed him in old age before he could reveal his secret. After attending Washington Academy, Jones began studying law under attorney John R. Eakin in January 1860, but the Civil War interrupted his legal education.

After Arkansas seceded from the Union in April 1861, Jones enlisted in Company A, Third Arkansas Regiment, and was elected captain. He took part in the battle of Oak Hill on 10 August 1861. He also served as captain of Company A of the Twentieth Regiment, which he had personally recruited and organized. At the battle of Corinth on 4 October 1862, he was shot below the heart during a charge and became a prisoner of war but was later exchanged for a Union soldier. By July 1863 he was a colonel and in command of his regiment at Vicksburg where he was again captured and held for a brief period by the Union army.

On 9 February 1864 he married Margaret P. Hadley of Ashley County at Hamburg. The marriage produced three sons—Claudius, Daniel W., Jr., Howard—and two daughters, Elizabeth and Bobbie. Jones resumed his law studies at Washington and was admitted to the bar in September 1865. The following January Gov. Isaac Murphy appointed him prosecuting attorney for Hempstead County. During the 1870s he practiced law in partnership with James K. Jones, a boyhood friend and future U.S. senator. Jones was elected prosecuting attorney for the Ninth Judicial Circuit in 1874, served as a presidential elector in 1876 and 1880, and won the office of attorney general in the 1884 and 1886 elections. In the latter office he initiated legal action in state and federal courts against the Iron Mountain Railroad to secure remuneration for unpaid property taxes for 1874–1883. His efforts led eventually to a compromise settlement that brought $250,000 into the state treasury. After practicing law in Little Rock for several years, in 1890 Jones was elected to serve in the state house of representatives for Pulaski County. He would return to this office again in his later years after the 1914 election. During the 1895 session of the general assembly, representing the Iron Mountain Railroad as an attorney and lobbyist, Jones appeared before a house committee to testify against the Railroad Commission bill. Ironically, the man who had forced the Iron Mountain to settle its tax account with the state and had helped to defeat the Robinson Railroad Commission bill in 1895 would later secure the establishment of such a commission during his administration as governor.

In 1896 Jones entered the county primaries as a candidate for the Democratic gubernatorial nomination. Despite his image as a genteel, planter-class, Bourbon Democrat and railroad attorney, he set out to champion those causes most dear to the rising agrarian agitators. He would be the last Civil War veteran to serve as governor, the last of the conservative Democrats, yet he came to be a moderately Populist and reform-minded governor. His administration set the stage for the more demagogic and less respectable agrarian reformism of Gov. Jeff Davis (1901–1907). With Jones populism lapped at the shores of the Democratic island while with Davis it swept like a tidal wave across the party.

Silver became the leading issue in the 1896 campaign in Arkansas. To the debtor classes the unlimited coinage of silver at a ratio of sixteen to one would provide enough inflation to ease the burdens of depression and low farm prices. During the primaries, Jones established himself as the leading silver proponent, and he defeated A. H. Sevier and James H. Harrod in the primary election. Sevier had aligned himself with Pres. Grover Cleveland's gold-standard views, opposed a railroad commission, promised a "business administration," and trailed the other candidates in the voting. Harrod had taken a position similar to that of Jones on silver and the railroads but had promised to stand by Cleveland and any other gold-standard Democrats who might be nominated. Taking a more militant position, Jones had refused to promise support to a gold-standard presidential nominee and had hoped to prevent even a single goldbug justice of the peace from winning nomination in the primaries. Early in the campaign Harrod stated he would only support Democrats, even if they "nominated the devil" and Rothschild wrote the platform. The statement provided effective ammunition for Jones who repeated it frequently in the primary campaigns. The *Helena Weekly World* asked a pertinent question, "What has the Governor of Arkansas to do with the settlement of the free coinage of silver?" For Jones, perhaps it was sufficient that this issue helped him to demolish his two opponents. The counties held primaries on dates of their own choosing running from February through June. Although Jones entered the race later than his opponents and did not have his name on the earliest primary ballot, he quickly outdistanced his opponents in the primaries and won nomination by acclamation at the state Democratic convention. The convention met on 17 June and adopted a platform calling for silver coinage at sixteen to one, a federal income tax, a tariff for revenue only, and a railroad commission.

During the August campaign Jones assured the Republicans and Populists that he supported a revision of the election laws to remove inequities. He easily won in the 7 September state elections, polling 91,114 votes to 35,836 for Harmon L. Remmel, the Republican, and 13,990 for A. W. Files, the Populist. The Populists had fused with the Democrats behind presidential candidate William Jennings Bryan. Since Bryan and Jones appealed to the prosilver agrarians, some of the former Populist voters apparently chose to vote for Jones instead of for their own candidate, Files.

Ten days before the governor-elect took office, he gave some indication of his intention to support the farming and agricultural interests in his administration. In a letter to the *Gazette* "on the Industrial Progress of the State," he warned that "great cities and powerful money combinations" were "the worst and last expressions of a character of progress not to be desired." Arkansas's future lay not in luring Northern capital or in industrialization but in maintaining agricultural strength.

In his inaugural address on 18 January 1897, Jones called on the general assembly to submit to the people an amendment to the state constitution providing for a truly secret ballot. The numbering of ballots compromised the confidentiality of the vote. The election law needed revision, he believed, to provide representation for the largest of the minority parties on state and county election boards. The minority election judges and clerks should be chosen by their own party rather than by the dominant Democrats. The law should also prohibit a candidate from purchasing votes by paying a citizen's poll tax. Jones proposed that illiterate voters be aided in marking their ballot by two judges of opposite parties. He believed a party that kept power by "unjust or unfair laws" did not warrant the people's support. He favored the creation of a temporary railroad commission to serve until the general assembly could submit to the people a constitutional amendment providing authority for creation of a permanent commission. The amendment would mollify critics who claimed that the constitution prohibited creating new governmental authorities. Jones also called for a constitutional amendment reducing the maximum permissible interest rate from 10 to 6 percent. This usury amendment would aid the farming class. He bemoaned the state's lack of authority to take action on the silver issue but proposed a law for the regulation and inspection of banks. The state, he declared, should put its convicts to work building two great trunk-line railroads. These lines, running north-south and east-west would be state-owned but could be leased, if his critics insisted, to private companies. The control of the state railroads would be in the hands of a board that could borrow money from state and other sources to construct the line. The state government was not to be held liable for any debts of the board. Jones's inaugural address also called for an insolvent law to aid debtors, payment of the state's debt, and building of a reform school so that juveniles would not be imprisoned with adult criminals.

The senate was not disposed to accept many of Governor Jones's suggestions. Although the house of representatives sent to the senate bills for lowering railroad passenger rates from three to two cents a mile and for a railroad commission, the upper house rejected them. In February the *Gazette* warned the legislature that the election of a full slate of Democratic officers on a platform advocating a commission and relief from railroad abuses had obligated them to fulfill the pledge. The assembly enacted a mild antitrust measure, created county normal institutes, allowed farmers to establish mutual insurance organizations, and submitted to the voters a constitutional amendment permitting creation of a permanent railroad commission.

Disappointed with the regular legislative session's lack of productivity, Jones called a special session to meet on 26 April 1897. In the special session, the assembly appropriated funds for the operation of the government that it had neglected to provide earlier. The extraordinary session also accepted the state railroad concept by passing the Bush bill. The bill, introduced by Populist Rep. J. O. A. Bush, had the support of all the Populists but one and incorporated Jones's basic proposals. The *Helena Weekly World* called Jones's railroad scheme a "Populite baby" nursed by a Democratic governor. Actually many businessmen supported the governor's plan as beneficial to the state's economy, and even the conservative goldbug Sen. R. W. Worthen joined hands with the Populists to pass the bill. Arkansas never built a state-owned railroad because the communities on the proposed routes did not make the financial contributions required before work could begin. The 1899 legislature repealed the Bush Act. Atty. Gen. Jeff Davis used the issue during his 1900 gubernatorial campaign. He charged that a state railroad board would place the government under huge debts despite the law's specific provision that the state would not have any financial liability for the board's bonds.

Many conservatives in the special session supported another measure, the Smith bill, which granted up to one thousand acres of land to the Springfield, Little Rock, and Gulf Railroad for each mile of track laid. The Populists lost a battle to defeat this land grant, and in June 1897 the state granted a charter for the new company. Businessmen hoped the Smith bill might lead to a north-south railroad, but as with the Bush Act, a lack of financial support killed the project.

The most important railroad measure from the governor's viewpoint was the commission bill. The house passed its version of this bill by eighty-one to three, but the prorailroad forces, continuing their domination of the senate, again killed the proposal. The governor expressed surprise and chagrin that the senate should repudiate the platform pledge of the Democratic party.

Jones suffered another defeat at the hands of the special session when it overrode his veto and accepted a debt-settlement compromise. Ever since Arkansas became a state it had accumulated debts to the U.S. government. The federal and state governments made claims and counterclaims against each other. In 1850 the U.S. Congress granted all the unsurveyed overflowed lands in Arkansas to state ownership, yet three years later the Congress made railroad grants of 273,000 acres of Arkansas swamplands that had previously been granted to the state. Gov. James Paul Clarke had reached a settlement of the debt controversy in negotiations with the Grover Cleveland administration. The U.S. House of Representatives accepted this compromise but, bowing to pressure from the railroads, added the proviso that lands granted to the predecessors of the Iron Mountain Railroad be confirmed in the hands of those holding the property. When the Arkansas General Assembly approved the congressional version with its so-called Meiklejohn Amendment, Governor Jones fired off a veto message labeling the deal an "Infamous proposition." The fifteen pages of legal argument in the message concluded with an estimate that the state would lose $1 million worth of property without any rational justification. In this debate Jones stood against the whole congressional delegation from Arkansas, which eventually cast its votes for the Meiklejohn Amendment. The *Pine Bluff Weekly Press-Eagle* believed Jones had become "perverse and obdurate" to a degree never reached by Governor Clarke, the most stubborn and pugnacious of all the governors. When Attorney General Davis made his 1900 bid for the governorship, he sided with Jones on this issue. Davis pictured the amendment as a steal by the railroads and corrupt politicians.

In April 1898 the United States entered into armed conflict with Spain. Governor Jones called for the creation of two new regiments of volunteers since the National Guard did not have sufficient recruits. Although the state responded with enthusiasm, the fighting came to an end in August before the Arkansas troops had completed their training. The war captured public interest at the expense of state politics, but Governor Jones continued to remind the state of the need for a railroad commission. He told the Democratic state convention that once the voters approved of the constitutional amendment making a permanent commission possible, the state legislature must "no longer hesitate." In the fall election the amendment passed, and Jones easily won reelection with almost three times the vote of his Republican opponent, H. F. Auten.

In his second inaugural address on 18 January 1899, Jones advised the legislature to create a railroad commission and lamented the failure of the Bush Act to lead to a new northerly railroad. He believed that if the act were revised to permit leasing of the railroad instead of direct operation by the government, the potential problem of political interference and frequent policy changes could be avoided. Although the Bush Act never produced a railroad, Jones won a major victory when the legislature enacted the commission bill in March. He appointed Robert Neill, Henry Wells, and Jeremiah Wallace to the commission. These men had little experience and naively accepted the published rates of the railroads as their basis for regulation, without considering the fact that the railroads often gave preferred customers lower rates. Some shippers actually experienced higher rates, but by 1901 the commission claimed it had achieved an overall lowering of rates.

The governor informed a *St. Louis Post-Dispatch* reporter that Arkansans were "rabid" in their opposition to trusts and "nothing but war on the evil" could satisfy them. The general assembly responded to the state's vindictive mood by passing the stern Rector Antitrust Act. Newly elected Attorney General Davis so vigorously prosecuted the trusts that many insurance companies fled the state. The act, according to Jones, made rate fixing (collusion to set prices) illegal only if such rates were enforced in Arkansas. But Davis thought a conspiracy anywhere would constitute loss of the privilege to do business in the state. According to Jones, Davis considered an insurance company to have violated the Rector Act if it "was a party to a rate agreement in Hong Kong." The Arkansas Supreme Court upheld Jones's interpretation of the act. The governor was disdainful of his new attorney general's demagogic behavior. Davis began a crusade to win the governor's chair almost as soon as he took office in 1899, and his blatant attacks on the governor created a serious rift within the administration and the party.

The Jones administration generated another controversy that raged for a decade. The governor repeated former Governor Clarke's request that the old statehouse be replaced by a new capitol. The old building had grace and charm but insufficient space. One senator noting its dilapidated condition referred to it as an "ancient rookery." The legislature provided $50,000 to begin construction on the penitentiary grounds in Little Rock. But Davis initiated a frenzied legal campaign in May 1899 to obstruct the project, which he viewed as boondoggle to enrich the wealthy "high-collared roosters" in Little Rock at the expense of the rural classes. Davis initiated quo warranto proceedings to prevent the capitol commissioners from carrying out their functions, sought an injunction to prevent the beginning of construction, and sued the auditor to prevent any payment for construction work. Although the courts resisted all these maneuvers, the 1900 state Democratic convention upheld Davis over Jones by rejecting a plank endorsing the capitol-construction project. Jones did manage to lay the cornerstone in November 1900, but the construction site remained inactive for a two-year period.

By May 1899 Jones's intention to run for James Henderson Berry's Senate seat became apparent. In June Davis solicited an alliance with Berry against Jones, but the old one-legged Civil War veteran refused the request. Davis set out not only to win the governorship but also to defeat Jones in his bid for the Senate.

On 29 January 1900 Jones officially announced his candidacy. In an address to the people he argued for an imperialist policy. Puerto Rico and the Philippines should be retained but given a large degree of self-government. The advance into Asia would provide a market for Southern cotton. He decried the timidity that would not "carry our Christian civilization beyond the eastern bounds of the Pacific." In his expansionist sentiments he stood squarely in opposition to Arkansas Senators Berry and James K. Jones whose views were more in accord with Bryan's. The Arkansas Democratic platform of 1900 condemned "the carpetbag government foisted on the people of Puerto Rico and Cuba." On most issues, such as direct election of senators, Berry and Governor Jones agreed. Of the first eight county primaries Jones lost all but one. His defeat can be explained as a result of the tendency to reelect an incumbent rather than as a rejection of his ardent expansionism.

In 1900 Jones turned his energies to the practice of law in Little Rock. His political star was rapidly eclipsed by Davis's meteoric rise. After his wife's death in 1913, the old veteran returned briefly to active political office as a Pulaski County representative in the 1915 general assembly. His work as a legislator gained scant attention from the newspapers. The *Gazette* once described Governor Jones as tall, slender, with iron gray hair and a "courtly manner." He was an Episcopalian, a Confederate veteran, and one of the last Arkansas politicians from the old patrician class.

Following a ten-day illness, he succumbed to pneumonia at Little Rock on Christmas Day, 1918, and was buried in Oakland Cemetery in a Confederate uniform to which he had attached an American flag.

JEFF DAVIS

1901–1907

JEFF DAVIS (6 May 1862–3 January 1913), attorney, was born in the Red River lowlands near the village of Rocky Comfort, Sevier County, Arkansas, on the first anniversary of Arkansas's secession from the Union. His father, Lewis W. Davis, was a Baptist preacher who had migrated to Rocky Comfort from Kentucky in 1850. Born in Todd County, Kentucky, in 1832, he was the son of Rebecca and Joshua Davis, a struggling blacksmith and farmer. In July 1861 Lewis Davis married a well-to-do young widow, Elizabeth Phillips Scott. Born near Tuscaloosa, Alabama, in 1832, Elizabeth Davis was the daughter of Bolen C. Phillips, a wealthy planter (he owned thirty-six slaves and $10,000 worth of real estate in 1850) who had moved to Sevier County from Alabama in 1835. Her first husband, William Scott, with whom she had three children, was a planter who owned nine slaves at the time of his death in 1860.

Lewis Davis was enough of a Rebel partisan to name his only natural son after the president of the Confederacy, but he did not see action in the Confederate army until he was drafted in 1864, a fact that later caused his son a good deal of political embarrassment. After serving briefly as a private, Lewis Davis accepted a chaplain's commission in the Nineteenth Arkansas Infantry. On his return from the war, he abandoned the ministry (though he remained active as a Baptist lay leader until his death in 1906) and took up the practice of law. In 1866 he was elected county and probate judge of Sevier County. After July 1867 when the southern half of Sevier became Little River County, his jurisdiction was limited to the new county. But with the advent of Radical Reconstruction in 1868, he and other local Democratic officeholders were swept out of office.

In 1869 the Davis family resettled in Dover, the small county seat located in the foothills of Pope County. The move to Pope County did not provide the Davises with an escape from Reconstruction politics—

Dover was the storm center of the Pope County Militia War of 1872—but it did bring them a measure of success and prosperity. By the early seventies, "Judge" Davis was the acknowledged leader of the Dover bar. In 1873 following the completion of the Little Rock and Fort Smith Railroad, the Davises moved ten miles south to the booming railroad town of Russellville. The coming of the railroad inaugurated an era of boosterism and development in Pope County that was ideally suited to Lewis Davis's talents and ambitions. As an attorney specializing in homestead cases, a real-estate agent, a newspaper editor, a state legislator (1877), and the leader of several local booster organizations, he played a central role in the economic modernization of the county. In the process he became one of Russellville's most prosperous citizens.

As the son of such a man, Jeff Davis enjoyed a relatively privileged adolescence. Educated in the Russellville public schools, he applied for an appointment to West Point but was rejected, allegedly because he was a chronically poor speller. In 1878 he enrolled at the University of Arkansas at Fayetteville, where he remained for two years. In 1880 he transferred to the law department of Vanderbilt University. While at Vanderbilt he completed the standard two-year law program in a single year, but the university administration refused to grant him a diploma because he had failed to meet a residency requirement. Undaunted, Davis returned to Russellville and immediately applied for admission to the bar, even though he was technically under age. Through his father's influence the minimum age limit was waived, and in the summer of 1881 he was admitted to the bar of Arkansas's Fifth Judicial Circuit. His college odyssey was not quite over, however. In the fall he returned to Tennessee to attend Cumberland University. The following spring, with his law degree finally in hand, twenty-year-old Davis became the junior partner of L. W. Davis and Son, Attorneys at Law.

In October 1882 Davis married Ina MacKenzie, the daughter of a Methodist minister and the stepdaughter of Judge Frank Thach, Lewis Davis's close friend who had served two terms (1874–1878) as county judge before his death in 1878. Ina Davis bore twelve children, eight of whom survived past infancy. The Davises' eldest son, Wallace (1888–1965), served as state attorney general from September 1915 to January 1917 and as a Democratic national committeeman from 1915 to 1921. Ina Davis died in 1910, and in October 1911, Davis married Leila Carter, the daughter of Dr. Wallace Carter of Ozark.

Davis was involved in local political campaigns as early as 1884, but his active political career did not begin until 1888. Selected as a presidential elector by the state Democratic convention, he stumped the state for Grover Cleveland, white supremacy, and "reform." The 1888 campaign whetted Davis's appetite for politics, and in 1890 he ran for district prosecuting attorney. Promising to rid the district of liquor-law violators and vowing to "fill the penitentiary so full of negroes that their feet would be sticking out the windows," he narrowly defeated his opponent for the Democratic nomination, Charles C. Reid of Conway County, a young Vanderbilt law graduate who later served five terms in Congress. Unopposed for reelection in 1892, Davis served as district prosecuting attorney until October 1894.

Buoyed by a flourishing law practice, Davis ran for Congress in 1896. Calling himself a free-silver Democrat and claiming to be the farmer's friend, he challenged William L. Terry, a popular three-term congressman from Little Rock. Unfortunately for Davis, the challenge proved to be short lived. When the Pope County Democratic convention convened in February, Davis expected to receive a unanimous endorsement. Instead, more than a third of the convention's delegates supported Terry. Stunned, Davis immediately withdrew from the race. Following his disappointing loss to Terry, he became totally absorbed in the presidential campaign of William Jennings Bryan. Selected as a presidential elector for the second time, he set out on the campaign trail like a political evangelist, preaching the Bryanist gospel of free silver to anyone who would listen. Because of a fusion agreement with the People's party, he was ultimately replaced by a Populist elector, but he continued to entertain the voters with his spellbinding oratory until the bitter end. Acknowledging his enormous contribution to the local Bryan campaign, his fellow electors gave him the honor of delivering Arkansas's official vote to the electoral college in Washington.

In 1898 Davis embarked on what initially appeared to be an ill-advised quest for the state attorney generalship. Slowed by a minor stroke that sapped his strength and temporarily paralyzed his left arm and part of his left side, he was given little chance of defeating the front-runner Judge Frank Goar, dean of the University of Arkansas law school and deputy commissioner of mines, manufactures, and agriculture. After the first four county primaries, Goar held a commanding lead over Davis and three other candidates. But on 6 April Goar suffered a fatal stroke. With this sudden twist of fortune, Davis's candidacy gained new life. By the time the last county primary was over, Davis, with 30,029 votes, enjoyed a large plurality over his three remaining opponents: J. B. Baker (17,513), John T. Hicks (14,672), and

E. P. Watson (8,093). In the general election Davis defeated his Republican challenger, J. J. Henley, by a margin of nearly three to one and carried all but two of the state's counties.

Davis's attorney generalship proved to be the most memorable in the state's history. By challenging the legality of the Kimbell State House Act, which provided for the construction of a new capitol building on the site of the existing state penitentiary, and by rendering a radical and highly controversial extraterritorial interpretation of the Rector Antitrust Act, he triggered a bitter political struggle that threw the attorney general's office into the spotlight and the state into an uproar. According to Davis, the Rector Act prohibited any trust from doing business in Arkansas—regardless of where the trust had been organized. To make his point, in March 1899 he filed suit against every fire-insurance company then doing business in the state, demanding that they withdraw from industrywide pricing agreements. The fire-insurance companies responded by threatening to cancel policies by the hundreds, and outraged businessmen, infuriated by Davis's economic secessionism, held mass protest meetings across the state. But Davis, supported by the legislature, refused to back down. On 27 May Davis's interpretation of the antitrust law was overruled by the state supreme court. Legally this ended the controversy, but politically it simply added fuel to the fire.

Styling himself a martyr, Davis took his case to the people. In June he announced for the governorship and embarked on an exhaustive year-long campaign. Visiting virtually every county in the state, he conducted a one-man crusade against the "Yankee trusts" and their local collaborators. He had tried to throw the rascals out, Davis told the voters, but he had been betrayed by the "five jackasses" of the supreme court and the "high-collared crowd" in Little Rock. "The war," he declared, "knife to knife, hilt to hilt, foot to foot, knee to knee, between the corporations of Arkansas and the people. . . . *If I* win this race I have got to win it from every railroad, every bank and two-thirds of the lawyers and most of the big politicians. But if I can get the plain people of the country to help me, God bless you, we will clean the thing out." Although Davis was ridiculed by the state press and branded as a demagogue by his four opponents—John Fletcher, Edgar Bryant, A. F. Vandeventer, and James Wood—the electoral response to his populistic rhetoric was overwhelming. Carrying seventy-four of seventy-five counties in the Democratic primary, he won the most resounding political victory in Arkansas history. Arkansas politics would never be quite the same again. In the general election, Davis won handily over Republican Harmon L. Remmel and Populist A. W. Files, even though several thousand anti-Davis Democrats, including ex-Gov. William Meade Fishback and ex-Sen. Augustus Hill Garland, refused to support him.

Davis's inauguration, which took place on 18 January 1901, was marred by the absence of outgoing Gov. Daniel Webster Jones, who broke custom and refused to participate in his successor's installation. In his inaugural address, Davis outlined an ambitious reform program, focusing on the two issues that had catapulted him into the limelight. He implored the new legislature to pass an extraterritorial amendment that would put some teeth in the Rector Antitrust Act, and he reiterated his opposition to the Kimbell State House Act. He recommended the abolition of the existing capitol commission, the firing of the architect hired by the commission, the creation of a new capitol commission made up of the governor and other state officials, and the use of competitive bidding and convict labor. Elsewhere in the speech, Davis called for a fellow-servant law, the establishment of a state reform school, the enlargement of the state lunatic asylum, increased appropriations for Confederate pensions, the abolition of the suicide clause in life-insurance policies, and the repeal of an 1897 act that provided for the construction of state-owned railroads by convict labor.

The Davis administration's first major task was to gain control of the legislature, which was in session from mid-January to mid-April 1901. At the outset, it appeared that most of the legislature was anxious to cooperate with the new governor; Thomas H. Humphreys, an ardent Davis supporter, was even elected speaker of the house. But in the end, several factors—a powerful business lobby, ideological conservatism, institutional inertia, concern for legislative autonomy, widespread distrust of Davis's motives, and the fact that personal factionalism was generally equated with bossism in Arkansas politics—combined to defeat Davis's legislative program. His one success came on the statehouse issue, and even there he won only a partial victory. After weeks of wrangling, the legislature ratified a compromise that, though leaving the basic structure of the Kimbell Act intact, established a new capitol commission consisting of the governor and three appointees, appropriated $1 million for the new state house, and called for the use of competitive bidding and convict labor. Davis was bitterly disappointed with the results of the 1901 legislative session, but he was careful to avoid a full-scale confrontation.

Despite his problems with the legislature, Davis's first six months in office were surprisingly peaceful. The savage conflict that had characterized the 1900 primary campaign had abated, and the party's wounds seemed to be healing. As summer approached, several prominent anti-Davis leaders admitted that the new administration had turned out to be a pleasant surprise. But as so often was the case during Davis's career, this period of calm was merely the lull before the storm.

The calm was shattered by a struggle for control of the state's penal system. Although the penitentiary controversy eventually encompassed several explosive issues, the conflict initially centered around Davis's opposition to the convict-lease system. When the penitentiary buildings were torn down in the summer of 1899 to make way for the new state-house, the state penitentiary board (made up of the governor and four other state officials) was obliged to find a new home for several hundred inmates. Consequently, the board leased nearly a third of the state's prisoners to the Arkansas Brick Manufacturing Company. W. W. Dickinson, the president of the brick company, insisted on a lucrative ten-year contract, even though long-term convict-lease contracts violated state policy. This situation outraged Davis who for political as well as humanitarian reasons demanded that the Dickinson contract be annulled.

A related controversy involved the purchase of a new state convict farm. Although the governor and a majority of the legislature agreed that the state should purchase a convict farm (which would serve as a replacement for the old penitentiary), there was widespread disagreement over how the purchase should be financed and where the farm should be located. In February 1901 Davis vetoed the "Sunnyside" farm bill, and in April the legislature rejected several measures that would have enlarged the governor's role in the administration of the penal system. The conflict escalated in June when Davis turned to the penitentiary board for help. When it became clear that a majority of the board supported the Dickinson contract and opposed Davis's plans for penal reform, he decided to force the issue by exposing the brutality of the convict-lease system. After an inspection of the convict-lease camp at England, where he allegedly witnessed unspeakable horrors, Davis created a sensation when he informed the press that the board was deliberately sabotaging his reform efforts and consigning the state's convicts to a living hell. In response, Atty. Gen. George Murphy, formerly a Davis ally, accused the governor of slander and demanded a full investigation of the charges.

While the penitentiary controversy simmered, Davis turned his attention to another potentially explosive issue, the proposed new statehouse. Under the terms of the statehouse act that Davis had signed in April, the original capitol commission had been disbanded, and a new capitol commission had been appointed by the governor. The new commission had a clear mandate from the legislature to begin construction of the new statehouse as soon as possible, but Davis had other ideas. Throughout the summer, with Davis leading the way, the capitol commissioners expended all their energy in a running feud with George Mann, the architect hired by the first capitol commission. Davis tried to force Mann to resign, but the architect made it clear that he would bow out only if the state made it worth his while financially. Proponents of the new statehouse urged Davis and the other commissioners to stop squabbling with Mann and to begin construction, but as the months passed not a shovelful of dirt was turned. By late summer, the statehouse advocates had just about run out of patience, when Davis suddenly threw them a curve. At a meeting of the commission in early September, Davis unveiled a plan to build a new statehouse on the foundation of the existing one. The proposal, which was tentatively endorsed by the other commissioners, would allegedly save the taxpayers a great deal of money and would thwart the plans of the special interests who had schemed to bleed the state dry. When Mann complained that the governor's proposal would short-change future generations by producing a statehouse of inadequate size, Davis retorted: "Damn the future, it's the present I'm interested in." Other critics charged that Davis knew that his proposal was unrealistic, that he was simply using it as a means to further postpone the construction of a statehouse on the old penitentiary grounds.

Davis's handling of the penitentiary and statehouse issues left many Democratic leaders disgruntled, but the controversy that shook the Arkansas Democratic party to its foundations was his interference in the Senate race between the incumbent Sen. James K. Jones and former Gov. James Paul Clarke. Overlooking an unwritten party rule against intermixing gubernatorial and senatorial politics, Davis threw his support to Clarke, east Arkansas's most powerful politician. Motivated by practical as well as ideological concerns, Davis realized that without increased support from the "swamp Democrats" of east Arkansas he had little hope of gaining firm control of state politics. His subsequent indictment of Jones, a former chairman of the Democratic National Committee, was unrestrained and unrelenting. According to Davis, Jones, who owned stock in the American Cotton Company, was a tool of the trusts. Before the campaign was over, Davis had accused the senator of a whole host of personal and political sins: declaring bank-ruptcy in 1868 in order to avoid paying a board bill, cheating a ward out of several thousand dollars, serving only one month in the Confederate army, and conspiring to defeat the administration's antitrust bill.

Davis's attack on Jones sent shock waves across the state. Many anti-Davis leaders charged that the governor had proven once and for all that he was an unprincipled, power-hungry boss. Jones himself fought back with everything he had; after issuing a point-by-point rebuttal of Davis's charges, he set up a headquarters in Little Rock that disseminated anti-Davis broadsides and pamphlets. Most impor-tant, he and other anti-Davis leaders convinced Elias W. Rector, the patrician reformer who had sponsored the 1899 antitrust act, to chal-lenge Davis for the Democratic gubernatorial nomination. Rector was a formidable adversary. An able campaigner, he was the only politi-cian in the state with trust-busting credentials that rivaled those of Davis. As long as Rector was his opponent, Davis could not rely on the antitrust issue that had figured so prominently in his 1900 primary victory. He had no choice but to turn to other issues.

Davis turned first to the class issue, emphasizing Rector's aristo-cratic background (his father was Henry Massie Rector, Arkansas's Civil War governor) and high-toned lifestyle. But he eventually focused on Rector's involvement in a conspiratorial "penitentiary ring" that was allegedly trying to take over the state. Davis claimed that because he had exposed the inhumane conditions in the penitentiary system, Rector and the ring had vowed to destroy his career. The most spec-tacular aspect of the penitentiary-ring controversy had more to do with racial demagoguery than penal reform. Early in the campaign Davis discovered that nothing excited the voters more than the charge that Rector had sanctioned the use of "negro guards" at state prison camps. In speech after speech, in varying degrees of hyperbole, Davis described the horrors he had discovered during his inspection of the England camp the previous July. "The first sight that greeted my eyes," he told a crowd at Hot Springs, "was a great, big, black negro with a pump gun guarding the white men and driving them down the row and saying: 'Hoe that cotton, damn you, or I will kill you.'" Rector tried to counter Davis's charges with racial demagoguery of his own, but he had little success.

Rector was most effective when he focused on the temperance issue. Charging that Davis was a shameless drunkard and a tool of the liquor interests, Rector scandalized the local Baptist establishment, which had elected Davis first vice-president of the Arkansas Baptist

Association in November 1901. During the final weeks of the campaign, several prominent ministers and temperance leaders echoed Rector's charges and called for Davis's defeat.

The Davis-Rector campaign was a political donnybrook, but in the end it was no contest. Davis won a sweeping victory on election day, garnering 66.1 percent of the vote and carrying seventy counties. To Davis's delight, his ally Clarke was also victorious, winning 54.3 percent of the vote in the senatorial primary.

Politically speaking, the results of the 1902 primary represented a great victory for Davis. By defeating Rector, he eliminated the only politician who had any hope of challenging his leadership of the local antitrust crusade. By engineering the defeat of Jones, he demoralized the conservative wing of the Arkansas Democratic party. And finally, by effecting an alliance with Clarke, he transformed an embryonic political organization into a powerful statewide machine. Nevertheless, Davis paid an enormous price for his double victory over Rector and Jones. His alliance with Clarke brought him added power and security, but it also compromised the ideological integrity of the Davis movement. With few exceptions, the "swamp Democrats" who entered the Davis organization through the alliance with Clarke had little sympathy for and little understanding of the revolt that had brought Davis to power. Perhaps even more important, the racial and moralistic turmoil that accompanied the Davis-Rector campaign diverted attention from Davis's crusade against New South colonialism.

Davis's landslide victory in the 1902 primary set the leaders of the anti-Davis coalition back on their heels but did little to still the controversies that had dominated the campaign. Nowhere was this more evident than in the continuing controversy over Davis's moral character. In late March Davis provoked a bitter feud with ex-Gov. James Philip Eagle, the president of the Arkansas Baptist Association and a member of the capitol commission. Davis demanded Eagle's resignation from the capitol commission, ostensibly because he had supported Jones in the senatorial primary. On 7 April, when Eagle refused to step down, Davis resigned as vice-president of the Arkansas Baptist Association. On 18 April Davis formally removed Eagle from the capitol commission, an action that infuriated the Baptist establishment and most of the legislature. To complicate matters, the entire controversy soon became hopelessly entangled in the affairs of the Second Baptist Church of Little Rock, to which both Davis and Eagle belonged. Less than a week after Eagle's ouster, a church disciplinary committee that included state Supreme Court Justice Carroll Wood, ex-attorney general W. F. Atkinson, and former Populist gubernatorial candidate A. W. Files drew up a list of formal charges against Davis, accusing him of public drunkenness, chronic intemperance, and generally immoral behavior.

Davis condemned the committee's proceedings as a political witch hunt, but on 28 May he was formally expelled from the congregation. An incident of this kind might have ruined a man with ordinary political skills, but Davis, who liked nothing better than assuming the role of a martyr, soon turned the situation to his advantage. After having himself readmitted to fellowship by his home church in Russellville, he implored the voters to strike down the "high-collared" pharisees in Little Rock who had persecuted him for his political beliefs. "I love the Baptist church of Arkansas," he told the state Democratic convention in mid-June, "and a few canting hypocrites of this church cannot drive me from its blessed folds."

The church-expulsion affair was an important episode in Davis's career. Coming as it did on the heels of the controversy over his intervention in the Senate race, the affair severed his few remaining ties with "respectable" society and all but completed the polarization of the Arkansas Democratic party. After his expulsion from the church, Davis was openly hostile toward what he derisively called "the morality crowd." Throughout the remainder of his career, he was solidly allied with the state's liquor industry; during his second and third terms he vetoed several temperance bills and pardoned hundreds of convicted liquor-law violators. In return for these favors, the liquor interests allowed themselves to be integrated into the Davis organization.

Like the temperance issue, the penitentiary controversy continued to rage during the closing months of Davis's first term. Pursuing his crusade against the convict-lease system and the penitentiary ring, Davis became embroiled in a bitter feud with penitentiary superintendent Reese Hogins. Although Hogins was a staunch Davis supporter when he took over as superintendent in December 1901, the relationship between the two men was soon poisoned by Davis's constant interference in penitentiary affairs. Davis claimed that the root of the trouble was Hogins's collusive relationship with Dickinson and the Arkansas Brick Manufacturing Company, but Hogins insisted that the feud was triggered by his refusal to hire the governor's brother-in-law.

The Davis-Hogins feud captured its share of headlines, but the most volatile aspect of the penitentiary fight was the ongoing struggle over the purchase of a state convict farm. The struggle turned into a full-scale political war in November when, over Davis's protest, the penitentiary board purchased the Cummins farm, an eleven thousand-acre tract in Lincoln County. Davis, who wanted the board to purchase a farm owned by Jefferson County Republican leader Louis Altheimer, insisted that the Cummins property was totally "unfit for a convict farm" and vowed to do everything in his power to nullify the Cummins farm contract. When the new legislature convened in January 1903, he devoted almost half of his inaugural address to the Cummins farm issue and other aspects of the penitentiary controversy. Using language that was usually reserved for the stump, he charged the penitentiary staff with mismanagement and fraud and excoriated the penitentiary board for obstructing his reform program.

Davis's unrestrained attack on the penitentiary ring triggered a storm of controversy that ultimately engulfed his entire legislative program. Although he successfully prodded the legislature into sending an investigative team to the Cummins farm, he alienated a number of legislators in the process. As his legislative support slipped away, Davis began threatening unruly legislators with political extinction, which just made matters worse. The more high-handed he became, the more the legislature stiffened its resistance.

Davis's struggle with the legislature and the penitentiary board led to a move for his impeachment. The leader of the impeachment forces was Atty. Gen. George Murphy, who outlined the case for Davis's removal at a massive anti-Davis rally in Little Rock on 12 February. Murphy focused on the Cummins farm controversy and Davis's attempts to bully the penitentiary board, misuse of the governor's contingency fund, and the unwarranted removal of Eagle from the capitol commission. The morning after Murphy's philippic, the house of representatives ordered its ways and means committee to conduct a full investigation of the charges and countercharges issued by Murphy and Davis. Davis claimed that he welcomed the investigation, but everyone concerned realized that the committee's hearings represented the first step of the impeachment process.

The investigation began on 18 February and lasted for more than five weeks. Meeting nightly in the chambers of the supreme court, the eleven members of the committee interviewed scores of witnesses and compiled more than eight hundred pages of testimony and evidence. Rigidly factionalized, the committee was composed of six anti-Davis legislators, three Davis supporters, and two members who tried to remain neutral. The atmosphere at the hearings was extremely tense, and Davis later claimed that he attended the committee's proceedings at the risk of his life. Throughout the investigation Davis was squarely on the defensive, which was probably where he wanted to be. For a politician like Davis, who thrived on persecution and who spent much of his career trying to cultivate an image of martyrdom, the nightly melodrama in the supreme court chambers was a dream come true. Recognizing that the charges against him were too trivial to sustain an impeachment, he provided his enemies with enough rope to hang themselves.

In the end, the hopelessly divided committee submitted four separate reports. The majority report, prepared by Chairman Edward Merriam and five other anti-Davis committeemen, defended the penitentiary board, endorsed the purchase of the Cummins farm, absolved Superintendent Hogins of any wrongdoing, contradicted Davis's claim that the state's prisoners were being mistreated, and condemned Davis for misusing his contingency fund, trying to intimidate state auditor T. C. Monroe, and accepting free transportation and other improper gifts. The report did not explicitly call for Davis's impeachment, but its implications were clear. Fortunately for Davis, when the majority report was submitted to the full house for approval, it was defeated by a vote of forty-three to forty-four. Thus ended any chance of Davis's impeachment.

In the aftermath of the impeachment attempt, Davis was full of bluster. The "high-collared roosters" had tried to skin him, he repeatedly declared, but they had lost their nerve. Nevertheless, he soon discovered that his troubles with the legislature were far from over. During the final three weeks of the legislative session, Davis's enemies in the legislature dealt him one defeat after another. Both houses overrode his veto of the Merriman State House Bill, which empowered the legislature to select five new capitol commissioners. When Davis, in a fit of pique, refused to acknowledge the new law and appointed five new commissioners of his own, the legislature filed a quo warranto suit against him. The administration's antitrust bill was defeated; the house refused to annul the Dickinson convict-lease contract; and the senate refused to confirm Davis's appointment of James G. Wallace as a chancery judge. These parting shots from the legislature provoked a savage counterattack. In late May, after announcing his intention to run for an unprecedented third term, Davis stunned the state by issuing an omnibus veto of more than three hundred bills. Attorney General Murphy immediately challenged the legality of the mass veto, and in June his challenge was sustained by a district judge. Undaunted, Davis appealed the decision to the state supreme court, which, to nearly everyone's surprise, ruled in his favor.

The mass veto set the stage for the most tumultuous primary campaign in the state's history. By mid-June 1903 three anti-Davis candidates had announced for the governorship: M. J. Manning, a former president of the senate; Vandeventer, the Morrilton lumber merchant and former speaker of the house who had opposed Davis in the 1900 primary; and Judge Wood. Neither Manning, who withdrew from the race less than two weeks after the opening of the county canvass, nor Vandeventer, who was simply searching for a measure of personal vindication, posed any real threat to Davis. But Wood's candidacy was another matter. The Wood campaign was well financed and extremely well organized. The anti-Davis press was mobilized as never before, the state was flooded with anti-Davis broadsides and pamphlets, and local organizations known as "Wood clubs" were formed in virtually every county in Arkansas. Anti-Davis rallies and parades were held in many of the state's larger cities and towns, and tens of thousands of small wooden buttons, the official emblem of the Wood faction, were distributed to the voters.

The factional split between pro-Davis and anti-Davis Democrats was never more intense or more sharply drawn than during the 1903–1904 campaign. As one observer described the situation, "no man could offer even for constable or school director, much less the higher offices, unless he in advance declared himself as between Davis and Wood." It was the kind of contest that Davis loved, a bruising, no-holds-barred brawl. Both sides repeatedly resorted to racial demagoguery and personal invective, and on two occasions Davis and Wood actually came to blows. Wood, the self-professed candidate of moderation and respectability, charged that Davis was an unprincipled demagogue who was morally unfit to be governor. Davis, relying on folksy rhetoric and a sharp wit, portrayed Wood as a dandified, trust-heeling city slicker. He also trumpeted the accomplishments of his first two terms, boasting that he had prevented a "million dollar state house steal," thwarted the designs of the penitentiary ring, and expanded governmental services without adding to the common man's tax burden. He was especially proud of the new state deaf-mute institute, which had been financed by increased railroad taxes. Davis also spent a great deal of time defending his liberal pardon record, which he claimed had been misrepresented by the press.

Despite Wood's monumental campaign, Davis won a convincing victory in the primary election, carrying fifty-eight counties and winning 57.8 percent of the vote. Wood's strong showing in his native south Arkansas, in the plantation lowlands of east Arkansas, and in urban areas was not enough to offset his poor support among farmers in the uplands and the backcountry. Once again "Our Jeff" had demonstrated that he was the undisputed champion of the rural stump.

Following the 1904 primary, Davis was at the peak of his power. With the opposition in disarray, his forces gained complete control of the 1904 state Democratic convention, during which they reorganized and formalized the party's primary system. In the general election Davis had no trouble defeating his Republican opponent, H. H. Myers, despite the fact that several thousand anti-Davis Democrats "went fishing" on election day. The voters also elected a predominantly pro-Davis legislature. Waylaid by an intense corporate lobbying effort and a systematic campaign of bribery and boodling, the 1905 legislature disappointed Davis on a number of occasions. But it did approve several of his pet projects, including an extraterritorial antitrust law, the establishment of a state reform school, and the reorganization of penitentiary management.

Most of Davis's third term was devoted to a race for the Senate. In the spring of 1905, Davis challenged Senator Berry, an aging one-legged Confederate veteran who had served in the Senate since 1885. Davis had supported Berry in the 1900 primary, but he now claimed that the senator was too old and feeble to stand up against the trusts. Hampered by poor health, Berry conducted a lackluster campaign and refused to meet Davis in joint debate. Most of the race's excitement was provided by Davis's constant interference in the gubernatorial primary, which pitted Davis's handpicked successor, Rep. John Sebastian Little, against Atty. Gen. Robert L. Rogers. The most dramatic episode of the senatorial campaign occurred in October 1905, when President Roosevelt made a brief visit to Little Rock. Davis, who had race-baited Roosevelt mercilessly during the 1904 presidential campaign, single-handedly turned the president's visit into a white supremacist publicity stunt. After devoting most of his welcoming speech to a defense of lynching, Davis refused to attend a banquet held in Roosevelt's honor because ex-Gov. Powell Clayton (whom Davis characterized as a villainous carpetbagger) had also been invited. In the months that followed, Davis turned the Roosevelt-Clayton incident into a major political issue, and Berry, one of the last of the Confederate brigadiers, found himself in the curious position of being branded a traitor to the South for having attended the presidential banquet. In the March 1906 primary, Berry—despite his considerable popularity—managed to carry only twenty-four counties. As in 1902 and 1904, Davis's charismatic style of personal politics had overwhelmed a seemingly powerful opponent.

Davis's senatorial career was, in the words of one historian, a "long anticlimax." Although Davis assured his followers that he would take Washington by storm, his plans quickly went awry. To Davis's dismay, the rough-and-tumble style of political combat that had proved so effective in the Arkansas backcountry seemed strangely out of place in the nation's capital. Soon after his arrival in Washington, Davis introduced an antitrust bill and, to the amazement of his colleagues, delivered a long and impassioned harangue against "the malefactors of great wealth." The speech was roundly criticized by the national press and by several senators who reminded Davis that senatorial etiquette proscribed long-winded speeches by newly elected members. Davis later claimed that his antitrust speech had "swept the cobwebs off the ceiling of the Senate chamber," but in truth he was bitterly disappointed by the Washington establishment's refusal to take him or his bill seriously. In April 1908 in an effort to get his antitrust bill out of committee, he apologized for his intemperate rhetoric and his breach of senatorial etiquette, but it was too late. The press continued to portray him as a wild-eyed, backwoods buffoon, and Davis retreated into stony silence.

Senator Davis's problems were compounded by a deteriorating power base in state politics. Little, a Davis ally, was elected governor in 1906, but poor health forced him to resign in February 1907. Consequently, during most of Little's two-year term, Xenophon Overton Pindall, the president pro tempore of the senate and an ardent anti-Davis Democrat, served as acting governor. Davis was determined to regain control of the governorship, and in February 1908, less than two months after his arrival in Washington, he returned to Arkansas to campaign for his close friend Atty. Gen. William F. Kirby, who was seeking the Democratic gubernatorial nomination. Kirby's major opponent was George Washington Donaghey, a prominent building contractor who previously had been on good terms with Davis, largely because he had echoed Davis's criticisms of the original capitol commission. Davis claimed that Donaghey had become a trust-heeling conservative and ordered everyone in the Davis organization to support Kirby. In the end, despite a monumental stump-speaking effort by Davis, Kirby was soundly defeated by Donaghey. Davis tried to save face by reversing himself and insisting that Donaghey was still a Davis man, but the new governor remained permanently disaffected. The Davis organization never recovered from the Kirby-Donaghey fiasco. With its leadership in disarray and without its gubernatorial patronage base, the once-powerful Davis machine went into permanent decline.

Davis spent the remainder of his career brooding about his lack of influence in Little Rock and Washington. In 1909 he gained a measure of notoriety by introducing a bill that prohibited speculation in crop futures, but his proposal was never enacted into law. In 1910, after supporting William Kavanaugh's unsuccessful bid for the governorship, Davis became embroiled in a bitter controversy over the disposition of public land in east Arkansas. Davis's apparent collusion with land speculators in the so-called sunk-lands controversy tarnished his reform image and further accelerated his political decline. During his final years in the Senate, Davis became increasingly absorbed in his family life and spent less and less time in Washington. In the 1912 senatorial primary, Davis faced a stiff challenge from Rep. Stephen Brundidge. Brundidge was the aggressor throughout the campaign, as Davis uncharacteristically refused to meet his opponent in joint debate, but in the end Davis eked out a narrow victory.

Davis's reelection seemed to rekindle his interest in public policy, but his comeback was to be short-lived. On 3 January 1913, two months before the expiration of his first term, he suffered a fatal stroke. He was only fifty years old. Although Davis had been bothered by a serious weight problem for several years, most observers were shocked by the suddenness of his passing. His funeral was one of the largest in Little Rock history, as thousands of mourners came to pay their respects to early-twentieth-century Arkansas's most engaging political folk hero. He was buried at Mount Holly Cemetery.

Davis was a genuinely paradoxical figure. He was a successful, college-educated attorney with a solidly upper-middle-class background, yet he sincerely and convincingly assumed the role of a hillbilly folk hero. He was a deeply religious man, yet he battled with preachers and prohibitionists throughout his career. Passionately egalitarian, he democratized party politics, yet he was also a ruthless political boss. He was a humanitarian reformer who tried to mitigate the excesses of an inhumane penal system, yet he was also a vicious Negrophobe who promoted black disfranchisement and defended lynching. An agrarian radical, he dramatized and personalized the problems of downtrodden farmers, yet for the most part his politics of catharsis and symbolic action probably inhibited radical change. He was an innovative politician who knew how to acquire and hold power, yet his administration produced more politics than government, more rhetoric than reform. He left an ambiguous legacy.

JOHN SEBASTIAN LITTLE

1907

JOHN SEBASTIAN LITTLE (15 March 1851–29 October 1916), attorney, was the son of Jesse and Mary Elizabeth (Tatum) Little, pioneer settlers in western Arkansas. Little, whose middle name derived from his being the first male child born in the newly created Sebastian County, grew up on his father's two-hundred acre farm near the village of Jenny Lind. Familiarly known as "Bass," he attended public schools in Sebastian County and enrolled for a single term at Cane Hill College in Washington County. For three years thereafter he taught school near his home while studying law under Judge C. B. Neal. Admitted to the bar in 1873, he briefly practiced law in Greenwood before transferring his practice to Paris in Logan County. On 4 January 1877 he married Elizabeth Jane Erwin of Paris. The couple had five children: Montie Olivia, Lizzie Lou, Paul, Thomas Eugene, and Jesse Edward.

Shortly after settling in Logan County, Little became active in Democratic politics and in 1876 was elected prosecuting attorney of the Twelfth Judicial Circuit on the Democratic ticket. Reelected three times to this position, he established himself as an effective courtroom performer and acquired a wide circle of politically influential friends in western Arkansas. After returning to Greenwood where he maintained a residence for the remainder of his life, he was elected in 1884 to represent his native county in the lower house of the general assembly. Two years later he ran for and was elected judge of the Twelfth Judicial Circuit Court, a post that he held until 1890.

Early in that year Little entered the Fourth Congressional District race against incumbent representative William L. Terry of Little Rock. Late in March 1890 he withdrew from the contest because of illness. Press reports implied that the nature of his malady was emotional as well as physical, claiming that his condition had been caused by overwork. Apparently fully recovered by the summer of 1894, he was elected to fill the unexpired term of Rep. Clifton R. Breckinridge who resigned on 14 August. Reelected to six succeeding Congresses, he served more than a dozen years in the House of Representatives. An ardent prohibitionist, he secured legislation outlawing the sale of alcoholic beverages in the Capitol building. Throughout his tenure in the House he displayed a keen interest in Indian affairs and consistently advocated greater federal regulation and supervision of railroads and large corporations. On 14 January 1907 he resigned his seat in Congress to become the twenty-first governor of Arkansas.

Little's competitors for the Democratic nomination for governor in 1906 were state attorney general Robert L. Rogers and S. Q. Sevier. Little's nomination owed much to the assistance of Gov. Jeff Davis and his former congressional colleagues from Arkansas. In 1906 the senatorial contest in which the colorful and controversial Governor Davis successfully challenged the incumbent, James Henderson Berry, tended to overshadow the gubernatorial race. Governor Davis aided Little's cause by verbally attacking Attorney General Rogers, Little's chief rival for the gubernatorial nomination.

Throughout the campaign Little projected the image of a man who would inaugurate an era of "harmony, decency and cooperation" in Arkansas's Democratic politics. The prospect of political peace and harmony was all the more appealing in view of the controversy that had characterized Davis's three terms as governor. Unlike Davis, Little was not hostile to the so-called high-collared roosters of Little Rock. In addition to the usual campaign rhetoric about justice, economy, dignity of labor, and care for Confederate veterans, Little focused special attention on the need for more adequate regulation of trusts and monopolies, an employers' liability law, free schoolbooks, election reforms, the establishment of a state textile school, and the suppression of gambling. Triumphant in his bid for the Democratic gubernatorial nomination, he defeated his Republican opponent, John I. Worthington, by a vote of 105,586 to 41,689. Two other gubernatorial aspirants in 1906, prohibitionist John G. Adams and Socialist Dan Hogan, polled fewer than 5,500 votes.

At his inauguration as governor on 18 January 1907, Little outlined a legislative program encompassing most of the proposals that he had discussed during the campaign. In addition, he called for abolition of the convict-leasing system, improvements in roads, and the establishment of a more comprehensive system of drainage and levees. But, two days after his inauguration, reports of the governor's "indisposition" circulated widely, followed by rumors of his death. In fact, Little had suffered what was termed a mental and physical collapse. On the advice of his physicians he returned home to Greenwood and left his son, Paul, who was his secretary, "in charge of the [governor's] office." Although the legislature displayed great sympathy for the governor and enacted a resolution authorizing payment of his salary during his illness, some individuals questioned the constitutionality of a governor's attempt to exercise the powers of the office "outside the seat of state government." The issue arose when it became known that bills passed by the general assembly were being taken to Greenwood for the governor's signature. An opinion by the attorney general disavowing any legal complications caused by this procedure appeared to settle the issue.

Despite optimistic reports regarding Little's condition and predictions that he would soon return to the capital city, he did not improve, and on 11 February 1907 he left for an extended period of recuperation on the Texas Gulf coast. On the day of his departure from the state he officially requested senate president, John Isaac Moore of Phillips County, to assume the executive office as acting governor. Less than two weeks later, news arrived that Little had suffered a relapse in Corpus Christi, Texas. Since he was unable to resume office by 14 May 1907, when the legislature adjourned, the newly elected president pro tempore of the senate, Xenophon Overton Pindall, became acting governor and served for the remainder of Little's term.

Despite treatment in various hospitals in Texas and Missouri, Little never recovered his health. He died in the Arkansas State Hospital for Nervous Diseases. Following funeral services at the Greenwood Methodist Church where he had been a member for a half century, he was buried in City Cemetery in Greenwood.

GEORGE WASHINGTON DONAGHEY

1909–1913

GEORGE WASHINGTON DONAGHEY (1 July 1856–15 December 1937), businessman, oldest child and first son of Christopher Columbus Donaghey and Elizabeth (Ingram) Donaghey, was born near the Oakland post office in Union Parish, Louisiana. The Donagheys came to America from Ireland, and the Ingrams from Scotland. Christopher Columbus Donaghey moved from Alabama to northern Louisiana and purchased land lying across the Arkansas-Louisiana border. Shortly following the birth of their first child, he and his wife moved across the border into Arkansas where their other five children were born: three daughters—Alice, Lenora, and Willis—and two sons, Columbus and James. Donaghey's father served in the Confederate army, was wounded at Vicksburg, and spent the last days of the conflict as a prisoner of war. Donaghey attended local schools only occasionally and found his role as the oldest son in a fatherless family demanding on his time and energies. After Appomattox, the family struggled to recoup the losses incurred during the war. At fifteen years of age Donaghey fulfilled his boyhood dream of going west to Texas. Penniless, he struck out on horseback without letting his parents know. He worked as a cowboy and farmer in Texas before returning to Arkansas. In 1875 he visited relatives in Conway, Arkansas, thus beginning an association with that growing railroad town that would last until his election to the governorship. The following year he raised sixteen bales of cotton on twenty acres of land in Faulkner County belonging to his uncle, William Ingram. In 1876 the appeal of the life of a cowboy and his health (he suffered from malaria) lured him back to Texas. Returning to Arkansas three years later, he settled in Conway where he became a carpenter. After a brief tenure as a student at the University of Arkansas in 1882–1883, he taught school, and met and courted Louvenia Wallace of Lonoke County. On 20 September 1883 they were married and established their home in Conway. The Donagheys had no children.

Donaghey's career as a builder grew out of his carpentry skills. He worked in John A. Pence's cabinet shop, becoming a partner in 1886. In November of that year a large portion of downtown Conway burned, including the Pence establishment. Donaghey's fortune literally rose out of the ashes of that fire. From furniture making and repairing he gradually branched out into construction. He served a term as town marshal and was an unsuccessful prohibition candidate for mayor in 1885.

Donaghey played a role in securing three institutions of higher learning for Conway: Hendrix College in 1889, Central College in 1890, and the State Normal School in 1908 (now the University of Central Arkansas). His interest in education was an enduring one, climaxed by his generous endowment of Little Rock Junior College (University of Arkansas at Little Rock) in 1929.

In 1890 Donaghey constructed the first bank building in Conway and after a temporary diversion into the mercantile business was awarded the contract to construct the main building for the new campus of Hendrix College. In its early years his construction business was not always profitable, and he suffered substantial losses on his contract for building the second Faulkner County Courthouse. But he recouped his fortunes supervising the reconstruction of the Arkansas Insane Asylum after it was destroyed by a tornado in 1894. He invested in farm and timber land but devoted most of his energies to construction. Success and profits increased as he contracted to build courthouses in Arkansas and Texas, ice plants and roads in Arkansas, and railroad stations and water tanks for the Choctaw, Oklahoma, and Gulf Railroad.

In 1899 Donaghey was appointed to the commission charged with constructing the new state capitol. The work was started by Donaghey but would not be completed for a dozen years. Gov. Jeff Davis opposed the construction and delayed its progress in whatever ways he could. Donaghey made completing the capitol part of his election campaign for governor in 1908 and in the face of considerable difficulties succeeded in fulfilling his pledge. The general assembly met in the new structure in 1911, and by 1914 the building was occupied by other state agencies.

The dispute over the capitol lured Donaghey into politics. To secure the Democratic party's nomination he had to fight not merely the other party hopefuls, such as former state senator William F. Kirby from southwest Arkansas, but Kirby's volatile supporter, newly elected U.S. Senator Davis. Donaghey won the nomination and defeated Republican John I. Worthington and Socialist J. Sam Jones in the general election, polling 106,512 to their 42,979 and 6,537 votes, respectively. He campaigned as a sound, hardworking businessman who would satisfactorily complete the construction of the state capitol.

The fulfilling of his promise was not a small accomplishment, especially in view of the controversy it generated, but his other contributions, while less spectacular, may well have been more significant. Donaghey had a meager formal education, but he prized learning highly and made educational advancements a goal of his administration. In 1910 Governor Donaghey cooperated with the Southern Education Board in bringing its campaign for public education to Arkansas. The board had already carried on successful programs in other Southern states, and its efforts in Arkansas succeeded in arousing public support for the implementation of many of the recommendations made by a commission that investigated educational conditions in the state. Among the achievements in education during Donaghey's administration were the establishment of a new state board of education, support for high schools, and the passage of a law making consolidation easier. In 1910 the governor also supported the creation of four agricultural high schools that developed into Arkansas Tech, Arkansas State, Southern State, and the University of Arkansas at Monticello.

Donaghey's administration also contributed to the improvement of public health. The death of one of the governor's sisters from tuberculosis helps to explain his interest in and support of the creation of the Booneville TB Sanitarium in 1910. In the same year he cooperated with the Rockefeller Sanitary Commission in its campaign to eradicate hookworm. The modern state board of health eventually grew out of this program in 1913. The progress in public health started by Donaghey continued in subsequent years. Among the Southern states, Arkansas became a leader in public health: it was the first state in the nation to require smallpox vaccinations of all schoolchildren and school personnel, and the Crossett malaria control experiment in 1916 served as a model for the campaign against the mosquito. Donaghey also supported the first conference of charities and corrections in 1912 that investigated, discussed, and informed the public about pressing social problems.

His efforts to persuade the general assembly to reform the state tax structure to better meet the demands of the expanding role of government in the lives of its citizens was as unsuccessful as similar appeals by subsequent governors. Donaghey was more successful in promoting the adoption of Amendment 10 to the state constitution, which provided for the initiative and the referendum, direct democracy devices high on the agenda of early-twentieth-century progressives. He brought William Jennings Bryan to the state to campaign for the amendment's adoption in 1910. By 1914 Arkansas was the only Southern state to enact the initiative and referendum.

The most spectacular move Donaghey made while governor was the blow he delivered against the notorious convict-lease system. After the Civil War the South turned to the practice of leasing the labor of state convicts to private contractors for pitifully small sums of money because it was less expensive than rebuilding and maintaining a penitentiary system. Repeated exposés revealed a rotten, corrupt system that enriched the contractors and offended humanity. Donaghey himself characterized the system as one in which the prisoners were kept in "burning, seething Hells." In the fall of 1912, at a Southern governors' conference in West Virginia, he heard South Carolina Gov. Cole Blease describe how he had used mass pardoning to attack the evils of the lease system in his state. Returning to Arkansas and keeping his intentions to himself, Donaghey asked the penitentiary superintendent for a list containing the names of all convicts, their crimes, and certain other data. The governor found a shocking pattern in the information. Many prisoners were serving long terms for petty crimes. On the basis of flimsy charges of disorderly conduct, others were being held in captivity after their sentences had expired. The prisoners' living conditions were not humane even by the most minimal definition. On 27 December 1912 Donaghey granted 360 pardons to the inmates he deemed most deserving. This number represented nearly half of the penitentiary population and was designed to ruin the value of the leases currently held. The notoriety generated by the mass pardoning produced the desired result. The lease system was finally ended in 1913 and a new, more realistic prison board was provided. The move away from the convict-lease system to the prison farm later proved to be little better, but that is another chapter in Arkansas penitentiary history. Donaghey, to his credit, had successfully terminated one of the worst abuses in that sordid and tragic story.

Donaghey won reelection in 1910, securing 101,612 votes to Republican Andrew I. Roland's 39,770 votes and Socialist Dan Hogan's 9,916. He persuaded himself to seek a third term in 1912, undoubtedly thinking that his work was unfinished and that he would have no trouble since Davis had already broken the informal two-term limit. His efforts at much-needed tax reform and his interest in statewide prohibition were the two issues that he believed would win him a third term. This time, however, he faced not only Davis and his allies as Democratic foes, but the emerging power broker in Arkansas politics, Joseph Taylor Robinson. The legislature rebuffed Donaghey's reforms and the electorate rejected his prohibition scheme. Robinson went on to secure the Democratic nomination and win the general election.

Donaghey's second term ended on 15 January 1913, but he continued to serve the people of the state in numerous official and unofficial capacities after his return to private life. He served as president of the Board of Control of State Charitable Institutions from 1922 to 1926, as president of the state board of charities and corrections for six years, and as chairman of Gov. Thomas Chapman McRae's Education (Study) Commission in 1921. He was chairman of the boards responsible for constructing two bridges across the Arkansas River between Little Rock and North Little Rock and continued his contracting activities. In the 1920s he built several office buildings in downtown Little Rock.

He became an officer or member of the board of trustees of numerous Arkansas businesses including banks, insurance companies, and dry-goods wholesalers. He was a Mason, Kiwanian, and lifelong member of the Methodist church.

Donaghey died at his home in Little Rock of heart disease. He was buried at Roselawn Memorial Park.

JOSEPH TAYLOR ROBINSON

1913

JOSEPH TAYLOR ROBINSON (26 August 1872–14 July 1937), attorney, was the son of James Madison and Matilda Jane (Swaim) Robinson. Born in a log house on a six-hundred-acre farm northwest of Lonoke, he was the fourth son in a family of ten children. His father, who studied medicine at Tulane University in New Orleans, settled in Arkansas in 1844, where he served as a country physician and a Baptist minister. His mother, who was part Indian, was a native of Maury County, Tennessee.

As a boy Robinson attended the rural schools of Lonoke County, where his fighting tendencies earned him the nickname, "Scrappy Joe." Although he possessed little formal education, he passed the Arkansas teachers' examination and at seventeen was a teacher in the rural schools of Lonoke. After two years of teaching, he had saved enough money to attend the University of Arkansas at Fayetteville. Enrolling in 1890 as a member of the freshman class, he remained at the university only two years. Returning to Lonoke, Robinson studied law with Judge Thomas C. Trimble, a veteran lawyer and friend of the family. He completed his legal studies at the University of Virginia School of Law, where he received a law degree in the spring of 1895. He was admitted to the Arkansas bar in September of that year.

Before his admission to the bar Robinson was elected to the state legislature in 1894 on the Democratic ticket. In the legislative session of 1895 he joined forces with those favoring railroad regulation. Following a single term in the state legislature, he returned to Lonoke to practice law. On 15 December 1896 he married Ewilda Gertrude Miller, daughter of Jesse and Sarah E. (Goady) Miller of Lonoke, Arkansas. They had no children.

Robinson remained out of elected office until 1902 when he won election to Congress from Arkansas's Sixth Congressional District. He served five terms in Congress (1903–1913) during a period of Republican domination. His tenure also witnessed the maturing of the reform effort known as progressivism that attempted to achieve honest, efficient government; improve the quality of life; and control big business. In Congress Robinson, a Democrat, generally aligned himself with moderately progressive elements, thus many times voting with those Republicans identified with Pres. Theodore Roosevelt. He favored measures that regulated railroads and child labor and supported the income-tax and woman-suffrage amendments to the U.S. Constitution. He also joined Roosevelt in advocating a large navy.

In 1912, while still in Congress, Robinson announced his candidacy for the Arkansas Democratic gubernatorial nomination. His campaign was based on a four-part platform that called for the appointment of a state budget committee, the placing of state government on a cash basis, the establishment of a state banking department, and the enactment of a corrupt-practices act. In the primary election Robinson defeated the incumbent George Washington Donaghey, who was seeking a third term, and in the general election he won by a vote of 109,825 to 46,440 for Republican Andrew I. Roland, and 13,384 for Socialist G. E. Mikel. Robinson resigned his seat in Congress on 14 January 1913 and was inaugurated as the twenty-third governor of Arkansas two days later.

But an element of uncertainty had been introduced into the political scene by the death of Arkansas's Sen. Jeff Davis on 3 January 1913. On 28 January, less than two weeks after his inauguration as the twenty-third governor, Robinson was elected by the legislature to succeed Davis in the U.S. Senate. Despite his election, Robinson did not resign the governorship until 10 March 1913. Consequently, he held the unique record of being congressman, governor, and senator-elect all within fourteen days. He was also the last U.S. senator in the nation elected by a state legislature.

During the interim when he was both senator and governor, Robinson remained in the state directing an active session of the Arkansas legislature. He was instrumental in the passage of a corrupt-practices act and the creation of a state banking department, both of which had been part of his campaign platform. He also aided in the establishment of a bureau of labor statistics and the creation of a highway commission within the state land department. Before departing from the governor's office he secured authorization for the building of dams across nonnavigable streams for hydroelectric power, an appropriation of $500,000 to complete the state capitol, a provision for the electrocution of criminals convicted of capital crimes, and the adoption of a state flag.

One issue with which Robinson was not in total agreement but one in which he acquiesced was the issue of prohibition. Prohibition was a growing national concern; by 1913 some states had already banned liquor sales. Robinson's position on prohibition was that it should be decided at the local level and thus he preferred a local-option policy for liquor regulation. However, during his tenure as governor he signed a statewide liquor licensing act.

Robinson took the oath of office as a U.S. senator on 10 March 1913. He was reelected in 1918, 1924, 1930, and 1936. In 1922 he was chosen Democratic leader in the Senate and in 1932, when Franklin D. Roosevelt and the Democrats gained control, he became majority leader, a position he held until his death in 1937. Known as a senator who was fiercely loyal to Democratic presidents, he consistently supported Pres. Woodrow Wilson's policies, particularly in regard to America's declaration of war in 1917. He also supported Wilson's unsuccessful attempt to bring the United States into the League of Nations.

During the 1920s as Democratic minority leader Robinson led the attack against Republican policies of high tariffs and tax cuts. He fought for increased veterans' benefits and flood control of the Mississippi River. Throughout the 1920s and into the 1930s he was known as an internationalist and retained his reputation as a big-navy advocate. In 1924 at the Democratic convention in New York City he was put forth by Arkansas as a possible presidential choice, but that honor went to a compromise candidate, John W. Davis, who was soundly defeated by Calvin Coolidge. In 1928 Senator Robinson reached the high point of his career: he was nominated as vice-president to run on the Democratic ticket with presidential candidate Alfred E. Smith of New York, a Roman Catholic and a foe of prohibition. The Republican, Herbert Hoover, won in 1928.

Disillusioned by Hoover's failure to deal more effectively with the Great Depression, the voters rejected his bid for a second term and swept Roosevelt and the Democratic party into office in 1932. Robinson, as Senate majority leader, became the spokesman for FDR and his New Deal administration and broke only once with the president over a major issue when he voted to override a veto of the Soldiers Bonus Bill in 1936. The greatest test of Robinson's loyalty came in 1937 when he tried to push through Roosevelt's Judiciary Reorganization Bill. An unpopular, poorly conceived measure, it was as politically motivated as anything Roosevelt had ever done. Ostensibly the bill was designed to appoint additional justices to the

Supreme Court, but most Republicans, as well as many Democrats, simply referred to it as the "court-packing plan." While some leading Democrats deserted FDR, Robinson held firm. Rumors claimed that Roosevelt had promised Robinson a seat on the Court if the bill passed. In the midst of this struggle on the president's behalf, Robinson was fatally stricken with a heart attack; he was buried in Roselawn Memorial Park in Little Rock. His death was attributed to overwork, but he died as he lived, trying to do the best he could with the job he had been given. In paying tribute to Robinson, President Roosevelt said: "A pillar of strength is gone, a soldier has fallen with face to the battle."

Robinson did not become a legend as FDR did, nor is he well known throughout America. Only one major piece of legislation bore his name: the Robinson-Patman Act Of 1936, which was designed to eliminate price discrimination tending to promote monopoly. Few would consider him a great man in his own right, but he was the kind of man that every so-called great man has to have around him. An adept parliamentarian, superb debater, and articulate spokesman for party policies, Robinson was, above all, a friend whose fidelity never wavered.

GEORGE WASHINGTON HAYS

1913–1917

GEORGE WASHINGTON HAYS (23 September 1863–15 September 1927), attorney, was born at Camden, Arkansas. His father, Thomas Hays, was a farmer and an early Arkansas settler from Alabama; his mother, Parthenia Jane (Ross) Hays, was brought to Arkansas from Kentucky at the age of two. After attending public school in Ouachita County, Hays farmed until he was twenty-five years old. He served as a store clerk for six years and as a teacher for three months. He received a legal education at Washington and Lee University in Lexington, Virginia, and then, after studying with the law firm of Gaughan and Sifford at Camden, he began his own law practice in that town in 1894.

On 20 February 1895 Hays married Ida Virginia Yarbrough at Buena Vista in Ouachita County. The couple's oldest son, born on 22 October 1896, George Grady, served as Sen. William F. Kirby's secretary (1916–1920) and as secretary of the Arkansas Railroad Commission. A second son, William Francis, was born on 17 August 1904.

Hays served as probate and county judge for Ouachita County from 1900 to 1905. He returned to his law practice in Camden until 31 October 1906, when he began serving as judge of the Thirteenth Judicial District. Reelected in 1910, he resigned before completing his second term when he won election as governor in 1913.

After Joseph Taylor Robinson succeeded Jeff Davis in the U.S. Senate, the general assembly passed a resolution calling for a special election to choose a new governor. The election was eventually set for 23 July 1913. The Democratic party chose 21 June as the date for its primary election. Hays faced two Democratic opponents, Charles Hillman Brough, a history and political-science professor at the University of Arkansas, and Stephen Brundidge, a former congressman from Searcy. As early as January 1913 Hays had written to Brough asking him not to make the race for governor, but the professor did not give up the battle until April.

Hays looked to remnants of the Davis faction for support, while Brundidge had greater strength in the towns and cities. Hays also allied himself with the politically powerful Eugene Williams, treasurer of the St. Francis Levee District Board. The board had strong influence in delta-region politics. Brundidge charged Hays with backroom dealings with the levee board. He also attempted to transfer to Hays some of the public resentment against Senator Robinson for his hasty abandonment of the governor's chair. Brundidge claimed that Hays's refusal to condemn Robinson's action implied an alliance between the two.

As the counties announced returns of the 21 June primary, the difference between the two candidates remained razor thin. Phillips County election officers held back on announcing their returns until 25 June. Knowing how the other counties had voted, they reported sufficient votes for Hays to barely turn the election his way. The Phillips County maneuver seemed transparently corrupt since the county had been a strong Brundidge area during the latter's congressional campaigns. Hays had not even bothered to campaign in the county. Brundidge appealed to the Democratic state central committee, but that body refused to grant sufficient time to collect poll books and prepare evidence of fraud. The Pulaski Chancery Court, which had granted Brundidge an injunction calling on the committee to give a fair hearing to the case, now said its injunction had been ignored and labeled the committee's hearing a "travesty." But on 11 July Hays won a victory in the supreme court when Judge Kirby wrote the majority decision declaring the primary election to be outside the court's jurisdiction. Despite the division and bitterness engendered by this dispute, Hays easily defeated his opponents, Republican Harry H. Meyers, Socialist J. E. Weber, and Progressive George W. Murphy, in the 23 July general election.

Hays came to the governor's chair at a time of rising reform sentiment in the state and nation. Woodrow Wilson's inauguration, his crusades for antitrust, banking, and tariff reform all occurred during Hays's election campaign and tenure as governor. But Hays showed much less interest in the goals of the progressives than one of his recent predecessors, George Washington Donaghey, or his successor, Brough, did. Hays did not actively press for change, and critics viewed his record as one of inactivity, irresolution, and vacillation. His major preoccupation seemed to be creating a loyal political machine by gaining control of the board of charities and the levee board. He found it almost impossible to stand firm when powerful pressure groups sought to exert influence. Reforms achieved by the legislature in his tenure were usually accomplished without leadership from the governor's office.

In September 1913 Hays announced that he would not call a special session of the legislature to deal with the government's financial needs. In 1914 his reelection was assured, and attention focused on the attempt of his friend Judge Kirby to unseat Sen. James Paul Clarke. The county officials rescinded an earlier announced tally to furnish Clarke, the delta favorite, with enough votes to ease him into the winner's column. Hays failed to influence either the Democratic state central committee or the state convention to deal with the questionable primary election. Clarke and Robinson had captured control of the state Democratic machine at the expense of Hays and Kirby. Hays had no opposition in the Democratic gubernatorial primary election held on 25 March 1914, and the campaign for the general election likewise elicited little public interest. Andrew L. Kenney, the Republican candidate, described Hays as a "man of high character" but condemned him for spending too much time "building up or attempting to build up a political machine." Hays called for a rigid economy to keep the state solvent. The governor enjoyed an overwhelming victory at the general election on 14 September 1914. One important initiative act accepted at the same election was a child-labor law. But Hays's attorney general decided not to enforce this act with vigor, lest he create difficulties for employers with special hardships.

In his inaugural address to the legislature on 14 January 1915, Hays identified revenue deficiencies as the state's main problem. With the state nearly a half-million dollars in debt he advocated severe economy. He opposed any increase in taxation but suggested adopting a more equitable method of assessment. Most of the property in the state was greatly underassessed. He called for a "square deal" for capital and labor. "The old days," he rejoiced, "of suspicion and misunderstanding between the people and the companies engaged in transportation and other public service is rapidly passing away." The governor praised Arkansas's corporations and asserted that capital must be encouraged to enter the state. He announced the completion of the new capitol building without debt and requested a small tax levy for its maintenance.

Prohibition continued to be a major issue in Hays's administration. Under the earlier Going Law in 1913, liquor licenses could not be granted in a community unless a majority of the white voters signed a local-option petition. Arkansas had become an almost totally dry state by 1915. The liquor forces determined to abrogate the Going Law by submitting the prohibition question to the people at a general election. During his campaign Hays joined forces with prohibitionists who opposed this measure, favoring instead a statewide prohibition law. In his inaugural address he vigorously assailed the evils of liquor, but in effect he aligned himself with the "wets" by asking the legislature to resubmit the question to the voters. He also supported the wet candidate for president of the senate, but the senate rejected his advice and chose a strong prohibitionist. Near the end of January 1915, several dry leaders met with the governor. George A. Thornburgh, a Methodist lay leader who served many terms as president of the Anti-Saloon League, joined with state senator Thomas C. White and B. H. Greathouse to press Hays to return to his earlier prohibitionist commitment.

Although the governor expressed his embarrassment to the delegation at the thought of rescinding the earlier appeal to the legislature for submission, he agreed to call for a strong prohibition measure. In a special message to the legislature, he explained that when he prepared his inaugural address, he had believed the liquor businessmen needed more time to "wind up their affairs" and had thought the legislature would not pass a statewide bill. Now, convinced that the general assembly favored total prohibition, he called for rejection of the submission concept. On 25 January the senate decided not to submit the question to the voters. With Hays's support the legislature passed the statewide prohibition bill making it illegal after 1 January 1916 to manufacture or sell liquor in Arkansas. On 6 February he signed the measure. Brough later accused Hays of trying to "run with the 'drys' and drink with the 'wets.'"

On 8 March 1915 the governor sent a veto message to the house of representatives. The rejected Sawyer Racing Bill would have legalized pari-mutuel betting at Hot Springs. "No act of mine," said the governor's message, "will ever legalize gambling." Mysteriously, along with the word "disapproved," the bill carried the governor's signature. Five witnesses favoring the bill testified to having seen the chief executive sign it. Hays admitted that he had signed it but added that later with nobler impulses he had written "disapproved." "I have never had such pressure brought to bear upon me in all my life to get me to do something that I did not feel was right," he explained. A few days later the governor, himself a Missionary Baptist, before a crowd at the Second Baptist Church in Little Rock, acknowledged that he deserved some criticism. "I meditated, I hesitated . . . when the test came I had the manhood to do what I thought right." Maneuvering by the Hot

Springs interests in the legislature and courts failed to establish that the racing bill had been legally signed into law.

In another controversial veto, Hays struck down a bill to make the membership of the St. Francis Levee Board elective. He had spoken in favor of an elected board in a speech to Crittenden County landowners in July 1913. Once in the governor's chair, he preferred to keep the appointive power intact despite the insistence of delta-area legislators on the board's reform.

Hays helped to bring about the defeat of a primary election reform bill designed to end the vote manipulation that had often occurred in eastern Arkansas. The governor apparently owed his 1913 primary election victory to the juggling of returns in the delta region. The so-called Brundidge bill provided for advance publication of the names of people holding poll-tax receipts and stipulated jail sentences for anyone involved in voting fraud. Although the senate passed the bill, Hays spoke out against it. His opposition helped to squelch the measure in the house by a close vote. An initiative drive led by Brundidge resulted in enactment of the reform in 1916.

During the 1915 session the legislature passed a number of significant progressive measures that received Hays's approval. The Alexander Road Improvement Act provided for creation of road-improvement districts governed by commissions with power to issue bonds. State elections were now consolidated with federal elections. Instead of a state election in September, both state and federal elections would be held on the Tuesday after the first Monday in November. Consolidation had long been opposed on grounds that it would lead to federal interference and black Republican domination. Governor Clarke had argued as early as 1895 that such fears were groundless, and by 1915 most legislators were now satisfied that the poll tax and white primary were sufficient to ensure white Democratic supremacy. The legislature also enacted a "blue sky law" to protect investors from stock and bond fraud, a law to permit and regulate chiropractic, and an act to regulate the method of weighing coal at mines. Women achieved important gains during the Hays administration. Their working hours were restricted to a nine-hour maximum day and a six-day maximum week. The legislature gave women the right to enter into contracts and to own property and submitted to the voters a woman-suffrage amendment.

During Hays's tenure he fought many battles over the charities board and the penitentiary board. When the 1915 general assembly convened in January, he had dismissed (or received resignations from) the seven members of the charities board and appointed new members. One of those removed claimed that Hays was using the dismissals "as a leverage for a third term." In his 1915 inaugural address the governor accused the old board of misusing funds and creating unnecessary debt, but he did not charge corruption. He called for the creation of a new three-member commission to operate the State Hospital for Nervous Diseases, the School for the Blind, the Arkansas Deaf Mute Institute, and the Confederate Home. In March 1915 the general assembly passed the Ruff bill that enacted the governor's plan. Three salaried officers, appointed by the governor without regard to districts, would be able to devote their full time to supervision of the institutions instead of meeting together only once a month. Advocates believed this reform would remove the charities from politics and put the board on a "business plane." Critics thought the measure would give more power to the governor and strengthen his "machine."

In May 1916 the *Gazette* condemned Hays for his dismissal of the superintendent of the State Hospital for Nervous Diseases, Dr. Mame Bledsoe. The governor explained that he first had doubts about Bledsoe when he heard that "the bodies of the poor, penniless and friendless were being used at the Hospital for experimental purposes and were being whittled upon, under the pretext of holding autopsies." The dean of the University of Arkansas medical school and many county medical associations condemned the dismissal and defended the autopsies as routine medical practice. In 1913 the penitentiary board had acquired the Tucker plantation to serve "as a white-convict farm." When Hays left office in January 1917 he boasted of having "at last achieved the purpose indicated by the Legislature of separating the white and colored convicts. This is in keeping, in my judgment, with the age and well advanced civilization."

After the death of Senator Clarke on 1 October 1916, Hays considered appointing his "close political and personal" friend, Kirby, to fill out the term. But he quickly cast aside this plan and decided to call a special election for 7 November, and the people of Arkansas sent the governor's friend to the U.S. Senate. When Hays left office in January 1917, he began practicing law in Little Rock and Camden but kept his residence at Little Rock. When Kirby completed his term in the Senate in January 1921, he joined Hays's law firm. This association continued until Kirby became a judge on the Arkansas Supreme Court in 1926.

During the last two years of his life, Hays published a number of articles in national periodicals. In *Scribners Magazine* he argued for the practical necessity of capital punishment. He viewed the taking of life by the state as a "remnant of barbarity that must surely disappear from the earth with the progress of civilization." Someday society would conform to the ethical principles of Christianity, but until that time capital punishment would be essential. In the South, "the sometimes unexplainable fiendish crimes of low-grade types of negroes" led often to lynchings. Without the death penalty "mob violence would be supreme." Hays wrote several articles during 1926 and 1927 calling for the nomination of Alfred E. Smith as the Democratic party's candidate for president in 1928. He ridiculed fears that the South would not stand solidly behind a "wet" Roman Catholic.

While the South preferred Protestantism and prohibition, it was also solidly Democratic; voting Republican would be almost sacrilegious for a Southerner. "It was the Republican party," he recalled, "that tried to force the social equality of the Negro upon the Aryan people of the South." To protect the white man's "social and racial interests," the South would unquestionably vote Democratic. Hays did not live to see the outcome of Smith's quest for votes in Dixie: Smith would capture six of the former Confederate states including Arkansas, but would lose in all the remaining states of the South.

In July 1927 Hays contracted influenza. During his recuperation he developed pneumonia and died on 15 September in Little Rock. He was buried at Camden, Arkansas.

CHARLES HILLMAN BROUGH

1917–1921

CHARLES HILLMAN BROUGH (9 July 1876–26 December 1935), educator and orator, was born in Clinton, Mississippi, the son of Charles Milton and Flora M. (Thompson) Brough. His father, a native of Adams County, Pennsylvania, was a Civil War veteran who had served as brevet captain in the Fifteenth Pennsylvania Volunteer Cavalry. By the time of his son's birth the elder Brough had become a prominent mine owner and banker in the Utah Territory. He subsequently was active in local politics in Ogden, Utah, serving as Weber County treasurer and as mayor during the 1890s. Flora Thompson Brough was born in Maine but spent most of her girlhood in Mississippi. She met Charles Milton Brough while visiting her brother in Utah.

Charles Hillman Brough's first six years were spent with his parents in Utah. At age six he returned to Clinton to live with his uncle, Dr. Walter Hillman, and his wife, Adelia, who was Flora Brough's sister. This arrangement was prompted in part by the illness of Mrs. Brough and in part by the excellent educational opportunities available in Clinton. Dr. Hillman was president of Central Female Institute, a Baptist institution; Mrs. Hillman had aided him in founding the school and was a highly regarded member of the faculty. Brough's mother had served on the staff before marrying and moving to Utah. She died in 1885, and Brough and his seven-year-old brother Knight remained in Clinton, being entrusted to the Hillmans for their upbringing and education.

At age fourteen Brough was admitted to Mississippi College, a Baptist men's school in Clinton. His scholastic record there was brilliant—he averaged almost 100 every quarter during his four years, graduating as covaledictorian in 1894. After graduation he spent a year in Utah with his father, and in the fall of 1894 he enrolled in the graduate school at Johns Hopkins University. One of Brough's history professors there was Herbert Baxter Adams, who had become widely known for directing students in scientific, objective research and writing. Brough earned high marks on his doctoral written examinations, and his dissertation, *Irrigation in Utah,* was published by the Johns Hopkins University Press. The work received favorable notices in a number of publications. In 1898 Brough was awarded the doctor of philosophy degree in economics, history, and jurisprudence.

In the fall of 1898 Brough began his teaching career at his alma mater, Mississippi College. He remained there three years, teaching a variety of courses, including European and American history, economics, ethics, and German. In addition to his teaching assignments Brough participated in recruitment programs for the college, prepared several scholarly articles, and delivered numerous lectures over the state. His published articles included studies of taxation in Mississippi and the Clinton race riot of 1875.

In 1901 Brough resigned his position at Mississippi College to enter law school at the University of Mississippi. He completed the two-year course in one year and graduated with second honors in the law class of 1902. He did not take up law practice, however, but returned to college teaching, this time at Hillman College in Clinton. In 1902 he unsuccessfully sought appointment as director of the newly created Mississippi Department of Archives and History, and in 1903 he left the state to accept a professorship of political economy at the University of Arkansas at Fayetteville. There he taught a variety of courses, including economics, law, transportation, tariff history, and principles of sociology. Brough maintained his interest in research and writing, publishing articles on finance, taxation, and Arkansas history. In 1904 he was admitted to the Arkansas bar, although he never actually practiced law.

In Arkansas, as in Mississippi, Brough continued to be in demand as a public speaker. He gave numerous addresses at commencement exercises and at meetings of civic, patriotic, and educational organizations. He also delivered political speeches on behalf of Democratic candidates for office. Brough's oratorical style was flowery, characterized by frequent use of ornate phrases, metaphors, and emotional appeals. His speaking ability of course served him well in his later political campaigns and eventually enabled him to become a headliner attraction for the Redpath Chautauqua.

During his youth Brough had developed a strong interest in religion and had joined the Clinton Baptist Church. At Fayetteville he continued to be an active church member, teaching Sunday school and, on occasion, "filling pulpits" of Baptist churches.

On 17 June 1908 Brough married Anne Wade Roark of Franklin, Kentucky. They had no children.

For a few months in 1913 Brough, encouraged by colleagues and former students, was a candidate for governor in a special election to choose a successor to Joseph Taylor Robinson, whom the general assembly had sent to the U.S. Senate. Brough withdrew from the contest in April, partly because he felt that he had not had sufficient time to place his views before the electorate. In 1915 he resigned his job at the university and began to campaign for the 1916 Democratic nomination for governor. His platform embraced a number of progressive goals, including a better primary election law, greater efficiency in government, better roads, prison reform, and support of statewide prohibition. The most heated rivalry in the primary campaign was between Brough and Secretary of State Earle W. Hodges. Hodges and his supporters indulged in mudslinging, asserting that Brough advocated race-mixing and wanted to give the university control over state affairs. The Brough forces refuted these and other charges and countered with some mudslinging of their own. Brough won the nomination by a plurality of over 13,000 votes over his nearest rival, L. C. Smith; Hodges was third, trailing Smith by 2,626 votes. In the general election Brough swamped the Republican and Socialist candidates by a majority of over 80,000 votes.

In 1918 Brough ran successfully for his party's nomination, defeating his only opponent, Smith, by more than 80,000 votes. The Republican party did not nominate a candidate but endorsed Brough, who defeated the Socialist candidate, Clay Fulks, by a margin of 62,273 votes.

As governor, Brough proposed sweeping reforms. He urged that a new constitution be framed and adopted and called for the passage of numerous progressive measures. In general, the legislature responded favorably to his proposals; the 1917 general assembly approved about seven-eighths of the governor's program. In accordance with Brough's wishes, an act was passed providing for a constitutional convention. Although the document framed by the convention was soundly defeated in a special election held in December 1918, Arkansas progressivism reached maturity during Brough's two terms. Measures that he steered through the general assembly in 1917 and 1919 read like a progressive litany.

In response to Brough's urging, an act was passed providing for a millage basis for the support of all state educational institutions. The legislature also gave its support to vocational education by enacting a measure that accepted federal benefits from the Smith-Hughes Act. Other accomplishments for education during Brough's administration included creation of an illiteracy commission, authorization for county boards of education, and a compulsory-attendance law.

The legislature created a state commission of charities and correction that was "charged with the oversight and study and improvement of the institutional life of the State, public and private." The agency's specific functions included assistance to private charitable organizations in standardizing their work, supervision of juvenile courts, and promotion of parole work for the industrial schools. Brough's support for public responsibility in the amelioration of social problems was shown by his active participation in the Southern Sociological Congress, which he served in various official capacities. Other progressive measures on behalf of society's less-fortunate members included the provision of limited financial assistance to needy mothers of dependent children, the establishment of a school for the care and training of the feebleminded, and provision of free medical care for needy persons who were sick, injured, or crippled.

In response to urging from the governor, the 1917 general assembly enacted a law allowing women to vote in all primary elections, a significant victory for Arkansas suffragists, since the winners in Democratic primaries were almost certain to win in the general election. Addressing a meeting of suffragists celebrating the passage of the measure, Brough expressed his belief that woman suffrage would "be a mighty factor in the education, social, and moral amelioration of our state."

Arkansas's "bone-dry" prohibition law, which Brough supported, was strengthened by the 1917 legislature. Other measures aimed at moral improvement included laws placing restrictions on the operation of billiard halls and pool rooms.

In Brough's opinion, one of the most progressive measures enacted during his administration was the creation of the Arkansas Corporation Commission, which was given authority to supervise and regulate public utilities in the state.

Throughout his two terms Brough worked to secure better roads for Arkansas. Convinced that progress for agriculture and business was impeded by an inferior system of transportation, he advocated generous state appropriations for the construction of a comprehensive highway system. Although twenty-five hundred miles of good roads were built in Arkansas during his administration, the governor's vision of a comprehensive system did not materialize. A major flaw in the program was the policy of allowing local road districts to handle planning and construction rather than assigning the state government overall supervisory responsibility.

On racial questions Brough shared the paternalistic attitudes of most Southern progressives. He had high regard for the moderate program of Booker T. Washington and commended blacks who adopted Washington's approach to racial progress. Before becoming governor, Brough served as chairman of the University Commission on Southern Race Questions, and in his report on the commission's work he referred to the inferiority of blacks and stated his support for segregation of the races. However, he insisted on the right of blacks to "life, liberty, and the pursuit of happiness" and to the protection of these rights. During his second term as governor one of the worst episodes of racial strife in Arkansas history occurred: the "Elaine riots" in Phillips County in October 1919 that resulted in the deaths of five whites and at least twenty-five blacks. Responding to the urging of local officials, Brough, after securing authorization from the secretary of war, sent federal troops to Phillips County to restore order. Of the several hundred blacks taken into custody, sixty-five were indicted and tried, and twelve were sentenced to death for first-degree murder. However, none of the sentences were ever carried out. Following the riots, Brough appointed a special commission, composed of both whites and blacks, whose duty was to promote more harmonious relations between the races.

Brough was an enthusiastic supporter of Pres. Woodrow Wilson's foreign policy. During World War I he delivered more than six hundred patriotic speeches, recruited the Fourth Arkansas Regiment, took an active part in Liberty Loan and Red Cross campaigns, and provided effective leadership for the Arkansas Council of Defense and the State Agricultural Preparedness Committee. Brough urged Arkansans to make sacrifices such as voluntary abstention from alcoholic beverages in the interest of both morals and grain conservation. He shared Wilson's idealism concerning the role of the United States in the postwar world, strongly endorsing American participation in the League of Nations.

Although a number of Brough's friends urged him to run for the U.S. Senate, he declined, partly because he felt he could not afford such a campaign. He chose instead to accept a position as publicity agent for a group interested in economic development. In addition to this job, which he began in 1921 after a period of illness, the ex-governor was employed for several years as a lecturer for the Redpath

Chautauqua and became widely regarded as one of the circuit's head-line speakers. His most famous lecture, "America's Leadership in the World," extolled Americanism and advocated a more active role for the United States in international affairs.

Brough's publicity job lasted until 1925 and consisted mainly in enhancing the state's image by making speeches on its agricultural resources, industrial opportunities, beautiful scenery, high level of morality, and other attractions. Even when on the chautauqua circuit he boosted the "Wonder State," often taking several minutes to talk about Arkansas before turning to his announced topic. Brough was well aware that Arkansas suffered from a poor image—that of a back-ward, hillbilly state—but insisted that the unattractive image was unde-served. He pointed out that such sources as Opie Read's stories and Thomas Jackson's *On a Slow Train through Arkansas* were largely responsible for the negative views that many people held about the state. While conceding certain deficiencies (in education, for example), Brough maintained that they were being overcome and emphasized the state's high rank in the production of cotton, timber, and mineral resources.

Brough was beset by ill health in the mid-1920s, but after he and his wife returned from a two-month stay in Europe in 1927, he resumed his usual brisk schedule of public-speaking engagements. One of his commencement addresses in 1928 was at Central College at Conway, a small Baptist two-year college for women. A few weeks later he was elected president of Central. His long-standing record as an outstanding Baptist layman, his prestige as "war governor," and his oratorical and public-relations skills were important assets that he brought to the job (which involved fund raising more than adminis-trative responsibilities). Brough's first few months as president of Central were perhaps the most controversial period of his life, for he alienated conservative Baptist clergymen and lay leaders by his stand on two highly emotional issues: prohibition and evolution. A staunch Democrat, Brough began making political speeches in support of his party's nominee for president, Gov. Alfred E. Smith of New York, and Smith's running mate, Senator Robinson of Arkansas. Many conser-vative Baptists strongly opposed Smith because he favored repeal of prohibition. The Arkansas Baptist Convention had pledged its mem-bers not to support any "wet" presidential candidate, and a number of leaders in the denomination asserted that Brough, as an employee of the convention, was out of place in publicly going against the convention's position. Brough refused to be muzzled, however, and continued to deliver speeches on behalf of the Smith-Robinson ticket. He accused his adversaries of religious bigotry and charged them with being more concerned about Smith's Catholicism than about his antiprohibition views. He further denounced them for trying to use their pulpits as political rostrums for Herbert Hoover, the Republican candidate.

The anti-Smith forces also attacked Brough for his opposition to an antievolution measure placed before Arkansas voters in the November election in 1928. Brough and several other educators in the state had taken a public stand against the bill, and since the Baptist convention had adopted resolutions repudiating evolution in any form, fundamentalist preachers considered Brough and "Broughism" a dangerous influence at Central. The hard feelings produced by the acrimony over the prohibition and the evolution issues were probably important factors in Brough's resignation from the presidency at Central in March 1929.

From 1929 to 1932 Brough worked for the University of Arkansas as a public-relations representative in Little Rock. He resigned this position to run for the U.S. Senate against six other contenders in the Democratic primary, including the incumbent, Hattie M. Caraway. The deciding force in this election was Sen. Huey P. Long of Louisiana, whose whirlwind campaign on behalf of Mrs. Caraway gave her an impressive victory. Brough placed only fourth among the candidates.

From September 1932 until June 1934 Brough worked for an insurance company and then accepted a presidential appointment as chairman of a federal commission charged with settling a border dispute between Virginia and the District of Columbia. While Brough was on this assignment, he and Mrs. Brough resided in Washington, and they remained there after the commission's final report was submitted on 30 November 1935. Brough suffered a fatal heart attack in their Washington apartment on 26 December 1935. He was buried in Roselawn Memorial Park in Little Rock.

THOMAS CHIPMAN McRAE

1921–1925

THOMAS CHIPMAN McRAE (21 December 1851–2 June 1929), attorney, was born in Mount Holly, Union County, Arkansas, the oldest of five children of Duncan L. and Mary Ann (Chipman) McRae. McRae's father, a native of North Carolina who had migrated to Arkansas in 1843, was a founder of the Mount Holly community. The McRaes, devout Presbyterians, eked out a modest living on a small farm and were considered stalwarts of the community.

The Civil War era brought considerable economic hardship to the family. In addition, McRae's father died in July 1863. Thereafter McRae had the responsibility of running the farm and providing for his family. For a brief time, however, he did serve as a courier for Confederate troops stationed in nearby Washington, Arkansas. Not until his mother's remarriage in 1868 did he entertain any thought of acquiring a formal education. For a year he attended private schools at Shady Grove, Mount Holly, and Falcon. Following twelve months as a store clerk in Shreveport, Louisiana, he attended Soule Business College in New Orleans (1870–1871). In the fall of 1871 he entered the law school of Washington and Lee University in Lexington, Virginia, graduating the following June with an LL.B.

Twenty-one-year-old McRae was admitted to the Arkansas bar in January 1873. He opened a law office in Rosston, the county seat of newly created Nevada County, and quickly developed a successful and profitable practice. Two years later, on 17 December 1874, McRae married Ameria Ann White, the daughter of the county clerk. Enduring nearly fifty-five years, their union produced six daughters and three sons, but only five of the nine children survived until adulthood. In 1877 the McRaes and their growing family moved to Prescott, Arkansas, to be near the Nevada County Courthouse, recently relocated in that community. The house they constructed, The Oaks, was the focus of family activity for the next half century.

McRae's public career began simultaneously with the move to Prescott. He was elected as a Democrat in 1877 to the state house of representatives. As the youngest member of that body, he won attention by opposing repudiation of that part of the state debt known as the Holford bonds. Thereafter he held a succession of offices in Prescott city government and in the state Democratic party. Utilizing this experience and exposure, he ran for and was elected over four opponents as U.S. representative from Arkansas's Third Congressional District in 1884. Taking his seat in Congress the following year, McRae served his sixteen-county constituency with diligence and distinction for the next eighteen years. As member and then chairman of the House Committee on Public Lands, he was responsible for the legislation that required railroads to return to the public domain unearned land grants, that reserved public lands offered for sale to actual settlers, and that established the basis for the national forest system. Moreover, he championed the free coinage of silver, a tariff for revenue only, the taxation of trusts, a constitutional amendment to authorize an income tax, single statehood for the Oklahoma and Indian territories, and the abolition of the sugar bounty. In sum, Congressman McRae advocated a quasi-populist legislative program that reflected both the needs and aspirations of his rural and poverty-ridden district. He voluntarily retired from office in March 1903, by which time his length of service in the Congress exceeded that of any prior Arkansas representative.

As a private citizen, McRae resumed his residence in Prescott. At first he devoted himself completely to the practice of law, but in 1905 he purchased and became president of the Bank of Prescott. His success in this endeavor and his statewide reputation caused him to be elected as president of the Arkansas Bankers Association four years later. Working with others, he then drafted model legislation adopted by the Arkansas General Assembly in March 1913 that regulated the state banking industry. In October 1913 he attended the American Bankers Association meeting in Boston, Massachusetts, and spoke in support of legislation creating the Federal Reserve System, an unpopular position for a member of that audience. Although McRae was one of the state's foremost bankers, he did not neglect his law practice, which was conducted through the firm of McRae and Tompkins. His partners included Charles H. and W. V. Tompkins, who was also active in the state Democratic party organization. McRae's stature within the legal profession accounted for his election in 1917 as president of the Arkansas Bar Association. In that year he was also elected as one of the

114 members of a convention that wrote and submitted to the elec-torate a new state constitution in 1918. Providing for woman suffrage, initiative petitions, and referendum votes, the constitution was imbued with the reform spirit that characterized the national progressive move-ment and that had shaped the constitutions of Oklahoma and other states. Arkansans, however, rejected the document in December 1918.

The voters' lack of interest in constitutional reform was not sur-prising. Emotions generated during World War I were redirected fol-lowing the armistice, resulting in a season of political turmoil, social reaction, racial tension, labor distress, and economic readjustments. In Arkansas this period saw demands for economy in government, final victory for the woman-suffrage movement, the Elaine race riot, the revival of the Ku Klux Klan, resistance to prohibition, strikes by rail-way workers, reduced incomes, and a tax rebellion. The postwar era in Arkansas also produced an unwillingness to address difficult issues and to provide services considered essential by state governments else-where. Functions and questions affected by this reluctance were edu-cational services, the highway system, the tax base, and the penal program. Thus, the rejection of the new constitution in 1918 was in keeping with the temper of the times and said less about the docu-ment itself than about the state and its people.

Given the social, economic, and political environment that existed within Arkansas, strong and respected leadership at the governor's level seemed absolutely essential. This need directed attention toward McRae. His long congressional service, stature within the legal and banking professions, and recent service in the constitutional conven-tion gave him qualifications and recognition that few men within the state possessed. In 1913 he had withstood his friends' pleas to run for governor, but in 1920 he succumbed to them and agreed to make the race. He did so reluctantly, for he was then sixty-eight years old. The Democratic primary campaign that followed was more strenuous than anticipated. One of nine candidates, McRae was accused of being the choice of vested interests, especially bankers, who would force the state to pay the so-called Holford bonds that had been repudiated some forty-five years earlier. He denied this charge and instead advo-cated a positive program of better schools, a more equitable road-building program, a fairer system of taxation, and more economy in government to be achieved by the abolition of useless offices. The pri-mary election on 10 August 1920 produced a record vote of more than 160,000, in large part because of the U.S. Senate race involving Thaddeus H. Caraway and William F. Kirby and the participation of

women for the first time in a statewide election. More important for
McRae, he won the Democratic gubernatorial nomination by more
than 11,000 votes over his nearest competitor, Smead Powell. In the
general election held on 2 November 1920, the nationwide success of
the Republican ticket headed by Warren G. Harding was barely felt in
Arkansas. Winning 65 percent of the vote, McRae buried both Wallace
Townsend, the regular or "Lily White" Republican candidate, and J. H.
Blount, the independent or "Black-and-Tan" Republican standard-
bearer.

On 12 January 1921 McRae was inaugurated as governor. His
address before the general assembly set the tone and established the
priorities for his administration. He urged the legislature to abolish
useless commissions and boards, especially the board of control, the
penitentiary commission, the tax commission, and the corporation
commission. As constituted, these were excessively expensive and
should be replaced with honorary boards that would represent the best
interests of the people at no cost to the state. The corporation commission, established two years before, was especially evil to McRae
because it centralized regulatory authority over all public utilities in
Little Rock and because it cost the people three times as much as its
predecessor, the railroad commission. McRae also urged a reorganization of the state highway department, objected to the practice of
building roads by organizing improvement districts and levying taxes
on property owners, and argued that those who used the roads should
be required to build and maintain them. The governor further recommended increased support for the state's educational program,
creation of a purchasing office, strict enforcement of the law, and
appointment of women to state offices. In sum, McRae urged that the
state conduct its business with more efficiency and that its essential
services be prudently expanded.

Though modest, the governor's legislative program was not well
received by the general assembly. To be sure, the corporation commission was abolished, the railroad commission was reestablished, and
the control of public utilities was returned to the municipalities. The
penitentiary commission was replaced by an honorary board, and the
state millage tax was readjusted to provide a definite source of revenue for educational institutions such as the University of Arkansas at
Fayetteville. The governor also proclaimed 23 January 1921 as Law
and Order Day. Beyond that, however, little else was accomplished. A
proposed severance tax on natural resources extracted from the land,
air, and water that would have been earmarked for the public school
fund was defeated. The governor's pleas for a workman's compensation

program and cessation of sales of school lands were ignored. And seventy-two hours after Law and Order Day was observed, a black resident of Osceola was lynched.

Even more significant was the failure of McRae's highway program to win legislative approval. Nothing had captured more attention during the session than the highway issue. During the previous administration of Gov. Charles Hillman Brough, the general assembly had sought to create a network of state highways by establishing hundreds of local improvement districts. These districts were authorized to sell construction bonds and then to build roads with only minimal supervision from the state highway department. Designed to be of little or no expense to the state, the district system encouraged widespread fraud and resulted in burdensome taxes for the owners of property bordering the road. When he assumed the governorship, McRae was well aware that the road program was a disaster and that supporting funds from the federal government were in jeopardy. For that reason he had invited officials from the U.S. Bureau of Public Roads to assess the situation in Arkansas and to suggest remedial legislation to be submitted to the general assembly. In February 1921 a model bill was speedily prepared and introduced; just as speedily, it was killed in the senate. McRae was able, however, to salvage part of his road program: the legislature approved a one-cent-per-gallon gasoline tax to be credited equally to county and state road funds, and it also increased registration and licensing fees on motor vehicles and allocated the revenue to the state highway fund. Because these measures shifted the taxation burden from property owners to road users, they did constitute small victories for the governor.

The general assembly adjourned in March 1921. Its failure to come to grips with the highway problem brought untold embarrassment to the state and to Governor McRae. The national press carried stories about the "Arkansas Road Scandals," and U.S. senators complained about the "rottenness in Arkansas." Additional revelations of fraud and shoddy construction in the improvement districts prompted federal officials to threaten to withhold all highway subsidies unless Arkansas acted to correct the irregularities. Unfortunately, McRae was powerless to respond to these demands, for the root of the problem— state laws establishing road-improvement districts—could not be changed without legislative action. The need became more acute in November 1921 when Congress mandated the withholding of federal aid for road construction from those states whose highway departments did not have sole supervision of road projects. Confronted with the prospect of losing federal funds, the governor appointed a forty member honorary commission in April 1922 to draft model legislation for presentation to the next general assembly that would bring credibility to the state's highway-building program.

While awaiting the recommendations of the commission, McRae turned his attention to the matter of reelection. Only token opposition materialized in the Democratic primary, a happy circumstance that on 8 August 1922 enabled the governor to defeat E. P. Toney of Lake Village by more than seventy thousand votes. His majority was all the more impressive since the Ku Klux Klan, an increasingly powerful force within the state, had apparently supported Toney. In the general election held on 7 November 1922, McRae easily outpolled his Republican opponent, John W. Gabriel, receiving 78 percent of the vote.

With his political position solidified, Governor McRae was able to address the opening session of the forty-fourth general assembly on 10 January 1923 much more forcefully than he had two years earlier. That the legislature must respond to the crisis in the highway program by increasing the gasoline tax and by concentrating administrative authority within the state highway department was clear. But it also had to address an educational crisis that had restricted public school terms to an average of 131 days and spawned one hundred thousand illiterate adults. To remedy this tragedy the general assembly had to provide significantly higher levels of state funding, which would only be feasible with a change in the traditional philosophy of taxation. McRae, therefore, recommended that the legislature consider taxing intangible property such as securities and instituting income, inheritance, and severance taxes. By robbing privileged "hen roosts" sufficient revenues could be generated to finance educational and other reform programs.

McRae's legislative recommendations fared only slightly better in 1923 than they had two years before. Despite opposition from the American Bauxite Company and the Crossett Lumber Company, a severance tax was passed and all revenue deriving from it was earmarked for the public school fund. Within three years, this tax produced some $3.5 million. The general assembly also enacted a personal-income-tax law that placed a 0.10 percent tax on all gross incomes exceeding one thousand dollars. Recognizing the importance of the newly discovered El Dorado oil field in southern Arkansas, it created an office of state geologist and authorized the railroad commission to regulate and inspect oil-production procedures. The legislature increased the tax on gasoline to three cents per gallon in an effort to provide more money for highway construction. But it made no attempt to abolish the multitude of road-improvement districts or to centralize administrative authority in the state highway department as had been recommended by McRae's honorary commission and demanded by the federal government. When the general assembly adjourned in March 1923, therefore, it had failed to act on the key element in the governor's legislative program.

Federal officials responded to the inaction by withdrawing highway-construction funds from the state and recalling technical personnel. With the improvement districts now threatened with bankruptcy, Governor McRae convened a special session of the general assembly on 24 September 1923 and demanded that it pass legislation necessary to stem the crisis. Strong opposition materialized, especially from the Farmer's Union, but the general assembly was finally persuaded to approve the so-called Harrelson Road Law in early October. In brief, the act established an honorary highway commission, granted the state highway department sole supervision over construction and maintenance of highways, and increased the gasoline tax to four cents per gallon with revenues to be used to retire the bonds of the old improvement districts and to finance the work of the reconstituted highway department. With this measure, one of the principal problems of the McRae administration was largely solved.

Another, however, remained unsolved—the lack of state support for the public school system. The income tax authorized in early 1923 had been challenged in the courts, leaving the status of the law uncertain and the projected funds for education unrealized. Even more committed to good schools than good roads, Governor McRae determined to devote the remainder of his administration to solving the financial distress of the state's educational system. On 24 March 1924, therefore, he convened yet another special session of the general assembly to deal with the funding crisis. The school districts, he told the legislature, had taxed themselves to the limit, but still 25 percent of the children of the state attended school less than a hundred days per year, one-room schools were predominant, and high schools were nonexistent in rural counties. From all sources the average expenditure per pupil was only $23.63, which compared to $64.34 in Oklahoma and $54.94 in Missouri. And of this amount the state supplied only $2.74 per child. To correct this shameful record, McRae recommended that the legislature assess a tax on net incomes, that is, on profits rather than property, and write the statute so that it would withstand any court test. The general assembly agreed that additional revenue was necessary, but it objected to raising it by income taxes. Instead, it preferred a tax on cigars and cigarettes. A first for the state, the tobacco tax was accepted by the governor as a reasonable substitute to his own recommendation. The financial distress of the school system, it seemed, had been relieved.

Like the income tax before it, the tobacco tax was promptly challenged in the state courts and just as promptly declared unconstitutional. Undaunted, McRae called a third special session of the general assembly to meet on 23 June 1924. Opposition was extreme, but he eventually persuaded the legislators to rewrite the tobacco-tax measure to meet the tests of its enemies. When the governor's term of office expired on 12 January 1925, his dream of a public school system reasonably well-financed by state revenues had become a reality.

In sum, McRae's four years as governor had a profound impact on the state. Three of his contributions were most notable: the highway construction program was reformed and the burden of cost placed on users rather than on property owners; a new philosophy of taxation was instituted that looked to intangible rather than tangible wealth as revenue sources; and the public school system received its first major infusion of state funds. In light of these and other successes such as an improved National Guard, a tuberculosis sanitarium for blacks, and a treasury surplus, McRae was personally satisfied with his performance as governor. On the completion of his term he returned to Prescott where he pursued his legal and banking interests. He died at the age of seventy-eight and was buried in De Ann Cemetery at Prescott.

THOMAS JEFFERSON TERRAL

1925–1927

THOMAS JEFFERSON TERRAL (21 December 1882–9 March 1946), attorney, was born in Union Parish, Louisiana, the son of George W. and Celia G. Terral. His father was a moderately successful merchant and planter who was able to provide his family with the advantages of a middle-class home. He instilled in his son traditional Southern values that included a commitment to hard work, sobriety, the Baptist church, the Democratic party, white racial superiority, economic conservatism, and education. Terral attended public schools in Louisiana and Mississippi and took college-level work at the University of Kentucky and the University of Arkansas, where he received the LL.B. in 1910. Determined to make Arkansas his adopted state and permanent home, he petitioned for and gained admittance to the state bar the year of his graduation from law school. Simultaneously, he opened an office and began private practice in Little Rock. He also supplemented his income by teaching public school.

Terral began his political career in 1911. In that year he was appointed assistant secretary of the Arkansas State Senate. Because he served the senate well, when the general assembly adjourned he was able to secure a position as assistant to the deputy state superintendent of public instruction. He filled that post through 1916, except during the periods in 1913 and 1915 when the general assembly was in session. On these occasions he resigned so that he could accept an appointment as secretary of the senate. During this early portion of his career, on 25 February 1914, Terral married Eula, the daughter of Nathanial Terral, a Pine Bluff resident who may have been a distant relative. The couple maintained a residence in Little Rock throughout their lives; they had no children.

In 1916 Terral made his first statewide political campaign. Eschewing all local races, he entered the Democratic primary as a candidate for the party's nomination as secretary of state. He proved to be an excellent campaigner, and by building on the friendships he had made as secretary of the senate he was able to win the nomination without serious difficulty. Given the predominance of the Democratic party within the state, this success ensured his victory in the general election held in the fall of 1916. Reelected in 1918, Terral served as secretary of state for four years. His record in the office was auspicious enough that he offered himself as candidate for the Democratic nomination for governor in 1920. He ran third in a field of nine, a showing that suggested considerable statewide support. During the next four years, while he practiced law, he maintained and even increased his political contacts across the state. By 1924 as Gov. Thomas Chipman McRae's term of office was drawing to a close, Terral prepared to make another bid for the Democratic gubernatorial nomination.

The 1924 primary race attracted six candidates, including Terral. It was especially significant because for the first time the Ku Klux Klan launched a major effort to influence the outcome of the campaign. As a consequence of a preferential vote among its membership, the Klan endorsed William Lee Cazort of Johnson County. With one exception the other candidates had hoped to win the support of the Invisible Empire. Terral himself so coveted it that he attempted to join the Arkansas Klan in 1923. When he was denied admission, apparently on a technicality, he succeeded in being "naturalized" at Bernice, Louisiana. Although this effort did not bring him the Klan's formal support, it did keep him from being opposed by its leadership. A vigorous campaign that included some two hundred speeches in sixtynine counties on a platform calling for reduced taxes, greater support for education, better roads, more law enforcement, and respect for the constitution ultimately spelled success for Terral's gubernatorial ambition. On 12 August 1924 he polled 53,628 votes of the 196,893 cast. Cazort, the runner-up, received some 12,000 votes less. Having won the Democratic nomination Terral was virtually guaranteed victory in the general election and on 7 October 1924 easily defeated his Republican opponent, John W. Gabriel, by a vote of 100,606 to 25,154.

Terral was inaugurated as governor on 13 January 1925. His initial address to the forty-fifth general assembly set the tone for his administration and revealed his legislative program. He declared himself in favor of the strict and impartial enforcement of state laws, especially those relating to the prohibition of alcoholic beverages and the carrying of concealed weapons. The governor urged the legislature to enact measures that would severely punish bootleggers and "Pistol toters." He recognized that the McRae administration had doubled the amount of state money expended per schoolchild annually to five dollars, but he believed that even more could be done. Accordingly, Terral recommended that the general assembly levy small taxes on certain luxuries like chewing gum and cosmetics for the purpose of increasing the per capita allocation to ten dollars per child. He also proposed that revolving loan funds be created at the University of Arkansas at Fayetteville and at other state colleges that would provide sources of monies from which students could borrow to help finance their educations. With reference to the public road system that had caused so much grief for his predecessor, the governor applauded the contributions of the McRae administration—especially the Harrelson Act and the four-cent-per-gallon gasoline tax—but he urged an additional one-cent-per-gallon tax on gasoline and a greater percentage allocation of tax revenue to the counties. The latter would help relieve the indebtedness stemming from the old road-improvement districts.

Despite recommendations for increased taxes to benefit education and roads, Governor Terral was primarily interested in economy and efficiency in government. His inaugural address contained numerous recommendations about how this could be achieved. Foremost of these was his demand that honorary boards and commissions utilized by state government be either eliminated or consolidated. The members of these groups served without pay, but their expenses incurred in attending meetings, which were reimbursed by the state, seemed unusually large. Accordingly, he suggested that eleven of the boards and commissions with a membership of sixty-two people be reorganized into a permanent three-member board of charities and correction. The members of this board would be paid, but their aggregate salaries would be less than the annual expenses of those who currently served on the honorary boards. Terral also recommended that the duties of six different revenue-collecting agencies be consolidated into one department of insurance and revenues. Moreover, he insisted that a department of conservation and inspection be created that would incorporate the inspection and chemical-analysis functions of three agencies. This plan, he said, would prevent duplication of effort and would eliminate the jobs of ten state employees. The governor also demanded that the legislature abolish the state game and fish commission, an agency that cost the taxpayers $80,000 per year. This money should be transferred to the educational system and utilized to protect "child life" instead of "wild life." Game and fish laws could be enforced by county sheriffs and deputies, Terral said. The governor made a host of other recommendations designed to foster efficiency in government; among these was a constitutional amendment increasing the number of supreme court judges from five to seven.

In the main, the general assembly responded favorably to the governor's principal recommendations. It consolidated the revenue collecting activities of the state government into a new department of insurance and revenues, and it combined all inspection and chemical-analysis functions into a department of conservatism and inspection. And despite the opposition of ex-Governor McRae who termed the enabling legislation "the most dangerous piece of political work ever proposed in the history of Arkansas," the general assembly abolished eleven honorary commissions and created in their place a salaried three-member board of charities and corrections. It also created the revolving loan fund for university and college students proposed by the governor, and even authorized building programs to be financed by revenue bonds at the university at Fayetteville and the colleges at Conway and Russellville. The legislature also adopted a measure permitting construction of a state general hospital in Little Rock, an action of vital importance to the university's school of medicine. But it did not approve additional excise taxes to increase the public school fund. At the same time, it did adopt and refer to the electorate a constitutional amendment increasing the number of supreme court judges. This amendment and one allowing initiative petitions and referendum ballots were later adopted by Arkansans. Not a part of the governor's program but one that he came to support, a measure creating Arkansas's first state park at Petit Jean Mountain was also approved.

In some matters, Governor Terral got less cooperation from the general assembly than he desired. This lack of cooperation was especially true with reference to the road program. Anxious to relieve the tax burden of those property owners who had borne the brunt of previous highway construction costs, some legislators urged that the state sell several million dollars worth of new bonds; the revenue from these bonds would be used to reduce the indebtedness of those counties where the construction had occurred. As such a plan would effectively transfer the debt from the local level where it had been incurred to the state level where it had not been, Terral adamantly opposed it. Only with the greatest of effort, which included a statewide conference called to consider the question, was the governor able to defeat the measure. The general assembly responded to Terral's opposition by refusing to levy the additional one-cent-per-gallon gasoline tax he recommended, which resulted in no additional money for the state's highway program. The legislature also declined to abolish the game and fish commission as well as other state offices the governor considered unnecessary. In other matters its spirit of independence was no less evident; over the governor's objections, it legalized Sunday baseball and licensed physicians who did not meet the requirements of medical examining boards. Terral vetoed these measures after the general assembly adjourned.

In comparison to the legislative sessions during the administrations of Governors McRae and Brough, the results of the session that convened in 1925 were hardly auspicious. In part, this situation was due to the fact that Governor Terral had asked so little of the general assembly. Its record was uninspired, because Terral had failed to challenge it with something other than a program designed merely to mark time and save money. Ironically, the governor considered these results more as signs of virtue than of failure. He was proud of his accomplishments and believed that he had kept faith with those Arkansans who had elected him to office. Indeed, he was certain that his record would guarantee him another two-year term as governor.

That Terral was not entirely wrong in his assessment of his administration became apparent during the Democratic primary campaign held in the summer of 1926. Only one candidate, John E. Martineau of Little Rock, came forward to challenge him. And had the election been held earlier than it was, Terral undoubtedly would have won. But Martineau proved to be a formidable opponent, and toward the end of a bitter campaign he accused the governor of malfeasance in office. Two of his charges seemed to be most telling: the governor had shown favoritism to the American Book Company in selecting books for use in public schools, and he had accepted a partially paid life-insurance policy in return for channeling the state's fire-insurance business to a particular agent. The governor largely ignored these accusations and tried to direct attention to the positive accomplishments of his administration. Specifically, he emphasized his support of prohibition and his opposition to a state bond issue to absorb the indebtedness of the independent road districts; he boasted that his administration was the first in twenty years not to raise taxes, that there had been no special sessions of the general assembly, that he had prevented Sunday baseball, that he had reduced the cost of state government by $35,000 per year, and that he had secured a student-loan fund and launched a building-construction program at the colleges and the university. Unfortunately for the governor, this record was not as compelling to the electorate as Martineau's well-timed charges were. On 10 August

1926 Terral received some 101,000 votes, but his opponent tallied more than 117,000. The governor had run well, but not well enough.

During the remaining four months of his term, Terral conducted his administration no differently than he had during the previous twenty months. He kept the offices of state government open and insisted that employees work economically and efficiently, merely marking time until others with a different vision for Arkansas assumed leadership. That transition occurred on 11 January 1927 when Martineau assumed the governorship. For almost two decades thereafter Terral engaged in the private practice of law in Little Rock, where he died on 9 March 1946 after a long illness. He was buried in Roselawn Memorial Park.

JOHN E. MARTINEAU

1927–1928

JOHN E. MARTINEAU (2 December 1873–6 March 1939), attorney, was born in a log cabin in Clay County, Missouri. After migrating to Missouri from Quebec, his father, Gregory Martineau, married Sarah Hetty Lamb in St. Louis on 5 February 1873. When Martineau was four years old, the family moved to an eighty-acre farm seven miles northwest of Lonoke, Arkansas, near the community of Concord, where Gregory and Sarah Martineau reared their ten children. Concord was also the community in which Joseph Taylor Robinson grew up. As youths, Martineau and Robinson established an important friendship that lasted for the remainder of their lives.

After attending public schools in Lonoke County, Martineau entered the University of Arkansas, from which he received a B.A. degree in 1896. He then moved to Tishomingo, Indian Territory, to become principal of Chickasaw Male Academy, an Indian school. In 1897 he returned to Arkansas to pursue a law degree, studying in the University of Arkansas law school at Little Rock while at the same time serving as principal of the North Little Rock schools, a post he held until 1900. He received his law degree and was admitted to the Arkansas bar in 1899.

In 1902, three years after beginning his law practice, Martineau was elected to represent Pulaski County in the Arkansas House of Representatives; he was reelected in 1904. He served as chairman of the house judiciary committee and as a member of the penitentiary committee.

In October 1907 James E. Riddick, associate justice of the Arkansas Supreme Court, died. Grasping the politically convenient opportunity to make two appointments instead of one, Acting Gov. Xenophon Overton Pindall named Jesse C. Hart of the First Chancery Court to the vacant supreme court seat, and on 21 October 1907 appointed Martineau to replace Hart as chancellor of the First Chancery Court (Pulaski, Lonoke, and White Counties).

As chancellor, Martineau acquired a reputation for fairness enhanced by an ability to cut directly to the core of the case before him. Often, he would come to a decision before testimony was completed, at which time he would disconcertingly begin filing his fingernails. Once, he even announced his ruling before defense arguments were finished and began to leave the courtroom. When the defense counsel protested, Martineau instructed him that he could continue to present his case to the court reporter, but that the decision would stand. The supreme court upheld his ruling. Thus, as a judge, Martineau became known for his simple way of settling what might otherwise have been long, drawn-out cases.

During his tenure as chancellor Martineau also acquired a reputation as a liberal. After race riots in Elaine, Phillips County, in 1919, Martineau signed a habeas corpus petition preventing the execution of twelve blacks sentenced at Elaine for their alleged participation in the riot. The case eventually reached the U.S. Supreme Court, which freed the blacks. Martineau's reputation for fairness marked by liberalism stood well with his constituency, who reelected him to three six-year terms as chancellor without opposition.

In 1909, early in his judicial career, Martineau married Ann H. Mitchell from Pine Bluff. That marriage ended tragically six years later, with her death. In 1919 Martineau married Mabel Irwin Thomas of Des Arc.

Meanwhile, a wave of reform aimed at eliminating prostitution swept across the country. Most major cities created commissions to investigate "the social evil," as it was called, and Little Rock was not long in emulating the example of big cities. In January 1912 the Little Rock Vice Commission was organized, with Martineau as chairman. Other members included prominent Little Rock doctors, businessmen, and religious leaders, all appointed by the mayor. Its report, presented 20 May 1913, recommended an end to the unofficial police tolerance of brothels and the creation of a special agency within the police department to combat prostitution.

In 1924, Martineau began a quest for statewide office by seeking the Democratic nomination for governor. In his first experience with competitive politics in nineteen years, he finished third in a field of five. During the following year and a half, the victor of that race, Thomas Jefferson Terral, alienated many Arkansas voters by abolishing the honorary boards for state institutions. Many considered his alternative, paid boards composed of three members each, as a needless extravagance. This plan, combined with questions regarding the handling of state contracts and public roads, made Terral subject to the charge of managerial incompetence. Mismanagement, therefore, became the central issue in the gubernatorial election of 1926.

With Terral vulnerable, Martineau entered his second race for the governorship. Since automobiles had begun to replace horses as the chief means of transportation in Arkansas in the 1920s, Martineau proposed reorganization of the state highway system to facilitate road building. This change, countered Terral, would mire the state in debt. Furthermore, Terral charged that Martineau supported the repeal of prohibition and labeled him the candidate of "Bonds and Booze."

In an unusually heavy turnout, Arkansas voters made known their preference in the Democratic primary of 12 August 1926. The race was so close that not until late the following night was it clear that Martineau had won; his victory made him the first man in Arkansas since Reconstruction to defeat an incumbent governor running for a second term. With no real Republican party in Arkansas, victory in the Democratic primary assured his election in November.

As governor, Martineau restored the honorary boards for state institutions. He also formed the Confederate Pensions Board to over-see the granting of pensions to Confederate veterans and provided for bonds to be issued to cover the pension program's cost. The greatest trial of his administration, however, came with widespread flooding that followed unusually heavy rains in April 1927. The flooding affected the entire Mississippi valley, and the destruction was so extensive that Pres. Calvin Coolidge named Secretary of Commerce Herbert Hoover to head relief efforts. Louisiana and Mississippi joined with Arkansas to form the Tri-State Flood Commission to coordinate planning, and Martineau was elected president. He worked closely with Hoover during the crisis, making several trips to Washington to brief the president and consult with Hoover.

Martineau's most lasting achievement, however, was laying the foundation of the modern state highway system in Arkansas. The rise of the automobile caused a road-building boom in the state early in the 1920s. Construction costs were met by taxing the land through improvement districts, causing skyrocketing property taxes throughout the state as well as heavy indebtedness by the road districts. Martineau proposed that the state assume the debt of the road-improvement districts and issue highway bonds for road construction. Instead of taxing the land to pay for the bonds, he urged user-related taxes, such as automobile-license fees or gasoline levies.

Proposals to this effect were placed before the Arkansas General

Assembly of 1927. The assembly authorized the state to issue $13 million of state highway notes a year for four years for road construction. It also directed the state to assume the road improvement district debt and authorized the return to counties of $1.5 million dollars a year for county road construction. The general assembly also raised gasoline taxes to a nickel per gallon and authorized state aid for highway construction within city limits. These steps, along with other associated measures passed by the general assembly, became collectively known as the "Martineau Road Plan" and initiated Arkansas's commitment to modern transportation.

The Martineau Road Plan had its critics who repeatedly offered legal challenges to the laws. Ironically, Martineau himself ruled on many of these challenges, for on 2 March 1928, fourteen months after taking office as governor, he resigned to become U.S. district judge for the Eastern District of Arkansas.

In appointing the Democratic Martineau, President Coolidge surprised almost everyone by breaking with the previously strict adherence to patronage. Martineau's appointment was strongly urged, however, by Hoover, who had come to know and respect him during their collaboration on the flood-relief program. Also, Senator Robinson used his influence as Senate minority leader to lobby hard for his old friend and saw to it that the Senate confirmed Martineau's appointment on the same afternoon that Coolidge announced it. On 14 March 1928 Martineau was sworn in and began his second career as a judge.

Martineau served on the federal bench for almost nine years. He became known for his strong support of the probation system, whereby the home life of the convicted person was investigated before sentencing.

On 28 January 1937 Judge Martineau came down with influenza and was confined to bed. Toward the end of February he appeared to rally, but during the first week of March he developed complications and turned suddenly worse. On 6 March 1937, after thirty-four years of public service to Arkansas, he died at the age of sixty-three. He was buried in Roselawn Memorial Park in Little Rock.

HARVEY PARNELL

1928–1933

HARVEY PARNELL (28 February 1880–16 January 1936), merchant and farmer, was born on a farm near Orlando, Cleveland County, Arkansas, the son of southern Arkansas farmers, William Robert and Mary Elizabeth (Martin) Parnell. He shared farm chores with four brothers and two sisters, attending rural schools until he was eighteen. He then moved to Warren, Arkansas, to attend high school and clerked in a hardware store. In 1900 he moved again, taking a position with E. P. Remley and Company in Dermott as a clerk and bookkeeper. After two years with that firm, Parnell struck out on his own and for the next eight years operated a dry-goods business in Dermott. On 2 June 1903 he married Mabel Winston who bore him two daughters, Martha and Mary Frances. In 1904 Parnell acquired 150 acres of farmland in Chicot County and returned to farming on a part-time basis. By 1910 he had increased his holdings to 1,750 acres and listed his occupation as cattle raiser. Parnell periodically added to Old Crooked, as he called his place near Crooked Bayou, so that at the time of his death the farm consisted of 3,000 acres. The businessman-turned-farmer took pride in his agricultural background, stating once, "the people of Arkansas called me from the farm to serve as their chief executive." Parnell was a member of the Methodist Episcopal Church South, a Mason, and a Democrat.

Parnell's initiation into state politics began in 1919 when he was elected to the forty-second general assembly as a representative from Chicot County. Though his voice was seldom heard on the floor, Parnell early demonstrated a tendency to support progressive measures such as health and safety standards for coal miners and an act granting women the right to hold civil office. After serving two terms as a representative, Parnell won election to the upper chamber of the Arkansas legislature in 1923. By this time he had matured as a legislator and for the next three years the senator from Chicot and Ashley

Counties not only supported but also introduced various reform bills. Labor leaders across the state urged his appointment to the Labor committee. Even suffragettes could call him a friend. He was one of fifteen state senators to vote for ratification of the Child Labor Amendment and was a consistent if not outspoken advocate of woman suffrage. In November 1931, during his second elected term as governor, Parnell appointed Hattie M. Caraway to fill the unexpired term of her late husband, Sen. Thaddeus H. Caraway. Mrs. Caraway would later earn the honor of being the first woman elected to serve in the U.S. Senate.

Parnell's legislative record met the requirements for inclusion in that genre of Southern politics called "business progressivism." Political leadership throughout the South in the 1920s took an opportunistic approach to reform by insisting that public health programs and social reforms would attract business and industry into the region. Parnell joined this crusade in 1923 when he attached his name to the cigarette-tax law that provided revenue for public schools. Typical of a business progressive, however, Parnell regarded such an act as a means, not an end; as he told the Arkansas Education Association, "all manufacturing establishments are in states with good school systems."

A court decision and a surprise federal appointment allowed Parnell to advance rapidly from a state senator to governor of Arkansas. On 12 April 1926 the Arkansas Supreme Court settled a dispute on state constitutional law, declaring that the office of lieutenant governor had indeed been approved by a majority of those voting on the measure in 1914. For twelve years, it had been assumed that the amendment creating that office had not passed since it had not received a majority vote of all the electors at the general election. A constitutional issue was resolved, the office of lieutenant governor was proclaimed vacant, and Parnell announced his decision to seek the post. What was described as a "Parnell machine" over the next few years began in 1926 as a collection of friends and acquaintances whom he had made as a member of the general assembly. Their support assured Parnell of a successful race for lieutenant governor, a race in which he was virtually unopposed. Furthermore, Parnell gained political mileage from his dual career: during his 1926 campaign he claimed that his background as both businessman and farmer gave him the distinct advantage of being the candidate representing both major elements of the Arkansas populace. In November 1926 he became Arkansas's first elected lieutenant governor. In the same election John E. Martineau was chosen governor.

As lieutenant governor, Parnell's duty was to preside over the senate, and his primary concern was enactment of the Martineau Road Law. Crisscrossing the state with a modern highway system fit squarely into Parnell's avowed mission to change the image of a benighted Arkansas. The lieutenant governor was to play an even greater part in the road program, however, for on 14 March 1928, Governor Martineau resigned to accept an appointment to a federal judgeship.

Parnell's message to the people of Arkansas on assuming the office of governor was a promise to continue the Martineau program. Between 1928 and 1933, however, Parnell emerged as the leader of a two-pronged attack on the political and economic structure of the state, seeking not an overhaul of the system, but a realignment. The failure to bring many of his plans to fruition was due more to economic and environmental disasters than to political obstacles. Surely no other chief executive in Arkansas's history dealt with the problems of weather more than Parnell did. Only a year before he succeeded Martineau as governor, Arkansas had experienced an extremely cold, harsh winter followed by unprecedented spring of flooding. The spring of 1929 brought several tornadoes that caused severe and widespread property damage. The Red Cross had barely finished administering aid to the flood victims when the southwestern portion of the United States suffered a drought in the summer of 1930. By all accounts the state hardest hit was Arkansas. The economic forecast was no better than the weather. With the stock-market crash of 29 October 1929 and the resulting Great Depression, Arkansas, a state that ranked forty-sixth in per capita income, sank for the next decade into a quagmire of unemployment, bankruptcy, farm foreclosures, and dire poverty. But in 1928 few people predicted clouds over the economic horizon, and Parnell's concerns were focused on highways and the politics of an election year.

After taking office Parnell called a special session of the legislature to authorize $18 million in bonds each year to expand the Martineau road program. A state highway toll-bridge-construction program also passed in that session, calling for the sale of $7.5 million in bonds. Other than increasing state indebtedness for highways, Parnell refrained from energetic and costly programs until he had been elected governor in his own right.

The August primary of 1928 gave Arkansas voters a choice of four candidates for the Democratic gubernatorial nomination, and in a race that hinged largely on personalities, Parnell received the greatest support. Shortly after the returns were tabulated, however, Parnell was charged with violating the Corrupt Practices Act by spending more than the $5,000 campaign limit. He denied the allegation, explaining that the attempt to disqualify him was the work of an interest group opposed to his toll-bridge program. Whether Parnell had correctly identified the opposition, or even whether the accusation could be substantiated is unknown because in the course of two weeks the whole matter was dropped.

Arkansans had other events claiming their attention. In the months between August and November the state was alive with feverish political activity. Since the Democratic presidential candidate, Alfred E. Smith, had chosen U.S. Sen. Joseph Taylor Robinson of Arkansas as his vice-presidential running mate, candidates for office in Arkansas felt compelled to state their opinions and preferences in terms of national issues. State and local politicians pooled their efforts in order to win a total Democratic victory. The 1928 election was composed of such a hybrid combination of characters that Parnell, a Protestant, urged Arkansas voters to ignore Smith's Catholicism and expressed his belief that the Irish politician and governor of New York would enforce the Eighteenth Amendment. To a predominantly rural population who abhorred urban bossism, Parnell delicately explained that even Smith's Tammany Hall connections were not brewed in the same kettle as Teapot Dome.

Running against the Republican party locally and nationally, Parnell was in league with other Democratic candidates who sought victory over the party of big business by rediscovering the electoral strength of the farmers. The gubernatorial hopeful who since first entering public office in 1919 had promoted industrial expansion and development declared in 1928, "the Governor's office can be made a strong force in securing legislation which will really benefit the farmer." That November Arkansas voters approved a measure forbidding the teaching of evolution in state-supported schools at the same time that they voted for Smith and returned Parnell to the governor's office.

Parnell had no set program geared to fit any one special interest. Instead he defined state development in terms of specific areas that needed attention. Only after the beginning of the Great Depression, when the Arkansas farmers' plight was magnified and publicized, was legislation for that group forthcoming from the governor's office. For the time being Parnell was satisfied that farmers and other elements of the population could be taken care of by an attack on what he called the three outstanding problems in Arkansas: taxation, education, and rural highways.

The newly elected governor sought to more equitably distribute the burden of paying for state government and services by instituting a tax on occupations. Previously, the tax load had only been shouldered by people with property that could be assessed; hence, the farmer or property owner was a frequent stop for the tax assessor. Perhaps Parnell did nothing directly to aid the distressed condition of agriculture in his first elected term, but he was at least familiar enough with the farmers' history of tax grievances to realize that he must find another source of revenue for his proposed construction projects. To citizens such as the Taxpayers' Protection Association who protested the income tax, Parnell replied in a speech made in 1929, "this state was ninety-three years old the other day and it seems to me that we have waited long enough before requiring those with large incomes and no property or practically none, to pay something for the support of our institutions."

Tax reform proved to be a bitter struggle, and the occupational-tax bill that Parnell first sent to the general assembly was thought to be so discriminatory and oppressive that the whole measure was in danger of being dropped. A compromise was reached, however, with passage of the Hall Net Income Tax Law in February 1929 that placed a reasonable tax on all net incomes.

With the funds provided from this "reasonable tax" Parnell forged ahead with his favorite projects. Construction began on a new hospital for the mentally ill near Benton, Arkansas. Additional buildings were authorized on Parnell's recommendation for the Arkansas Tuberculosis Sanitarium at Booneville, and a glaring deficiency was rectified with the completion of a new school for deaf children at Little Rock. The auditorium at that school, Parnell Hall, was named for the governor whose tax program had helped to build it.

Due to his own rural background and meager formal education, Parnell was particularly sensitive to the needs of rural school districts. With newly found revenue he undertook programs to upgrade the state school system. The one-room schoolhouses that operated barely six months out of a year were consolidated into larger school districts maximizing the use of money and resources. Seventy-two such mergers occurred in the 1929–1930 school year. Streamlining the public school system could hardly have taken place, however, if the school bus had not been put to optimum use. In that same period the number of children being transported nearly tripled. High-school enrollment across the state increased 20 percent, and the school term was lengthened to eight months. Attention was also given to higher education with the creation of Henderson State Teachers College at Arkadelphia in 1929. Parnell's plans for education were more ambitious than the economy would allow in 1930 and thereafter the changes he wrought were of a cosmetic and less-expensive nature. For example, in 1931 the office of superintendent of public schools was renamed state commissioner of education and the position obtained by appointment from the state board of education, rather than popular vote.

Parnell had worked in state government for over ten years and knew the difficulties of legislating and administering the state's needs within the constitution of 1874. His attempts to improve the state's departmental and bureaucratic machinery offered additional clues to his business progressivism. In his own words, "state government is a business organization for the people of the state, providing services which the people need and demand." Parnell wanted state government reorganized along the lines of corporate management and to this end he commissioned in August 1930 a New York City firm, the Bureau of Municipal Research, to conduct a survey and make recommendations for a more efficient and coordinated system of administration. By extending an invitation to "outsiders" to walk into Arkansas and rearrange state government, Parnell encountered a regional bias that put him on the defensive. Though he maintained that many progressive states such as New York, New Jersey, Illinois, and Virginia operated under similar plans, the majority of Arkansans resented those "slick brain trusters" from New York City. Once the bureau's recommendations were submitted to the general assembly, the house of representatives refused approval because under the new plan only the governor, lieutenant governor, and attorney general would be elective officers, with the governor appointing twelve department heads. A bill calling for a constitutional convention passed both houses in 1931 only to be vetoed by Parnell because in the midst of economic distress, the state simply could not bear the expense of a constitutional convention. Once again, the Great Depression had thwarted business progressivism.

In fact business progressivism contributed to the Great Depression. Parnell's energetic efforts to improve state services and facilities meant that the state treasury had no reserve funds for emergency relief. The state's bonded indebtedness became a much debated issue in the August 1930 Democratic primary between the two leading contenders, Brooks Hays and Parnell. To Hays's charges that further bond issues for highway construction would bankrupt the state, Parnell responded with a promise to appoint a commission to audit the highway department. Arkansans did not seem concerned about bonded indebtedness;

they were interested in roads and gave Parnell a decided majority over Hays in the primary.

The drought of the previous summer and election-time rhetoric induced the governor to remind his fellow Arkansans, "I am just a plain farmer." Throughout the fall of 1930, Parnell campaigned against the Republicans at home by blaming the Republicans in Washington for the farmers' distress and for the depression in general. No Republican was in danger of being elected governor of Arkansas during the Great Depression.

Yet the relief that Parnell offered was neither immediate nor direct; it bore a striking resemblance to federal aid, Herbert Hoover–style. Parnell argued that agriculture had ceased to be profitable in Arkansas because the farmer had not kept up with the times. "The farm is strictly a business institution," lectured the governor, and failure to apply the marketing tactics of modern business resulted in poor returns on the farmers' investment. To help the farmer modernize, Parnell suggested construction of county roads to get the goods to market. This was the last of Parnell's bond issues because in 1931 the state of the economy precluded additional bond sales.

The winter of 1930–1931 was Arkansas's lowest point in the depression. In 1930 alone over a hundred banks across the state closed their doors. Without the Red Cross or federal funds the state would have been unable to help its destitute and homeless. In November 1930 Governor Parnell established the state committee on unemployment to study and make recommendations. He asked for contributions to charitable organizations and urged employed persons to contribute one day's pay per month to the needy. Encouragement of voluntary programs, however, was simply not sufficient. On Saturday, 3 January 1931, around three hundred farmers marched into England in Lonoke County, Arkansas, and demanded food from the local merchants. There was some shouting, a store window was broken, but after bread was given to them, the farmers dispersed. The national press recorded the incident as a full-scale bread riot and for a time the nation's eyes were turned on what one periodical called, "Famine in Arkansas." As a governor who had spent nearly three years sprucing up his state to make it attractive to industry and immigration, Parnell resented the unfavorable publicity. A comedy of errors ensued when he sent telegrams to certain national newspapers denying that Arkansas was experiencing serious economic difficulties. To Senators Robinson and Caraway the England riot was just the publicity they needed to secure congressional approval of an additional $5 million relief appropriation for Arkansas drought victims. Hence, after assuring readers of the *Baltimore Sun* and the *New York Times* that Arkansas was fully capable of handling relief, Parnell had to send a telegram to Congress stating that he did not mean to imply that Arkansas did not need assistance.

The situation in Arkansas demanded that the 1931 session of the general assembly be sensitive to the severe economic problems, yet neither the legislature nor executive branch expressed much interest in public-relief projects. Like President Hoover who saw prosperity around every corner, Parnell announced in 1931 that there were "signs of the dawn." The governor cut the wages of state employees 10 percent and called for a 20 percent reduction in state spending. In August Parnell attended a conference of Southern governors in New Orleans and agreed to promote a cotton-acreage-reduction program in Arkansas. He called a special session of the legislature to deal with the deepening financial crisis but showed more interest in the debates over how much authority should be vested in the highway audit commission. The legislature, however, enacted a cotton-control measure that restricted the cultivation of crops in 1932 to 30 percent of the previous year's acreage.

In that year agriculture received increasing attention. First, Parnell joined other Southern governors in advocating crop diversification and in pointing out the devastating economic and environmental effects of the one-crop farm system. Acreage previously taken up with unprofitable, soil-depleting cotton was put into corn and grains. Parnell also joined the back-to-the-land movement of the 1930s by advising his constituents to practice the self-sufficient farming of the Arkansas pioneers. Each family, he proposed, should be an independent unit, raising enough vegetables and livestock to feed and clothe its members. Certainly the Great Depression had altered the governor's opinion of just how farming in Arkansas should be conducted. Back-to-the-land was a far cry from agribusiness.

No appreciable economic gains were made in 1932, either in agriculture or industry. The average annual farm income had fallen to $230, and only 62.7 percent of the labor force remained employed. Deposits in state banks fell from $137 million to $62 million, yet the state's bonded indebtedness was over $105 million. Seventy-five percent of the revenue the government did receive that year went to the highway department. In March 1932 Parnell again called a special session of the legislature, but he presented no emergency-relief programs, and the issues raised, whether to refund the highway debt or to raise taxes, were futile in dealing with financial chaos. As many schools closed as banks, and by October 1932 private charities had exhausted their funds. Between February and August Arkansas received more farm loans from the Reconstruction Finance Corporation (RFC) than any other state. Parnell created an emergency-relief commission to disburse RFC money for public-works projects in every Arkansas county; that agency depleted its financial resources in eight months.

As far as Parnell was concerned, the situation was improving. The charismatic governor of New York, Franklin D. Roosevelt, had just won the Democratic nomination for president and pledged a new deal for the American people. The Arkansas governor was honored with a position on the platform committee of the Democratic party. In a speech to the Rotary Club, Parnell concluded that the only obstacle left to be overcome in Arkansas was unemployment; the financial, agricultural, and industrial outlook was bright. The greatest factor contributing to this economic upturn was, Parnell insisted, the Martineau Road Law.

The people of Arkansas did not share Parnell's optimism, and the action of the house of representatives revealed that many blamed Parnell for much of the suffering in the state. On 20 February 1933 the lower chamber of the general assembly adopted a resolution describing the Parnell administration as "the most corrupt since the days of reconstruction and the most extravagant and wasteful in the history of the state." Furthermore, the representatives asked in this memorial that Parnell's name be deleted from President Roosevelt's patronage list. Parnell had fallen from grace, but the legislature in a moment of passion had acted as a grand jury. Cooler and calmer heads prevailed in the house, and a few days later the resolution was rescinded.

When Parnell left public office on 10 January 1933 and returned to his large farm near Halley in Chicot County, he did not retire from public service. The ex-governor whose attitude toward relief had resembled the self-help philosophy of ex-President Hoover, spent his remaining three years as an appraiser for the RFC. He traveled throughout Arkansas, Louisiana, Mississippi, and other sections of the country reviewing the applications of levee-and-drainage districts for refunding loans. The transition in career for the twenty-ninth governor represented a political and economic transition for Arkansas as well. State government for the remainder of the depression was headed by a governor whose predecessor was now employed by a New Deal agency. Parnell died 16 January 1936 in St. Vincent's Infirmary in Little Rock after suffering two heart attacks. He was buried in Roselawn Memorial Park in the capital city.

JUNIUS MARION FUTRELL

1933–1937

JUNIUS MARION FUTRELL (14 August 1870–20 June 1955), attorney, was born in the Jones Ridge community in Greene County, northeastern Arkansas. His parents were among the pioneer settlers and planters of eastern Arkansas. His father, Jeptha Futrell, migrated from Kentucky to eastern Arkansas in 1843, and his mother, Arminia Levonica (Eubanks) Futrell, a Georgia native, moved to the area with her parents in 1856. Married in 1864, Jeptha and Arminia had three children, two sons and one daughter; Junius Marion Futrell was their second child.

Educated in the public schools of Greene County, Futrell attended the University of Arkansas in 1892–1893. He returned to eastern Arkansas and taught in the public schools of Greene, Independence, and Craighead Counties until 1896 when he began farming and entered the timber business. While pursuing these interests, Futrell also began the independent study of law and was admitted to the Arkansas bar in 1913.

During his brief career as a public school teacher, Futrell met and married Tera A. Smith, daughter of W. D. Smith, a prominent citizen of Independence County, on 27 September 1893. The couple had six children: Nye, Prentiss, Byron, Ernie, Janice, and Daniel.

Futrell's first political victory came in 1896 when he was elected state representative from Greene County. He was reelected in 1900 and 1902. Elected circuit court clerk in 1906, he served in that post for four years. In 1912 the voters of the First District (Greene, Clay, and Craighead Counties) chose him as their state senator. In the following year the senate elected him president pro tempore, and when Gov. Joseph Taylor Robinson resigned to become U.S. senator, Futrell served as acting governor from March until July 1913. A special election in 1914 resulted in the election of George Washington Hays as governor.

After leaving the Arkansas senate, Futrell returned to his home in Paragould and practiced law until 1921 when he was appointed circuit judge for the Second Judicial District. Elected chancellor of the Twelfth District two years later and reelected to a second six-year term in 1930, he resigned to run for governor in 1932. In the summer Democratic primaries he defeated Dwight H. Blackwood who headed the state's highway commission. In the general election of 1932, Futrell defeated his Republican opponent, J. O. Livesay, by a vote of 200,612 to 19,713. Renominated two years later, he again won election, defeating his Republican challenger, C. C. Ledbetter, by a vote of 123,920 to 13,121.

When Futrell was sworn in as Arkansas's thirtieth governor in January 1933, he faced the monumental task of coping with the ravages of the Great Depression. Arkansas was on the verge of bankruptcy and in danger of losing its national credit. Funds requested by various state departments for fiscal 1933–1934 totaled $39,680,993.47, while state income for the period was projected at only $24,000,000.00 and the general-revenue fund, which supported all state agencies, faced an outstanding highway-bonded debt of $146,000,000.00 by January 1933. In addition to the state's debt problem, Futrell had the problem of finding funds to support public education and relief for the state's unemployed and poor.

In his inaugural address of January 1933, Futrell called for retrenchment and outlined a program based on a mixture of Jeffersonian-Hooverian philosophy. Believing that the primary purpose of government was to protect people's natural rights to life, liberty, and property, Futrell pledged his administration to the discontinuance of all activities not within the proper purposes of government; to the reduction of state employees and salaries; to the elimination of duplication of services; and to the expulsion of graft, waste, and mismanagement. He also promised to pay off the state's debts and to put Arkansas's government on a cash basis.

Futrell believed that the key to achieving his objectives lay in the payment of the state's highway debts, and he began to push for a new highway-funding system. His plan called for the consolidation of all highway debts with all claimants to highway revenues having equal status. Increased fees on the sale of oil and gas, truck and auto licenses, and licenses for commercial vehicles would be used to finance the new system and to keep the existing highway system operational. Due to strong opposition from some legislators and from out-of-state highway bondholders who feared the loss of funds owed them from previous Arkansas bond issues, the legislature of 1933 failed to enact the governor's plan. However, a special session of the general assembly in 1934 passed Futrell's proposal as the Highway Refunding Act.

Highway refunding had been his first priority as governor, and he considered the passage of the Refunding Act as the greatest achievement of his administration. Convinced that the state's highway indebtedness resulted from excessive and unauthorized spending on the part of the legislature, he moved to prevent such spending in the future. To put Arkansas on a cash basis, Futrell proposed two amendments to the state constitution. Both were designed to limit the taxing-and-spending authority of the legislature.

The proposed Nineteenth Amendment limited the taxing-and-spending power of the legislature by requiring a majority vote in each house before enactment of new laws. It also limited legislative appropriations to a fixed amount and required the approval of the voters in a general election or a three-fourths vote in each house of the legislature before state taxes could be increased. The proposed Twentieth Amendment simply required voter approval before new state bonds could be issued. With little debate the legislature passed both proposals and submitted them to the voters in the 1934 general election; both were approved. In Futrell's opinion, Arkansas could now meet its obligations without fear of excessive legislative spending in the future.

Even though Futrell took the lead in the fight to save the state's credit and to prevent future financial instability, he was slow to take action to meet the needs of public education and to ease the plight of the aged, the poor, and those on relief rolls. He believed that poverty was the result of a lack of individual initiative and that the huge unemployment rolls were due to the use of modern labor-saving machinery that Futrell felt was unnecessary. Arguing that public education was also unnecessary beyond the primary grades (grades 1–8), in 1935 Futrell asked the legislature to cease funding of public education above the eighth grade. He was convinced that a primary education was altogether sufficient to prepare a person to assume a useful role in modern society. Due to Futrell's agrarian conservatism, Arkansas was one of the most difficult states to organize for participation in the relief program administered by the Federal Emergency Relief Administration (FERA) created by Congress in March 1933. He was content to let the FERA shoulder the cost of education and poor relief in Arkansas.

The FERA provided matching federal grants to the states for relief and readily came to the aid of needy individuals and school districts in Arkansas. FERA officials, however, believed that education and relief were the responsibilities of the state and began to push Arkansas to pay its share of the costs. Near the end of 1934, Harry Hopkins, FERA director, informed Futrell that Arkansas would lose not only funds for education and relief, but "all" federal funds if the 1935 legislature did not appropriate $1,500,000 as its share of relief and educational costs. Hopkins set 1 March 1935 as the deadline for compliance. In an effort to prevent the loss of federal funds, which the depressed economy of the state could scarcely afford, and to avoid any new direct taxes, Futrell and the legislature began work on three controversial measures to raise the required revenues: sales taxes, prohibition repeal, and legalized gambling. Only the liquor and gambling measures had the initial support of the governor.

The sales-tax bill, which levied a 2 percent tax on all retail sales except specified foods and medicines, passed the senate without Futrell's endorsement. In the house, however, the bill was held up beyond the 1 March deadline, resulting in the loss of federal funds. Futrell, who placed a low priority on education and relief for the poor, only urged house passage of the measure after federal funds had been terminated. With the governor's belated support, the house passed the sales-tax bill on 15 March 1935. Of the $2,250,000 the tax was expected to generate, $1,500,000 was set aside for public education.

While the sales-tax bill was being debated, three other measures were making their way through the general assembly—prohibition repeal and two separate gambling measures. All had the support of the governor. Although not an avowed "wet," Futrell openly supported prohibition repeal, which he believed would both reduce bootlegging and provide the state needed additional revenues. In fact, the governor proposed a plan calling for the conversion of one of the state's penal institutions into a state-owned distillery for the manufacture and sale of corn whiskey; convicts would provide the labor. The legislature rejected the proposal, which critics quickly labeled the "Convict Corn Plan." Instead, it passed a bill that repealed prohibition on a local-option basis and that included an excise tax on liquor sales.

Along with the passage of the liquor bill, the legislature created the Arkansas Department of Public Welfare to administer aid to the aged, the unemployable, and those on relief. To fund the agency, $500,000 from expected liquor revenues was set aside for the remainder of 1935. To ensure adequate funds for relief and education, Futrell also urged the general assembly to enact one of the controversial gambling measures. The legislature responded by passing both. Parimutuel betting was legalized on dog racing at West Memphis and on horse racing at Hot Springs. Responding to public protest, Futrell allowed the dog-racing bill to become law without his signature. However, the horse-racing bill, which passed the legislature with an attached emergency clause, was immediately signed into law. The passage of the sales-tax bill and the liquor and gambling measures satisfied federal require-ments, and Hopkins restored federal funding to Arkansas on 17 March 1935. Futrell then reluctantly turned his attention to the plight of des-titute tenant farmers and sharecroppers in eastern Arkansas who had formed the Southern Tenant Farmers Union (STFU) for their own protection. The STFU was organized in July 1934, when eighteen sharecroppers—eleven whites and seven blacks—met behind closed doors on the Fairview plantation of Hiram Norcross at Tyronza, Arkansas. Its initial goals were to protest the wholesale eviction of ten-ant farmers and sharecroppers by local landlords in order to avoid sharing Agricultural Adjustment Administration (AAA) cotton parity payments, and to increase wages for cotton pickers from forty cents to one dollar per hundred pounds. To achieve its objectives, the union filed suits against landlords who evicted their tenants without reason and staged cotton-picker strikes. The reaction of the local landlords was violent.

Because of its organizational activities, in 1935 STFU leaders and members were victimized by mob action and mass arrests. Appeals to Futrell for help and protection fell on deaf ears. Born into the conser-vative planter aristocracy of eastern Arkansas, the governor's sympa-thies clearly lay with the landlords. At no time during his administration did he take positive action to aid eastern Arkansas's destitute tenant farmers and sharecroppers. But the nationwide sympathy aroused by their plight finally prompted Futrell to appoint a state commission to investigate farm tenancy in eastern Arkansas in 1936. The commission did little to improve the situation. In fact, the condition of eastern Arkansas tenants did not improve significantly until the federal gov-ernment intervened in 1936, when Pres. Franklin D. Roosevelt appointed his commission on farm tenancy and developed a program for the rehabilitation and resettlement of displaced farmers.

In 1937 Futrell's second term expired. To his credit was the state's improved financial condition, largely due to the Highway Refunding Act of 1934 and the adoption of the Nineteenth and Twentieth amendments to the state constitution. As a result of Futrell's efforts, the state was on a cash basis and possessed a treasury surplus when he left office. He remained in Little Rock after leaving the governorship and served as the attorney for the Dyess Colony, Incorporated, a cooperative farm in Mississippi County organized under the resettlement program of the New Deal.

On 4 July 1948 Futrell suffered a stroke while en route to the funeral of an older brother, J. David Futrell. He remained in poor health thereafter and died on 20 June 1955. He was buried in Linwood Cemetery in Paragould, Arkansas.

CARL EDWARD BAILEY

1937–1941

CARL EDWARD BAILEY (8 October 1894–23 October 1948), attorney, the son of William Edward and Margaret Elmyra (McCorkle) Bailey, was born at Bernie, Missouri. His father earned a modest living as a logger and hardware salesman. The Baileys moved to Campbell, Missouri, soon after Carl was born. Although he lived briefly in Paragould, Arkansas, and in Paducah, Kentucky, Bailey grew up at Campbell, where he graduated from high school in 1912. After graduation he taught at a country school, the first of a series of jobs. Even as a young man he was headstrong and independent, always ambitious to improve himself. Leaving home, he worked at a St. Louis shoe factory and as a railroad brakeman in Texas. For a time he operated a café at Campbell. In 1915 he attended Chillicothe Business College in Missouri but lacked the money to complete the course of study. Returning to Campbell, he worked as a deputy tax assessor and read law in his spare time. On 10 October 1915 he married Margaret Bristol at Paragould, Arkansas. The marriage produced six children, five sons and one daughter. In 1917, with a family to support, Bailey moved to Trumann, Arkansas, where he worked as a bookkeeper for a lumber company but soon went to Augusta to take a similar job.

While living at Augusta, Bailey continued to read law and in 1922 passed the Arkansas bar exam. In the same year he moved to Little Rock, where he held two successive jobs, first as manager of the Arkansas Cotton Growers Cooperative Association and then as deputy commissioner in the Department of Mines, Manufactures and Agriculture. In 1924 he opened a private law practice.

Bailey played his first active political role in 1926 when he worked for Boyd Cypert in a successful race for prosecuting attorney of the Sixth Judicial District (Pulaski and Perry Counties). Although Bailey had not intended to give up his law practice, Cypert persuaded him to take a job as deputy prosecuting attorney. Bailey's ambition inevitably drew him further into politics. In 1930 he won his first campaign, succeeding Cypert as prosecuting attorney, an office that he held for two terms.

When Bailey took office in January 1931, the Great Depression held a tight grip on Arkansas, a state already poor by every national standard. As business activity stalled and unemployment mounted, people grew desperate. In 1932 Arkansas defaulted on the interest payments of highway-construction bonds issued in the late 1920s. The state treasury was empty.

As prosecuting attorney, Bailey won wide attention with sensational criminal cases. His best-known case was that of A. B. Banks, the owner of a banking empire that collapsed in late 1930. Before the depression, the American Exchange Trust Company of Little Rock was the largest bank in the state and the capstone of Banks's empire. The failure of the American Exchange Trust Company set off a domino effect that brought down sixty-six other banks around the state. In 1931 Bailey prosecuted Banks for accepting deposits in a bank he knew to be insolvent. The defense counsel was Sen. Joseph Taylor Robinson, who believed that Banks was being made a scapegoat for the depression. The Banks case had obvious political potential, and Bailey was a young man out to make a name for himself. In a dramatic trial Banks was found guilty and sentenced to one year in prison; he received a pardon before his term began.

While prosecuting attorney, Bailey began to exercise an influence in state politics. In 1932, facing no opposition for a second term, he worked actively for Cypert, who ran against Hal L. Norwood for attorney general. Norwood was a veteran campaigner, and he beat Cypert handily. Despite his personal political success, Bailey was an outsider as far as the Arkansas political establishment was concerned. Moreover, his prosecution of Banks had earned him the enmity of Robinson, the state's most powerful political figure.

Although embarrassed by highway scandals and the state-debt default in the early 1930s, the political establishment quickly emerged in a stronger position than ever. In 1933 Gov. Junius Marion Futrell restored fiscal respectability to state government with a program of severe retrenchment. After the coming of the New Deal under Pres. Franklin D. Roosevelt, the federal government began filling scores of new jobs in the state and pumping in millions of dollars to combat the depression. As Senate majority leader, Robinson dominated federal patronage in Arkansas. Although sympathetic to the New Deal, Bailey found himself gravitating toward men like Brooks Hays who opposed the power structure.

During his second term as prosecuting attorney, Bailey and Hays formed an alliance. In 1933 two unexpected vacancies—a seat on the state supreme court and the Fifth Congressional District seat—had to be filled. Governor Futrell urged the Democratic state committee to fill the positions by nomination, hoping to control both choices himself. Although Futrell did have his way with the supreme court vacancy, Hays and Bailey led a successful fight for a congressional primary. With Bailey's support, Hays entered the race but ultimately lost in a controversial runoff to David D. Terry. Behind the scenes Terry had the support of a powerful federal-state coalition consisting of Senator Robinson, Internal Revenue Collector Homer Martin Adkins, and Governor Futrell. This race was the first clash between Bailey and Adkins, who were to develop a rivalry that dominated Arkansas politics for the next decade.

After four years as prosecuting attorney, Bailey entered the race for attorney general in 1934. Despite having to run against the incumbent, Norwood, he felt confident. When the ballots were counted, he had won by twelve thousand votes. It was a spectacular feat that experienced politicians considered impossible.

As attorney general, Bailey displayed an interest in social welfare— a problem that the depression forced Arkansas to face for the first time. In 1935 Congress created the social security program to assist the nation's "unemployables," a class of relief clients such as dependent children and the aged who could not provide for themselves. The Works Progress Administration (WPA) would provide work relief for the able-bodied, but states were to assume some responsibility for their own unemployables under the auspices of the social security board. To qualify for federal matching money, the legislature passed the state's first sales tax and set up the Department of Public Welfare. A conservative, Governor Futrell reluctantly backed a state welfare agency. Bailey, on the other hand, was an enthusiastic supporter of welfare. Besides the humanitarian considerations, the political stakes were enormous. In Bailey's mind, Futrell intended to use welfare to bolster the political establishment; in turn Futrell, suspecting that Bailey had further political ambitions, tried to keep him from getting any credit for the welfare system.

While attorney general, Bailey benefited from another sensational criminal case. In 1936 Charles "Lucky" Luciano, a New York gangster, fled to Hot Springs to escape arrest for prostitution. When Luciano was discovered in Arkansas, Governor Futrell ordered him arrested and held for extradition hearings. But after Hot Springs officials released the gangster on a token bail, New York Special Prosecutor Thomas E. Dewey appealed to Bailey, who ordered the Arkansas State Police to take Luciano into custody and transfer him to Little Rock. One of Luciano's friends approached Bailey with a $50,000 bribe if he would make certain that extradition was denied. Bailey publicly revealed the offer. Futrell approved Luciano's extradition, and the gangster went back to New York for trial. He was ultimately sent to prison and later deported.

As his term neared its end, the attorney general grew restless. He wanted to be governor. With Futrell retiring at the end of his second term, the race would be wide open. When Bailey opened his campaign in 1936, his chance for victory was a long shot. Several events, however, worked in his favor. The Futrell administration could not agree on whom to support. After some indecision, Futrell supported Secretary of State Ed F. McDonald. In addition, a large number of candidates divided the vote, and the provision for a runoff primary had been dropped, making it possible to win with a plurality.

Bailey ran as an antiadministration candidate, sharply criticizing the Futrell administration. The Banks and Luciano cases had enhanced his reputation. In the primary Bailey polled only 32 percent of the votes cast, but he beat McDonald by 3,939 votes. In another surprise victory Bailey had taken on the state's political establishment and won.

As Arkansas's thirty-first governor, Bailey rode a wave of goodwill into office. He served notice that he intended to be an activist governor with a positive program. "The people who pay taxes are buying services, not surpluses," he said. In his inaugural speech, he questioned the value of political freedoms without economic security.

> What good is the right peaceably to assemble to a child so crippled that he cannot look forward to a normal life? What good is freedom of the press to the harassed, careworn mother of hungry, tattered, fatherless children? Of what use is freedom of speech to the aged who, through the miscarriage of an economic system they do not understand and are not responsible for, find themselves in the declining years of a respectable life without the means of support?

Scorning the "puppets of privilege" who opposed social security, he asserted that government must assume responsibility for helping its citizens to achieve "a decent, civilized existence."

The general assembly enacted his program in a stormy session. Bailey gave top priority to creating a state civil-service system. By filling state jobs with qualified personnel on a merit basis, the civil-service commission would end the political spoils system and, not incidentally, break the hold of the old guard on state politics. Social welfare also held a high priority. The legislature restructured the Department of Public Welfare, enlarging and centralizing all state welfare activities in this single agency. The new welfare department qualified Arkansas for full participation in all federal welfare programs.

The legislature enacted Bailey's plan to refinance the state's highway debt. He proposed to sell new bonds at lower interest rates and to pay off the old ones, hoping to save the state $20 million. Opponents of refinancing delayed the sale of new bonds by filing suit against the plan. The state supreme court upheld the legislation, but a recession in late 1937 destroyed the bond market. Although the refinancing plan failed, the general assembly left an impressive record of social and economic legislation.

After Bailey had served just over six months, Senator Robinson's death in 1937 threw state politics into confusion. The lines quickly formed for the fight over Robinson's vacant Senate seat. Bailey could not resist the chance to go to the U.S. Senate. Since he controlled the state party machinery, the Democratic state committee nominated him for the office, citing the cost of a special primary. Bailey would still have to win a special election, but he would be the Democratic nominee. He knew the contest would be bitter. "My friends may expect the best of me," he warned, "and my enemies may fear the worst."

The old-guard politicians could be expected to oppose Bailey. In addition, federal officials who ran the state offices of New Deal agencies had gained their positions through Robinson's influence, and many feared that they would lose their jobs if Bailey won. They actively opposed him, despite the fact that several members of Roosevelt's cabinet gave the governor written endorsements.

The anti-Bailey forces coalesced around Adkins, who recruited Rep. John E. Miller to run as an independent. Seizing on the committee nomination, Miller pictured himself as fighting for the right of the people to elect their own representatives. The governor's manipulation of the committee, he charged, was political arrogance. Bailey campaigned on his record and on his loyalty to the New Deal. The real issue, however, was Bailey himself, not the method of his nomination; neither side could point to a consistent record favoring primary nominations. On 18 October Miller won easily, with a margin of twenty-one thousand votes.

Outwardly Bailey was philosophical about the defeat, but privately he was bitter, blaming the defeat on the political machine that had always opposed him. Having lost prestige, he feared that he might be a one-term governor.

In March 1938 Bailey risked calling a special session of the general assembly to deal with highway matters, a perennial concern of the 1930s. The legislature removed the tolls from the state's toll bridges— an action that qualified Arkansas for additional federal highway funds—and increased highway taxes. The special session was a success, the first step in Bailey's political comeback.

Although Arkansas customarily gives its governors a second term, Bailey entered the governor's race in 1938 unable to take a second term for granted. To disarm opposition, he publicly admitted that he had made political mistakes. In a campaign of personalities Bailey defeated R. A. (Bob) Cook, former Pulaski County Judge, by thirteen thousand votes. Apparently Adkins did not play a major role in the governor's race, since he devoted his efforts to the reelection of Sen. Hattie M. Caraway, who won over Rep. John L. McClellan.

In his second inaugural address, Bailey disclaimed any intention of requesting "experimental" legislation. Nonetheless the general assembly session generated considerable turmoil. Bailey favored a decentralization of the state welfare department, but the plan ran afoul of the social security board, which threatened to cut off federal aid to Arkansas. The existing organization was continued without major changes. Another source of discord was civil service, which had grown increasingly unpopular. Aware of public sentiment, Bailey urged that civil service be modified but not repealed. The legislature repealed it anyway, and Bailey let the bill become law without his signature. In truth he had come to realize that he could not command support in the legislature without political patronage to dispense.

Beginning with Bailey's first term, Arkansas politics experienced increasing polarization. Bailey and the political establishment had always been at odds. The Senate election in 1937 intensified the conflict between the state administration and federal officeholders. After safely winning a second term, Bailey used his influence to fire W. A. Rooksbery, the unemployment-compensation director, who was believed to favor job applicants recommended by federal officials. With Rooksbery's firing, Bailey and the federal faction declared an open war. For months the governor carried on a public feud with state WPA director Floyd Sharp. Bailey accused Sharp of using WPA workers as a political machine to oppose him. In the 1939 legislature, Bailey's supporters tried to embarrass Sharp by investigating Dyess Colony, a WPA project in Mississippi County that seethed with unrest, but Sharp's friends filibustered the bill to death.

In July 1939 Bailey made his final effort to refinance the state highway debt. At a special session, the legislature passed another refinancing plan, but from behind the scenes, Adkins blocked refinancing by tying up the plan in court.

The leader of the federal faction since Robinson's death, Adkins resigned his collectorship in 1940 and entered the governor's race. Bailey decided to break an Arkansas tradition and run for a third term. He was loath to turn the statehouse over to Adkins, and he did not want to let his supporters down. He knew no honorable way to get out of politics except to be defeated.

At last the two antagonists came out to challenge each other openly. Adkins put his opponent on the defensive by attacking the highway-refinancing plan and the third-term issue. He still controlled the federal officeholders in the state and had the endorsement of the entire congressional delegation. Although Bailey had always supported the New Deal, he campaigned for states' rights as opposed to federal control of state politics through patronage. The campaign was brief but full of acrimony. In the end Adkins won by 31,500 votes. Against the combined strength of federal officeholders and dissatisfied factions within state government, Bailey was easily beaten.

Out of public office, Bailey still exercised an influence in state politics. In 1944, at the end of two terms as governor, Adkins ran for the U.S. Senate. Bailey supported Rep. J. William Fulbright, whom Adkins had fired as president of the University of Arkansas. Fulbright's victory gave Bailey a sweet revenge.

As a private citizen, Bailey resumed his law practice in Little Rock. He also operated a cattle farm and founded the Carl Bailey Company, an International Harvester franchise. After he left office, he and his wife were divorced, and on 27 October 1943 he married Marjorie Compton. A union man since his youth, he served as the legislative representative of the Brotherhood of Railway Trainmen. Near the end of his life he taught legal medicine at the University of Arkansas medical school. He died of a heart attack just after turning fifty-four and was buried in Roselawn Memorial Park in Little Rock.

Bailey governed Arkansas in a period of change and unrest. He was a controversial governor who evoked sharply divided emotions, arousing deep loyalty in some and intense hatred in others. His opponents saw him as an egotist, a would-be dictator, and they fought him bitterly. In turn he opposed them with equal relentlessness. The irony of his career was that the New Deal, which redefined liberalism in American political life, used its influence to defeat, instead of to support, him. He possessed a sound understanding of state problems, and his willingness to face them squarely set him apart from other Arkansas governors of his time. Bailey was one of Arkansas's most progressive governors.

HOMER MARTIN ADKINS

1941–1945

HOMER MARTIN ADKINS (15 October 1890–26 February 1964), pharmacist and businessman, was the son of Ulysses and Lorena (Wood) Adkins. Born on a farm near Jacksonville, Pulaski County, Arkansas, he attended public schools in Little Rock and on graduation from high school enrolled in Draughon's Business College in that city. In 1911 he completed a course of study at the Hodges Pharmacy School of Little Rock. Licensed as a pharmacist at the age of twenty, he was granted special permission to practice his profession for six months prior to his twenty-first birthday.

Adkins was first employed by a drugstore in Little Rock and later became a drug salesman. In 1915 he began studying law but, when the United States entered World War I, abandoned it to join the army. Assigned to the medical corps, he rose from the rank of private to captain by the time of his discharge in 1919. While stationed at Camp Beauregard, Louisiana, awaiting shipment overseas, Adkins met Estelle Smith, a Red Cross nurse from Jackson, Mississippi. Both served in France; they were married on 21 December 1921. They had no children.

Adkins' political career began in 1923 when he was elected sheriff of Pulaski County on the Democratic ticket with heavy support from the Ku Klux Klan. Adkins claimed that he joined the Klan solely for political expediency. Unsuccessful in his bid for reelection in 1926, he returned to private life and entered the insurance business. His second venture into politics came in 1932 when he was persuaded by the Arkansas Democratic Committee and the Democratic National Committee to work as a campaigner for Democratic presidential candidate Franklin D. Roosevelt. As a reward for his efforts in Roosevelt's 1932 victory over Herbert Hoover, Adkins was appointed collector of internal revenue for Arkansas. He held the post until 1940 and used it to build a strong political base throughout the state. In 1940 he resigned to run for governor. The support he had cultivated during his years as collector was evident in the governor's race.

His principal opponent in the 1940 Democratic primary was Gov. Carl E. Bailey who was seeking a third term. Adkins and Bailey were old rivals in state politics. In 1937 when a special election was called for the purpose of filling the Senate seat left vacant by the death of Joseph Taylor Robinson, Bailey was the candidate of the state's Democratic organization. A leader of those opposed to Bailey's candidacy, Adkins supported John E. Miller who campaigned for the Senate as an independent Democrat. Miller won the election in 1937. Three years later Adkins defeated Bailey by a large majority in the Democratic gubernatorial primary and triumphed in the general election over his Republican opponent, H. C. Stump, by a vote of 184,578 to 16,000. In 1942 Adkins was reelected without Republican opposition for a second term. After two terms in office, he chose not to seek a third term in 1944.

His election in 1940 made him Arkansas's wartime governor (1941–1945) in a period of dramatic economic and social change. At the beginning of his tenure, Arkansas was still suffering from the chilling effects of the Great Depression and the weight of a $137 million highway debt that was, in part, due to the economic impact of the depression. In his inaugural address, Adkins gave refunding of the highway debt first priority. Even before he was sworn into office, he began work on a new highway refunding plan. To ensure legislative support without extensive floor debate, Adkins consulted with members of the legislature in small groups explaining his plan. When the legislature convened on 13 January 1941, his refunding plan (Act No. 4) was passed unanimously by both houses of the legislature. Because highway refunding involved the expenditure of public funds through the issuance of state bonds, voter approval was required by law. In 1943 Arkansas voters, in a special election, approved the new highway-refunding plan by a vote of eighty-nine thousand to one thousand. The entire $136 million bond issue was purchased by the federal government's Reconstruction Finance Corporation.

Before Arkansas voters had approved the governor's scheme, the United States was at war. During the war years, due to the untiring efforts of the governor, the business community, and the Arkansas congressional delegation in Washington, D.C., some $300 million worth of defense plants and installations were located in Arkansas. At war's end, many of the plants were purchased by private firms and converted to peacetime production thus providing continued employment for

Arkansans. The establishment of war plants, together with increased military spending and growing demand for Arkansas agricultural products, enabled the state to recover from the depression. The state's treasury surplus rose from $21 to $45 million. The workmen's compensation act, approved by the voters in 1940 and supported by outgoing governor Carl Bailey and by Adkins, enabled the latter to obtain war manufacturing facilities in Pine Bluff, Jacksonville, and other cities.

In addition to improving the state's financial situation, Adkins, a devout Methodist, also attempted to improve the state's moral climate. In 1942 he authorized the state police to seize gambling equipment in Garland County (Hot Springs) and in Little Rock without benefit of search warrants. He even threatened to declare martial law in Hot Springs and to send in the National Guard in order to prevent illegal gambling. When Adkins' crusade against gambling was rebuffed by the state courts, he tried unsuccessfully to persuade the legislature to outlaw betting on horse and dog races at Hot Springs and West Memphis, respectively.

In sharp contrast to his crusade for moral purity, Adkins displayed little respect for the rights of minorities. The governor's attitude toward minority rights was clearly revealed by his treatment of the approximately twenty thousand Japanese-Americans who were interned in Arkansas during World War II. When the federal government requested permission to establish two Japanese-American relocation centers in Arkansas, Adkins refused to accept the camps until he was officially requested to do so as a patriotic duty and was assured that the internees would be kept under guard and would be promptly evacuated after the war. Although Arkansas suffered from a severe labor shortage during the war years, Adkins repeatedly refused requests from businessmen and farmers to allow the internees to work in Arkansas. He did, however, allow them to leave Arkansas to accept employment in other states. In addition to insisting that they be kept under close guard during their stay in Arkansas, Adkins also pushed for legislation to deny the internees access to public education and property ownership in Arkansas. In 1943 the state legislature, with strong support from Adkins, enacted a law denying Japanese-Americans the right to own property in the state. The measure, however, was later declared unconstitutional. It mattered little to the governor and to the legislature that the vast majority of the Japanese-Americans who were forcibly interned in Arkansas were loyal American citizens.

Adkins' attitude toward the civil and political rights of blacks in Arkansas was only slightly different from his attitude toward the

Japanese-Americans. Blacks were not denied property rights and educational opportunities (although such opportunities were minimal), but they were denied equal suffrage and employment opportunities. When President Roosevelt issued Executive Order 8802 in 1941 outlawing racial discrimination in federal job-training programs and in employment by industries with federal contracts, Adkins declared that the order violated states' rights and was unenforceable in Arkansas. He was enraged by the U.S. Supreme Court's decision in the *Smith v. Allwright* case of 1944. The decision outlawed the "all white" Democratic party primary in Texas and prepared the way for black voting in Democratic primaries throughout the South. In most Southern states the winner of the Democratic primaries usually won the general election because of the lack of strong Republican opposition. In an outburst of anger Adkins declared that the Democratic party in Arkansas and the South was a white man's party and urged the party in the state to change its rules in order to circumvent the Court's decision. He also sent a letter to the governors of other states requesting them to urge their legislatures to petition Congress to enact laws limiting federal authority and to call for a constitutional convention that would repeal Executive Order 8802 and the *Smith v. Allwright* decision. Undoubtedly, Adkins' attitude toward the political and civil rights of Japanese-Americans and blacks was consistent with the racial philosophy of the Klan, an organization to which he had once belonged.

In 1945 the Arkansas legislature, encouraged by Adkins and his successor, Benjamin Travis Laney Jr., passed a double primary law that attempted to thwart the Supreme Court's decision in *Smith v. Allwright*. Under this law regular and runoff primaries were held separately for state and federal officials. Blacks could only vote in the primaries being held for federal offices, not in those held for local ones.

In 1944 Adkins decided to make a bid for Hattie M. Caraway's U.S. Senate seat. In a spirited and expensive contest—the so-called million dollar race—he was defeated in the Democratic primary by Rep. J. William Fulbright, who was supported by Adkins' old political rival, former Governor Bailey. Returning to private business, Adkins became something of a political broker for Arkansas politicians aspiring for higher office. He was instrumental in the election of Sidney Sanders McMath as governor in 1948 and in McMath's reelection in 1950. Adkins also served as consultant and adviser to Orval Eugene Faubus during the latter's successful bid for the governorship of Arkansas in 1954.

Adkins remained in private business until 1948 when his political ally, Governor McMath, appointed him administrator of the Arkansas Employment Security Division, a post that he held until 1952. Though plagued by poor health, he continued to be active in Arkansas politics for almost a decade thereafter. In 1956 he established a public-relations firm in Little Rock and was associated for a time with Stephens, Incorporated, an investment company. Adkins spent much of his later life on the 250-acre farm near Malvern that he had acquired in the late 1930s. An active member of the Malvern Chamber of Commerce, he devoted much effort to attracting industry to the town and its environs. Admitted to a Malvern hospital for treatment of a heart ailment on 17 February 1964, he died nine days later and was buried in Roselawn Memorial Park in Little Rock.

BENJAMIN TRAVIS LANEY JR.

1945–1949

BENJAMIN TRAVIS LANEY JR. (25 November 1896–21 January 1977), businessman, was born on a small farm in the Jones Chapel community (commonly called Cooterneck), Ouachita County, Arkansas, one of eleven children of Benjamin Travis Laney Sr. and Martha Ella (Saxon) Laney. His father farmed marginal land and, though without formal education, saw six of his children receive college degrees. Laney described his father as hardworking and thrifty, a man who kept his promises and never bought anything he could not afford. His example may help to explain Laney's later public fiscal policy.

Laney did not finish high school, but his ability earned him a teaching job and admission to Hendrix College in 1915 where he was an honor student. He left Hendrix in 1916, taught again briefly, and joined the U.S. Navy in 1918. Following the armistice, Laney entered Arkansas Teachers College (now the University of Central Arkansas) and received the A.B. degree in 1924. He took graduate courses at the University of Utah. In 1925 Laney and one of his brothers bought a Conway drugstore; Laney also worked in a local bank. On 19 January 1926, in Conway, he married Lucile Kirtley, a student at Arkansas Teachers College and daughter of a Lewisville (Lafayette County) businessman. This union produced three sons: Benjamin Travis III, William David, and Phillip.

Five years after oil was discovered on the family farm in 1922, Laney moved to Camden where in addition to his farming and banking interests, he entered the oil business and acquired cotton gins and oil mills, as well as feed, grocery, and hardware stores. In a 1935 special election he was elected mayor of Camden, a post he held until 1939. Appointed to the Arkansas Penitentiary Board by Gov. Homer Martin Adkins in 1941, he served in that capacity until 1944. His first major activity in state politics was on behalf of John L. McClellan's bid for the U.S. Senate in 1942.

When Laney announced as a candidate in 1944 for the Democratic nomination for governor, he was not well known in the state. But he had consulted with political leaders and was supported by the Arkansas Public Expenditures Council, a private conservative organization. The other major candidates were State Comptroller J. Bryan Sims and David D. Terry, former five-term congressman. Terry and Laney accused Sims and his allies of using the state police for partisan political purposes and the charge of "Gestapo tactics" was added to a more traditional attack on machine politics. Terry's only criticism of Laney was his inexperience; Laney's campaign ignored Terry. Sims's appeals emphasized his many years in state government. All three candidates promised to impose economies in government, lower taxes, promote industrialization, protect states' rights, and support veterans' legislation.

Launching his campaign, Laney had said "I am not a politician" and his organization reflected the amateurism of many of his supporters. He characterized himself as "conservative yet progressive" and called for the preservation of "old-fashioned Americanism." He led the July preferential primary with 38.5 percent of the vote, while Sims trailed by only 7,511 votes. The stage seemed set for the 8 August runoff election. Sims took the offensive, hammering at Laney's "inherited, not earned" wealth. Then, suddenly, on 29 July 1944, in a move without parallel in Arkansas politics, Sims withdrew from the race. Denying rumors of a negotiated withdrawal, he simply said "I am definitely of the opinion I cannot win this fight." His action made Laney something of an "accidental governor." In the November general election Laney received 85 percent of the vote against the Republican H. C. Stump. In 1946 Governor Laney easily defeated challenger J. M. Malone in his bid for renomination and was elected to a second term by an 84 percent to 16 percent margin over Republican W. T. Mills.

During the 1944 campaign Laney emphasized efficiency, economy, and consolidation in state government and promised as governor to translate such policies into law. He also announced his intention to make all state appropriations from a single general fund. Existing practice allotted fractions of various taxes to more than one hundred separate funds and accounts. This arrangement prevented shifting funds when conditions required more or less money for particular programs.

To deal with this problem the governor submitted the revenue-stabilization plan to the legislature in February 1945. Worked out by Laney's chief fiscal advisers, Julian Hogan and Frank A. Storey, the measure was the governor's major legislative proposal, and he asked the press "not to print anything that would hurt the bill." Goals of the plan included paying off the state's nonhighway debt, reducing taxes and eliminating the state ad valorem property tax, and protecting services against possible future depressions. The governor believed that emphasis on economy and tax reduction would favorably impress business and help to lure capital to Arkansas. Hardly mentioned at the time was the possibility of the program's preventing deficit spending. Balances in various state funds (about $40 million) would remain undisturbed for emergency use by the agencies or services to which they were credited. The new single fund was intended only for future revenues.

Public and legislative response to the concept was favorable. The senate passed the bill with only one negative vote, house approval was unanimous, and Laney signed it in February 1945. Despite subsequent revisions, the law's essential features have remained intact. Some felt that the Revenue Stabilization Law was "so business-like and so non-political" that it would not survive. Such fears proved groundless and revenue stabilization became Laney's greatest achievement—a monument to fiscal responsibility.

The 1945 general assembly in response to administration requests consolidated the corporation commission and the utilities commission into a single agency, the Public Service Commission. Laney also created a fiscal control board to replace and incorporate the responsibilities of ten existing boards and commissions and reorganized the state police and pardon and parole processes. The Arkansas Resources and Development Commission was formed in 1945 to consolidate agencies dealing with the development and promotion of resources and to encourage industrialization to balance the state economy. The commission helped to formulate the "Arkansas Plan," a cooperative effort by science, business, government, and individuals toward the common goal of development.

Returning veterans' activities in the elections of 1946 triggered the so-called GI Revolt against entrenched politicians. Laney remained officially neutral in these factional fights and limited his role to sending the state police to maintain order at the polls in a few machine counties.

Reorganization had been the dominant theme in Laney's first term; the administration turned to tax revision in the second. Tax measures included increasing liquor, cigarette, state income, and severance taxes. Homestead exemptions were raised from $1,000 to $2,000, inheritance taxes were lowered (Laney hoped this would bring wealthy investors to Arkansas), and the state income-tax credit for federal taxes paid was reduced from 100 to 50 percent. State ad valorem property taxes were abolished effective 31 December 1948 because the governor wanted this revenue source left to local governments and school districts. Laney declined to introduce legislation to raise sales and gasoline taxes for highway purposes. Although he believed the increases necessary to avoid highway bond issues, he was convinced that the people would not support them.

To improve the quality of legislation, Laney sponsored a bill passed in February 1947 that created a legislative council. Its members were selected by the governor and the general assembly and would meet on a regular basis when the legislature was not in session. The council was to employ a full-time research director and to make recommendations on proposed legislation.

Laney thought that the lack of an official residence for the state's chief executive was an embarrassment to Arkansas, and in 1947 he sought and obtained appropriations for a governor's mansion.

One of the bitterest fights in the 1947 legislature was over a bill providing for construction of War Memorial Stadium, which Laney supported. Foes described the project as a waste of money and "nothing more than an institution of debauchery" but were unable to overcome strong administration backing. Laney signed the measure on 19 March 1947. A nine-member commission was authorized to issue revenue bonds, to select a site, and to proceed with construction. The state fiscal control board received permission to purchase part of the revenue bonds.

Debate over enabling legislation for Arkansas's "right to work" constitutional amendment of 1944 outlawing the closed union shop strained the governor's relations with organized labor. Amendment Thirty-four had been pushed by the Christian-American Association, a Texas-based antiunion organization that unsuccessfully sought an enabling act in the 1945 session. Two years later the general assembly passed a bill with little discussion. Although Laney had said in 1945 that such legislation was not necessary, he promptly signed the bill. Labor leaders charged collusion between the governor and organized conservatives.

Veterans received little attention from the 1945 general assembly, and even though the 1947 session contained many newly elected ex-servicemen, consensus was seldom reached. Frequent disagreements occurred among the three major veterans' organizations (American

Legion, Veterans of Foreign Wars, and American Veterans of World War II); Laney, himself a Legionnaire, usually supported legislation favored by the Legion. Among the few 1947 proposals that became law were provisions for educational benefits for the children of men killed in action during World War II, enrollment preference for veterans at state schools, and bonus points for veterans on local and state merit examinations.

In dealing with legislators, Laney's style was personal and effective. Frequent lunches, private conferences, and easy access to the governor's office facilitated passage of administration bills. Laney enjoyed major successes in both the fifty-fifth and fifty-sixth general assemblies, thus laying to rest the political cliché that Arkansas governors are "dictators in the first term and spectators in the second." Veteran legislators led the 1945 session while the 1947 body contained a majority of freshmen, but the change in composition caused Laney little difficulty.

A self-styled "economy bloc" in 1947 opposed some of the governor's proposals, but their victories were largely limited to delaying appropriations bills. A few legislators complained about steamroller tactics and one newspaper announced that "Laney's Control of the Legislature Astonishes Assembly Veterans." Careful groundwork and behind-the-scenes maneuvering prompted one columnist to remark that Laney "kept his intentions concealed better than an old maid's birthmark." And the policy paid off. William J. Smith, Laney's chief assistant, could "watch the Senators pop up like rabbits in a hat to rush through the governor's legislation." By May 1947 Laney himself said the "business governor" title was a misnomer and added "I'm a politician now, I've found that to hold this job successfully you have to be a politician."

Despite supporters' urgings and widespread speculation to the contrary, Laney chose not to seek a third term in 1948. But national events would keep him in the center of Southern politics. Pres. Harry S. Truman's 2 February 1948 civil-rights message to Congress ignited smoldering Southern hostility toward the federal government. Laney was prominent in the region's reaction.

States' rights concerns were the basis for Laney's opposition to Truman's call for an antilynching law, federal action to abolish the poll tax and eliminate racial discrimination, and the creation of a permanent fair employment practices commission. The governor said that change was inevitable but insisted that any action should originate with the states.

Southern governors, after a meeting in Florida in February 1948, unsuccessfully tried to persuade the national Democratic leadership to ignore Truman's proposals at the party's national convention that was to convene in Philadelphia on 12 July.

Reconvening at Jackson, Mississippi, on 10 May the Southern governors chose Laney as permanent chairman of the resistance that took the title "States' Rights Democrats" (Dixiecrats). Accepting the chairmanship, Laney reaffirmed his support of racial segregation but admitted that blacks in the South had not been given equal opportunities.

Laney, as a member of a small group of liberal New Dealers and Southern conservatives, worked to convince Dwight D. Eisenhower to seek the Democratic presidential nomination. Eisenhower declined and states' rights leaders looked back to Dixie for a protest candidate. Laney withdrew his name from consideration, and Sen. Richard Russell of Georgia was defeated soundly by Truman at the Democratic convention.

After that convention in Philadelphia adopted a strong civil-rights plank in its platform, the states' rights Democrats gathered in Birmingham, Alabama, on 17 July and chose Govs. Strom Thurmond of South Carolina and Fielding Wright of Mississippi as presidential and vice-presidential candidates, respectively. While present at the Birmingham gathering, Laney was not active in the proceedings. His decision not to seek either spot on the ticket was compatible with his assessments that the South would not solidly support a third party, that the effort lacked adequate organization and money, and that radicals such as Wright would discredit the movement. The former Arkansas governor believed that the only chance of defeating the civil-rights program would be through official Democratic organizations in the states. Although he chaired the Dixiecrats' executive committee and served on the party's steering committee, he was always distressed by the movement's lack of sophistication. He campaigned for the states' righters in Arkansas but Sidney Sanders McMath, the Democratic gubernatorial nominee, was able to hold the state's Democratic convention and presidential electors for Truman. Petitions placed the Dixiecrat slate on the general-election ballot, but Thurmond and Wright received only 16.5 percent of the vote.

Laney's bitterness toward McMath and his administration was no secret, but his 1950 effort to unseat the governor surprised many. The challenge meant that Laney had the dual problem of facing a popular governor seeking a traditional second term and of seeking a nontraditional third term for himself (accomplished only once previously in

Arkansas). Further complicating the situation was the former governor's identification with the Dixiecrats. Laney dealt with two of these
problems by charging that McMath had flaunted too many Southern
traditions to expect a traditional second term while he, Laney, had
always been a loyal "Arkansas Democrat." McMath was accused of
having bolted the party in supporting independent candidates in the
1946 elections. The third-term issue was skirted with a tortured campaign slogan: "Let's Re-Elect Ben Laney Governor, for a Second Time."

There was little serious disagreement between the two candidates
on issues such as improving education and highways, aiding the needy
and elderly, and attracting industry to Arkansas, but they differed over
their respective records in these areas. McMath was linked to the
allegedly "socialistic" Truman administration, and Laney was called a
do-nothing governor who represented privileged interests. A newly
mobilized black electorate, first active in 1948, gave strong support to
McMath. This support outraged racists and led one pro-Laney editor
to accuse McMath of furthering "the invasion of the white bedroom
in the South." Laney was made the champion of the vocal, radical,
and crude element with which he was often uncomfortable. The outcome was predictable: the voters decided not to reelect Ben Laney for
a second time by a two-to-one margin.

After his 1950 campaign loss, Laney remained active in politics and
the states' rights cause, although he disapproved of Gov. Orval Eugene
Faubus's handling of the integration question and supported Faubus
in only one of his eight gubernatorial races (1974). In 1969 Laney
served as a delegate to the Arkansas constitutional convention and was
a member of the finance and taxation committee. He was also active
in the reelection campaigns of Sens. John L. McClellan (1972) and
J. William Fulbright (1974), but his antipathy toward the national
Democratic party caused him to support the presidential candidacies
of George Wallace (American party) in 1968 and Gerald Ford (Republican) in 1976.

Laney managed the Arkansas rice farms of Winthrop Rockefeller
in the 1960s and spent his last years in Magnolia looking after his own
business affairs. Following a long illness, he died of a heart attack on
21 January 1977 at his Magnolia home and was buried in Camden
Memorial Cemetery.

SIDNEY SANDERS McMATH

1949–1953

SIDNEY SANDERS McMATH (14 June 1912–), attorney, was born in Columbia County, Arkansas, the son of Hal McMath, a farmer, and Nettie (Sanders) McMath. In 1922 the family moved to Hot Springs, where McMath's father operated a barbershop. After graduation from the local high school, McMath worked his way through the University of Arkansas at Fayetteville by waiting tables, washing dishes, and fighting exhibition boxing matches. In his last year at the university he starred in student theatrical productions and served as the business manager of the school's yearbook and president of the student body. He graduated with an LL.B. degree in 1936.

The next year McMath married his high-school sweetheart, but the union ended in tragedy when Elaine (Broughton) McMath died of nephritis in 1942 following the birth of the couple's only child, a son. Already on active duty with the U.S. Marine Corps, the future governor spent the next three years in military service during World War II. As an operations officer in the Third Marine Division in the Pacific theater, he fought at Guadalcanal, in the battle of the Solomons, and at Bougainville, where he received a battlefield promotion to lieutenant colonel. Over the course of the war, McMath received both the Silver Star and the Legion of Merit Award and several years later achieved the rank of major general in the marine corps reserve.

In 1944 McMath married Anne Phillips of Slate Springs, Mississippi, and the following year the couple moved to Hot Springs, Arkansas, where the ambitious young veteran opened a law practice and launched his political career. In the mid-1940s, Hot Springs was a thriving resort town with a nationwide reputation for medicinal mineral water and wide-open gambling. Politically, the city and surrounding Garland County were controlled by a clique headed by Mayor Leo P. McLaughlin. Backed by the gambling interests, the mayor's political machine had dominated the Hot Springs area for twenty years by openly flaunting election laws and by manipulating the poll-tax system. In 1946 McMath and several other recently returned veterans set out to overthrow McLaughlin's corrupt administration. Under McMath's leadership the group organized the Government Improvement League, conveniently abbreviated the organization's name to "GI" and entered a slate of nine candidates for various local offices in the summer primary. The subsequent election was known as the "GI Revolt." McMath filed for prosecuting attorney. Following an exceptionally rough campaign in which some of the GIs were threatened for publicizing political corruption in Garland County, the veterans won a narrow but complete victory. By far the chief beneficiary of the revolt was McMath, who emerged from the election with the popular image as a reform leader and as a tough-minded prosecutor with unlimited political potential.

After two surprisingly undistinguished years as prosecuting attorney for Garland and Montgomery Counties, McMath, who was still regarded as a popular progressive, entered the 1948 gubernatorial race. Temporarily shedding his image as a reformer, he conducted a conventional campaign by welding together factions of older political machines, stressing traditional issues like roads and schools, and relying on his charismatic personality and style. As he campaigned to the strains of the "Marine Hymn" in a patriotic blue suit, red tie, and white shirt accented by a white Panama hat, McMath projected an image of youth, vigor, and good looks that caused several observers to comment that even if he lost the race for governor, he probably had a considerable future as a movie star.

After leading a field of nine candidates in the July primary, McMath deviated from his traditional and conservative strategy when his opponent injected the issue of race into the runoff campaign. Rather than adopting the race-baiting stance that was typical of Southern demagogues of the era, McMath met the challenge as one newspaper said, "on the high ground of racial tolerance," and this decision marked the beginning of his reputation as a Southern liberal and racial moderate. Winning a narrow victory in 1948, McMath at thirty-six became the youngest governor of Arkansas since the Civil War.

During his four years in the statehouse at Little Rock, McMath promoted a variety of progressive measures and won a nationwide reputation as a spokesman for what some historians have called the "Southern reform tradition." Throughout the late 1940s and early 1950s he resisted the efforts of the extreme states' rights Dixiecrats to capture the Democratic party in Arkansas and, partly as a result of

McMath's efforts in the 1948 election, the voters of Arkansas refused to follow their fellow Southerners in Alabama, Mississippi, South Carolina, and Louisiana in abandoning the national Democrats for the Dixiecrat presidential slate. After the election McMath remained an ardent supporter of Pres. Harry S. Truman's administration and a bitter opponent of those who wanted to form a regional states' rights party. In 1950 McMath won reelection by a wide margin over former Gov. Benjamin Travis Laney Jr., the leading advocate of the Dixiecrat movement in the state.

In contrast to the conservative philosophy of the Dixiecrats, McMath promoted a relatively progressive program during his four years in office. With an emphasis on highway construction, health care, educational improvement, and economic development, McMath's plan for Arkansas was closely related to the "business progressivism" that had swept the South in the 1920s. The cornerstone of his program was his effort to save the state's deteriorating highway system. As a result of several factors, Arkansas's roads, often the object of ridicule in other parts of the nation, were in desperate condition when McMath became governor in 1949. In the 1930s the state had defaulted on a series of highway bonds, and there was little money for road construction. Because of the lack of labor and material during World War II, the highway system had become totally inadequate to meet the needs of a modern state. In January 1949 the legislature, under McMath's leadership, authorized the issuance of general-obligation bonds for the construction and maintenance of highways and bridges. The governor then called for a special bond election, which was held on 15 February. Over the objections of fiscal conservatives, McMath campaigned vigorously for the measure, and the voters approved the governor's program by a margin of almost four to one.

The bonds were the basis of an unprecedented highway-construction boom that provided a foundation for the state's accelerated modernization in the postwar era. During his tenure, McMath built more miles of highway than any previous governor. This construction included the first hard-surface roads connecting seven separate county seats with the state highway system. Prior to 1949 these areas had been forced to rely exclusively on gravel or dirt roads.

Another hallmark of the McMath administration was improved health care for the citizens of Arkansas. Under the governor's leadership construction was begun on a new medical center in Little Rock, the university medical school was upgraded, and the state's mental-health system was revised. McMath's program in this area included an extensive survey to determine centers of potential patient density and possible locations of mental-hygiene clinics. Calling for increased training facilities for professional personnel, the plan established a department of neuropsychiatry in the state medical school.

Along with improved health care, McMath saw electric service as a major factor in the state's overall modernization. Like other Southern progressives, he regarded electricity as one of the keys to improving rural life and felt that without electric power Arkansas farmers could never compete with those of surrounding states. Consequently, along with efforts to attract industry to Arkansas, McMath's economic program focused on support for the rural electric cooperative movement. Believing that private power companies had neglected this area, the governor felt that the cooperatives offered the farmers the most effective and inexpensive electrical service available. His unyielding support of the cooperatives, however, provoked the opposition of the state's major private power company and led to a series of dramatic confrontations over issues such as the use of multiple-purpose dams and the role of the Public Service Commission. The most widely publicized of these conflicts centered on the construction of a steam-generating plant near the town of Ozark. Early in 1949, when the Arkansas Electric Cooperative Corporation had applied to the federal government for a loan to build the Ozark plant, the loan was vigorously opposed by executives of the Arkansas Power and Light Company, the state's largest private utility. In a series of tension-filled hearings before the Public Service Commission, opponents of the plant accused the coops of being socialistic and threatening private enterprise. When, despite a favorable PSC ruling, the construction of the Ozark facility was delayed by a series of complex maneuvers in both state and federal courts, Governor McMath entered the controversy on the side of the cooperatives. He contacted President Truman and other federal officials to ensure rapid approval of the loan application and spoke at numerous rural electric cooperative meetings challenging the idea that public power was detrimental to private enterprise or to the state as a whole. Several years later the Ozark plant was completed, and McMath emerged from these controversies with a strong reputation as a proponent of public power.

McMath's interest in the problems of the state's rural citizens was matched by his concern for the welfare of Arkansas's urban workers. He sponsored legislation that more than doubled the annual budget of the labor department, increased minimum-wage laws, and strengthened industrial-safety codes. In October 1949 the governor also played a key role as a conciliator in a Missouri-Pacific Railroad strike that had damaged a variety of economic activities in a ten-state area. Because of these and other efforts, McMath received tremendous support in each of his campaigns from labor organizations within the state.

Along with his support for labor and public power, McMath's image as a Southern liberal was enhanced by his stance on issues involving Arkansas's black citizens. Although operating within the framework of a racially segregated social system, he attempted to improve the educational, political, and economic status of the state's black community. He attacked the diversion of state funds from black schools to white schools and supported efforts to improve the quality of education at Arkansas's only all-black, state-supported college. He also fought for the repeal of the poll tax, which was used to disenfranchise blacks, supported a state antilynching law, and appointed a limited number of blacks to previously all-white boards and commissions. Despite the fact that he never challenged the inequitable system of segregation, McMath set a relatively liberal tone in race relations that later provided a foundation of moderation in an era of racial turmoil.

Despite its overall record of achievement, the McMath administration suffered severe internal problems. In January and February of 1952 a highway audit commission conducted a series of public hearings in Little Rock and uncovered several improprieties within the Arkansas Highway Department. Along with some inefficient and wasteful practices, the commission revealed an unsavory pattern of political contributions to the governor by contractors and vendors of heavy machinery and road equipment. When the governor's executive secretary refused to reveal the complete campaign records to the commission, the administration was tarnished by accusations of scandal. McMath loyalists contended that the investigation was initiated by the governor's political enemies and pointed out that no one was ever convicted of a crime involving the conduct of the highway department. Nevertheless, the findings of the audit commission indicated a misuse of power and a lack of judgment in the relationship between political contributions and the awarding of state contracts.

The highway audit also played a major role in the gubernatorial election of 1952. Against the advice of his closest associates, McMath defied Arkansas's two-term tradition and ran for an almost unprecedented third term as governor. While his opponents hammered at the theme of corruption in the statehouse, the governor charged that the highway audit had represented the efforts of special interests to discredit his administration and campaigned on his record of road construction, educational improvements, and economic development. Although he led a strong field of candidates in the first primary, McMath lost to Judge Francis Adams Cherry of Jonesboro in the August runoff.

Despite his defeat in 1952, McMath remained a forceful and popular figure in Arkansas politics for several years. His family had grown to include two more sons and twin daughters, and the former governor maintained a successful law practice and an active civic life. In 1954 he was narrowly defeated in a race for the U.S. Senate by the incumbent senator, John L. McClellan, and in 1957 and 1958 he was one of the state's most outspoken critics of Gov. Orval Eugene Faubus's conduct during the crisis surrounding the desegregation of Little Rock Central High School. In 1962 McMath unsuccessfully ran for governor against Faubus in one of Arkansas's most dramatic postwar elections. (Faubus had begun his career in state government as part of the McMath administration.) After the 1962 election McMath withdrew from the political arena and returned to private law practice. Regarded as one of the state's most prominent attorneys, he was elected president of the International Academy of Trial Lawyers in 1976.

During his two terms as governor, McMath combined numerous elements of the South's Democratic heritage and served Arkansas in the capacity of a transitional liberal. By contributing to a more progressive image of the state in the post–World War II era and by breaking precedent with the series of conservative chief executives who preceded him in the statehouse, McMath provided a valuable legacy for the state's reform-minded leaders who emerged in the 1960s and 1970s.

FRANCIS ADAMS CHERRY

1953–1955

FRANCIS ADAMS CHERRY (5 September 1908–15 July 1965), attorney, was born in Fort Worth, Texas, the youngest of five children of Haskille Scott and Clara Belle (Taylor) Cherry. When Cherry was only a few months old, the family moved to El Reno, Oklahoma, where his father was employed as a railroad conductor on the Rock Island Lines. Another move was made to Enid, a prosperous city in the Oklahoma wheat country, and after graduation from Enid High School, Cherry attended Oklahoma A & M College in Stillwater where he undertook a prelaw curriculum between 1926 and 1930. Because of the depression he was forced to postpone plans for law school and instead spent the next three years working at a miscellany of occupations including washing dishes and driving an ice truck through the Ozark Mountains. He had moved to Fayetteville in 1932 and with the slender savings of thirty-seven dollars enrolled in the University of Arkansas law school the following year.

Despite having to support himself with various outside jobs, Cherry made an excellent academic record. Popular with his classmates, he was elected president of his senior class. He also found the time to become engaged to Margaret Frierson of Jonesboro, Arkansas, who had been selected campus queen at the university in 1933. They were married on 10 November 1937; they had three children: Haskille Scott III, Charlotte, and Francis, Jr.

After graduation from law school in 1936, Cherry spent a year in Little Rock where another young attorney, Leffel Gentry, gave him a desk in his office. Gentry would become Cherry's campaign manager in the 1952 gubernatorial race. In 1937 Cherry settled in his wife's hometown of Jonesboro and accepted a junior partnership in the Marcus Feltz law firm. He gained administrative and political experience when he was appointed U.S. commissioner for the Jonesboro Division of the Eastern District in 1939; the following year that experience was broadened when Gov. Carl E. Bailey named him referee for the workmen's compensation commission. In 1942 he decided to try for elective office and ran for chancellor and probate judge of the Twelfth Chancery District, which was composed of Clay, Greene, Craighead, Mississippi, Poinsett, and Crittenden Counties. He led the voting in the first primary and easily won the runoff over the incumbent. He enjoyed his judicial post, but with the nation's entire energies focused on winning the Second World War, Cherry waived his judicial immunity and requested induction into the armed services. When his efforts proved futile through the selective-service system, he applied directly for a naval commission and was appointed a lieutenant (j.g.). After serving in the navy for two years, he returned to Jonesboro in 1946 and resumed his duties as chancellor. He was reelected to the position without opposition in 1948.

Cherry's decision to abandon the security of his judgeship and to enter a crowded field for the Democratic gubernatorial nomination in 1952 was related to both state and national politics. At the state level Gov. Sidney Sanders McMath was completing his second term amid accusations of scandal and corruption in the highway department; McMath who had decided to defy Arkansas political tradition and to run for a third term was further handicapped by his association with the unpopular Truman administration. Truman had come to Arkansas in 1952 to dedicate Bull Shoals Dam. It was the first time the president had made a public speech in a Southern state since the Dixiecrat revolt of 1948, and he used the occasion to praise McMath's moderate policies and to give him a warm personal endorsement. The governor's challengers tagged him as "Harry's Boy."

Three prominent state Democrats joined Cherry in challenging McMath. They were conservative Rep. Boyd Tackett whose House seat was being eliminated as a result of the redistribution imposed by the results of the 1950 census; Ike Murry, the state's attorney general; and Jack Holt, a former attorney general who had lost to McMath in the 1948 Democratic runoff. All the governor's opponents attempted to take advantage of the increasingly conservative political climate.

The anti-Communist hysteria fueled by the charges of Sen. Joseph McCarthy had labeled Truman's Fair Deal program as "creeping socialism" and would culminate in a return of the Republicans to the White House after a twenty-year absence. In Arkansas, where the Republican party was so minuscule as to be an insignificant election factor, the conservative tide manifested itself within Democratic ranks and severely impaired McMath's chances for a third term.

Cherry's principal problem was lack of recognition. He had no statewide reputation, had not been active in state politics, and had no political organization that could command both workers and votes. To remedy the situation Cherry and Gentry contracted with Houck & Company, a Miami advertising agency, to provide a radio format aimed at establishing Judge Cherry's credentials. The result was the "talkathon"—a series of marathon appearances over a radio network in which the candidate fielded questions called in by listeners and appealed for funds to carry on the campaign. The initial talkathon on 2 July lasted for twenty-four-and-a-half hours. Before the 29 July primary, Cherry had conducted twenty more, all of which were at least three hours long. The tactic was an unqualified success and catapulted the handsome jurist from obscurity to statewide prominence. While the talkathon's appeal owed something to its novelty, Cherry's adroit handling of the device was equally important. Altogether he answered over thirteen thousand questions and was able to project the image of a candid candidate who was personally interested in the everyday concerns of the average voter. In a matter of four weeks Cherry came from last place in the polls to finish second behind McMath in the primary. In the 12 August runoff election the judge's momentum carried him to victory over the incumbent by almost a hundred thousand votes, the largest majority ever given an Arkansas gubernatorial candidate in a primary. He won easily over a nominal Republican opponent, Jefferson W. Speck, in the November general election.

Cherry brought with him to the governor's mansion a moderately conservative political philosophy that had as its basic tenet the idea that the business of state government could and should be operated with maximum fiscal efficiency and economy. This belief was to become the cornerstone of his legislative program. Complementary to this emphasis on frugality and sound management was his insistence that the future lay in industrialization, and he planned a determined program to "Build Arkansas" by encouraging manufacturing firms to locate plants in the state. Industrial growth and an efficient state government would reinforce each other and would create a favorable business climate. Cherry was also a strong advocate of states' rights, especially in relation to revenue and taxation. "I don't like the taking of money out of the states through taxes," he declared, "taking it to Washington, then turning around and giving it back to the states on the provision that the states raise additional funds to match the federal money." But he was also dubious about reversing the trend. Government, he believed, should be limited and as local as possible.

When he denied the charge in March 1954 that he had told Hot Springs gambling proprietors that they could "open up," he also added that cities and counties should be custodians of their own morals.

To Cherry, unlike many other Southern leaders of the day, a states' rights posture was not a cover for maintaining white superiority. Well in advance of the 1954 Supreme Court decision outlawing public school segregation, Cherry had announced that "we will have to abide by the decision handed down because that will be the law." Arkansas, he later said, would not become an outlaw. The governor also possessed a humanitarian streak that tempered his faith in limited government. He was appalled by the conditions he encountered at the Boys' Industrial School in Pine Bluff and called for state action to improve conditions. Certainly, his political philosophy was neither uncommon nor profound, but he considered it logical and common-sensical. It seemed in keeping with the wishes of an electorate that had just elevated Dwight D. Eisenhower, a man with similar perceptions, to the White House.

In his inaugural address Cherry outlined a three-point legislative program to implement his campaign promise to streamline the machinery of state government. The key proposal was the creation of a department of finance and administration; a second was to enact reforms in the highway commission; and the third was to ask the general assembly to place on the ballot in 1954 a constitutional amendment requiring property-assessment reform. Cherry believed that the plan to create a new finance department under a revamped fiscal code was fundamental to the success of all other administration projects.

As envisioned by Cherry and as eventually enacted by the legislature, the new department of finance and administration would take over the functions of the fiscal control board. It was to be a budget-control and executive budget-writing agency. It would supervise all travel by state employees, maintain the inventory of state properties, and operate a motor pool for state vehicles. A collateral measure, partially designed to soothe state legislators, created a legislative post-audit division that would audit every state agency and would be responsible to the general assembly rather than to the governor. Cherry lobbied vigorously for the program's passage, even taking the unprecedented step of personally appearing as a witness before a senate committee and testifying for two-and-a-half hours in support of his reorganization scheme. The bill passed both houses by unanimous vote.

The governor was also able to persuade the general assembly in the aftermath of the problems of the McMath administration to institute reforms in the highway commission. This step had in part been mandated by the voters in the November 1952 election when they had approved the Blackwell Amendment to the constitution that required the commission to designate all state roads for either inclusion within or exclusion from the state system. Since Cherry had made highway-commission abuses a campaign target, he proposed additional reform measures aimed at removing the commission from political pressures and at plugging loopholes in existing regulations. The most controversial was a bill that allowed the commission to give priority in road construction to localities that provided right-of-way land without cost. After the passage of most of the highway bills, many legislators had second thoughts and urged the calling of a special legislative session to consider restricting commission authority. Cherry's refusal became a campaign issue in 1954.

Even more crucial as a potential campaign controversy was the governor's proposed constitutional amendment to equalize the property tax. In February 1953 he submitted to the general assembly a plan that would assess all property at 100 percent of market value but would limit the millage cities and counties could impose. Opponents argued that the scheme would result in an exorbitant tax increase and would be especially harmful to farmers while Cherry contended that the present tax structure was a patchwork of inequality and that enactment of his proposal would actually result in a tax savings. The administration was obliged to make an all-out effort to persuade the assembly to place the tax amendment on the ballot. In an ironic declaration that later seemed prophetic, Cherry said: "I would rather see this tax provision go through than to be governor of Arkansas." When the tax measure was endangered by a house filibuster, the governor was forced to compromise by signing special-interest bills he had threatened to veto. Almost as soon as the general assembly had given its reluctant approval, Cherry began to back away from his previous commitment to stump the state on behalf of the amendment. By May 1953 he foresaw defeat for the plan, and in January 1954 he announced that he would not campaign for it, saying that "it was up to the people now." However, he could not escape identification with what rapidly became an unpopular idea.

In spite of the Arkansas political tradition that an incumbent governor was automatically elected to a second term, several factors were coalescing in early 1954 that would deny Cherry another two years in the governor's mansion. Most important was his lack of political skill combined with a failure of leadership. Examples of each are plentiful.

Politically, he never attempted to build an organization. When he was asked by a reporter whether he would seek to have one of "his" men elected speaker of the house of the 1955 legislature, Cherry replied that he considered all the legislators his men and that he would not intervene in a strictly legislative process. On another occasion in cautioning agency heads to refrain from political activity, the governor declared, "you are going to learn after the next election that the best political organization a man can have is no organization at all." Essentially a passive chief executive, he had no dedicated following in the general assembly; consequently, legislators felt free to attack him and to appeal to their own constituencies.

Assaults on the governor and his program were directed at four principal targets, each of which was the result of Cherry's philosophy of fiscal efficiency and nonpolitical management. One of his projects to cut unnecessary expenditures had been the trimming of welfare rolls. The governor had supported seven bills in the legislative session aimed at accomplishing this objective, the most stringent of which would have required welfare recipients to give the state a lien on all real property as a condition for receiving aid. While this extreme measure was not adopted, the administration nevertheless was able to drop twenty-three hundred people from the rolls in four months. Cherry was accused of being indifferent to the problems of the poor and aged and the epithet "deadheads" that he had used to characterize some of the people on the welfare rolls did not help his image.

The governor had also made some controversial agency appointments, going out of state to name Herbert Eldridge of Texas as highway director and Dr. H. G. Crawfis of California as superintendent of the state hospital. Cherry received great criticism for hiring nonresidents at large salaries and for insisting that state agencies should be immune from patronage pressures and that management should be directed by competent professionals. These policies irked legislators from all areas of the state.

Northwest Arkansas was particularly upset by the governor's veto of a bill that would have exempted feed, seed, and fertilizer from the state sales tax. Cherry contended that the state could not afford the estimated loss of $3 million in revenue, but the poultry industry remained adamant in its opposition and was ready to support a candidate who promised repeal. These issues combined with the growing apprehension concerning the proposed constitutional amendment to assess property at 100 percent of value contrived to make a primary challenge appear attractive to potential opponents.

Rumors about the formation of an anti-Cherry coalition began to surface by February 1954 with the names of Jim Snoddy and Orval Eugene Faubus most frequently mentioned as possible rivals of the governor. Both men were from northwestern Arkansas. Snoddy, a former Cherry aide and state senator, operated an auto-supply business in Van Buren; Faubus, a highway commissioner in the McMath administration, published the Madison County *Record* in Huntsville. After much speculation Snoddy announced on 17 March that he would not make the race; Faubus, after withdrawing from the contest on 3 April, reentered the primary on 28 April, the deadline for filing. Also joining the fray were state senator Guy "Mutt" Jones of Conway, J. M. Myers of Springdale, and Gus McMillian of Sheridan. The campaign, however, quickly developed into a two-man struggle between Cherry and Faubus.

At first the gubernatorial primary race attracted little attention, being overshadowed by the more dramatic confrontation between incumbent John L. McClellan and ex-Governor McMath in the Democratic primary for the U.S. senatorial nomination. Faubus took the offensive by emphasizing the issues of welfare; executive appointments; the veto of the sales-tax exemption on feed, seed, and fertilizer; and the property-tax amendment. Then in June Faubus introduced the issue of school desegregation, declaring in a formal statement that any sudden mixing of the races in Arkansas's public schools would jeopardize harmonious race relations. Cherry only said that the school boards should wait before they implemented desegregation plans. Faubus also accused the governor of responsibility for a controversial utility-rate increase granted to the Arkansas Power and Light Company. Although Cherry pointed out that the Public Service Commission and not the governor had permitted the rate hike and promised to do everything in his power to negate it, that charge along with the others placed him on the defensive, and in the 31 July primary Faubus succeeded in gaining a runoff spot against the incumbent by carrying twenty-nine counties and running strongly in rural precincts.

The runoff proved as heated as the weather. With temperatures reaching record levels throughout the state, the Cherry campaign introduced the sensational charge that Faubus had attended the Communist-leaning Commonwealth College at Mena, Arkansas, in 1935 and had been president of its student body. After first denying the allegations, Faubus eventually admitted that he had been at Commonwealth a short time but had left the school when he discovered its true character. Cherry's employment of a McCarthy-like tactic indicated the desperate straits of his reelection campaign and undoubtedly generated a sympathy vote for Faubus who won the 10 August balloting by seven thousand votes. In the November general election the Cherry debacle was completed when the property-tax amendment was rejected overwhelmingly by the voters.

Cherry never again ran for political office. He was appointed by President Eisenhower to the subversive activities control board in October 1955; Pres. John F. Kennedy named him the board's chairman in 1963. That same year he underwent heart surgery and never regained his full vigor. The last two years of his life were spent in failing health. His body lay in state in the capitol rotunda in Little Rock before burial in the Oaklawn Cemetery at Jonesboro.

ORVAL EUGENE FAUBUS

1955–1967

ORVAL EUGENE FAUBUS (7 January 1910–14 December 1994), teacher
and newspaper publisher, was born in the northwest corner of
Arkansas near the village of Combs in the Ozark Mountains. Faubus
was even more specific about his birthplace in later years when political campaigns made it profitable to talk of his origins in terms of
Greasy Creek close to Combs. The county seat of Madison County,
Huntsville, with a population of about one thousand people, dwarfed
tiny Combs, which in turn was larger than Greasy Creek. Faubus used
the fact that he was a country boy at least three times removed from
city "contamination" to advantage in rural Arkansas during his campaigns for governor.

His parents, John Samuel and Addie Joselyn Faubus, reared their
son in an atmosphere of borderline poverty and political radicalism.
Faubus's father was a poor independent hill farmer who worried con-
stantly about family finances and tried to instill into his family the
principles of honesty and egalitarianism. A follower of the Socialist
Eugene V. Debs, he was jailed during World War I for his antiwar activities. Faubus frequently compared his childhood to that of Abraham
Lincoln, and there were some parallels: Faubus, too, was raised in a log
cabin where "to enclose the small fields we split hundreds of rails
much as Abraham Lincoln had done a hundred years earlier."

Faubus's formal education took place in a one-room school in
Greenwood (Greasy Creek) and a two-room facility in Combs. After
completing eight grades, he walked to Huntsville where he passed the
teachers' examination. While teaching, the young man enrolled in various high schools in Madison County on a part-time basis and received
his diploma from Huntsville Vocational High School in 1934. The next
year he spent a brief period at Commonwealth College near the southwestern Arkansas town of Mena but departed without enrolling for
classes. His association with this small college, which was later desig-

nated as a Communist-front organization by the U.S. Justice Department, played a prominent part in his first gubernatorial campaign in 1954. During the first years of his local political career, he completed the formal phase of his education by taking night courses through the extension service in Huntsville.

Faubus's informal education was at least as extensive as his formal training. During the summers from 1928 to 1938 he attended Citizens Military Camp at Fort Leavenworth, Kansas, and Camp Robinson at Little Rock, Arkansas; was an itinerant fruit picker in the Midwest; lived as a hobo in various parts of the country; did some sawmill work, farm labor, and timber work in the Ozarks; and labored as a lumberjack in Washington State. During this period of itinerant summer toil Faubus taught school in the academic year, mainly at Pinnacle, the second largest one-room school district in the county. While employed as a teacher he married Alta Haskins, a minister's daughter from Ball Creek near Combs, on 12 November 1931.

Faubus's political career began inauspiciously in 1936 when he ran for the Arkansas legislature in the Democratic primary and lost by four votes. His first successful race came two years later when he was elected Madison County circuit clerk and reporter, a post to which he was reelected in 1940. He received the nomination for county judge, the most important local political office, in 1942.

He left his political career and a son, Farrell Eugene Faubus (born 5 April 1939), behind when he joined the U.S. Army shortly after the Japanese attack on Pearl Harbor. Faubus's military career helped to set the stage for his subsequent political forays. He entered the war as a private and came out three years later as a major. He served with distinction in Gen. George Patton's Third Army, 320th Infantry, Thirty-fifth Division. Perhaps just as important, he wrote a column for the Madison County *Record* during his time in the army; the column kept his name before the home folks and provided a base for later political activities.

Shortly after returning home from the war, Faubus was named postmaster of Huntsville. With his first six months' salary he bought the Madison County *Record*. Faubus was a successful newspaperman and quickly built the *Record* into the third largest weekly newspaper in Arkansas. The weekly provided a permanent platform from which he could gather political allies and launch future campaigns. He was soon able to attract the attention of another GI politician named Sidney Sanders McMath who had led a post–World War II political revolt in Hot Springs that had given him statewide publicity as a reformer with liberal ideas about governing Arkansas. McMath parlayed this attention into a successful campaign for the Democratic gubernatorial nomination in 1948. The nomination assured him of victory in the November general election since Republican political strength was virtually nonexistent in Arkansas until the mid-1960s. Faubus was attracted to McMath's moderate New South approach and supported him in the Madison County *Record*. As a reward for his support, McMath appointed him to the Arkansas Highway Commission. In March 1951 he became director of the Arkansas Highway Department. McMath was defeated in a bid for a third term in 1952 partly because of charges that highway-department funds had been diverted to the governor's campaign chest. As a highway commissioner, Faubus had kept his district free from corruption, and he became director too late to be credited with involvement in the scandal.

While McMath's political career was in eclipse in the early 1950s, Faubus's was just beginning to take shape. In 1954 speculation centered on Faubus or Jim Snoddy, a northwest Arkansas merchant and politician, as potential opponents of Francis Adams Cherry, the former judge from east Arkansas who had defeated McMath in 1952. Followers of Faubus and Snoddy met several times in an attempt to come to an understanding that would place one of the two at the head of an anti-Cherry coalition. The coalition fell apart when Snoddy declined to run for governor or to support any other candidate. Faubus apparently decided that he would postpone his statewide entrance into elective politics when he announced in early April that he would not run for governor in 1954.

But on 28 April, fifteen minutes before the filing deadline, Faubus changed his mind. He was given little chance to unseat the incumbent because of a strong two-term tradition in Arkansas and because of his association with the recently repudiated McMath. Faubus brought some advantages into the contest, however. Cherry was a poor politician who had alienated many supporters during his first term. His personality was austere, and his prematurely white hair gave him an aura of aristocracy not altogether attractive in a political campaign. In contrast, Faubus was seen as just a toothpick-chewing boy from the hills who preferred to identify with the common man in Arkansas.

Both candidates tried to grab an issue that would stimulate the interest of Arkansans. Perhaps inspired by the *Brown v. Topeka Board of Education* decision on desegregation of the public schools, Faubus, early in the first primary, attempted to make political use of the race issue. He inserted advertisements in both predominantly white newspapers in Little Rock that claimed that the principal issue in the current campaign was desegregation. Faubus suggested a local-option solution that would leave whites in control of Arkansas public school systems but would provide for the possibility of some desegregation in the future. When the *Arkansas Gazette,* the state's leading paper, criticized him for attempting to insert race into the campaign, Faubus chose to de-emphasize the issue for the remainder of the contest.

While his attempt was ineffectual, it was not damaging to his candidacy. He was able to force Cherry into a runoff, which was unusual in Arkansas in the 1950s. Faced with this uncommon circumstance, the Cherry camp decided to pin the red label on Faubus by dredging up his youthful connections with Commonwealth College. Faubus at first denied Cherry's charges, but he later admitted that he had spent time on the campus and had been elected student-body president in an election rigged by the faculty in order to boost the attendance of Arkansans at the school. On discovering the true nature of Commonwealth College, Faubus claimed, he left immediately without enrolling.

Whatever the impact of the Commonwealth College issue, and it may have engendered sympathy for Faubus and contributed to his narrow victory, the tactic did enliven a heretofore dull campaign and transform the second primary into one of the most scurrilous elections in Arkansas history. Faubus emerged from the primary with a seven-thousand-vote victory and went on to defeat a surprisingly tough Republican opponent, former Little Rock mayor, Pratt Remmel, in November.

Despite his attempt to insert the race issue into his 1954 campaign, Faubus was classified throughout his first term as a moderate in the McMath mold. He appointed several blacks to the Democratic state committee and resisted pressure to get involved in the controversial desegregation of Hoxie, a small northeastern Arkansas community. Faubus consistently avoided any commitment on the race issue in his early gubernatorial career. He leaned toward segregation when it was politically expedient but refused to embrace extremist policies until the Little Rock desegregation crisis of 1957. He qualified as a moderate in other ways, too. In 1955 he led the fight to regulate the Arkansas Power and Light Company, succeeded in establishing a children's colony for mentally retarded children at Conway, and appointed millionaire Winthrop Rockefeller to head the Arkansas Industrial Development Commission, which was designed to attract new businesses to the state.

Faubus was aware that his moderate stance on desegregation would draw segregationist opposition in the Democratic primary in 1956 and that his weakest area of support was eastern Arkansas, home of the planter class that was most adamantly opposed to public school integration. Early in that year he began to mend his fences with the east and sought to cut the ground from under any potential segregationist political foes. In January, with the governor's approval, five east Arkansans went to Virginia, the leader in massive resistance, to study ways to postpone desegregation legally. Faubus not only endorsed their findings but also produced a poll that purported to show that 85 percent of Arkansans opposed desegregation of their school systems. Faubus said that he could not give his backing to desegregation because it was heavily opposed by the people.

Faubus's strategy was successful. He was opposed in the Democratic primary by, among others, Jim Johnson, who had led the fight against the integration of the Hoxie School District. Faubus characterized the evangelistic Johnson as a "purveyor of hate" in contrast with his own "reasonable" brand of segregation. Faubus won renomination easily and was reelected in November. He had successfully co-opted the segregationist doctrine and superimposed on it his own moderate image.

Faubus continued his drift into the east Arkansas orbit in early 1957. He wanted the Arkansas legislature, dominated by eastern Arkansas planters, to pass a $22 million package that included provisions for raising teachers' salaries and for providing increased benefits for the elderly. In exchange for eastern sponsorship of his program, Faubus agreed to support a series of laws designed to delay desegregation, a goal especially desired by white residents of east Arkansas where the black population was concentrated. Both Faubus and the east got what they wanted when the segregation laws and the governor's $22 million program were passed by a cooperative legislature.

For a time in early 1957 race ceased to be a major concern in Arkansas. Much of this was due to Faubus's tactics. He refused to implement Arkansas's new segregation laws and in other ways modified his recent radical stance on desegregation of the public schools. The imminent integration of Little Rock Central High, however, once again pushed the race issue to the front and forced Faubus to take action. The Little Rock School Board had voluntarily presented a plan for gradual desegregation of the Little Rock public school system shortly after the *Brown* decision in 1954. Their plan called for desegregation to begin at Little Rock Central in September 1957. Increasing pressure by radical segregationists disenchanted with Faubus came to

a head in August when Georgia Gov. Marvin Griffin and his aide, Roy
Harris, made speeches before the Capital Citizens Council in Little
Rock. They said that no school in Georgia would have to open its doors
to blacks and that this should also be true in Little Rock. They singled
out Faubus, governor of Arkansas, as the man who had the power to
cancel school desegregation in Little Rock under the sovereign power
given to him by the state of Arkansas. After the Griffin-Harris speeches,
some people began to look to Faubus to do something about Central's
impending integration.

Faubus had already begun to look at the matter in terms of political survival. He had contacted a federal official in the Justice
Department and stated the fear that there might be violence if Central
was desegregated. The department official, Arthur B. Caldwell, himself
an Arkansan, met with Faubus late in August to explain the federal
position. Instead, Faubus did most of the talking. He told Caldwell of
a plan that would delay desegregation at Central. He had induced a
newly formed segregationist group, the Mothers League of Central
High School, to file a suit in Little Rock Chancery Court that would
delay Central's integration on the grounds of imminent danger of violence. The chancellor, Murray Reed, a Faubus appointee, would be
certain to grant the delaying injunction. The case, if appealed, would
then go to the federal district court in Fort Smith where the judge
would be John E. Miller, who had earlier refused a bid by the National
Association for the Advancement of Colored People (NAACP) to
force desegregation on Little Rock the previous year. If the Fort Smith
judge upheld the injunction, desegregation would be delayed until
sometime in the future when someone other than Faubus would be
forced to act. Caldwell expressed disapproval of the plan, and the governor's first confrontation with federal authorities ended in a stalemate.

The next day the Mothers League asked for an injunction and
called the governor as its only witness. Just as Faubus had forecast to
Caldwell, Chancellor Reed granted the delaying injunction. The case
then went to Judge Miller in Fort Smith. Miller, perhaps weary of
making integration decisions, requested that the case be transferred to
the Little Rock district presided over by newly appointed federal Judge
Ronald Davies from North Dakota who was not connected with
Faubus in any way. The new judge summarily ordered desegregation
to proceed at Central.

Faubus's plans for avoiding the Central situation had collapsed,
and he only had a short time to improvise. He met with his advisers on
30 and 31 August to decide what to do next. If he did nothing and

allowed the desegregation of Central to proceed on schedule, he would become the governor who stood by while blacks entered the state's largest school. Conversely, if he intervened with Arkansas militia and prevented Central's integration, he risked being branded as a radical of the stripe of the recently repudiated Johnson. Despite the potential risk, political logic had long been leading Faubus in that direction. In the past he had consistently succumbed to political reality when his moderate stance was shown to be strategically inadequate. He now wanted to become the first governor since Jeff Davis to be elected to a third term and the Little Rock Central issue might give him the impetus to accomplish his goal. He finally decided on 31 August to call out the Arkansas National Guard.

On the evening of 2 September, Faubus made his decision public when he addressed the people of Arkansas on television. He told of his fear of violence at Central. He spoke of caravans of white resisters poised to descend on Little Rock if blacks tried to enter the high school. In order to prevent bloodshed he had ringed Central with troops. The next morning the Arkansas National Guard, under the orders of the governor, turned back Elizabeth Eckord, one of the nine blacks scheduled to enter Central. The eight other blacks were eventually denied entrance into the all-white school, and Faubus's political maneuver precipitated a crisis of monumental proportions.

The troops remained at Central for three weeks while the courts, the federal government, Southern governors, Arkansas Rep. Brooks Hays, and Faubus tried to work out an acceptable solution. Hays was able to bring President Eisenhower and Governor Faubus together on 14 September at Newport, Rhode Island, where the president was vacationing. The conference produced no conclusive results, and after Faubus and his lawyers walked out of a hearing called by Judge Davies on 20 September, the federal government and Faubus were on a collision course. Faubus complied with a federal injunction that ordered the removal of troops and promptly left for the Southern governors' conference in Sea Island, Georgia. On 23 September blacks entered Central unprotected for the first time. The next day when Eisenhower ordered troops into Little Rock to shield the nine black students, he set a precedent that helped to ensure the success of the public school desegregation movement.

Accusations and bitterness were the order of the day in the aftermath of the Central crisis. Woodrow Wilson Mann, the mayor of Little Rock, summed up one side of the story when he publicly stated that Faubus "perpetrated a hoax on the people of Arkansas." Mann felt that the governor had called out the National Guard to further his own political ambitions. Faubus countered by saying that he was sincerely afraid of violence if Central were integrated. He pointed to the unrest that had accompanied Central's integration on 23 September and said that FBI accounts would eventually validate his position. There is little evidence to support Faubus's contention. The FBI interviewed over five hundred people, including the Arkansas governor, and found little indication of potential violence. Faubus presented to the FBI only a few well-known and well-worn scraps of evidence to support his impending-bloodshed theory.

Whatever can be said about Faubus's motives, the results of the Central crisis were of immediate political benefit to him. He was reelected to a third term by a wide margin in 1958. The crisis continued to gain votes for him until he finally retired as governor in 1967. Faubus also enjoyed national prestige. In December 1958 the Gallup organization published the results of a poll that named the ten people most admired by Americans: Faubus ranked in the company of Eisenhower, former President Truman, Winston Churchill, Charles de Gaulle, and Dr. Albert Schweitzer.

In the aftermath of the trouble at Central, Faubus enthusiastically took on the role of defender of segregation. When a federal court denied the Little Rock School Board's request to delay desegregation of the capital city's schools until the early 1960s, Faubus, armed with legislative endorsement, closed Little Rock's educational facilities in the fall of 1958.

The result was bitterness, acrimony, and a protracted battle for control of the Little Rock School Board. In December 1958 the board resigned en masse and Superintendent Virgil Blossom moved to San Antonio, Texas. Three moderates and three segregationists replaced the old board and a deadlock resulted. Faubus attempted to break the impasse by asking the Arkansas legislature to empower him to appoint another three board members, but his effort failed.

On 5 May 1959 events were set in motion that would break the board's logjam. The moderate faction (Ted Lamb, Everett Tucker, and Russell H. Matson) moved that all teachers' contracts be approved as prelude to starting the new school year in the fall. Instead, the segregationists on the board moved to fire forty-four teachers and administrators including newly appointed Superintendent Terrell E. Powell and veteran Central principal, Jess Matthews. The three moderates walked out of the meeting, and the rump board fired the teachers and supervisors.

The reaction was immediate. Many prominent businessmen and other concerned citizens formed an organization called Stop This Outrageous Purge (STOP). The segregationists responded with their own group: Committee to Retain Our Segregated Schools (CROSS). Both school board factions were subject to recall elections in May 1959. Faubus supported CROSS and described members of STOP as the "Cadillac brigade." Despite Faubus's sentiments, the moderate faction survived the recall while their segregationist counterparts did not.

Faubus followed his attempt to oust the leaders of the Cadillac brigade by backing legislation designed to provide financial support for Arkansas districts that had closed their schools to avoid integration. Once again, in 1960 the voters repudiated the Faubus position, this time in overwhelming fashion.

These results did not affect Faubus's personal popularity. In 1960 the incumbent ran against four segregationist opponents and campaigned under the slogan "Keep the Faith." While opponents talked about what they would do about public school desegregation, Faubus ran on his record. The majority of the people of Arkansas evidently felt that Faubus had kept the faith on the desegregation issue, and he was easily reelected.

His closest contest came in 1962 when he defeated former Governor McMath, segregationist Dale Alford, and three others in the Democratic primary by garnering 52 percent of the vote. During the 1962 campaign, Faubus once again displayed his political skills by casting himself as the moderate alternative to liberal McMath and conservative Alford. This was after he had publicly stated on 31 March 1962 that he would not run for a fifth term. Ironically his statement appeared in the press on April Fools' Day.

Again in 1964 the governor demonstrated his remarkable political flexibility. The key issue in that year was illegal gambling in Hot Springs. The resort town had long sanctioned betting at Oaklawn Park Race Track as well as many types of illegal gambling. Faubus had avoided the issue for years by calling it a local problem to be solved within the confines of Garland County. The previous year the governor's supporters had killed an antigambling bill introduced in the legislature. But in 1964, an election year, Faubus changed his mind and told Hot Springs officials to shut down illegal gambling or face the possibility of intervention by state police. Once again he had preempted an important political issue prior to a gubernatorial campaign.

The governor's main threat in 1964 came from the Republicans in the person of former Faubus appointee Rockefeller. For years

Rockefeller had been pouring money into the token Arkansas Republican party. In 1964 he decided to do more than finance the party. Rockefeller ran for governor on a platform of change. Faubus countered by contrasting the immensely wealthy Yankee with his own hillbilly origins. He mentioned Rockefeller's divorce ten years earlier and hinted that liquor was served at Petit Jean, the Rockefeller residence. Innuendo prevailed over plans for change, and Faubus was handily reelected with 57 percent of the vote; Rockefeller could console himself with the fact that he had polled more votes than any Republican in Arkansas history.

Faubus's last two years in office proved to be painful. The opposition successfully chipped away at his political power base as scandal touched his administration for the first time. Two million dollars worth of secret pay raises in the Arkansas Highway Department were publicized. Meanwhile, Rockefeller was again assembling his forces for another campaign for governor. Because of a concerted effort to register black voters and the experience Rockefeller had gained in his losing campaign, it was obvious that the millionaire ex-Yankee would be a formidable opponent in 1966. Late in March, Faubus again announced his intention not to run for governor "for strong personal reasons and because of some administrative difficulties." Speculation continued up until the filing deadline that Faubus would run again, especially since he had set the stage in late 1965 by appointing blacks to various state boards and commissions. But this time he did not change his mind and actually left the governor's mansion after twelve years in office.

Faubus has not led an easy life since he left office. His exit was bitter and somewhat sensational. He made a self-laudatory farewell speech to the Arkansas legislature. When it was over, he stalked out without waiting to greet Rockefeller, the new governor. His string of misfortunes actually started shortly after he announced his retirement, when his father died on 24 August 1966 at the age of seventy-eight. Even the purchase of a new home the following year produced speculation that turned into criticism when Faubus opened his new mansion to tourists for an admission price of $1.25. He insisted that his new home cost about $100,000, but opponents contended that the price was in the $250,000 range.

On 23 January 1969 Alta, his wife of thirty-seven years, sued Faubus for divorce, citing abuse and consistent neglect. The uncontested divorce was handled by Farrell Faubus, the estranged couple's son. Almost two months later, on 21 March, Faubus married a young divorcée, Elizabeth Westmoreland, originally from Holyoke, Massachusetts.

Later in 1969 the former governor refurbished his rustic image by becoming director of a new amusement park located near Harrison in northern Arkansas called Dogpatch, U.S.A. The following year political fever struck, and he entered the Democratic gubernatorial primary against seven opponents. He led the ticket in the first primary but was forced into a runoff by an obscure lawyer with Faubus-like origins in northwest Arkansas (Charleston) named Dale Leon Bumpers. Bumpers defeated Faubus easily and went on to foil Rockefeller's bid for a third term in November.

Faubus managed to avoid the spotlight during the early 1970s, but in 1974 he made one more bid for the office he had controlled for so long. Campaigning on a platform dominated by references to drugs and to the need for law and order, he narrowly missed a runoff with David Hampton Pryor, former congressman from Camden in southeastern Arkansas.

The last years of the seventies saw Faubus's life marred by personal tragedy, financial woes, and failing health. In June 1976 his son Farrell died near Seattle of a drug overdose. Early the next year, Faubus's deteriorating financial situation forced him to accept a job as a bank clerk in Huntsville for a meager salary of $5,000 a year. Later in 1977, in perhaps the most ironic twist of his long career, Ernest Green, one of the original blacks to enter Central High School and the first to graduate, was appointed by newly elected Pres. Jimmy Carter to a federal position with an annual salary of $50,000.

Failing health continued to plague Faubus. In 1977 and again in 1979 he underwent surgery; the first time to install a pacemaker and the second to correct a prostate condition. His poor health eventually forced him and his wife to move to Houston where the ex-governor could have ready access to the area's excellent medical facilities. He left unannounced in late August 1978 and was tracked down by an enterprising journalist in October. He reappeared in Arkansas for the inauguration of Gov. Bill Clinton in January 1979.

It is an undeniable fact that the Little Rock Central desegregation crisis of 1957 was the most important event in Faubus's political career. It is doubtful that the governor would have been more than a two-term official without the publicity lavished on him in September 1957. Yet the crisis has tended to overshadow his other accomplishments. There were positive aspects to Faubus's long tenure in office. During his administration teachers' salaries increased from an average of $2,264 in 1954 to $5,100 in 1966; Arkansas became one of the first states to equalize its standards for the assessment of property taxes, which benefited education; monthly welfare payments to the elderly increased from $30 in 1954 to $75 in 1966; an industrialization program, led in part by Rockefeller, resulted in an estimated ninety thousand new jobs in Faubus's twelve years; the Arkansas State Mental Hospital was rebuilt and escaped major scandal during his administration; the governor hired several dozen blacks for state jobs, and all but 9 of 410 school districts were desegregated in his years in office.

Ex-Governor Laney was once quoted as saying that Faubus "was a complete political creature" and perhaps his most impressive accomplishments were in that area. Unquestionably the results of his political maneuverings were impressive. He defeated twenty-five opponents in twelve years, appointed every member of every state board, and managed to portray himself in an attractive light in every election. He projected the image of a moderate alternative in most of his campaigns before and after the Central crisis and of the down-home country boy who would protect the rural interests from invasion from outsiders whether they were Yankee or rich or both.

Yet in the late days of August 1957 Faubus made the decision that will forever dominate historical evaluation of his tenure as governor. In words attributed to his longtime antagonist, Harry S. Ashmore, executive editor of the *Arkansas Gazette* during the Central crisis, "Faubus will never sit easy on the tiger he has chosen to ride." After all these years Faubus's legacy is still sitting uneasily astride that Little Rock Central tiger.

Orval Faubus died in Conway and was buried in Orval E. Faubus Memorial Gardens, Combs, Arkansas.

WINTHROP ROCKEFELLER

1967–1971

WINTHROP ROCKEFELLER (1 May 1912–22 February 1973), financier and farmer, was born in New York City, the son of John D., Jr., and Abbey (Aldrich) Rockefeller. The fourth of five children, Winthrop grew up in an affluence unsurpassed in America. His father held numerous executive positions in the business empire established by John D. Rockefeller Sr.

Rockefeller was educated at Lincoln School of Columbia University Teachers College, New York City, and at Loomis School, Windsor, Connecticut. Although popular with his classmates, Rockefeller was not a gifted student. He withdrew from Yale University during his third year without taking a degree.

Unwilling to immediately accept a post in the family business, Rockefeller went to Texas in 1936 where he took a job as an apprentice roughneck in the oil fields. He was in later years to consider his Texas interlude as the best year of his life. In 1937 he took a position in the foreign-trade department of Socony-Vacuum, thereby signaling his willingness to conform to family traditions and expectations.

Although Rockefeller had obviously decided it was impossible to have a life outside the family, he nonetheless continued to be somewhat unorthodox in personal tastes and preferences. Nowhere was this more evident than in his service record during World War II. Any Rockefeller could have spent the war performing valuable stateside duty, but Winthrop was attracted to the freedom and challenges offered by the uniformed services. He enlisted as a private in the army almost a year before Pearl Harbor on 22 January 1941. He attended Officer Candidate School, graduating on 22 January 1942 as a second lieutenant. For a time he served as a machine-gun instructor at Fort Benning, Georgia. In August 1942 he was named commander of H Company, 305th Infantry Regiment, Seventy-seventh Division, Fort Jackson, South Carolina. He was promoted to captain in December 1942 and to major in November 1943.

The tall, rugged Rockefeller, replete with a handlebar mustache, had the appearance of a swashbuckling commander. He saw extensive action in the South Pacific, participating in the battles of Guam and the Philippines. He was wounded in the invasion of Okinawa during a kamikaze attack. By the end of the fighting he had reached the rank of lieutenant colonel and had received the Bronze Star with Oak Leaf Cluster and the Purple Heart.

Military life, with its camaraderie and anonymity, continued to appeal to Rockefeller even after his discharge. For a time he served in the Seventy-seventh Division Reserve in New York City, and with the approval of Secretary of War Robert J. Patterson, he spent several months after V-J Day compiling an extensive nationwide survey of veterans' readjustment problems. He also kept in touch with his old infantry buddies, and during the 1960s he helped to raise funds for an infantry hall of fame to which he was also elected.

With the war over, Rockefeller again faced the long-postponed choice of a career. He resumed his work with Socony but found his new desk job stultifying. To compound matters, he chaffed under the pervasive influences of his family. The only one of the Rockefeller brothers who refused to follow unquestioningly in their father's footsteps, Rockefeller was a nonconformist in a family that placed great emphasis on adherence to family tradition. Gradually, he began to seek solace outside the tightly knit family, turning increasingly to alcohol. He also circulated in the chic café society of postwar New York, frequently dating actresses and other women from outside the old family circle of friends.

On Valentine's Day, 1948, Rockefeller married an attractive blond divorcée named Barbara "Bobo" Sears. In September of that year the couple had a son, Winthrop Paul Rockefeller. The marriage was actually little more than another impulsively defiant act on Rockefeller's part, and it soon began to fall apart. The couple separated within a year after the birth of their son.

Despondent over his broken marriage and playboy image, Rockefeller reached his emotional nadir in the early 1950s. Although the family rallied to his aid, the forty-one-year-old Rockefeller obviously had to pull his life together for a second start. Eventually, he chose the exact antithesis of New York City—Arkansas—for his new home.

Rockefeller came to Arkansas in early 1953 to visit an old army friend, Frank Newell of Little Rock, who introduced him to the area. While it might not have been love at first sight, the New Yorker was attracted to the state's pleasant rural atmosphere and natural beauty.

He was especially drawn to Petit Jean Mountain, a beautiful flattopped mountain in the Arkansas River valley near Morrilton. Soon he purchased over nine hundred acres atop the mountain and started work on his own version of Pocantico, the Rockefeller family estate north of New York City. Winrock Farms became a prosperous functioning farm—producing thoroughbred Santa Gertrudis cattle—and one of Arkansas's most popular tourist attractions.

Shortly after his arrival in Arkansas, Rockefeller was divorced from his estranged wife. Besides a sizable monetary settlement, reported to be more than $6 million, Mrs. Rockefeller received custody of their son, who was educated primarily in Europe. After the much-publicized divorce and subsequent separation from his son, Rockefeller concentrated his energy on building his new home and on becoming familiar with his adopted state.

Rockefeller's initial efforts went into developing Winrock Farms. Interested in many facets of agriculture, he devoted particular attention to his Santa Gertrudis cattle. "Rock," his first Santa Gertrudis bull purchased at a cost of $31,500, was to serve as a sire for a large herd. Soon Winrock Farms was a magnificent oasis with six artificial lakes, an extensive irrigation system, an airfield, numerous barns, a farm headquarters, and, most impressive of all, a huge stone-and-glass home perched on the edge of the mountain with a panoramic view of the Arkansas River. By 1966 Rockefeller's farming interests included 24,587 acres in Arkansas and over 15,000 acres in other states. Besides Santa Gertrudis cattle, his farms also produced rice, feed grains, and hay. Eventually, Rockefeller's annual cattle auctions became popular social events with buyers attending from throughout the United States and foreign countries.

Rockefeller did not confine himself to farming activities. As the grandson of John D. Rockefeller and the son of John D., Jr., he could not escape the family traditions of diverse investments coupled with extensive philanthropy. Real-estate and housing development held a strong attraction for Rockefeller. Under a parent company known as Winrock Enterprises, he founded Winrock Realty Company as well as Pleasant Valley, Inc., and the Arkansas Realty Company, which built Little Rock's first skyscraper, the eighteen-story Tower Building. His most unusual development, but far from being the most profitable, was the Museum of Automobiles atop Petit Jean Mountain. By 1965, Rockefeller had established himself as a businessman-farmer without peer in the state.

Rockefeller's interest in philanthropy preceded his entry into farming. Before World War II he had served as vice-chairman of the Greater New York Fund. After the war, he became an enthusiastic officer of the National Urban League, his first of many efforts to benefit American blacks. On moving to Arkansas, he found the state in desperate need of Rockefeller largesse. He established the Rockwin Fund and endowed a wide variety of worthy causes including the Arkansas Arts Center, a new school in his hometown of Morrilton, and a plethora of scholarships and grants. By 1966 Rockefeller had funneled more than $8 million into his adopted state.

Rockefeller's impact on Arkansas's development went much further than his benevolent contributions to worthy causes. His service on the Arkansas Industrial Development Commission probably touched more lives than any other aspect of his career.

The 1950s was a decade of extraordinary economic growth in most of the nation, and this new growth was especially true of Arkansas. Arkansas, like the remainder of the South, had been searching, without much success, for an industrial base for almost one hundred years. However, with the election of Gov. Orval Eugene Faubus in 1954, Arkansas had a leader with a firm determination to bring economic change. He persuaded the legislature to create the Arkansas Industrial Development Commission (AIDC) and named Rockefeller as its first chairman. During his nine years as head of the AIDC, Arkansas experienced an industrial revolution. Over six hundred new industrial plants were built, and more than ninety thousand new jobs, with an annual payroll of almost $300 million, were created. While the nation experienced a gain of less than 5 percent in industrial workers, Arkansas underwent an astronomical growth of 47.5 percent. Significantly, manufacturing wages climbed by 88 percent compared to a national rise of 36 percent.

Industrial development was definitely a mixed blessing for the state. Many of the new factories locating in Arkansas found the state's low wages and large, unorganized work force attractive. Most of the plants including numerous factories produced unsophisticated products. Among other negative effects of the industrial transformation was unplanned urban growth. Despite these problems, Rockefeller and the AIDC did much to bring Arkansas closer to America's economic mainstream. Rockefeller gave up the chairmanship of the AIDC in March 1964 as he prepared to enter the gubernatorial campaign.

When Rockefeller arrived in Arkansas in 1953, he found a state so solidly wedded to the Democratic party that the famous political scientist V. O. Key cited it as the archetypal one-party Southern state.

The tiny Republican party was led lethargically by a small coterie of elderly businessmen and lawyers who were primarily interested in dispensing patronage during the tenure of Republican presidents. Widely known as "Post Office Republicans," the Arkansas GOP consistently failed to challenge the Democrats. As a result, the Democrats had become callous to the frequent abuse of power found in state government. Fraudulent elections and maladministration by elected public officials were common phenomena in Arkansas.

Rockefeller gradually came to believe that many of Arkansas's problems could be directly attributed to the lack of a competitive two-party system. His first effort was to establish the supposedly nonpartisan Committee for Two Parties. He then funded the Arkansas Election Research Council, described as nonpartisan and charged with monitoring electoral corruption. In 1961 Rockefeller was elected Arkansas's Republican national committeeman much to the chagrin of many old-guard party leaders. He immediately set about to invigorate the small party. A large party headquarters was opened in the Rockefeller-owned Tower Building in Little Rock, and a professional staff was employed with Rockefeller funds.

Many Arkansans, both Democrats and Republicans, now urged Rockefeller to seek public office. Despite the overtures from Democrats, he refused to switch his party allegiance. By 1964 Rockefeller believed that he could no longer postpone his entry into politics. He had already made a clean break with longtime Democratic Governor Faubus whom the Republicans had already identified as their chief target. Many observers predicted a close race when Rockefeller announced his gubernatorial candidacy in the spring of 1964.

Rockefeller threw himself into the campaign with total commitment. He tried to visit every county, every political barbecue, every ground breaking and dedication. Traveling around the state in a plush bus, he called on Arkansans to enter a new era and to abandon their traditional allegiance to the Democratic party. But his efforts were to no avail: Faubus won with 56 percent of the vote. Undaunted, Rockefeller announced that he would run again on the same day he made his concession speech.

Between 1964 and 1966 Rockefeller maintained a hectic travel schedule working on behalf of himself and the Republican ticket. The GOP kept up a steady attack on the Faubus administration and won a resounding victory when the administration's $150 million highway bond issue was defeated in a special election. Scarcely a week passed when the Rockefeller forces did not disclose some new abuse of the

"Faubus Machine." The Republicans were especially successful when they disclosed that Faubus was constructing a huge home at Huntsville, despite the fact that the governor's salary was a mere $10,000 per year.

Even though Faubus retained much of his personal popularity and his political organization remained operative, he decided not to seek reelection in 1966. After a heated Democratic party primary, Supreme Court Justice Jim Johnson emerged with the nomination. "Justice Jim" was especially strident in his opposition to court-ordered desegregation. Early in the campaign, he went so far as to refuse to shake hands with blacks. With the Democratic party in disarray, the Republicans found their chances greatly enhanced.

In 1966 the Republican party fielded a formidable slate of candidates for offices ranging from congressman to justice of the peace. Rockefeller's running mate was Maurice L. "Footsie" Britt, a former University of Arkansas football star and World War II Congressional Medal of Honor winner. Perhaps the most aggressive GOP candidate was Kerry Thomasson, the bright, articulate nominee for attorney general.

The 1966 general-election campaign presented Arkansans with a diversity of choices uncommon in any state, much less one-party Arkansas. The Democratic nominee, especially when it became clear that he was falling behind, became increasingly vitriolic in attacking the Republican nominee. Describing Rockefeller as a "prissy sissy" who got his haircuts in New York City, Johnson appealed to Arkansans' longtime distrust of nonconformists and out-of-staters. Rockefeller countered by noting his many accomplishments and his personal commitment to his adopted state. Rockefeller's well-funded campaign organization made extensive use of television and radio. The GOP camp also benefited from extensive public-opinion polling. One crucial result of the polling was the discovery that Arkansans actually preferred integration to racial strife. Rockefeller, who was a personal liberal but a theoretical conservative, set about winning black votes. This decision in effect won the election for Rockefeller and his running mate. The Republicans received nearly 90 percent of the black vote, thus offsetting a deficit among white voters and assuring Rockefeller an overall victory of over 54 percent. Rockefeller carried the state's urban areas along with the indigenous Republican mountain counties of northwestern Arkansas. In the ninety-eight largest towns in the state, Rockefeller garnered 61 percent of the vote. Meanwhile, Britt captured the lieutenant governor's office by a mere 3,696 votes. The Republicans could also rejoice over the unexpected victory of John

Paul Hammerschmidt for the Third Congressional District seat long held by liberal Democrat James Trimble. Significantly, Thomasson, the GOP nominee for attorney general, lost to reform Democrat Joe Edward Purcell. Thomasson's defeat was to bode ill for the party since he had the potential to be a Republican successor to Rockefeller.

The new Republican administration faced numerous challenges, the most obvious being the stranglehold the Democrats held on the legislature (the GOP held only 3 of 135 seats). Even with its disproportionate composition, a total of 741 acts were adopted during Rockefeller's first term. In a special session meeting in February 1968, an additional 67 bills were passed. While most of this legislation was routine, some of it marked a significant break with the past. Rockefeller was successful in winning passage of tightened insurance regulations, the state's first general minimum-wage act, a freedom of information act, and stronger regulation of state banks and securities trading. Always a believer in planning, Rockefeller obtained authorization to establish a governmental efficiency-study commission. In a related development, a state administration department, with a personnel division, was created to bring order to the burgeoning state bureaucracy.

Many of Rockefeller's reform efforts were directed toward more aggressive enforcement of existing laws. His most dramatic success came when the new state police director, Lynn Davis, set out to stop illegal gambling in Hot Springs. In the glare of television lights, Davis led raids throughout the resort city. By the end of Rockefeller's administration, illegal gambling in Hot Springs had been stopped, and the city was beginning to enter a new era of prosperity based on tourism and industry.

Rockefeller's efforts at prison reform were not so successful. Arkansas's prisons had long been ranked among the worst in the country, and the new governor was determined to bring change. The state prison board was given extensive powers and a professional penologist, Tom Murton, was hired to oversee the reforms. Murton, to the chagrin of legislators, and later to Rockefeller, introduced many innovations that were unpopular. Later, as Murton grew impatient with the pace of reform, he set about dramatically illustrating the plight of the prisoners. He was fired after allowing the press to witness exhumations of what he described as the bodies of murdered inmates. (In actuality, the cemetery contained bodies of paupers and unclaimed prisoners.) After Murton's firing, prison reform proceeded at a slower pace and successive administrations have been unable to find permanent solutions to the state's correctional problems.

During his first term Rockefeller devoted an inordinate amount of time to trying to remove several members of the state game and fish commission. Allegations of purchasing and personnel abuses in the commission received extensive coverage during the 1966 campaign, and Rockefeller became obsessed with the need to remove some offending commissioners as well as the commission's director, Hugh Hackler. The fight continued for months with charges and counter-charges. Finally, an independent investigation cleared some of the members; others either resigned or left after their terms expired.

The governor had more success in his efforts to bring minorities into the political and governmental process. Blacks were appointed to numerous state boards and commissions, including public welfare, pardons and paroles, and corrections. Blacks were also hired to fill a sizable number of state jobs and served as state troopers.

No one doubted that Rockefeller would be the GOP nominee for a second term in 1968. The Democrats were as divided as ever. The leading Democratic contender was state representative Marion Crank, an ally of former Governor Faubus, who eventually won the gubernatorial nomination after defeating Virginia Johnson, the wife of Justice Jim Johnson, in a runoff election. Crank proved to be a formidable candidate, but he was tainted by his long association with the Faubus organization. The Rockefeller campaign, well organized and heavily funded, made effective use of computerized mailings. The campaign involved a number of questionable practices. Despite numerous references to Rockefeller's drinking problem, the Republicans turned out such a heavy black vote that the governor was able to win reelection with 52 percent of the total vote. As in 1966, the GOP nominee for lieutenant governor barely edged out his opponent.

Rockefeller's second term was, if anything, more controversial than his first. While the first Republican administration found the Democratic legislature to be merely recalcitrant, during the second term it was blatantly obstinate. Rockefeller made matters worse by failing to follow a consistent course. By nature he was a private man who believed in reasoned persuasion. However, the general assembly, accustomed to Faubus's firm guiding hand, was in no mood for quiet diplomacy. Rockefeller began his second term by inviting the legislators to his farm for a round of parties and lobbying. When that technique failed, the governor lost his patience and roundly condemned their partisan provincialism. A bitter fight had begun that was to grow more strident with each passing day.

On no subject did the governor and legislature disagree more than on Rockefeller's proposal to raise taxes. In his second inaugural address, the governor called for a wide-ranging revenue program to include a broadening of the sales tax and its increase from 3 to 4 percent; putting the income tax on a graduated basis; phasing out of the personal tax credit; an increase in the tax on cigarettes, beer, and parimutuel betting; as well as a number of other increases. The program was calculated to produce $90 million the first year and $105 million the second with 50 percent of the new revenues going for educational spending.

Calling on the public to demonstrate its faith in government, Rockefeller started a lobbying campaign with the slogan "Arkansas is worth paying for." The 1969 legislature flatly rejected most of the tax program and instead enacted a few minor bills that produced only $20 million. Rockefeller was deeply hurt by the defeat of his revenue program. However, later governors, notably Bumpers, were to benefit considerably from the revenue measures enacted during Rockefeller's tenure. Other than modest tax increases, Rockefeller's second term produced little substantive legislation.

Before the 1969 legislature finally adjourned, it had not only rejected the governor's tax program, but it also made the defeat more galling by assuming control over drafting the Revenue Stabilization Act, the law that determined how state revenues would be spent. Unwittingly, Rockefeller had significantly weakened the governor's office and had strengthened his own opponents.

Although he had always promised not to seek a third term, by early 1970 Rockefeller was hinting that he might be a candidate for reelection. His fights with the legislature, along with the lack of an obvious Republican successor, caused him to embark on one last campaign.

Rockefeller's growing unpopularity with the electorate spawned a wide variety of potential opponents in the 1970 Democratic primary. Faubus entered the race as did Attorney General Purcell. But, Bumpers, a young, unknown lawyer from the little town of Charleston, eventually won the nomination. Bumpers' major asset was his freshness and vitality. Untainted by any prior electoral experience, he was able to unite his party and to defeat Rockefeller by the huge margin of 375,648 to 197,418. The remainder of the GOP ticket, with the exception of Congressman Hammerschmidt, suffered a similar defeat.

Rockefeller left office without establishing the "Era of Excellence" he had sought. He was successful in bringing about many changes, most of them beneficial to the state. His insistence on firm regulation of insurance and security companies marked a radical departure from the old system whereby regulators were often inseparable from those they were regulating. The Freedom of Information Act proved to be an important piece of legislation in opening up state and local government in Arkansas to public scrutiny. Rockefeller was able to bring black voters into the mainstream of Arkansas politics. The need for restructuring state government was demonstrated during the Republican interlude and was later adopted during the Bumpers administration.

But not all of Rockefeller's efforts brought the results he sought. Without doubt his greatest defeat was the failure to develop a viable two-party system. The governor succeeded in building a large personal following, but he was unable to transfer that support to his party.

Rockefeller was shaken by the magnitude of his defeat in 1970. After several weeks of isolation, he emerged to resume a modest role in public affairs. Although he continued his heavy contributions to the Republican party and played a minor role in the 1972 reelection campaign of Pres. Richard Nixon, it was obvious that the former governor was no longer a political force. He returned to his home on Petit Jean Mountain where he was subsequently divorced from his second wife, Jeanette Rockefeller. Rockefeller died in California of cancer in 1973 and was buried at Winrock Farms. The major portion of his estate was bequeathed to a charitable trust.

DALE LEON BUMPERS

1971–1975

DALE LEON BUMPERS (12 August 1925–), attorney, was born in Charleston, Arkansas, a small town in the foothills of the Ozark Mountains. He was the youngest of three children born to William Rufus and Lattie (Jones) Bumpers. His father was a hardware merchant who was active in politics. He represented Franklin County in the state house of representatives in 1933. From his father Bumpers learned to love politics and to respect it as a noble profession.

Bumpers' childhood was spent in Charleston during the lean years of the depression. He helped out by working part-time in cotton and bean fields and, in his later youth, as a butcher at a local grocery store. According to his sister, Elizabeth, the Bumpers children lived in a "very close-knit family with a very fine Christian father and mother. . . . We were brought up with the work ethic, encouraged to get an education, and we were told we could do anything we wanted."

After graduating from Charleston High School, Bumpers briefly enrolled in the University of Arkansas at Fayetteville in 1943 but joined the U.S. Marines later that year. Discharged from the marines in July 1946 he reentered the University of Arkansas and graduated two years later with a major in political science. He then studied law at Northwestern University at Evanston, Illinois, where he received a law degree in 1951. During his studies, tragedy entered his life when both of his parents were killed in a car crash on 21 March 1949. Later in 1949, on 4 September, Bumpers married a former Charleston classmate, Betty Lou Flanagen. They have three children: Brent, William Mark, and Margaret Brooke.

Following his graduation from law school, Bumpers and his wife returned to Charleston where he took over the operation of his father's store, the Charleston Hardware and Furniture Company. He sold the store in 1966 and began operating a 350-acre Angus cattle ranch.

Admitted to the Arkansas bar in 1952, Bumpers proved to be an able attorney and during his years of practicing law (1952–1970), he lost only three jury cases. In addition to serving as choirmaster and Sunday school teacher in the local Methodist church, he also held other positions in the community including those of city attorney, member and later president of the school board, and president of the chamber of commerce. To Charleston residents, Bumpers was an important part of their community. They described him as a "man they never hesitate to ask to sing at a funeral, a man older people go to for help with understanding computerized utility bills. . . . To them he is the hamburger chef at the Sunday school picnic."

Those who knew him best probably realized that Bumpers was cut out for something bigger than being a small-town attorney. His personal horizon extended beyond his hometown. However, his first attempt at moving beyond local politics provided a rude shock. In 1962 Bumpers ran for the seat in the state house of representatives that his father had once held. Although he won over 90 percent of the vote in Charleston, Mike Womack, his opponent, defeated him. Ironically, the man who was later to become known as Arkansas's "Giant Killer" had suffered a humbling political debut.

Bumpers considered running for the governor's office in 1968 but decided to wait. He began preparing for the 1970 race early. He spoke to civic clubs, youth groups, and local bar associations, making contacts throughout the state. One of his more fortuitous meetings occurred at a state Jaycee convention when he became acquainted with Deloss Walker, a public-relations man who had been establishing himself as an astute political adviser. Walker later agreed to manage Bumpers' 1970 gubernatorial campaign.

When the filing deadline for the primary election passed in June 1970, eight candidates had stepped forward to seek the Democratic nomination for governor. At the beginning of the race, three major candidates seemed to have the best chances to win the nomination. Former Gov. Orval Eugene Faubus, who had retired from office undefeated after six terms in 1966, was the acknowledged front-runner. Arkansas's Atty. Gen. Joe Edward Purcell and the speaker of the Arkansas House of Representatives, Hayes McClerkin, had both enjoyed statewide publicity and had attracted a large enough following to be creditable candidates.

Bumpers started the primary campaign sandwiched in a field of five dark-horse candidates, all of whom had little political experience, exposure, or chance to win the election. The early days of the campaign could not have been encouraging. A poll at the time showed

Bumpers beginning with about 1 percent of the vote. Bumpers and McClerkin emerged as the two "progressive" candidates during the campaign. McClerkin energetically called for new and expanded programs and vigorously attacked Faubus. Bumpers proposed state programs to improve health care, to upgrade education, and to solve the prison problems. Taking a "high road" in the campaign, he did not attack Faubus directly. Purcell, with the polls indicating that he would win a place in a runoff with Faubus, conducted a low-key campaign. He called himself "The People's Choice" and said he was not running against anyone, but "for the state and for its people."

Bumpers proved to be an effective campaigner, and his charismatic personality, combined with his progressive image, began to win him enthusiastic support, especially in his home area, northwest Arkansas. Bill Lewis, writing in the *Arkansas Gazette,* observed that Bumpers' main asset was himself; "exposure to the voters was all it took." His appeal was also transmitted effectively over television. Bumpers proved to be a master of the medium. Lewis commented, "his aura of honesty, integrity, sincerity, and candor flowed almost tangibly to the camera and into Arkansans' homes." Most of Bumpers' $95,000 campaign budget was spent to purchase television time during the last two weeks of the campaign. Bumpers scored a stunning upset by edging out Purcell for the runner-up spot. He received 20 percent of the vote compared to Purcell's 18.9 percent. Faubus, the old political master, led all candidates with 36.4 percent of the vote.

The runoff election thus pitted the old politician against the political newcomer. Bumpers proved to be an elusive target for Faubus. In the two weeks before the runoff, Faubus launched a barrage of charges at Bumpers. He called him a "country clubber" who was a "tool of bogus liberals and newspaper editors" and charged that Rockefeller was funding Bumpers' campaign. Faubus also attempted to stir up racial passions by emotionally denouncing urban violence and busing. In contrast Bumpers talked about the need for new leadership and said that his election was a means of ridding the state of "the old machine and the money machine." Voters opted for the fresh face and handed Faubus his first electoral loss. Bumpers defeated him with 58.7 percent of the vote. Faubus later commented that no one could have defeated Bumpers in 1970 because "a man and the mood of the voters suddenly and inexplicably got in tune."

Polls conducted after the runoff election showed Bumpers with over 70 percent of the vote in a trial run with Rockefeller, the Republicans' gubernatorial nominee. Though disappointed that he could not do battle with his political archenemy, Faubus, Rockefeller marshaled his considerable resources and used them freely. His campaign dominated the airways and mailboxes with radio and television advertisements and computerized mailings. Bumpers conducted a low-key campaign, keeping quiet until two weeks before the election. He complained about his opponent's profligate spending and called it a threat to democracy. His candidacy destroyed the coalition of voters that had previously elected Rockefeller. Urban moderates returned to the Democratic fold, leaving a small core of the Republican faithful and the black voters supporting Rockefeller. In the election Bumpers scored a lopsided victory, defeating Rockefeller with 61.7 percent of the vote.

In his inaugural address on 12 January 1971, Bumpers pledged to confront the state's problems and promised that his administration would not waste the "new awakening of our people." Moving quickly to keep that promise, he first proposed a reorganization of state government to drastically reduce the number of state agencies reporting to him. Sixty of the largest agencies would be assigned to thirteen departments that would make up the governor's cabinet. Bumpers saw reorganization as a means of strengthening the governor's ability to manage the growing state bureaucracy. Reorganization had been sought by Rockefeller and other governors, but special-interest groups and some legislators had resisted any change in the status quo.

After successfully guiding a reorganization measure through the general assembly, Bumpers turned his attention to an even larger challenge: reforming the state income-tax structure to make it more progressive. He had concluded that a tax increase would be necessary to provide needed increases in teachers' salaries. He proposed to lower the income-tax rates for people with small incomes and to raise the rates for higher-income households. The maximum income-tax rate would be increased from 5 to 7 percent. The change in rates would yield additional revenues for the state. Bumpers proposed other smaller tax increases, including a five-cent increase in cigarette taxes, but eschewed a sales-tax increase, calling it "regressive." Despite the need for approval by a three-fourths majority in both houses, the tax measures were passed. The revised income tax has had a profound impact on Arkansas state government, increasing tax revenues as industrial growth and inflation pushed income in Arkansas rapidly upward.

In addition to these two major changes, Bumpers won the approval of the general assembly for other significant legislation during his first term: large increases in teachers' salaries, a home-rule law giving larger cities more power to determine their own fates, creation of a consumer-protection division in the attorney general's office, repeal of the "fair trade" liquor law, expansion of the state park system, and a construction program at the prison. A special session of the general assembly held in early 1972 approved a far-reaching program designed to improve social services for elderly, handicapped, and mentally retarded citizens. In his first term, Bumpers was rebuffed on few of his major programs: among his projects that failed to win legislative approval were those related to state employees and to a limitation on campaign expenditures.

Bumpers' phenomenal success with his ambitious legislative program was aided by several factors. First, he came into office with a huge reservoir of goodwill. He had defeated a Republican governor disliked by the legislature, and the vast majority of voters had given him their stamp of approval. Second, the general assembly that met in January 1971 was more open to change than its predecessors. Over 30 percent of its members were newly elected, and there were more urban-oriented legislators. The old guard had been decimated. Third, Bumpers had an outstanding ability to use personal persuasion. He was excellent in one-on-one meetings with legislators and cultivated cordial relationships with key members of the general assembly. Finally, Bumpers came into office unbeholden to special-interest groups. He had not needed the support of the traditional Democratic party machinery to win his election. His independence and lack of political debts made him extraordinarily free to pursue his own programs.

Bumpers easily won reelection in 1972. His major opponents in the primary were Q. Byrum Hurst of Hot Springs, a state senator since 1951, and Mack Harbour, a young, conservative, political newcomer. Hurst was supported by many old Democratic mainstays who were not pleased with the treatment that they had been receiving from the new governor. Harbour presented himself as a Wallace-type conservative. Bumpers not only won the primary with over 65 percent of the vote but also trounced his Republican opposition in the general election, Len Blaylock, with 75 percent of the vote.

At the beginning of 1973 the income-tax revision adopted two years earlier was creating an unprecedented situation in the state: the general assembly confronted the prospect of appropriating about $100 million in surplus funds. Bumpers formulated proposals for the use of these funds and in his inaugural address appealed to the legislators to avoid giving in to special-interest groups seeking large chunks of the surplus. Such groups did indeed exert tremendous pressure. A coalition of city-county forces made the strongest drive for the surplus funds. Led by the county lobbyists, traditionally strong in the legislature, the group gained legislative approval of a statute that automatically guaranteed them 7 percent of the state's general fund each year. In 1973 about $70 million would have gone to the cities and counties. Since approval of the legislation would have drastically reduced the state's surplus, wiping out most of Bumpers' plans for use of the funds, the governor vetoed the legislation. The general assembly did not override the veto.

Following Bumpers' recommendations, the 1973 general assembly enacted a broad legislative program. Major actions included creation of a state-supported kindergarten program, free textbooks for high-school students, increased assistance to help educate handicapped children, raises in teachers' salaries and retirement benefits, a major construction program at the state's colleges, elimination of the trustee system at the state's prisons, and encouragement of a community-college system through increased state payment of operational costs of the institutions. Bumpers' request for $10 million to purchase wilderness and scenic lands in the state and his recommendation to approve the Equal Rights Amendment were rejected by the general assembly.

Bumpers proved himself to be an able administrator even though he came to office with no real experience in state government or in the management of large organizations. As might be expected, in the beginning he was slow to delegate responsibilities and created a "horizontal organization" in which everyone in the governor's office reported to him. As a result of his initial management style, Bumpers spent fifteen to eighteen hours a day on the job taking care of the minute details of the office. At one point in these early months, he was grumbling about the back-breaking work load and was saying that he was seriously considering not running for reelection.

After seeking advice about how he should operate his office, Bumpers slowly began to delegate some of the work load. He brought in a professional manager, Tom McRae, to head up his program staff.

Bumpers promoted improvement of the management systems of the state. The reorganization created a cabinet that Bumpers used extensively. He also expanded the use of program-budgeting systems instituted by Governor Rockefeller and introduced the "management by objectives" budgeting technique into state government. In regard to personnel management, Bumpers avoided reversion to the spoils system, instead insisting that employment decisions be based on merit. By executive order, he created a central personnel agency to assist in the recruitment of state employees and to help ensure implementation of the state's affirmative-action program.

In reviewing Bumpers' administration, Doug Smith, veteran political reporter for the *Arkansas Gazette,* observed that it "was damn near revolutionary, but hardly anybody noticed." According to Smith, "there was more substantive progressive legislation enacted than in any other four year period in Arkansas history, probably, and while that was going on, Bumpers was casually establishing himself as one of the more skillful politicians the state ever produced." Walter DeVries and Jack Bass, in their analysis of the "transformation of Southern politics," claimed that Bumpers personified "the emerging politics of progressive moderation" in the South, while *Current Biography* described Bumpers as "one of that new generation of moderate and liberal Southern politicians who have cast off the albatross of race to enter the mainstream of American politics." Both descriptions seem appropriate. Bumpers' election marked a turning point in Arkansas politics. While Rockefeller began a transition to political moderation in the state, Bumpers established it as the norm. In 1970 Arkansas could have easily reverted to the politics of race and old-guard conservatism. The election and sustained popularity of Bumpers promoted popular support for the politics of moderation.

Bumpers' political style set a new tone in the state's public life. He talked about the high ideals of leadership and spoke of a moral code that guided his decisions. Christopher Lyon, a *New York Times* writer, characterized his style as "secular evangelism." Another person described him as a "civil religionist."

Bumpers' mode of operation as governor was usually to determine in his mind what was right and to act accordingly. As a "common man in politics," a person who had lived the first forty-five years of his life as a small-town lawyer, he tended to see the "right" as relating to the needs of the common people rather than of the power brokers or corporations. Another label that came to be applied to Bumpers was that of a "moralist-populist."

Lyon called Bumpers a "caricature of blandness" who was known for "tortured temporizing over big decisions." Smith noted that in the midst of controversy, Bumpers could be "maddeningly noncommittal in his public utterances." Bumpers' style was to try to get as much information as possible before making a commitment on a controversial issue. Sometimes this quest for information interfered with prompt stands on issues and slowed down the decision-making process.

However, in his own time, Bumpers usually took firm stands on even the most controversial issues.

DeVries and Bass accuse Bumpers of not providing "bold leadership that helps shape public opinion." However, few people would describe Bumpers' legislative program as being timid. Also, he led some spirited fights for issues that were not popular in Arkansas, including proposals to implement land-use regulations in the state. Bumpers' personality and style struck a deep-seated, responsive chord in the Arkansas electorate. At the end of his second term in office, polls showed that 90 percent of the electorate approved of his performance as governor.

In spring 1974 Bumpers successfully challenged Sen. J. William Fulbright in the Democratic primary for the senatorial nomination, receiving about 65 percent of the vote. He easily defeated Republican John Harris Jones in the general election.

Since taking office as Arkansas's junior senator in January 1975, Bumpers has acquired national prominence.

DAVID HAMPTON PRYOR

1975–1979

DAVID HAMPTON PRYOR (29 August 1934–), newspaper publisher and attorney, was born in Camden, Arkansas, the son of William Edgar and Susan (Newton) Pryor. Both his father, who had an automobile dealership, and his grandfather served as county sheriff. His mother became one of the first women in Arkansas to seek public office when she ran an unsuccessful race for circuit clerk in 1926. With such a strong political background, it is not surprising that Pryor has made a career in politics and public service.

After graduation from high school in Camden, Pryor briefly attended Henderson State Teachers College (1952–1953), then the University of Arkansas at Fayetteville where he majored in government and graduated with a B.A. degree in 1957. On 27 November 1957 he married Barbara Jean Lunsford of Fayetteville. The couple returned to Camden to establish and publish a weekly newspaper, the *Ouachita Citizen,* and to start their family of three sons: David, Jr., Mark, and Scott.

In 1960 Pryor was elected state representative on the Democratic ticket, a position to which he was reelected in 1962 and 1964. While serving in the legislature, he became identified as one of the Young Turks, pushing for constitutional and other reforms and frequently challenging the old guard's proposals and techniques. Also while in the legislature, he began studying law at the University of Arkansas at Fayetteville, from which he earned his LL.B. in 1964. He passed the bar in 1964, and from 1964 to 1966 he practiced law in Camden in the firm of Pryor and Barnes. In 1966, however, when longtime Rep. Oren Harris resigned to become a federal judge, Pryor entered the crowded race for his seat in the U.S. House of Representatives. At age thirty-two, he defeated four Democrats and one Republican to become the representative from Arkansas's Fourth Congressional District.

With a seat on the House Appropriations Committee, Pryor quickly established a record so satisfactory to his constituency that he was reelected without opposition in 1968 and 1970. Electing young men to Congress and leaving them unchallenged to build seniority has been an Arkansas tradition, but Pryor was not a conventional Southern congressman. As a member of the credentials committee at the 1968 Democratic National Convention he voted against seating the regular all-white Mississippi delegation; in his last term in Congress he had what labor described as a 100 percent prolabor voting record; and he challenged the entire congressional establishment to force attention to what he considered to be the neglected problems of the elderly. When the House refused to establish a committee on aging, Pryor compiled considerable evidence of mistreatment and mismanagement while working weekends in nursing homes disguised as an orderly, then created his own committee, which held well-publicized hearings in a trailer parked on Capitol Hill. Undoubtedly, Pryor could have had a lengthy career in the House of Representatives.

In 1972, however, he chose instead to challenge Sen. John L. McClellan's bid for a sixth term. In a Democratic primary memorable for the determination of its candidates and the fervor of their supporters, Pryor forced the traditionally invincible McClellan into a runoff but lost the runoff election by eighteen thousand votes. At the age of thirty-eight, after six years in the Arkansas legislature and six years in Congress, Pryor was again a private citizen. For two years he lived and practiced law in Little Rock, and for several months he commuted to Fayetteville to teach a political science course at the university.

To nobody's surprise, in 1974 he reentered the political arena, this time seeking the Democratic nomination for governor. It could have been a classic liberal-conservative confrontation, with former Gov. Orval Eugene Faubus accusing Pryor of being "soft" on such issues as amnesty for Vietnam draft evaders and gun control. Pryor, however, was supported not only by his usual constituents (educators, blacks, labor) but also by many of Faubus's former backers. Pryor defeated Faubus and Lt. Gov. Bob Cowley Riley by winning 51 percent of the votes, thereby avoiding a runoff. He won 66 percent of the votes against Republican candidate Ken Coon in November 1974 to become Arkansas's thirty-ninth elected governor.

Since much of Pryor's preceding political career had been characterized by challenges to the political establishment, many observers anticipated that his gubernatorial administration would be highly innovative and reformist. In some respects, this expectation was realized. Pryor continued to advocate reform of Arkansas's 1874 constitution.

The proposed constitutional convention he persuaded the legislature to authorize in 1975 was shortly struck down by the state supreme court as unconstitutional, due to its use of appointive rather than elected delegates. However, in 1976 Arkansas voters responded favorably to a citizen-initiated ballot question on whether to hold a constitutional convention, and Pryor was instrumental in shaping the subsequent legislation authorizing the funds and format for the elected convention that began work in 1979.

Pryor also saw to the establishment of several new governmental units: the Department of Local Services to coordinate state assistance to cities and counties; the Department of Natural and Cultural Heritage, combining six previously separate agencies dealing with such programs as historic restoration and stream preservation; a housing-development agency to finance home loans for moderate-income families; a health planning and development agency to coordinate planning for health facilities and services; an energy-conservation and policy office to develop and implement a statewide energy-conservation plan; and an overseas office in Brussels, Belgium, of the Arkansas Industrial Development Commission.

However, Pryor showed the most flair for the unexpected in the appointments he made to various boards and commissions. He appointed the first woman and the first black to serve on the state supreme court (Elsiejane Trimble Roy and George Howard Jr.); the first woman to serve in the cabinet (Anne Bartley as director of the new Natural and Cultural Heritage Department); the first women to serve on either the highway commission or the industrial-development commission (Patsy Thomasson and Helen McCarty); and two men with reputations for consumer sympathies to the Public Service Commission (John C. Pickett and L. Scott Stafford). By the time Pryor left office, both women and blacks had substantially upgraded their status in state employment, and at least one black and one woman served on each of the boards governing Arkansas's institutions of higher education. In December 1977, following Senator McClellan's death, Pryor first offered to appoint McClellan's widow to the vacant seat. When she declined, Pryor ignored the strong pressures brought by numerous aspirants and their supporters and persuaded Kaneaster Hodges Jr., a lawyer from Newport, to accept the appointment. Hodges quickly earned the respect of his Senate colleagues and the affection of Arkansas citizens, confirming the widespread assessment that Pryor's appointments were a strikingly superb aspect of his administration.

There were, then, some surprises and innovations in the Pryor years, and some dramatic moments when unexpected events presented new challenges. Several thousand Vietnamese refugees were temporarily housed at Fort Chaffee in 1975, creating numerous governmental problems. Pryor was praised in the national press for his warm welcome to the refugees, but later he made clear to the federal government that he did not expect the refugees' presence to be permanent. Also in 1975 Pryor made a difficult decision to send the National Guard into Pine Bluff to replace striking firemen, a move that rankled the leadership of organized labor.

For the most part, however, the Pryor administration was characterized by careful stewardship of what his predecessors had established, rather than by expansion and creation. Addressing the legislative council the day after his election victory in November 1974, Pryor surprised and relieved this group of senior legislators who remembered him as an insurgent by advocating austerity and caution and by promising that his single highest priority would be fiscal responsibility. In his first inaugural address, delivered on the steps of Arkansas's first state capitol, Pryor outlined his hopes for constitutional reform, educational improvements, better delivery of health services, a closer state-local partnership, and a greater commitment to the elderly. Throughout the speech, however, he emphasized frugality and common sense, pointing out that, "we shall be judged not by the addition of new state programs, but by the efficiency with which we have met our present needs."

Fiscal restraint became, in many ways, the guiding theme and the clearest legacy of the Pryor administration. In a "Summary of Accomplishments" published by Pryor at the end of his tenure, he proudly pointed to numerous money-saving efforts (a state building services agency, a new system for investing idle state funds, a freeze on hiring new state employees) as having seen Arkansas safely through a time of national economic recession without cutting state services, without raising taxes, and with a "projected $80 million surplus." While both the actual size and the contributing causes of the surplus were disputed, and while teachers in particular complained that this frugality was primarily at their expense, Pryor's achievements as guardian of the public purse are unquestionable.

However, in terms of legislative leadership, another major responsibility of contemporary governors, Pryor's record was mixed. During his four years as governor, the state legislature met an unusually frequent five times: the regular sessions beginning in January of 1975 and

1977; an "extended" session in January 1976 to complete the work of the 1975 regular session; a special session in September 1976 necessitated by the U.S. Supreme Court's invalidation of a federal law under which some state employees had received overtime pay; and a special session in September 1977 to cope with problems arising out of actions taken and not taken at the 1977 regular session. Due to the informal but rarely broken Arkansas tradition of two-term governors, a governor's second regular legislative session usually has something of a lame-duck atmosphere. In fact, former Gov. Sidney Sanders McMath has observed that whereas in the first regular session the governor is something of a "dictator," in the second session he tends to be a "spectator." Certainly Pryor's legislative leadership seemed to diminish with each succeeding session.

Pryor's first regular legislative session in 1975 was fairly successful. The legislature adopted his appointive constitutional convention plan, authorized establishment of the Local Services and Natural and Cultural Heritage departments, passed his "natural areas" bill, and adopted several of his proposals for aiding the elderly (such as tuition-free attendance at state colleges). Although the legislature did not enact his labor and political-ethics proposals, Pryor kept them from enacting measures that would have exempted the highway commission from proposed constitutional reform, lowered the state's air- and water-pollution standards, established a West Memphis branch of Arkansas State University, and "packed" the Pulaski County Election Commission. At the session's end, the *Arkansas Gazette* editorialized that Pryor had turned in a "more-than-adequate performance."

The "extended" session in January 1976 was primarily used to make budget adjustments in light of less-than-anticipated revenues and to propose constitutional amendments, since the appointed convention had been aborted. In both areas, Pryor's preferences generally prevailed.

Clearly, most Arkansas voters were well satisfied with Pryor's first-term performance. In 1976 he easily overwhelmed three opponents in the Democratic primary and gained 83 percent of the general-election vote to earn a second term as governor.

It was during his second term that Pryor's relationships with the legislature became less cooperative and productive. The keystone of the program Pryor presented to the legislature in January 1977 was a package of proposals, termed "the Arkansas Plan," for drastically shifting powers as well as taxing responsibilities, from state to local government. At the heart of the plan was a 25 percent permanent reduction in the state income tax, theoretically providing a logical additional resource for local governments and a psychological environment encouraging citizens to tax themselves locally. Despite a series of "town meetings" personally conducted by Pryor throughout the state in an effort to explain and build popular support for the Arkansas Plan, it was vehemently criticized by education associations, city and county officials, highway interests, and organized labor. Defended by Pryor as a revolutionary breakthrough, denounced by its opponents as a reactionary disaster, the Arkansas Plan generated fierce controversy that dominated the entire legislative session. The plan was repeatedly modified by Pryor and thoroughly emasculated by the legislature; except for legislation reorganizing the minimum foundation aid program of state aid to school districts, little else was accomplished.

The special session held in August 1977, primarily necessitated by oversights and errors in the regular legislative session, was not much more productive. Because erroneous figures had been used, kindergartens had been massively underfunded; because no authorization had been enacted for expenditure of a controversial new antilitter tax, a much-protested levy was being assessed for no programmatic purpose; because Pryor had vetoed the law mandating a general-election referendum on the proposed 1980 constitution, no time for ratification had been set. At the special session, kindergartens received their funds, the antilitter tax was repealed, and the question of when to vote on the proposed new constitution was referred to a vote of the people. At this session's conclusion, in a highly critical editorial, the *Arkansas Gazette* charged that the "key figure in the spoiling of the special session was the same governor, David Pryor, who had made a ruin of the regular session with the abortive Arkansas Plan."

On the other hand, the *Southern Standard* at Arkadelphia praised Pryor's "courage and wisdom" and rendered the following judgment on his overall performance: "Much to the pleasant surprise of many, the 'Old Liberal' David Pryor turned out to be a true fiscal conservative. He held the line with a tight fist against runaway spending and helped Arkansas weather the storms of recession and inflation that wracked the nation in 1974-75."

This latter judgment seems to have prevailed among the Arkansas voters who elected Pryor over two attractive and well-qualified opponents, Rep. Jim Guy Tucker and Ray Thornton, for the Democratic nomination for the U.S. Senate in June 1978 and then to the office itself in November 1978. The Democratic nomination was very closely contested, and for the first time in his political career Pryor ran without the backing of most labor and education interests. To a majority of Arkansas voters, however, the scandal-free, cost-conscious Pryor administration was to their liking, as was Pryor himself.

Even Pryor's critics acknowledge him to be a warm and friendly person of worthy motives and personal integrity. Some political commentators complained that "Pryor has never been one to present a very strong and identifiable image except as a politician ambitious for higher office." For the people of Arkansas, however, the image was clear enough. Despite an entire adult life spent in politics, Pryor still seemed less a professional politician than a genuinely concerned and caring individual.

WILLIAM JEFFERSON CLINTON

1979–1981, 1983–1992

WILLIAM JEFFERSON CLINTON (19 August 1946–), attorney and public servant, was born William Jefferson Blythe IV in Hope, Arkansas, the son of William Jefferson III and Virginia (Cassidy) Blythe. Bill Blythe died in an automobile accident three months before his son was born. Young Clinton spent his earliest years in Hope in the care of his maternal grandparents while his mother completed training in New Orleans as a nurse anesthetist. At age four he moved to Hot Springs following his mother's marriage to Roger Clinton, whose surname he legally took for himself at age fifteen.

Clinton excelled in his studies in the Hot Springs public schools and participated enthusiastically in a variety of activities, including student government and music, honor, and service societies. His 1963 selection as Arkansas's delegate to Boy's Nation, an experience which included a visit with Sen. J. W. Fulbright and a now-famous handshake with Pres. John F. Kennedy in the White House Rose Garden, fueled his interest in public affairs and his attraction to Washington, D.C., where he entered Georgetown University in 1964. Clinton immersed himself in student governance again and earned tuition money through work for Senator Fulbright. He graduated with a B.S. in international affairs in 1968 and won a coveted Rhodes Scholarship, permitting him to pursue his studies at Oxford University for the next two years.

In 1970 Clinton entered Yale Law School; he spent much of 1972 in Texas as a state coordinator of George McGovern's unsuccessful presidential campaign. Upon graduation in 1973, Clinton originally intended to begin a solo practice in Hot Springs but decided instead to join the faculty at the University of Arkansas School of Law at Fayetteville. Early in 1974 he declined an offered position on the congressional committee investigating Pres. Richard Nixon's possible impeachment, recommending instead his Yale Law classmate and

McGovern campaign coworker, Hillary Rodham. Clinton himself, at age twenty-seven, took on the challenge of seeking incumbent Third District Republican John Paul Hammerschmidt's seat in the U.S. Congress.

Clinton's non-stop stamina, populist themes, engaging oratory, personal charm, and enthusiastic volunteer organization (including many of his law students and Hillary Rodham, who joined the law school faculty that fall) swept him past three opponents in the Democratic primary. His surprisingly close general election finish, 48.5 percent, was the closest any opponent ever came to beating the popular Hammerschmidt. While Clinton's first race ended in defeat, the defeat established him as a political heavyweight and serious future contender.

On 11 October 1975, Bill Clinton and Hillary Rodham were married, and soon thereafter he announced his candidacy for attorney general. In his first statewide race, Clinton carried sixty-nine of Arkansas's seventy-five counties in the Democratic primary, beating a former secretary of state and a deputy attorney general with a sufficient margin (56 percent) to avoid a runoff. With no Republican opponent, Clinton's attorney generalship was insured. He coordinated Jimmy Carter's fall presidential race in Arkansas while recruiting and organizing an activist attorney general's staff. Positioning himself as a foe of the always-suspect utilities and a champion of the rate payer and consumer, Clinton opposed the twenty-five-cent phone call, supported victim compensation legislation, chaired a national panel on the rights of the elderly, and advocated a tough ethics law for state officials.

Given the statewide visibility resulting from his vigorous pro-consumer agenda and a tireless public-relations operation, Clinton entered the 1978 governor's race from a position of strength, over-powering (with 60 percent) all other contestants in a five-man Democratic primary. He then amassed 63 percent and sixty-nine counties against Republican state chairman Lynn Lowe in the general election. So certain was Clinton of victory that, in a year when taxpayer revolts were sweeping the country, he successfully campaigned against a ballot proposal to repeal the sales tax on food and drugs, citing the dire public consequences of a $60 million revenue loss. Using both his attorney general's staff and young policy makers recruited from around the country, he immersed himself in the budget-making process and began constructing an ambitious agenda.

At age thirty-two, after an elaborate three-day sequence of inaugural events entitled "Diamonds and Denim," Clinton became the second youngest governor, after nineteenth-century John Roane, in Arkansas history. A lengthy and eloquent inaugural address was written largely by Clinton himself on inaugural eve. It reflected his ideals, "For as long as I can remember, I have believed passionately in the cause of equal opportunity, and I will do what I can to advance it"; his policy priorities, "In education, we have lingered too long on or near the bottom of the heap in spending per student and in teacher salaries"; and, repeatedly, his determination to provide a brighter future for Arkansas, "We can bring on a new era of achievement and excellence—we can fashion a life here that will be the envy of our nation."

In a fifty-five-minute "State of the State Address" to the legislature, a self-confident Clinton outlined a lengthy and wide-ranging legislative program that included over seventy measures. In economic development, he emphasized small business development and international marketing over traditional smokestack-chasing activities. His educational measures would require new teachers to take the National Teacher's Examination, require statewide regular testing of students, and insure access to challenging programs for gifted and talented youngsters. In conservation, he called for a variety of innovative programs in a newly established Energy Department and the creation of a Natural and Scenic Rivers Commission and a State Land Bank. Priorities in health were the establishment of a Rural Health Development Office for medically underserved rural communities, funding for a state perinatal intensive-care nursery, and expanded in-home services for the elderly. To ensure that the state was receiving its fair share of federal funds, he established a Washington, D.C., office for Arkansas. Most significantly, to address the state's pressing road-building and repair needs, he proposed and persuaded the legislature to enact a program which, after heavy lobbying from the trucking industry and Highway Commission, raised revenues. This new revenue came primarily from increases in title transfer, especially vehicle registration fees.

By any measure, it was one of the most productive legislative sessions in the state's history. Clinton received plaudits not only from the state press but also from national news magazines, noting this "rising star" in Arkansas. His personal cup of good fortune flowed over with the birth of a daughter, Chelsea, in February 1980. By this time, however, his administration confronted national and state economic recession, a series of natural disasters, including severe tornadoes and a killer summer drought, political problems, and a rising tide of press criticism. Clinton's bright young aides were better at policy innovation than personal outreach, a serious mistake in the homegrown style of Arkansas politics. A number of their legislative and administrative innovations had infuriated many of the state's most powerful economic interests including utilities, timber, trucking, poultry, construction, and medicine. Clinton himself, by angrily denouncing the police when his state car was stopped for speeding and the press for questioning his extensive travels on national political business, seemed arrogant and insensitive.

Then came the Cuban refugees: in May 1980 the White House informed Clinton that the federal installation at Fort Chaffee had been selected as a resettlement site for some of the estimated 120,000 "Freedom Flotilla" Cuban refugees. Clinton's initial response was that the state, as it was obligated to do, would meet its responsibilities. However, when the White House repeatedly ignored Clinton's requests for sufficient federal security forces to keep the rioting refugees within the fort and repeatedly reneged on promises not to send additional refugees, Clinton's previous close ties with Pres. Jimmy Carter were seen as having inflicted rather than prevented this infuriating "exploitation" of Arkansas. Meanwhile, discontent emerged when more and more Arkansans encountered hefty increases in vehicle registration and license fees. This was especially true in rural areas because vehicles in the heaviest and oldest classes were subjected to the biggest hikes. What amounted to a rural rebellion caught fire.

Although Clinton lost only six counties and easily defeated Monroe Schwarzlose (a retired turkey farmer) in the Democratic primary, in the 1980 general election, Republican businessman and former Democratic Arkansas Industrial Development Commission director Frank White scored the most stunning upset in Arkansas political history. White became only the second Republican governor since Reconstruction. Clinton became only the second twentieth-century governor to be denied his bid for a second, sometimes called courtesy, two-year term. He was the youngest ex-governor in Arkansas and American history.

It was a humiliating halt to what had seemed an endlessly upward trajectory. Many close friends, concerned over Clinton's deep personal devastation, counseled a respite from public life. Clinton, however, while putatively practicing law with a Little Rock firm, almost immediately began making plans for a rematch. He endlessly sought the opinions of both politicos and ordinary citizens on why he had failed; and he hired Betsey Wright, a Texan who had worked with the Clintons in the McGovern effort and was the founding executive director of the national Women's Education Fund, to help organize his comeback effort.

In February 1982, preceding any formal announcement, Clinton effectively opened his campaign with two television commercials in which he apologized for past errors—especially the car-tag fee increases and some controversial commutations—asked for forgiveness, and assured voters that he had learned he could not "lead without listening." Clinton got only 42 percent of the vote in a five-man Democratic primary, and only narrowly (54 percent) defeated longtime Lt. Gov. Joe Purcell for the nomination. The general election was equally bruising. Both Clinton and White raised and spent record amounts, and both waged largely negative media campaigns, arguing who would be least likely to raise taxes, who would be least lenient with pardons and commutations, who would be least accommodating to the power companies, and who would create the most jobs in Arkansas. Clinton's final victory, with 55 percent of the vote, was a personal triumph and historic first—the first Arkansas governor to have recaptured the office.

Clinton and his supporters were understandably jubilant, but the Clinton who prepared to resume the governorship seemed much less certain that he could take the state in dramatic new directions through the force of his own personality and intellect. He repeatedly reminded supporters and cautioned himself to "avoid arrogance" and maintain "maximum accessibility." At his first meeting with the legislative council he shook hands longer than he spoke, and what he said was how much he needed their advice and assistance. The 1983 inaugural was a one-day rather than three-day event; the inaugural address stressed hard times and austerity. Immediately after his swearing in, he told the assembled legislators that he was "humbled to be given another chance to serve the people."

All of this was effective public relations, but it was also reality. It was in fact a much more restrained and pragmatic governor who presented to the 1983 legislative session a much more modest program, which dealt primarily with utilities, prisons, and budget cuts. In everything from staff (older, and almost all Arkansans), to appearance (shorter haircut), speaking style (harsher and twangier), travel and intergovernmental associations (frequent in the first term, almost nonexistent in the second), to his wife's last name (Clinton rather than the Rodham she had initially retained, disquieting traditionalists), the comeback governor had "gone native."

To those former supporters disappointed in this seeming new

passivity, Clinton explained that he had learned the importance of focusing on one major issue at a time, with budgetary matters necessarily assuming priority, and that "just getting by," although it might not sound very imaginative, was much better than many of the state's citizens were doing. Above all, he had learned how to do things "that are achievable, that are understandable, and, by all means, involve the people in them."

Many observers point to the 1980 defeat and carefully planned comeback as the most crucial episode in Clinton's gubernatorial, perhaps entire political, career. Certainly he learned from these experiences some strategic lessons that guided the rest of his governorship: mandates must be fashioned rather than imposed; accomplishments must be publicized or they will not be known; criticism, no matter how farfetched, must be instantly and massively refuted. Others, more critically, suggest that from 1980 onward he excessively courted the economic interests he had once fearlessly challenged, that he lost not only his naiveté but his nerve. According to Arkansas political journalist Mike Trimble, for example, "Some people said his first administration had gone out of its way to offend people; some now said that his second had a pathological fear of offending anybody." However, a fortuitous combination of events soon made it possible for Clinton's inherent activism to reassert itself.

Amid the more heated and protracted issues of utility rate regulation and permissible highway weight limits which dominated the 1983 legislative session, a bill was passed establishing a fifteen-person Education Standards Committee. This committee was to recommend new and higher standards to the Department of Education, for adoption by 1984. School districts not in compliance by June 1987 would be forced to consolidate. Suspecting, correctly, that a coming state supreme court decision would declare unconstitutional the existing formula for distributing state school aid, Clinton decided to use this "crisis" as an opportunity for the dramatic educational advances he had long envisioned. He would use the Education Standards Committee—to which he named his wife, Hillary, as chair—as the central engine of reform.

When the supreme court ruled on 31 May that the existing education aid formula unconstitutionally denied equal educational opportunity for all children, both Clintons swung into high gear. Hillary Clinton's committee held public hearings in all seventy-five counties, collected criticisms and recommendations, shaped and publicized proposed new standards, and secured their preliminary approval by the

State Board of Education. Clinton himself began systematically building public and legislative support for the tax increases necessary to pay for them. Using the skills and staff acquired in his previous political campaigns—opinion surveys done by professional pollsters, brochures prepared by public-relations professionals, fund raising, and targeted mailings—Clinton's "campaign for educational excellence" activated and intensified public opinions already aroused by a highly publicized national report on the alarming condition of American schools and by repeated publicity over Arkansas's last or next-to-last ranking in most comparative education measures.

In a thirty-minute speech telecast over every station in Arkansas on 19 September, Clinton outlined the proposed education reforms (smaller classes, longer school day and year, more demanding curriculum, mandatory examinations before certain promotions, testing of all teachers) and the compelling reason for them—the job future of every Arkansan. Increased taxes would be necessary, but they would be dedicated to educational improvements, and therefore would be "an investment in the future of our children and in the economic development of the state."

Resisting attempts to place anything but education into the special session which began on 4 October, Clinton fought successfully through heated battles for a new aid distribution formula; for teacher competency testing; and finally, for the revenues to pay for the new formula, new standards, and higher teacher salaries. Clinton's insistence on teacher testing, which he saw as strongly coalescing public support for the new programs and higher taxes, earned him the passionate and long-lived enmity of the Arkansas Education Association. However, by the end of the longest special session on record (twenty-eight days), the legislature had adopted a new and fairer formula, more challenging school standards, and the first sales tax increase in twenty-six years, from three to four cents.

The 1984 elections, both primary and general, were essentially referenda on whether to weaken or preserve the new school standards, and the public clearly sided with Clinton. He got 64 percent of the vote against three opponents in the Democratic primary, 63 percent against Jonesboro businessman Woody Freeman in the fall, and thereby became only the third governor in Arkansas history elected to a third term.

Instructed by these electoral expressions of public opinion, the 1985 legislature followed Clinton's lead in resisting fervent attempts to weaken the new school standards and cancel teacher testing.

Clinton's primary focus for this session, however, was economic development. In his inaugural address Clinton strongly emphasized "that our primary goal is growth: more jobs and higher incomes. We will not sacrifice our commitment to equal opportunity, a clean environment or other important objectives to achieve growth but all our policies should be directed toward maximizing it." Rather than a State of the State speech, Clinton reviewed with legislators a 312-page booklet containing summaries of more than eighty bills he was proposing in education, crime, utility regulation, and especially economic development. This complicated, innovative package would create an Arkansas Development Finance Authority empowered to issue tax-exempt bonds to finance development projects, would mandate investment in Arkansas by the state's biggest retirement systems, and would provide substantial new tax incentives for in-state investment by business. Most of the economic development package passed with little debate giving Clinton some of his most clear-cut and consequential legislative achievements.

Other events, however, reflected less well on Clinton's legislative leadership. When the legislature overrode Clinton's veto of gasoline and diesel taxes to fund highway construction, it was the first time in history that the general assembly had supported a revenue raise opposed by the governor, and Clinton was widely criticized for having played politics to his own rather than the state's advantage. Two bills, permitting home schooling by parents and giving income tax write-offs for college contributions, were so flawed in the form signed by Clinton that a special session was necessary for remedial action. And with respect to the latter measure, Clinton appeared considerably less than gubernatorial when it was revealed that he had sent a state trooper to retrieve the bill, with a coat hanger slid beneath a legislative office door, in order to "undo" a veto.

Most troublesome to Clinton, and repeatedly identified by him as the single most frustrating event of his gubernatorial career, was the final, highly unsatisfactory resolution of the Grand Gulf affair. Although Arkansas never requested and was not to receive any power from the $3.5 billion Grand Gulf nuclear power plant in Mississippi, the Federal Energy Regulatory Commission (FERC) ruled in June 1985 that Arkansas Power and Light would have to pay for 36 percent of Middle South Energy's 90 percent share of it. This allocation was bitterly protested by Arkansas officials but was upheld in federal court. Clinton argued against and angrily denounced first the FERC and then the federal judiciary, but in September 1985 he reluctantly went along with a state Public Service Commission settlement, as "the best deal Arkansas could get under the circumstances." The settlement made AP&L rate payers responsible for 80 percent and stockholders responsible for 20 percent of the Arkansas-assigned costs.

This settlement, as well as the school consolidations that would be caused by the new school standards, were the principal issues used against Clinton in both the Democratic primary and general elections in 1986. However, he won first over ex-Governor Orval Faubus (by 61 percent), then over ex-Governor Frank White (by 64 percent); and, since Arkansas voters also approved a ballot issue changing gubernatorial terms from two to four years, Clinton won not only his fourth term but a four-year term.

Seemingly, Clinton had a solid popular mandate to perform in a significantly strengthened office. He presented to the 1987 legislature a comprehensive set of initiatives for "Making Arkansas Work: Good Beginnings, Good Schools and Good Jobs." "Hard economic times and slumping tax collections might once have suggested cutting back on education and human development spending," Clinton noted in his inaugural, but "that will not work today. In our highly integrated, highly competitive world economy . . . either we press ahead or we are pushed back. There is no status quo." However, almost as though weary of being nagged, the legislature, under concerted pressure from affected interest groups, balked at the price tag (about $200 million in new taxes) for such "investments." Eventually, in this and a subsequent special session, sufficient funds were eked out to sustain implementation of the school standards. Clinton resolved to address two problems which had long confounded Arkansas governance and had been especially evident in the 1987 session.

First, because Arkansas's constitution requires that changes in all taxes other than the sales tax require a three-fourths legislative majority, the tax system inevitably tilts in a regressive direction. Revenue increases supported by majorities of legislators can be thwarted by very small oppositional minorities. In June 1987 Clinton appointed a blue-ribbon Tax Reform Commission which recommended a constitutional amendment requiring a 60 percent majority for all tax changes. He assisted in securing the necessary signatures for its place on the 1988 ballot, and then campaigned, unsuccessfully, for its adoption.

Second, because relationships between legislators and lobbyists had been less regulated in Arkansas than in any other state and these relationships had seemed particularly visible and obstructionist in the 1987 session, Clinton appointed a special Code of Ethics Commission in June 1987 and directed it to develop a strong, comprehensive state code of ethics. When a special session Clinton called for this purpose failed to enact the commission's recommendations, he took the issue to the people, chairing the campaign to collect signatures to get the measure on the ballot, and chairing the successful 1988 campaign for passage.

On 15 July 1987, after weeks of excited speculation and strong hints that the governor would seek the 1988 Democratic presidential nomination, Clinton announced that he would not. He cited his daughter's youth as the major factor weighing against running. A year later, at the Democratic National Convention, Clinton seemingly ended whatever presidential prospects the future held in his speech "introducing" nominee Michael Dukakis. Arkansans in the convention hall in Atlanta and at home watching television eagerly anticipated the national display of Clinton's easy oratorical gifts. They were then horrified as a speech scheduled to last only fifteen minutes ran for what seemed an interminable thirty-two minutes and was greeted with increasingly vocal disapproval and derision by delegates and television newscasters alike. Clinton's subsequent appearance on the Johnny Carson show, where he displayed his saxophone-playing skills as well as his self-deprecating wit, somewhat salvaged both the Arkansas psyche and Clinton's reputation—over one-fourth of the state's population watched, the highest ratings in the history of Arkansas television.

That fall, however, Dukakis lost Arkansas and voters rejected the Fair Tax Initiative. Confronted with rising criticism of his out-of-state trips, Clinton proposed an ambitious agenda to the legislature, but midway into the twentieth-century's first four-year gubernatorial term, no electoral mandate existed. Many legislators and lobbyists were also smarting from the rhetoric and impact of the ethics initiative campaign, and the legislative environment was further poisoned by disputes between powerful senators and Clinton's top aides.

Into this unfriendly atmosphere, Clinton proposed an ambitious plan to "Move Arkansas Forward" through educational and economic development initiatives to be financed by making the tax system both more equitable and more productive. This would be done by removing 264,000 low-income taxpayers from the income tax rolls, modestly increasing income taxes on the middle class and rich, and increasing the sales tax one cent. The progressive income tax reform was an absolute prerequisite to the regressive sales tax increase, a requirement acceptable to the House, but narrowly stymied in the Senate. While a large number of innovative programs were enacted—a new system of juvenile justice and "boot camps" for juvenile first offenders, school choice for students and annual report cards on the schools, and, after much contentious debate, school-based health clinics—the entire legislature balked when presented with a $119 million bill as final settlement on long-standing Little Rock school desegregation costs.

Despite warnings that federal court judgments could ultimately run much, much higher without this settlement, it took four votes to finally get majority approval in the session's waning hours. To Clinton's dismay, the battle had to be fought again when the constitutionality of all spending bills passed in the regular session was judicially challenged. It took two additional special sessions and enormous time and energy to resolve this issue, identified by Clinton as second only to Grand Gulf in its frustration quotient. His further efforts in a special session to provide additional funding for education, prison problems, and the war on drugs through a temporary surcharge on personal and corporate income taxes produced little but talk of legislative gridlock and gubernatorial burn-out, and a widespread assumption that Clinton would and probably should move on to other pursuits.

However, on 1 March 1990, while acknowledging that "the fire of an election no longer burns in me," Clinton announced his belief that "more than any other person who could serve as governor, I could do the best job"; and therefore, he would ask the voters for a fifth term. If elected again, Clinton pledged to serve out the four-year term, a promise repeated during the campaign. In both the Democratic primary, where his major opponent was ex-Winthrop Rockefeller Foundation president and grandson of a 1920s Arkansas governor, Tom McRae, and in the general election, against former Democrat and ex-Arkla president Sheffield Nelson, the chief battle cry of opponents was "Ten Years Is Enough." Nelson also portrayed Clinton as a liberal tax-and-spender whose expensive educational initiatives had produced few results. Clinton's winning percentages in both the Democratic primary (54 percent) and the general election (57 percent) were his slimmest victories in ten years, suggesting dim prospects for the subsequent legislative session.

However, energized by a victory which seemed a positive referendum for the path on which he had long been leading the state and facilitated by the defeat of some of his most entrenched legislative opponents, Clinton renewed his familiar inaugural reminder that "when we are as healthy and well-educated as the rest of America, our incomes and opportunities will rise to and beyond the national average." He also asked lawmakers to enact a program making the 1990s "a decade of destiny for Arkansas." By session's end Clinton was exuberantly describing it as "the best regular session of the legislature in my lifetime," and even Clinton's usual critic Sen. Nick Wilson called it "the most progressive session since 1971."

Using the themes of opportunity, investment, citizen choice, and government accountability, lawmakers increased the sales tax by one-half cent, with all increased revenues targeted for an Education Trust Fund, and the corporate income tax by 1/2 percent to overhaul and upgrade technical education. The gasoline tax was also increased for a $2.4 billion highway program. At the same time, 25 percent of low-income Arkansans were removed from the state income tax rolls. Educational initiatives ranged from new early childhood programs and dropout prevention measures to a statewide residential math and science high school, thousands of new college scholarships, and an average teacher pay increase of $4,900 over the biennium. New health services for Arkansans extended from the very youngest (income withholding for children's health care coverage and expansion of school-based health clinics) through the oldest citizens (new and more flexible services funded by a cigarette tax increase). For the first time since 1978, Clinton seriously addressed Arkansas's growing environmental problems with measures to restructure the Pollution Control and Ecology Commission, establish a cohesive state landfill system, encourage recycling through income tax credits, and prohibit permits to companies with bad environmental records from other states.

While Clinton could legitimately claim credit for "enacting every single legislative commitment in the campaign," by late summer he was clearly contemplating breaking another commitment, his pledge to serve the full four-year term. In early autumn he toured the state "consulting" with longtime supporters regarding the pros and cons of a presidential bid, warning them that "Republicans would run against him by trying to run the state down." He found release from his pledge in the vocal approval of supporters and decided to ignore critics who, he noted, "spent ten years trying to get rid of me and now they can't do without me." Clinton next insured the cooperation of Lt. Gov. Jim Guy Tucker, who constitutionally would become acting governor during any absence from the state. Then, on 3 October 1991, Clinton announced his bid for the Democratic presidential nomination in a highly produced event on the grounds of the Old State House in Little Rock.

As predicted, the state itself and Clinton's record as its governor came under exhaustive scrutiny during both the Democratic nomination battle and the three-way general election contest between incumbent Republican George Bush, independent billionaire businessman Ross Perot, and Democratic nominee Clinton. By campaign's end, Bush and Perot were competing over who could portray Arkansas in the most unflattering light. Opponents charged that despite 128 tax and fee increases during Clinton's governorship, Arkansas still ranked last or next to last in family median income, average weekly wages, literacy rates, teacher pay, infant health, and environmental quality.

The Clinton campaign issued data-filled documents arguing to the contrary: Arkansas had the second-lowest state and local tax burden in the country with taxes as a percent of personal income actually lower than when Clinton took office. By July 1992 the state ranked fifth nationally in job creation and ninth in wage and salary growth, with median income increasing twice as fast as the nation generally. Arkansas had achieved the highest high-school graduation rate in the region and was sending 34 percent more students to college than it did ten years previously, and such students were better prepared in smaller classes with a more demanding curriculum. Arkansas teachers received the highest percent salary increase in the country the preceding year. The state's infant mortality rate had declined 43 percent from 1978 to 1990, to virtual parity with the national average, while over 60 percent of the state's children were being served in free preschool programs as a result of Clinton initiatives. And Arkansas, one of only eight states meeting all federal standards under the Clean Air Act, had developed some of the most progressive water quality standards in the nation and was among the top ten states in wetlands protection and energy research.

President Bush repeatedly characterized Clinton as the "failed governor of a small state," and in the final presidential debate said that what worried him most was that Clinton would "do to America what he did to Arkansas." Apparently the nation's governors felt otherwise; they repeatedly elected Clinton to leadership positions and ranked him as "the most effective" governor in June 1991. And Arkansas voters also signaled a very different assessment on 3 November 1992, giving their favorite son his largest margin (53.8 percent) in any of the fifty states. On election night, thousands of Arkansans gathered at the site where Clinton had begun his campaign thirteen months previously and cheered with fervor when President-elect Clinton emerged victorious through the Old State House doors and emotionally thanked the people of "this wonderful, small state."

By the time Clinton left office to become the nation's chief executive, he had run fifteen statewide elections in Arkansas and won fourteen of them; and, by one informed estimate, he had met over half the people in the state. He had made over five thousand appointments, had proposed the state's first billion dollar budget, and had piloted six regular and thirteen special sessions. But neither statistical summaries nor lists of legislative enactments could adequately measure the impact of his twelve-year governorship.

Clinton himself, and most of those who have assessed his record, point first to the state's educational advances. According to a doctoral dissertation by Charles F. Allen, which examines these reforms, "During the Clinton years, more significant changes affecting the role of education in the growth of Arkansas were made than during the previous 140 years combined." This and other analyses point not only to the specific programs catalogued above, but also to a massive increase in the state's investment in education, rising by 1991 to 71 percent of the total budget, third highest in the nation, and to seventh in the nation in per capita state spending on schools. A comprehensive 1990 study of Clinton's education reforms also "starred his report card" because "he brought such inseparable issues as prenatal health, early childhood development, teen pregnancy, and drug abuse into the overall discussion of education." Most important, for over a decade Clinton put the state's schools at the very center of public debate, igniting an overwhelmingly positive change in public interest, attitudes, and priorities.

In terms of hours expended, Clinton frequently noted that he spent more of his "time trying to generate jobs for Arkansas than anything else," and here, too, it seems the efforts were productive. In one 1992 analysis and summary in the *Wall Street Journal,* Jeffrey Birnbaum concluded that Clinton was "better than average at finding jobs for his constituents" and that "Arkansas's economy and fiscal health has made slow but steady progress during Mr. Clinton's governorship, and the state has done better than its neighbors and better than the nation as a whole." While Arkansas remained one of the poorest states in the nation, to have made progress during years dominated by national economic recession and stagnation and sharply declining federal assistance to the states was a noteworthy accomplishment. Certainly Clinton's numerous initiatives for upgrading the work force, stimulating internal development, increasing exports, and creating public-private partnerships all eased Arkansas's transition from a predominantly agricultural and low-wage, low-skill manufacturing economy to an economy better prepared to compete in a technologically advanced global market.

Again, however, the most critical advances may have come in attitudes and expectations rather than per capita statistical measurements. In hundreds of speeches and messages delivered in an endless variety of forums over more than a dozen years, Clinton encouraged Arkansans to aspire to greater heights, to expect more from their children, themselves, their state government, and their future. "So many people in Arkansas have seemed to believe as long as I've been alive that in some sort of strange way God meant us to drag up the rear of the nation's economy forever," Clinton said in one typical statewide telecast. But, he repeatedly insisted, "The future need not be fate. It can be achievement. Let us move Arkansas from the economic backwaters to the crest of prosperity and opportunity in America."

The message was hardly a novel one in Arkansas, but it may have had particular impact coming from one who himself had risen from modest circumstances to public heights through education, hard work, ambition, and persistence. Furthermore, Clinton made a particular point throughout his governorship of bringing into power many who had traditionally been excluded. He demonstrated by example that women and blacks could effectively fill the most responsible positions in state government if given the opportunity. Throughout his tenure Clinton named blacks to the most prestigious and powerful cabinet positions, including the heads of the Departments of Health, Finance and Administration, Human Services, and the Development Finance Authority. In addition to the unprecedented responsibilities entrusted to his wife, Hillary, Clinton's longest-tenured chief of staff was Betsey Wright, who also ran most of his campaigns. Numerous other women served in his cabinets and in key campaign and staff positions.

Clinton's election to the presidency insured that every aspect of his personal life and public record would continue to be exhaustively scrutinized, rigorously criticized, and vehemently debated by partisans, journalists, and historians. What seems beyond question, however, is the energy, imagination, and passion which Clinton brought to the job he often described as "the best in America." At the 12 December 1992 swearing-in ceremony for his successor, Lt. Gov. Jim Guy Tucker, as Clinton left the major occupation of his adult life, he emotionally described his dozen years as governor as "an affair of the heart." He told those assembled, "I loved being governor. I love our state and I love you all."

FRANK DURWOOD WHITE

1981–1983

FRANK DURWOOD WHITE (4 June 1933–), banker, was born in Texarkana, Texas, the son of Durwood Frank Kyle and Ida Bottoms (Clark) Kyle. He was given the name Durwood Frank Kyle Jr. In 1940 the elder Kyle died; his seven-year-old son was an only child. Two years later his mother married Loftin E. White of Dallas, Texas, who adopted his stepson, and Durwood Frank Kyle Jr. changed his name to Frank Durwood White. He attended Highland Park High School in Dallas until his stepfather died in 1950, whereupon his mother moved back to Texarkana, and young Frank enrolled in the New Mexico Military Institute, Roswell, New Mexico. Graduating from NMMI in 1951, White studied briefly at Texas A & M University before accepting an appointment to the United States Naval Academy. His favorite subject was Spanish, though he received the obligatory engineering training. Graduating from the Academy in 1956, ranked 273rd in a class of 681, White took a commission in the air force, where he served as a pilot for five years and was discharged with the rank of captain in 1961. In April of that year White married Mary Blue Hollenberg of Little Rock. They had three children, Elizabeth Clark, Rebecca Hollenberg, and Kyle Everette.

The Whites settled in Little Rock where Mrs. White's family, the Hollenbergs, were a well-known fixture in the business and cultural community. Frank took a job as an account executive with the Merrill-Lynch firm where his gregarious personality helped him excel. In 1973, at the urging of prominent banker William (Bill) Bowen, White joined the management of Commercial National Bank. Bowen, a confirmed Democrat who would later oppose White politically, was White's Sunday school teacher. Despite their political differences, White and Bowen were to have a persistent business relationship.

White threw himself into his business career with the enthusiasm that typified his life in general. As his career developed, he involved himself in a variety of civic activities. He served as president of the Little Rock Jaycees during 1965–66, a time when that organization was full of intense young men of political and business ambition. For over a decade he was on the board of the Arkansas Children's Hospital, including a term as treasurer, and served on the national board of the Family Ministry Division of the Campus Crusade for Christ.

Religion was important to Frank White. He grew up in the Baptist Church, being baptized as a youth in the Beech Street Baptist Church in Texarkana, later pastored by the Rev. Mike Huckabee who was elected lieutenant governor of Arkansas in 1993 as a Republican. When White and his first wife divorced in 1973, he turned to religion for comfort, a process that was reinforced by his marriage to Gay Daniels, a devout and fundamentalist Christian, whom he married in 1975. She and her first husband had worked for the Campus Crusade for Christ. Frank and Gay White had no children of their own, but they eventually gained custody of White's three children. The Whites were members of the First Methodist Church, a historic but progressive congregation located in downtown Little Rock. A few years later the Whites and four other couples established the Fellowship Bible Church, a fundamentalist congregation that quickly grew in size and political influence. White's intense religious faith would later have a profound impact on his tenure as governor.

Frank White's first foray into state government was as a member of the cabinet of popular Democratic governor David H. Pryor. In 1975 White was named director of the Arkansas Industrial Development Commission. His tenure at AIDC was not particularly successful. Few new jobs were created during his administration, a situation that White later attributed to an economic recession and oil price increases. His major accomplishment as AIDC director was in convincing the legislature to create a state trade office in Europe. That success, however, was marred by his appointment of an inexperienced young Jaycee friend to head the office in Brussels, Belgium.

White left the AIDC directorship after little more than two years. He assumed the presidency of Capital Savings and Loan in Little Rock in 1977, and though he had no experience in the savings and loan business, he quickly used his salesmanship skills to build up the total deposits. Later, during White's first campaign for governor, his detractors noted that Capital Savings and Loan dropped from eighth to twelfth in the state in total assets during White's presidency. Despite his considerable skills in salesmanship, White found elective politics more appealing than the boardroom.

On 16 March 1980 the *Arkansas Gazette* published an article specu-
lating that first term governor Bill Clinton could expect "no serious
opposition" to reelection. That prophecy was reinforced when the filing
period ended and Clinton's only opponent in the Democratic primary
was Monroe Schwartzlose, a rustic turkey farmer from rural Cleveland
County. The Republican opposition seemed no more threatening—a
little known one-term former state representative from Johnson
County, Marshall Chrisman, and an almost equally obscure Little
Rock businessman named Frank White.

White was especially unknown in Republican circles. His previous
political activity was on behalf of Democrats, primarily Governor and
later U.S. Sen. David Pryor. White said he ran as a Republican because
he was a conservative and felt more comfortable among Republicans.
Additionally, running as a Republican offered the advantage of a much
longer period of time to mount a campaign against an entrenched
incumbent.

Though White won the GOP primary with more than a two-to-one
majority, the low turnout must have been discouraging: only 8,177
people voted in the Republican primary while almost one-half million
votes were cast in the Democratic contest. But Frank White was not
easily discouraged. The general election campaign was full of fury.
White was tutored by the GOP National Committee in the art of
aggressive television campaigning, and he put that new knowledge to
good use.

Two issues dominated the general election campaign of 1980: "Car
Tags and Cubans." During his term, Governor Clinton increased automobile license fees in order to raise funds for highway construction.
The Cuban issue arose when the federal government sent several thousand Cuban refugees to a resettlement center at Fort Chaffee near
Fort Smith. Discord erupted at Fort Chaffee, and near riots ensued
among elements of the refugees. White relentlessly harried Clinton,
accusing him of thoughtlessly raising taxes and at the same time failing to stand up against the refugee center at Fort Chaffee.

White also kept Clinton off balance by periodically attacking on
other fronts. A million dollar grant request by the Ozark Institute at
Eureka Springs to train people to farm, organize farm cooperatives,
and conserve energy was portrayed as wasteful if not subversive. The
SAWYER project, a program to train woodcutters, was ridiculed by
White who pointed out that only twelve cords of firewood had been
produced.

Buoyed by polls that showed him far ahead, Governor Clinton

failed to respond to Republican charges until it was too late. With only two weeks left in the campaign, Clinton counterattacked with a vengeance. He blasted White's support for increasing truck weight limits to 80,000 pounds. And, at the same time, Clinton ridiculed White's business record, gleefully noting that more jobs were created in Arkansas during his term as governor than while White was director of AIDC.

When the dust cleared after what was probably the most negative campaign of the modern era in Arkansas, Frank White was the winner. With the third congressional district of northwest Arkansas providing the Republican with a 60 percent majority, Clinton was lucky that his overall defeat was only 435,684 to 403,242. Although the Democrats carried such traditional strongholds as Crittenden, Lee, Mississippi, Phillips, Saline, Jefferson, and Pulaski Counties, the margins were usually slight, and they lost some counties that Democrats normally carried handily, such as Craighead, Jackson, Hot Spring, and even Garland County where Clinton grew up. Frank White was headed for the governor's mansion, and Bill Clinton entered a painful period of depression and self-analysis.

Frank White turned out to be much more adept at running for office than serving as governor. He got off to a rough start by proclaiming a few days after the voting that his election was "a victory for the Lord," a statement that drew a chorus of criticism and was to be typical of the verbal faux pas that trailed Frank White like beagles following a rabbit.

Since no one expected White to win the election, little thought had been given to putting together his legislative program. To complicate the situation further, the state faced a projected revenue shortfall of $80 million. Fortunately for the governor-elect, two Republican legislators were available to meet the challenge. State representative Preston Bynum of Benton County took over as head of a transition team and representative Carolyn Pollan of Fort Smith, a member of the powerful legislative council, assumed responsibility for compiling the governor's biennium budget recommendations. In the end, White's legislative program was, to use the words of Representative Bynum, "a very minute program."

Due to the expected revenue shortage, the governor-elect, at the suggestion of Representative Pollan, implemented a plan to restrict agency budgets to "continuing level minus five percent." This across-the-board approach meant that all state agencies suffered relatively equally. White did find money to set up a separate division of vocational-technical education within the huge Department of Education. Increases were also given to the Department of Corrections, reflecting White's promise to fight crime.

If car tags and Cubans dominated the 1980 campaign, then creation science and utility regulation were the hallmarks of the White administration. Nothing during the White tenure so divided the state as the question of creation science. Though Act 590 of 1981, which required schools to give "balanced treatment" to "creation science" and "evolution science," was not an administration bill, Governor White agreed to sign the legislation if it passed. With heavy pressure from the Moral Majority and other fundamentalist organizations, the Arkansas General Assembly passed the legislation by sizable majorities after very little public debate.

The sponsor of the bill, state senator James L. Holsted of North Little Rock, admitted that he did not consult with the Department of Education or the attorney general prior to introduction of the bill. In an interview published in the *Baltimore Sun,* Senator Holsted admitted that his own personal religious beliefs prompted his introduction of the bill: "we legislators have prejudices and beliefs that affect what legislation we introduce."

When the bill reached Governor White's desk, he signed it. Later, he commented that he acted without reading it. A firestorm of condemnation resulted from White's action. The governor tried to explain his position, saying that he promised to sign the bill if it got through the legislature. He correctly noted that it is impossible for any governor to read every bill he signs. His explanations did nothing to prevent George Fisher, editorial cartoonist for the *Arkansas Gazette,* from portraying White as a narrow-minded fundamentalist buffoon. His cartoon of White with a half-eaten banana in his hand did much to discredit the governor.

Eventually the Arkansas branch of the American Civil Liberties Union took the state to federal court over the matter. Governor White found himself supporting creation science along with the likes of television evangelist Pat Robertson and Ku Klux Klan leader Thom Robb. A man in a gorilla suit roamed the halls of the Federal Courthouse on the day the trial opened, further adding to the outlandish nature of the trial. Eventually Federal Judge William R. Overton, after conducting a lengthy trial that included testimony from such scientists as Harvard paleontologist Stephen Jay Gould, found Act 590 to be unconstitutional. The trial not only sullied Arkansas's reputation, it also embarrassed Governor White.

Utility regulation, the second great defining issue of the White administration, had been a hot topic in Arkansas for years. Governor White had a long association with the power companies, even serving for a time in the late 1970s as a member of the Board of Directors of Arkansas Missouri Power Company. On the very day of his inauguration Governor White fired three of the top leaders of the Arkansas Energy Department. Later, he abolished the Energy Department entirely, combining it with the Arkansas Industrial Development Commission.

As dramatic as these actions were, they paled when compared to the controversy generated by White's appointments to the Public Service Commission, the state agency charged with regulating the various utilities. Everyone knew that Frank White was pro-business; indeed, he campaigned on the slogan of running Arkansas like a business— or "bidness" as his detractors mockingly put it. Yet even the most conservative Republicans must have blanched when word leaked out during White's reelection campaign that he helped arrange meetings between an Arkansas Power and Light Company executive and three women whom he was considering appointing to the Public Service Commission (PSC). Though Governor White vigorously denied any wrongdoing, the public perception was that he had given AP&L veto power over his PSC appointment. That perception increased when voters were reminded that the PSC vacancy had occurred in the first place when Governor White's political ally state senator Joe Ford blocked the confirmation of Governor Clinton's appointment of Frank Newell to the PSC. White's ultimate PSC choice, Ms. Sandra Cherry, was one of the commissioners who signed a May 1981 order granting AP&L an unprecedented $104 million rate increase.

Even before the PSC appointment controversy erupted, White was well aware of his weakness in the area of utilities regulation. In November 1981 he called a special session of the legislature to consider utility reform. Though his detractors complained that White's efforts were halfhearted, he did secure passage of laws to prohibit utilities from imposing rate increases under bond. Also, the practice of "pancaking" was outlawed, thereby preventing utilities from filing additional rate increases before a pending increase could be considered.

Creation science and utility regulation were not, of course, the only issues to occupy the time of Governor White and his detractors. Not only did developments on the national level intrude on the state scene on more than one occasion, but White's personal style detracted from his administration. For example, in the spring of 1981 word leaked out thatWhite wanted to reshape the Governor's School, a summer school for gifted students held at Hendrix College in Conway. Led by the respected educator RobertW. Meriwether, the Governor's School had come under attack from religious extremists. Coupled with the creation science controversy, the attack on the Governor's School made White look caustic and narrow-minded. Like his predecessor, Frank White made many enemies during his first term. He even alienated many within his own Republican base. His appointment of former Democratic governor Orval Faubus to a high state position caused many "Rockefeller Republicans" to viewWhite as a turncoat. Faubus's appointment sulliedWhite's generally good record in appointing competent directors for major state agencies.

To achieve a second term, White had to vanquish again his old nemesis—Bill Clinton. After his defeat in 1980, Clinton endured a painful period of self-analysis. Traveling throughout the state, the former governor met with thousands of people; he asked questions, sought advice, made amends. And then he went on television to declare his candidacy for his old job, staring into the camera and promising that he would not try to "lead without listening."

The 1982 gubernatorial campaign was completely different from that of 1980. Clinton, utilizing the considerable skills of BetseyWright, an old friend from Texas, ran a flawless campaign. Governor White, who was best when campaigning as a scrappy outsider, had to run as an incumbent. Also, the nation was suffering from a severe recession with high unemployment, which the Democrats effectively blamed on Pres. Ronald Reagan and the Republican party.

The 1982 campaign also witnessed the transformation of Bill Clinton into an effective hardball politician.WheneverWhite unleashed an attack, Clinton responded in kind. For example, when Governor White attacked Clinton as a supporter of gun control, Clinton hit back by saturating the radio airwaves with his own counterattack in which he accusedWhite of trying to use sportsmen's fees to balance the state budget.

Another problem plaguingWhite was the public perception that he lacked vision, that he only stood up to oppose rather than to lead Arkansans toward specific goals. For example, White completely neglected the growing concern about education in the state, leaving that issue for Clinton to adopt as his own cause.

Governor White faced only token opposition in the 1982 Republican primary, which he won with 83 percent of the vote. The story in the November general election was far different. Clinton won the election with a comfortable margin of almost 55 percent, winning three of the four congressional districts. Clinton, who never tired of reminding African-American voters that Governor White had appointed Orval Faubus to a state position, garnered huge margins in the black precincts. Even white women abandoned the Republican nominee, leaving only older white men as the demographic base in the GOP camp.

Though Bill Clinton returned to the governorship in 1982, he was not the same governor he had been during his first term. Gone from his political life were the young and idealistic associates who had done battle during his first term. The new Bill Clinton was much more tentative and cautious. He came to terms with corporate Arkansas. Never again as governor would he raise his voice against clear-cutting timber companies or polluting corporate agriculture. Perhaps that transformation of Bill Clinton was Frank White's major impact on Arkansas politics.

JAMES GUY TUCKER JR.

1993–

JAMES "JIM" GUY TUCKER JR. (June 13, 1943–) was born in Oklahoma City, Oklahoma, to James Guy and Willie Maude (White) Tucker. His family moved to Little Rock where Jim Guy was educated in the public schools. After graduating from Harvard with a B.A. in government in 1964, he enrolled in the University of Arkansas Law School. Graduating with a J.D. degree in 1968, he was admitted to the Arkansas bar later that same year. An officer in the U.S. Marine Corps Reserves, he became a civilian war correspondent in South Vietnam during 1965 and again during 1967. He wrote about his experiences in *Arkansas Men At War,* which was published in 1968.

Tucker became an associate attorney with the Little Rock firm of Rose, Barron, Nash, Williamson, Carroll, and Clay from 1968 to 1970. He began his career in public service in 1970 when he became the prosecuting attorney for the Sixth Judicial District. Two years later he was elected to the first of two terms as attorney general of the state of Arkansas. He won election to the U.S. Congress in 1976 from the Second Congressional District. While in Congress he served on the House Ways and Means Committee, the Social Security Subcommittee, and the Speaker's Task Force on Welfare Reform. He ran for the U.S. Senate seat vacated by Sen. John McClellan in 1978 but lost to Gov. David Pryor.

After nearly a decade in public service, he returned to private practice in 1979 and became a partner in the Tucker and Stafford firm. From 1982 until October 1991, he was a senior partner in the Mitchell, Williams, Selig, and Tucker firm. His specialty was corporate and commercial litigation, and he wrote and published articles in *The Arkansas Banker* and *State Government Quarterly*. He became chairman of a cable and television management company in 1982 with interests across the United States and abroad. While his business acumen gained him prestige and wealth, Tucker devoted time to various civic activities including the Boy Scouts of America, the Girl Scouts of America, the Jaycees, and the American Legion. With a particular interest in health issues, he was State Fund Drive chairman of the Arkansas Association of Retarded Citizens and was a member of the National Advisory Committee of the Multiple Sclerosis Society.

Elected lieutenant governor of Arkansas in 1990, Tucker served in October 1991 as acting governor of the state during Gov. Bill Clinton's campaign for the presidency. Exemplifying a reputation for decisiveness that he established as a young prosecuting attorney and attorney general, acting Governor Tucker called a special session of the legislature to address a shortfall in Medicaid funding. Demonstrating certain political "courage" he raised taxes in order to meet the crisis. But during his first regular legislative session as governor, after Bill Clinton assumed the presidency in 1993, Tucker promoted a particularly conservative approach to spending. Rather than raise taxes again, he cut the budgets of agencies which could generate their own revenue to offset their reduced allocations from the state. For example, Parks and Tourism saw its budget cut and began charging entry fees to various state parks. By paring the budgets of agencies like Parks and Tourism, Tucker was able to funnel the revenues into primary and secondary public education.

Although Tucker courted the labor vote in his 1978 campaign for the Senate against Governor Pryor, he has not endeared himself to that particular interest group since that time. He coauthored a usury law for the Chamber of Commerce and for the bankers association, and as governor he sponsored changes in the Workers Compensation Law which left labor embittered. The new law made it more difficult for injured workers to be deemed eligible for compensation by tying benefits more directly to specific injuries on the job. Stress related injuries, such as carpel tunnel syndrome, might not be covered.

Early in his public career, Tucker expressed reservations about the death penalty, reservations he no longer professes. After assuming the governor's office in December 1992, he supported prison reforms including more stringent sentencing guidelines and indicated that he was willing to consider eliminating "good time" paroles. Ironically, it was over the pardoning of certain African-American convicts while Tucker was out of state that his governorship experienced its greatest controversy to date. As acting governor, senate president pro tempore Jerry Jewell extended executive clemency to three convicts and pardoned two others while Tucker was in Washington attending inaugural festivities for Bill Clinton in January 1993. Tucker returned to the state to face a public uproar. Expressing surprise at Jewell's actions, he called for limits on actions by acting governors, and a spate of legislative bills was introduced by various representatives to curb the power of acting governors and to limit executive clemency. Within ten days of returning to the state after the Jewell pardons, Tucker signed a clemency and pardon delay law which requires a thirty-day notice on all such actions.

Tucker's most dramatic act as governor, however, was to call a special session of the legislature in August 1994 to deal with the rising crime rate among juveniles. Addressing the concerns of children's rights activists who raised questions about the "punishment" rather than "prevention" focus of his juvenile crime package, the governor promised to address the issue of prevention in the January 1995 regular session of the legislature. In his special session which met 15–25 August, he sponsored bills designed to facilitate the apprehension and punishment of juvenile offenders. At the end of the session, he had signed thirty-one bills into law and several others awaited his signature. Among those passed by overwhelming majorities in both the house and the senate was a bill that allowed minors to waive the right to counsel without first consulting their parents. Other measures addressed the issue of the confidentiality of certain juvenile offenders, the seizure and forfeiture of firearms found in the unlawful possession of minors, and the removal of the $2,000 cap on the amount a juvenile might be required to pay as restitution. Another measure approved by the general assembly provided for an increase in the penalty for the unlawful possession of a firearm by a minor.

Although the senate judiciary committee amended certain measures because of concerns over constitutionality (for example, a measure that established it as a crime to solicit membership to a gang), the legislature enthusiastically supported Tucker's package. Republicans generally gave high praise to the governor, except for Sheffield Nelson, the Republican candidate for governor, whom Tucker defeated in the November election by 60 percent of the vote (carrying seventy-three of seventy-five counties). Nelson charged that Tucker had privately confided to certain legislators that the package would require a $100 million tax increase. Tucker had indicated that the crime measures would have a $18.5 million price tag "which would come from unspent revenues and the state's general improvement fund."

While the special session was ostensibly called to focus on juvenile crime, adult crime was also addressed. For example, while one measure authorized the expansion of facilities for juveniles, a similar bill called for an expansion of adult facilities. Meanwhile, law enforcement officials were gratified by the passage of a bill which authorized the purchase of an expensive automated finger-printing system to be used for adult as well as juvenile offenders. In the final analysis, Tucker laid undisputed claim to the governorship and emerged from the Clinton shadow with the success of the special session of the legislature on juvenile crime.

Jim Guy Tucker married Betty Allen on 8 November 1975 and they have four children and one grandchild. The Tuckers are members of the Second Presbyterian Church in Little Rock where both teach Sunday school.

ACTING GOVERNORS OF ARKANSAS
1836–1994

Official state records listing the names of individuals who served as acting governor of Arkansas and indicating precisely the dates of such service apparently do not exist. Although proclamations filed with the Secretary of State's office are helpful, they by no means provide a comprehensive list of acting governors. But insofar as can be ascertained from research in a variety of primary and secondary sources, especially newspapers, the acting governors whose biographical sketches appear here constitute a complete list of those who have served in that capacity between 1836 and 1994.

Because of the extraordinary circumstances under which certain individuals laid claim to the governorship, it has sometimes been difficult to determine those who should be included in a list of acting governors. For example, in 1908 Allen H. Hamiter, speaker of the house, had himself sworn in as governor while acting Gov. Xenophon Overton Pindall was attending a conference in Washington, D.C. Because Hamiter occupied the governor's office and functioned as the state's chief executive for five days, he is generally considered an acting governor and his biographical sketch appears here. On the other hand, Volney Voltaire Smith, who proclaimed himself governor in 1874 but who never actually occupied the office, is not identified as one of the acting governors. A native of Ohio who migrated to Arkansas shortly after the end of the Civil War, Smith became politically allied with Powell Clayton and was elected lieutenant governor in 1872 on the Republican ticket with Elisha Baxter for a four-year term. The new constitution of 1874 not only paved the way for the return to power of the Democrats and eliminated the office of lieutenant governor but also had the effect of reducing both Smith's and Baxter's terms from four to two years. A few days after the inauguration of Augustus Hill Garland, a Democrat, as governor on 12 November 1874, Smith staged what some called a coup d'état by issuing a proclamation that asserted

his claims to the governorship. The document contended that the proceedings of the convention that drafted the constitution of 1874 were
illegal and that since Baxter had vacated the office, he, Smith, as the
lieutenant governor was legally entitled to it. When Governor Garland
ordered his arrest, Smith quickly left the state. After receiving appointment to a consular post in the Caribbean from Pres. U. S. Grant, he
largely disappeared from public view. Smith spent the last several
months of his life in the Arkansas Lunatic Asylum where he died on
17 April 1897.

Some sources also suggest that James C. Tappan of Helena, a
former Confederate general who was speaker of the house during
the regular (11 January–11 March) and special (26 April–16 June)
legislative sessions of 1897, was for a time acting governor, but evidence to support that contention is lacking. The confusion apparently stems from the fact that at the close of the regular session in
1897 the senate failed to elect a president pro tempore so that pre-
sumably Tappan would have been acting governor if the occasion
had arisen between the end of the regular session in March 1897 and
the election of Jerry C. South as president of the senate on 16 June
1897. But a thorough search of the press as well as of other relevant
sources failed to reveal any reference to Tappan as acting governor.

When Gov. John E. Martineau resigned on 4 March 1928 to accept
appointment as a federal judge, Harvey Parnell succeeded to the governorship. Parnell had been elected lieutenant governor in 1926 under
a constitutional amendment voted on in 1914 and declared in force by
the courts a dozen years later. Since Parnell was elected governor in
1928 and reelected in 1930, he is the subject of a full-length essay
included earlier in this volume and does not appear in the appendix
devoted to acting governors. For similar reasons sketches of Junius
Marion Futrell and James Guy Tucker do not appear in this appendix.

ACTING GOVERNORS OF ARKANSAS, 1836–1994

SAMUEL CALHOUN ROANE (27 February 1793–8 December 1852),
    attorney and planter, was the son of Hugh and Hannah
    (Calhoun) Roane. Born in Mecklenburg County, North Carolina,
    he grew up in Tennessee where members of his family held
    important political offices. He was an admirer of Andrew Jackson
    and the two men were reputedly friends. Following service in the
    War of 1812, Roane moved to Kentucky where he married Ann

Hobbs. Three years after her death in 1815, he migrated to the Arkansas Territory, settling first at Arkansas Post and later at Little Rock. Active in political and civic affairs from the beginning of his residence in Arkansas, he served as president of the territorial legislative council in 1821 and 1823. Beginning in 1820, he served for more than fifteen years as U.S. attorney in the territory except for a brief tenure (1827–1828) as circuit judge. Following his marriage to Julia Embree of Jefferson County in 1825, he resided on a large plantation near Pine Bluff. A member of the convention that drafted the Arkansas constitution of 1836, Roane was elected to the state senate that year. As the president of that body, he became the first acting governor of Arkansas, serving from May until September 1838, during the illness of Gov. James Sevier Conway. For many years thereafter he remained a power in state politics and helped his younger brother, John Selden Roane, win election as governor in 1849. He died on his Jefferson County plantation at the age of sixty.

SAMUEL ADAMS (5 June 1805–27 February 1850), planter, was the son of Sylvester and Fanny (Smith) Adams. Born in Halifax County, Virginia, he grew up in Humphreys County, Tennessee, where his parents settled in 1810. He moved to Arkansas in 1835 and settled in what became Johnson County. He acquired considerable wealth in land and slaves and for a time headed a bank in Van Buren that went defunct in the 1840s. A member of the state's first general assembly in 1836 as a representative from Johnson County, he was reelected to that post two years later. In 1840 he went to the state senate where he served two terms. Elected president pro tempore of the senate in the session of 1843, he became acting governor (from 29 April to November 1844) because of Gov. Archibald Yell's resignation. In 1844 he was elected state treasurer, a position that he retained until his retirement in January 1850. Adams died on his plantation in Saline County a month later.

JOHN WILLIAMSON (14 April 1786–25 June 1861), farmer, was born and reared in Tennessee. He moved to Arkansas about 1830 and settled near present-day Russellville in Pope County. He acquired considerable property and became one of the county's most prominent citizens. A devout member of the Cumberland Presbyterian Church, he built a church campground on the

banks of Shiloh Creek shortly after settling in Pope County.
Elected to the territorial legislative council in 1833 and 1835, he
served as president of that body in 1833. He represented Pope
and Johnson Counties in the first state senate in 1836 and
remained a member of that body through the session of 1851. As
president pro tempore of the senate, he was acting governor from
9 April to 7 May 1846 in the absence of Gov. Thomas Stevenson
Drew. Williamson died at his residence in Pope County.

RICHARD C. BYRD (1805–1 June 1854), planter and banker, was born
in Alabama. Migrating to Arkansas, he settled first in Little Rock
where he became active in territorial politics. He served as auditor of the territory (1829–1831) and as representative from
Pulaski County in the lower house of the territorial general
assembly of 1833. He was elected to the same post in the state's
first legislature in 1836. Chosen a director of the Bank of
Arkansas in that year, he figured prominently in the sale of state
bonds. From 1839 through 1843 Byrd represented Pulaski
County in the state senate. In 1844 he ran unsuccessfully for governor as an independent Democrat. Moving to Jefferson County
where he owned a large plantation and a mercantile business, he
was twice elected senator from Arkansas, Jefferson, and Desha
Counties (1846–1849). As president pro tempore of the senate,
he became acting governor on the resignation of Governor Drew
and served in that capacity from 10 January to 19 April 1849.
Shortly afterward he met with "an unfortunate accident by which
he was rendered a cripple." Following a protracted illness, he died
on his Jefferson County plantation.

JOHN ROBINSON HAMPTON (1 April 1807–9 February 1880), printer
and planter, was the eldest son of George W. and Cornelia
Hampton. Born and reared in Charlotte, North Carolina, where
he learned the printer's trade, he moved to Tuscaloosa, Alabama,
as a young man. Early in the 1840s, he settled in Union County,
Arkansas, near the town of El Dorado and later moved to
Bradley County near Johnsville. An active Presbyterian layman,
Hampton entered politics shortly after his arrival in Arkansas and
was elected in 1846 to the state senate. Reelected to the senate in
1848, 1850, 1852, 1856, 1858, 1862, 1876, and 1878, he was twice
chosen president pro tempore (in 1850 and 1856) and served as
acting governor during the administrations of Govs. John Selden

Roane and Elias Nelson Conway. His longest tenure as acting governor was from 21 April to 14 September 1857 while Governor Conway was out of the state for reasons of health. A member of the constitutional convention of 1874, Hampton was senator from the Eighteenth District (Bradley and Union) at the time of his death.

THOMAS FLETCHER (15 May 1815–25 February 1880), attorney and planter, was born in Nashville, Tennessee. Following graduation from the University of Nashville in 1836, he studied law with his father, Thomas H. Fletcher, and was admitted to the bar in 1838. He first settled in Natchez, Mississippi, where in 1843 he became probate judge. Two years later he was appointed U.S. marshal of the southern Mississippi district. In 1850 Fletcher moved to Desha County, Arkansas, and acquired a sizable plantation near Red Fork. Elected state senator from Desha, Jefferson, and Arkansas Counties in 1858, he served in that capacity through 1862 and again in 1864 in the Confederate general assembly. Chosen president of the senate on three occasions, he was acting governor 4–15 November 1862, following the resignation of Gov. Henry Massie Rector. After the Civil War, Fletcher practiced law in Little Rock, where he died.

OZRO A. HADLEY (10 June 1826–18 July 1915), farmer and merchant, was the son of Alvah Hadley, a respected farmer, whose ancestors were pioneers in western New York. Born at Cherry Creek, Chautauqua County, New York, he attended public schools and Fredonia Academy until the death of his father forced him to seek employment to support the family. In 1855 he migrated to Minnesota and settled near Rochester, where he engaged in farming. Appointed county auditor in 1859, he was elected to the post in the following year and reelected in 1862. Though reared a Whig, Hadley joined the Republican party shortly after it was organized. In 1865 he moved to Little Rock, Arkansas, where he established himself in the mercantile and commission business.

Closely allied with Powell Clayton, the Republican leader in post–Civil War Arkansas and labeled a "carpetbagger" by Democrats, he was active in the affairs of the Republican party and Union League throughout the tumultuous Reconstruction era. He was a delegate to the Republican National Conventions of 1872, 1876, and 1880. When a struggle developed within the state's Republican party between Clayton's forces, known as the Minstrels, and a faction led by Joseph Brooks that was called the Brindletails, Hadley remained loyal to Clayton and incurred the enmity of the Brooks faction. First elected to the state senate from the Tenth District (Pulaski and White Counties) in March 1868, he served two terms in the upper house where he functioned as a legislative spokesman for Clayton who was then governor. At the opening of the stormy session of the legislature in 1871, Lt. Gov. James M. Johnson, as president of the senate, recognized Brooks, the anti-Clayton leader, rather than Hadley, as the duly elected senator from the Tenth District. The senate later reversed this decision, and Hadley was seated, whereupon Governor Clayton, who had been elected to the U.S. Senate by the legislature of 1871, induced Johnson to become secretary of state, leaving the post of lieutenant governor (and president of the senate) vacant. The senate then chose Hadley as its president, which meant that, on Clayton's departure for Washington, Hadley became acting governor from 17 March 1871 until 6 January 1873. Such an arrangement, according to Democrats and anti-Clayton Republicans, allowed Senator Clayton "to direct affairs in Arkansas" from Washington. During Hadley's tenure in the governor's office partisan strife was "at white heat." Not the least of the problems that he confronted was the so-called Pope County War. In the view of less partisan observers, his "conservative course" in regard to the affair was largely responsible for preventing large-scale bloodshed.

Denied the Republican gubernatorial nomination in 1872, Hadley left office the following year and purchased a large farm in Lonoke County that he personally operated until his appointment as register of the U.S. Land Office in Little Rock in 1875. Two years later, on 6 June 1877, he became postmaster of Little Rock and was instrumental in bringing free mail delivery to the city in 1880. Retired from the postmastership two years later, he moved west and finally settled in Watrous, New Mexico, where he engaged in the cattle business. He died at the age of ninety at the home of his daughter in Los Angeles where he had resided since 1910.

BEN T. EMBRY (19 April 1820–26 January 1892), attorney and merchant, was the son of Samuel P. and Mary (Fowler) Embry. Born in Greene County, Kentucky, where he lived until he was twenty-eight years old, he attended Center College and graduated from St. Joseph College in 1837. After reading law with Judge Richard A. Buckner, he was an attorney for seven years in Greensburg and Murfreesboro, Kentucky. He moved to Memphis in 1848 and later in the same year settled in Des Arc, Arkansas, where he cleared swampland and engaged in farming. In 1850 he was elected to the state house of representatives from Prairie County. Three years later he moved to Pope County where he conducted extensive farming operations and ran a large store at Galla Rock. In 1861 Embry entered the Confederate army, rising to rank of colonel. When his unit, the Second Arkansas Cavalry, was reorganized after the battle of Corinth in 1862, he returned to Pope County, which he represented in the state senate of the Confederate general assembly in 1862 and 1864. From 1870 to 1874 he was a wholesale grocer in Little Rock, but in 1874 he returned to Pope County and established a mercantile business in the new town of Atkins. A Whig who became a Democrat, he was a delegate to the Democratic National Convention in 1880. Elected state senator two years later he was chosen president pro tempore of the senate in 1883 and served as acting governor (25–30 September 1883) during the absence of Gov. James Henderson Berry. Embry retired from business in 1880 and died in Atkins a dozen years later.

JOHN WILLIAM STAYTON (6 November 1835–6 November 1896), attorney, was the son of Thomas N. and Esther (Harns) Stayton. Born and educated in Helena, Arkansas, he studied law under Maj. Coleman Palmer and was admitted to the bar in 1857. He was for a time city recorder of Helena. In 1866 he moved to Jacksonport and engaged in the mercantile business until 1874 when he returned to the practice of law. He served as mayor of Jacksonport in 1868 and as county judge of Jackson County (1874–1878). First elected state senator in 1884, he was reelected two years later. In 1885 he was chosen president pro tempore of the senate. Late in April of that year while Gov. Simon P. Hughes was in New Orleans, he served briefly as acting governor. From 1885 until his death Stayton resided in Newport where he practiced law with his son.

DAVID EDWARD BARKER (8 July 1836–26 December 1914), planter, was the son of James and Mariah Louisa Grant (Simpson) Barker.

Born and educated in Carroll County, Tennessee, he migrated with his family to Drew County, Arkansas, in 1855 and settled at a place that became known as Barkada. The family prospered and acquired considerable property in land and slaves. At the outbreak of the Civil War, Barker joined the Third Arkansas Regiment. He served throughout the duration of the conflict and was wounded at the battle of Gettysburg. On returning to Drew County in 1865, he engaged in farming and the steam-mill business and became active in Democratic politics. Elected in 1878 to represent Drew County in the lower house of the general assembly, he was reelected to that office in 1880, 1882, and 1884. Elected to the state senate in 1886 and reelected two years later, he was chosen president pro tempore in 1887 and served briefly as acting governor in that year in the absence of Governor Hughes. Twice defeated in his bid for a seat in Congress, he shifted his allegiance from the Democratic to the Populist party. He served as president of the Arkansas State Farmers' Alliance in 1892–1893 and ran unsuccessfully for governor on the Populist ticket in 1894. Returning to the Democratic party in the late 1890s, he again represented Drew County in the state house of representatives in the sessions of 1905, 1907, and 1911. Following a stroke he died in the Confederate Home in Little Rock.

CHRISTOPHER COLUMBUS HAMBY (14 September 1851–31 January 1921), attorney, was the son of T. J. and Nancy Elizabeth (Byers) Hamby. Born and reared in Calhoun, Mississippi, he was a brakeman on the Illinois Central Railroad at the age of eighteen. He moved to Arkansas in 1872, settling first in Logan County where he attended high school for a single term. He taught school in Ouachita County in 1874. He read law and was admitted to the bar two years later. In 1878 he settled in Prescott where he practiced law. Widely known for his skill as a criminal lawyer, he entered politics and was twice elected to the state senate (1890 and 1892). Chosen president pro tempore of the senate in 1891, he served as acting governor for four months during the illness of Gov. James Philip Eagle in the summer of 1892. A strong advocate of education, Hamby was a member of the University of Arkansas Board of Trustees for a dozen years. Active in a variety of civic and fraternal organizations, he was one of the founders of the Citizens Bank of Prescott and served for a time as its president. He died in Prescott.

CLAY SLOAN (21 August 1861–14 February 1942), planter and banker, was the son of James F. and Bertha (Shaver) Sloan. Born and reared in Lawrence County, Arkansas, he graduated from Arkansas College in 1881. Twice elected county clerk of Lawrence County (1886 and 1888), he was a member of the lower house of the general assembly in 1891 and was a state senator in the legislative sessions of 1893 and 1895. Elected president pro tempore of the senate in 1893, he served as acting governor for thirty days in 1894 while Gov. William Meade Fishback was out of the state. From 1897 to 1901, he was state auditor, and for seventeen months (June 1911–October 1912) was commissioner of mines, manufactures, and agriculture. He also served for a time as a member of the state board of charities. An ardent prohibitionist and civic leader, he was for many years president of the First National Bank at Black Rock. Sloan died at his home in Strawberry.

JOSEPH C. PINNIX (23 September 1863–26 July 1942), attorney, was born in Caswell County, North Carolina. A graduate of Trinity College (Duke University), he settled in Murfreesboro, Pike County, Arkansas, in 1891, where he practiced law for a half century. He served one term (1893) in the lower house of the general assembly and four terms (1895, 1897, 1903, and 1905) in the senate. Elected president pro tempore of the senate in 1895, he served briefly as acting governor the following year. He was prosecuting attorney of the Ninth Circuit Court (1908–1912) and a member of the constitutional convention in 1917–1918. Pinnix organized the Pike County Bank in 1910 and served as its president until his death.

JERRY C. SOUTH (20 March 1867–24 September 1930), attorney, was the son of Samuel and Malvery (Jett) South who migrated from Kentucky to Arkansas. Born in Baxter County, Arkansas, he was a graduate of Kentucky Military Institute and attended the University of Louisville. After completing his law degree at the University of Virginia, he became an attorney in Mountain Home. In 1890, before he was twenty-four years old, he was elected to the lower house of the Arkansas legislature. After three terms in the house (1891, 1893, and 1895), he served two terms in the state senate (1897 and 1899). As president of the senate in 1897, he served briefly as acting governor during a visit to New Orleans by Gov. Daniel Webster Jones in September of that year.

Though captain of a volunteer infantry company during the Spanish-American War, his unit never left the United States. He was a delegate to every Democratic National Convention from 1896 through 1912. Following his tenure as chief clerk of the U.S. House of Representatives (1911–1915), he practiced law in Washington, D.C., where he died.

ROBERT L. LAWRENCE (1869–24 October 1904), attorney, was born in Saint Francis County, Arkansas, and grew up in Pope County where he resided for the remainder of his life. Educated at the University of Arkansas and Vanderbilt University law school, he entered politics as a Democrat and was elected circuit court clerk of Pope County in 1894. After serving in that capacity for four years, he won election in 1898 to the state senate and at the close of the legislative session of 1899 was chosen its president pro tempore. In this capacity, he was acting governor for the week ending 23 September 1899 during Governor Jones's absence in St. Louis. At the close of his second term in the senate in 1901, Lawrence declined renomination in order to run for prosecuting attorney of the Fifth Judicial District. He was completing his first term in that office at the time of his death.

MICHAEL PLEASANT HUDDLESTON (2 August 1872–3 January 1938), attorney, was the son of Rev. J. M. Huddleston, a Baptist minister. Born in Tennessee, he moved to Arkansas when he was seventeen years old and lived in Paragould for almost forty years. A graduate of the University of Arkansas School of Law at Little Rock, he was a well-known attorney who at one time was a law partner of Junius Marion Futrell. From 1893 to 1897 he was chief clerk in the U.S. Land Office in Little Rock. Elected to the senate in 1900 and reelected in 1902, he was chosen president pro tempore in 1901. In that capacity Huddleston served as acting governor on a half-dozen occasions, lasting from a few days to over a month, during Gov. Jeff Davis's absences from the state. So frequently was he called on to fill the governor's office that one newspaper suggested that he "take up permanent residence in the city of Little Rock." While acting governor in July 1901, Huddleston attracted considerable publicity by a rigid enforcement of the Wilson antigambling law that for a time closed down all "gambling dens" in Little Rock. Defeated by Thaddeus H. Caraway in 1908 for the position of prosecuting attorney of the

Second Judicial District, he was elected to that office four years later. In 1916 he entered the race for attorney general but later withdrew. Thereafter, he practiced law in Paragould.

OLIVER NEWTON KILLOUGH (18 February 1865–23 August 1926), attorney, was the son of John W. and Mary Eliza (Rooks) Killough. Born at White Hall, Poinsett County, Arkansas, he was educated at the University of Mississippi (1881–1885) and the University of Virginia School of Law (1888–1890). Settling in Cross County, he began the practice of law in Wynne where he resided for the remainder of his life. Elected as prosecuting attorney of the Second Judicial District in 1896, he served in that capacity for four years. He was a member of the lower house of the state legislature in 1901 and 1907 as the representative from Cross County. First elected to the state senate in 1902, he was reelected for a second term in 1904. Chosen president pro tempore of the senate in 1903, he served as acting governor on several occasions during the administration of Governor Davis. Killough was for many years prominently identified with the work of the St. Francis Levee Board on which he served for a time as president. He died at his residence in Wynne.

JOHN P. LEE (8 November 1868–30 March 1941), attorney and banker, was the son of John R. and Elizabeth (Greene) Lee. Born in Itawamba County, Mississippi, he was a graduate of the University of Mississippi and the Cumberland University law school. He began the practice of law in Clarendon where for thirty-five years he was active in civic and business affairs. He was for many years president and director of the Bank of Clarendon. Following two terms in the lower house of the state legislature as the representative from Monroe County (1897 and 1899), he was elected to the state senate in 1904 and reelected in 1906. Chosen president pro tempore of the senate in 1905, he served briefly as acting governor during the interim between the resignation of Governor Davis who went to the U.S. Senate and the inauguration of Gov. John Sebastian Little. For thirty-five years he was chairman of the school board in Clarendon.

JOHN ISSAC MOORE (7 February 1856–18 March 1937), attorney, was the son of Esom D. and Nancy Ann (Vineyard) Moore. Born in Lafayette County, Mississippi, and reared in Phillips County,

Arkansas, he graduated from the University of Arkansas in 1881 and studied law at Cumberland University. Admitted to the bar in 1882, he won election to the lower house of the Arkansas legislature in the same year and served a single term (1883). He was police chief of Helena (1890–1894) and Phillips County probate judge (1894–1900). He returned to the lower house of the legislature in 1901 and in 1903 was elected speaker. Elected to the state senate in 1904, he served four terms (1905, 1907, 1913, and 1915). As president of the senate, he served for four months (7 February–15 May 1907) as acting governor because of the illness of Governor Little. In 1909 he was appointed to a commission in charge of constructing a new state capitol. He was a member of the constitutional convention of 1917–1918. By the time of his death he had been a member of the Arkansas bar for over a half century.

XENOPHON OVERTON PINDALL (21 August 1873–2 January 1935), attorney, was the son of Lebbeus and Nora (Snell) Pindall. Born in Monroe County, Missouri, near Middle Grove, he grew up in Arkansas where his father and uncle were well-known attorneys. He attended Missouri Military Academy and Central College (Missouri) and received his law degree from the University of Arkansas in 1896. Shortly afterward, he began the practice of law with his cousin in Arkansas City in Desha County where he served as deputy prosecuting attorney. First elected to the state house of representatives in 1902, he was reelected two years later. In 1906 he was a candidate for attorney general of the state and claimed to have received "the largest popular vote ever balloted for that office but was defeated in a delegated convention." In 1906 he was elected to the state senate and at the close of the legislative session in May 1907 was chosen its president pro tempore. Governor Little, elected in 1906, was forced to resign his office less than a month after his inauguration on 18 January 1907 because of a physical and emotional breakdown. Senate president Moore served as acting governor from 11 February 1907 until 15 May 1907, when Pindall, the newly chosen president of the senate, became acting governor. For a year and seven months, he functioned in this capacity except for five days in 1908 (9–14 May) when Speaker of the House Allen H. Hamiter had himself sworn in as acting governor during Pindall's absence from the state capital. When Pindall's term as president of the senate expired on January 1909, his successor, Jesse M. Martin of Pope County, was acting governor for three days until the inauguration of Gov. George Washington Donaghey. Of his accomplishments as acting governor, Pindall manifested special pride in the enactment of a pure food and drug law, the imposition of a franchise tax on foreign corporations, and the passage of a measure designed to prevent price discrimination. At the expiration of his term in 1909, he returned to the practice of law in Little Rock and acquired a statewide reputation as a criminal lawyer. He was a popular lecturer and civic leader until his death.

ALLEN H. HAMITER (27 November 1867–9 February 1933), attorney and businessman, was the son of John Hodges and Florence (Lafayette) Hamiter. Born in Walnut Hill, Lafayette County, Arkansas, he was educated at Hendrix College. Admitted to the bar in 1895, he established a lucrative practice in Lewisville where he also engaged in insurance and real estate. He served as mayor of Lewisville and was appointed to fill the unexpired term (1900–1902) of A. S. Lester as treasurer of Lafayette County. First elected to the lower house of the general assembly in 1904, he served two terms and was chosen speaker of the house in the session of 1907. In the latter capacity, he took the occasion of acting governor Pindall's absence from Little Rock to have himself sworn in as acting governor on 9 May 1908. The following day Hamiter issued a call for a special session of the legislature to consider what he termed pressing needs regarding the new capitol building and changes in the revenue laws. When Pindall, who was in Washington to attend Theodore Roosevelt's National Conservation Congress, returned to Little Rock on 14 May 1908, Hamiter abandoned the governor's office. Pindall revoked the call for a special legislative session. Hamiter returned to Lewisville where he spent the remainder of his life.

JESSE M. MARTIN (1 March 1877–22 January 1915), attorney, was the son of Jasper J. and Martha (Johnson) Martin. Born in London, Arkansas, he was educated at Hendrix College and the University of Arkansas. After four years (1902–1906) as circuit court clerk of Pope County, he began the practice of law in the firm of Brooks, Hays, and Martin. He served two terms (1907 and 1909) in the state senate. Chosen president of the senate at the beginning of his second term, he served as acting governor of Arkansas

(11–14 January 1909) from the expiration of the term of acting governor Pindall until the inauguration of Governor Donaghey. Elected judge of the Fifth Circuit Court in 1914, Martin died the following year in Mineral Springs, Texas, where he had gone for treatment of Bright's disease.

JAMES T. ROBERTSON (12 October 1857–28 March 1935), businessman, was the son of James Robertson of Scotland and Ann Lewis (Dale) Robertson. Born in Phillips County, he grew up in Lee County where he attended public schools. He served three terms as mayor of Marianna and was a delegate to the Democratic National Convention in 1908. Elected to the state senate in the same year, he was chosen president pro tempore of the senate in 1909 and served briefly as acting governor during the administration of Governor Donaghey. During his second term as state senator in 1911, he co-sponsored a bill (Robertson-Hardage) providing the "grandfather clause as a requisite for suffrage." After 1911 he devoted his attention primarily to his business affairs.

WILLIAM CHAMP RODGERS (15 October 1863–15 December 1961), attorney, was born in Grand Saline, Texas, where his father was head of the Confederate salt works. He grew up in West Point, White County, Arkansas, where his family settled in 1865. He moved to Nashville, Howard County, Arkansas, in 1886 and was admitted to the bar the following year. A charter member of the Arkansas Bar Association, he was for many years a lecturer in the Arkansas law school in Little Rock and wrote a widely used textbook on domestic relations. After serving as mayor of Nashville, he was elected to the state senate in 1910 and served two terms. Chosen president pro tempore of the senate in 1911, he functioned briefly as acting governor in Governor Donaghey's absence. He practiced law in Nashville where he died in a nursing home at the age of ninety-eight.

WILLIAM KAVANAUGH OLDHAM (29 May 1865–6 May 1938), planter, was the son of William K. and Catherine (Brown) Oldham. Born in Richmond, Kentucky, he attended Central University in that city and settled in Pettus, Lonoke County, Arkansas, in 1885. A cotton planter and civic leader, he was a member of the lower house of the Arkansas General Assembly in 1907 and served in the upper house in 1911 and 1913. He was chosen president of the senate in 1913. When Gov. Joseph Taylor Robinson resigned his office to become U.S. senator, Oldham claimed that he, rather than Futrell who had been chosen president of the senate at the close of the legislative session of 1913, should become acting governor. Both Oldham and Futrell functioned for a time as acting governor. The state supreme court ultimately ruled in Futrell's favor. A prominent Baptist and a trustee of Ouachita College, Oldham was also a member of the Arkansas Cotton Growers Cooperative Marketing Association and was chairman of the Cotton Reduction Commission. He died at his home in Pettus.

ROBERT LEE MAY BAILEY (7 August 1892–23 December 1957), attorney, the son of John Marshall and Mollie (French) Bailey, was born in Hindman, Kentucky, and educated in the grade school of Hindman. When he was sixteen years old, his family moved to Russellville, Arkansas. Bailey attended Kentucky Wesleyan College and the University of Michigan Law School. Like his father, he became a lawyer and began his practice in Russellville where he served as city attorney beginning in 1919. Elected to the Arkansas Senate in 1922 on the Democratic ticket and reelected two years later, he was selected president pro tempore in 1925. In that position he served as acting governor on at least one occasion. Again chosen to represent Johnson and Pope Counties in the state senate in 1932, he was elected lieutenant governor four years later and reelected in 1938. Bailey apparently also served on occasion as acting governor between 1937 and 1941.

WILLIAM LEE CAZORT (1888–6 October 1969), attorney, was the son of James R. and Belle (Garner) Cazort. Born at Lamar, Johnson County, Arkansas, he attended Hendrix College and the University of Arkansas and obtained his law degree from Washington and Lee University. He served two terms in the lower house of the Arkansas General Assembly (1915 and 1917) and was house speaker in 1917. Elected to the state senate in 1918 and reelected two years later, he was chosen president of that body in the session of 1921. An "avowed Klansman," he had the endorsement of the Ku Klux Klan in his unsuccessful bid to win the Democratic gubernatorial nomination in 1924. He was elected lieutenant governor in 1928. He did not seek reelection in

1930 but was elected lieutenant governor again in 1932 and 1934. In June 1933 he served briefly as acting governor. Appointed federal referee in bankruptcy in 1937, he remained in federal service until his retirement in 1964.

LAWRENCE ELERY WILSON (7 July 1884–23 June 1946), teacher and businessman, the son of L. T. and Mattie (Booth) Wilson, was born in Village, Columbia County, Arkansas. A graduate of the local schools and Southwestern Academy in Magnolia, Arkansas, he taught school for several years in Columbia County prior to going into the lumber business, which he pursued for eight years. In 1917 he moved to Camden, Arkansas, in Ouachita County where he was associated with Watts Brothers, a mercantile establishment. Active in Democratic politics and various fraternal orders, Wilson was elected circuit and chancery clerk of Ouachita County in 1922. After four years in this office, he was elected to the lower house of the Arkansas legislature, a position that he held until 1929. Elected lieutenant governor in 1930, he served a single two-year term in that office and was acting governor on several occasions.

JAMES LAVESQUE SHAVER (17 May 1902–1 August 1985), attorney, the son of W. W. and Irene (Morgan) Shaver, was born in Vanndale, Cross County, Arkansas, but grew up in nearby Wynne. Following graduation from Wynne High School, he attended Hendrix College in Conway, Arkansas, and received his law degree from Washington and Lee University in Virginia in 1921. Admitted to the bar in Arkansas in 1923, he entered politics as a Democrat and was elected to the state house of representatives from Cross County in 1924. Reelected twice he served in the lower house in the sessions of 1925, 1927, and 1929, and later served two terms in the state senate. In addition to being legal counsel for the St. Francis Levee Board, he was legislative secretary for Govs. Homer Adkins and Orval E. Faubus. First elected lieutenant governor in 1942, he occupied that office for two terms. He was "called upon a number of times to serve as acting governor." He maintained a law practice in Wynne until his death.

NATHAN GREEN GORDON (4 September 1916–), attorney, the son of Edward and Ada Ruth (Bearden) Gordon, was born in Morrilton, Arkansas. He attended the city's public schools, Columbia

Military Academy in Columbia, Tennessee, and Arkansas Poly-
technic College in Russellville, Arkansas. After receiving his law
degree from the University of Arkansas at Fayetteville in 1939, he
began practicing law in Morrilton. In May 1941 he entered the
Naval Air Corps; he later qualified as a navy pilot and did more
than two years of service in the Southwest Pacific theater in
World War II. The pilot of a fighter plane named the Arkansas
Traveler in the Black Cat Squadron, Gordon received numerous
citations for gallantry in action, including the Congressional
Medal of Honor and the Distinguished Flying Cross. Returning
to Morrilton after the war, he entered politics as a Democrat and
was elected lieutenant governor of Arkansas in 1946. Reelected
nine times, Gordon served in that office from January 1947
to January 1967 during the administrations of four governors.
During his twenty years as lieutenant governor, he reputedly
functioned as acting governor more often than any other individual in Arkansas history.

MAURICE L. BRITT (30 June 1919–), manufacturer, the son of Maurice
Lee and Virgie (Oliver) Britt, was born in Carlisle, Arkansas, and
grew up in Lonoke. An outstanding athlete in high school, he
attended the University of Arkansas on an athletic scholarship.
His nickname, "Footsie," derived from his size thirteen foot.
Following graduation from the university in 1941, he briefly
played professional football with the Detroit Lions. Called into
military service in December 1941, he was seriously wounded in
February 1944 and suffered the loss of his right arm. His numerous military honors and decorations, including the Distinguished
Service Cross and the Congressional Medal of Honor, testified
to his distinguished service record. Retired from active duty on
31 December 1944, Britt entered the University of Arkansas law
school where he was a student in 1945 and 1946. He abandoned
law school to become associated with a furniture manufacturing
company in Fort Smith. In 1963 he moved to Little Rock where
he organized and headed the Beautyguard Manufacturing
Company, which specialized in aluminum building products.
Three years later Britt left the Democratic party and waged a
successful campaign for the office of lieutenant governor on the
Republican ticket. Reelected in 1968, he served as lieutenant governor during the tenure of Republican Gov. Winthrop Rockefeller. Although Britt was acting governor on several occasions, he

did "not keep a record of the dates" in which he served in such a capacity. Deciding not to run for reelection in 1970, he acted as Rockefeller's campaign manager in his unsuccessful bid for a third term in that year. Appointed district director of the Small Business Administration, Britt thereafter continued to be involved in a wide variety of civic and charitable causes.

BOB COWLEY RILEY (18 September 1924–16 February 1994), educator, the son of Columbus A. and Winnie (Craig) Riley, was born in Little Rock, Arkansas. Educated in the city's public schools and at the University of Arkansas (B.A., 1950; M.A., 1951; Ed.D., 1957), he was briefly in the insurance business prior to embarking on a career in college teaching, first at Little Rock University (1951, 1953–1955) and then at Ouachita Baptist University. A veteran of World War II, active in political, educational, and civic affairs, he entered politics as a Democrat and was elected to the state house of representatives from Pulaski County in 1946 and was reelected in 1948. A member of the city council of Arkadelphia (1960–1966), he served as the city's mayor in 1966–1967. Elected lieutenant governor in 1970 and reelected in 1972, he was defeated in his effort to win the Democratic gubernatorial nomination in 1974. As lieutenant governor, Riley served as acting governor in the interim (2–14 January 1975) between the resignation of Gov. Dale Leon Bumpers who entered the U.S. Senate and the inauguration of the new governor, David Hampton Pryor. Returning to Ouachita Baptist University on expiration of his term, he resided in Arkadelphia until his death.

JOE EDWARD PURCELL (29 July 1923–), attorney, is the son of Edward L. and Lynelle M. (Cunningham) Purcell. Born in Warren, Bradley County, Arkansas, he graduated from Little Rock Junior College. Following service in the U.S. Army during World War II, he entered law school at the University of Arkansas and graduated in 1952. In that year he began the practice of law in Benton, Saline County, which has been his legal residence ever since. Beginning in 1955 he served for four years as city attorney of Benton. In 1959 he became municipal judge, a post that he held until 1966 when he was elected attorney general of Arkansas on the Democratic ticket. He was reelected to that post in 1968. Two years later he was an unsuccessful candidate for the Democratic nomination for governor. First elected lieutenant governor in 1974, he was reelected to the office in 1976 and 1978. Purcell served as acting governor from 3 January when Governor Pryor resigned in order to take his seat in the U.S. Senate until 9 January 1979 when Gov. Bill Clinton was inaugurated. Actively involved in a variety of civic affairs, Purcell did not seek reelection as lieutenant governor in 1980.

WINSTON BRYANT (3 October 1938–), attorney, was born in Donaldson, Hot Spring County, Arkansas. After graduating from Ouachita Baptist University, he earned a law degree at the University of Arkansas at Fayetteville and a master of law degree at George Washington University. A practicing attorney since 1963, he served in the U.S. infantry and later as assistant U.S. attorney for the eastern district of Arkansas. Following his tenure as legislative assistant to U.S. Sen. John L. McClellan (1968–1971), he resumed the practice of law in Malvern, Arkansas, in 1971 and was appointed deputy prosecuting attorney of Hot Spring County in the same year. In 1972 he was elected on the Democratic ticket to the Arkansas House of Representatives from Thirty-sixth District and reelected two years later. In 1976 he won election as secretary of state and served in that office until 1981. Elected lieutenant governor in 1980, he remained in that position for a decade (1981–1991). During his tenure as lieutenant governor, he served on several occasions as acting governor and a term as chairman of the National Conference of Lieutenant Governors. Elected the state's attorney general in 1990, he continues to occupy that office.

NICK WILSON (12 March 1942–), attorney and businessman, was born in Monette, Arkansas. After graduation from high school in Pocahontas, Arkansas, he received his undergraduate education at Arkansas State University and his law degree from the University of Arkansas at Fayetteville. Elected on the Democratic ticket to the Arkansas Senate in 1970 from the Fifteenth District, he has occupied that position since 1971 and was reelected in 1994. A member of many important senate committees, Wilson served periodically as acting governor during 1987–1988 in the absence of both the governor and lieutenant governor as a result of his position as president pro tempore of the senate. As acting governor, he on occasion sparked controversy by making appointments. He appointed the members of the Arkansas Health

Services Commission, a member to the board of trustees of Arkansas Tech University, and a member to the Arkansas State University board of trustees. His most controversial action was the transfer of Gov. Bill Clinton's chief of staff, Betsey Wright, to the staff of the Arkansas Transportation Commission in April 1988.

JERRY DONAL JEWELL (30 September 1930–), dentist, was born in Chatfield, Arkansas, and attended public school in West Memphis, Arkansas. After obtaining a bachelor's degree in chemistry from Arkansas A.M.&N. College in Pine Bluff, Arkansas, he attended the School of Dentistry of Meharry Medical College in Nashville, Tennessee. Awarded the D.D.S. degree, Dr. Jewell settled in Little Rock where he practiced his profession and was active in civic affairs, especially through his role in the National Association for the Advancement of Colored People. The first African American to serve on the Little Rock Public Service Commission, he also became the first African American since the 1890s to serve as a member of the Arkansas General Assembly. Elected to the senate in 1972, he remained in that position for two dozen years, being defeated in the Democratic primary in 1994 by another African American, representative Bill Walker. As president pro tempore of the state senate, he served as acting governor for four days in January 1993 when Lt. Gov. Jim Guy Tucker, who succeeded to the governorship after Gov. Bill Clinton's election to the presidency of the United States, was in Washington for Clinton's inauguration as president. As acting governor, Jewell organized an economic development group and sparked a heated controversy by granting executive clemency to three individuals, one convicted of cocaine possession. He also pardoned two other prisoners during his tenure as acting governor.

L. L. "DOC" BRYAN (31 January 1920–), businessman, was born in Coal Hill, Arkansas. A World War II veteran and a businessman in Russellville, he served as director of industry of the Arkansas Poultry Federation for some years. Elected to the lower house of the general assembly from Pope County in 1966, he has remained a member of the legislature to the present. In January 1993 while Bryan was speaker of the house, he was acting governor for about twenty-four hours when Gov. Jim Guy Tucker was in Washington attending the inauguration of President-elect Bill Clinton and senate president pro tempore Jerry Jewell had to make a trip out of state. Senator Jewell turned the governorship over to House speaker Bryan who occupied the office during 20–21 January. Bryan's most notable action as acting governor was an appointment he made to the state's Livestock and Poultry Commission.

MIKE HUCKABEE (24 August 1955–), minister, was born in Hope, Hempstead County, Arkansas. An ordained Baptist minister who occupied the pulpit of Beech Street Baptist Church in Texarkana, Arkansas, he served as president of the Arkansas Baptist State Convention in 1989 and 1990. A Republican, Huckabee challenged veteran U.S. Sen. Dale Bumpers in the election of 1992. Although Bumpers won reelection, Huckabee polled about 40 percent of the vote. A special election was called in 1993 to choose a lieutenant governor because Lt. Gov. Jim Guy Tucker had assumed the office of a governor after Gov. Bill Clinton's election to the presidency of the United States. Nominated for lieutenant governor by the Republican party, Huckabee defeated the Democratic nominee. As lieutenant governor he has served as acting governor on several occasions. On one such occasion he proclaimed a "Christian Heritage Week" which elicited both praise and criticism from residents of the state.

BIBLIOGRAPHY

GENERAL SOURCES

Several general secondary sources have proved to be very valuable for background information on Arkansas history. Many contain information on the governors' lives as well as on their times. These books apply to so many of the governors and acting governors that we extract them here rather than continually repeat them throughout the bibliography.

The most useful general works on Arkansas history and politics are John Hallum, *Biographical and Pictorial History of Arkansas* (Albany, 1887); Fay Hempstead, *Historical Review of Arkansas: Its Commerce, Industry, and Modern Affairs*, 3 vols. (Chicago, 1911), and *A Pictorial History of Arkansas from the Earliest Times to the Year 1890* (St. Louis, 1890); Dallas T. Herndon, *Centennial History of Arkansas*, 3 vols. (Chicago and Little Rock, 1922); Dallas T. Herndon, ed., *Annals of Arkansas, 1947*, 4 vols. (Hopkinsville, Ky., c. 1947); O. E. McKnight and Boyd W. Johnson, *The Arkansas Story* (Oklahoma City, 1955); John H. Reynolds, *Makers of Arkansas History* (Little Rock, 1918); Josiah H. Shinn, *Pioneers and Makers of Arkansas* (Washington, D.C., 1908); William S. Speer, ed., *The Encyclopedia of the New West* (Marshall, Tex., 1881); David Y. Thomas, *Arkansas and Its People: A History, 1541–1930* (New York, 1930); Diane D. Blair, *Arkansas Politics and Government: Do the People Rule?* (Lincoln, Neb., 1988); Marvin E. DeBoer, ed., *Dreams of Power and the Power of Dreams: Inaugural Addresses of the Governors of Arkansas* (Fayetteville, 1988); and Richard L. Niswonger, *Arkansas Democratic Politics, 1896–1920* (Fayetteville, 1990).

General biograpical sources that contain sketches of many of the governors' lives are *Appleton's Cyclopedia of American Biography* (New York, 1894); *Encyclopedia of American Biography* (New York, 1934, 1939); Allen Johnson and Dumas Malone, eds., *Dictionary of American Biography* (New York, 1927, 1930, 1936); and *The National Cyclopedia of American Biography* (New York, 1909, 1927, 1930).

In addition to these reference works, consult the more specific primary and secondary sources given on the following pages under each governor's or acting governor's name.

GOVERNORS OF ARKANSAS, 1836–1994

James Sevier Conway

Apparently the state's first governor left no collection of personal or public papers. For a more detailed analysis of Conway's record as governor, see D. A. Stokes, "Public Affairs in Arkansas, 1836–1850" (Ph.D. diss., University of Texas, 1966). Some references to Conway's activities as land surveyor are included in Lonnie J. White, *Politics on the Southwestern Frontier, 1819–1836* (Memphis, 1964).

Articles that provide insights into individual aspects of Conway's career include W. David Baird, "Arkansas' Choctaw Boundary Survey: A Study of Justice Delayed," *Arkansas Historical Quarterly* 27 (Autumn 1969): 203–22; Michael Dougan, "A Look at the 'Family' in Arkansas Politics, 1856–1865," *Arkansas Historical Quarterly* 29 (Summer 1970): 99–111; Jack B. Scroggs, "Arkansas Statehood: A Study in State and National Political Schism," *Arkansas Historical Quarterly* 20 (Autumn 1961): 227–44.

Newspaper accounts of Conway's activities include the *Arkansas Gazette*, 17 May, 5 June, and 5 July 1936; the *Texarkana Gazette*, 27 May 1936; and the *Lafayette County Democrat*, 26 July 1979.

Archibald Yell

A collection of Archibald Yell Papers exists in miscellaneous manuscripts, Library of Congress, Washington, D.C. Among the most valuable treatments of Yell's career is Melinda Meek, "The Life of Archibald Yell," *Arkansas Historical Quarterly* 26 (1967): 11–24, 162–84, 226–43. Significant information on Yell is also found in Margaret Ross, *The Arkansas Gazette: The Early Years, 1819–1866* (Little Rock, 1969); and Clarence Edwin Carter, ed., *The Territorial Papers of the United States, the Territory of Arkansas*, vol. 21 (Washington, D.C., 1954). Also of significance are "A Message of Archibald Yell to His Constituents, April 5, 1838," *Arkansas Historical Quarterly* 3 (Winter 1944): 373–82; Gene W. Boyett, "A Letter from Archibald Yell to Henry A. Wise, July 12, 1841," *Arkansas Historical Quarterly* 32 (Winter 1973): 337–41; Walter L. Brown, "The Mexican War Experience of Albert Pike and the 'Mounted Devils' of Arkansas," *Arkansas Historical Quarterly* 12 (Winter 1973): 301–15.

Thomas Stevenson Drew

Drew's personal papers were destroyed at Dardenelle, Arkansas, during the Civil War. Extant primary sources relating to his career are mainly letters published in contemporary newspapers, official public documents, and a few scattered papers in several collections at the Arkansas History Commission, Little Rock. The principal secondary sources are Lawrence Dalton, "Thomas Stevenson Drew of Arkansas," *Arkansas Gazette*, 18 April 1948, p. 13B;

Margaret Ross, *The Arkansas Gazette: The Early Years, 1819–1866* (Little Rock, 1969); and Margaret Ross, "Thomas S. Drew Became Fourth [*sic*] Governor of State, But Resigned in Second Term," *Arkansas Gazette,* 26 May 1968, p. 6B.

John Selden Roane

Few primary sources relating to Roane's career exist. If any personal papers survived his death, they were probably lost in a turn-of-the-century fire that destroyed his widow's home in Tulip, Arkansas. Extant primary sources are mainly letters published in contemporary newspapers, official documents, and a few scattered letters in several collections at the Arkansas History Commission, Little Rock. Among the most useful works in providing biographical data on Roane are Maurice Garland Fulton, ed., *Diary & Letters of Josiah Gregg: Southwestern Enterprises, 1840–1847* (Norman, 1941); and Dewey A. Stokes, "Public Affairs in Arkansas, 1836–1850," (Ph.D. diss., University of Texas, 1966).

Elias Nelson Conway

The best sources on the administration of Elias Nelson Conway are the newspapers of the day, in particular the *Arkansas True Democrat* and the *Arkansas State Gazette and Democrat*. Richard H. Johnson, the editor and Conway's personal secretary, spoke for Conway in the *True Democrat*. Conway himself probably wrote some of the editorials; at least the *Gazette* saw his style more than once. The *Journals* of the regular sessions of the general assembly also provide information on the governor's relationship with the legislature. See also the obituaries in both the *Arkansas Democrat,* 29 February 1892, and the *Arkansas Gazette,* 1 March 1892, as well as a long feature article in the *Arkansas Gazette* on 27 November 1927.

Most of the histories of Arkansas deal in some way with the banks and their adverse effect on the state's reputation. *The Arkansas Gazette: The Early Years, 1819–1866* (Little Rock, 1969), by Margaret Ross, is the best of the modern histories for this period; it is especially valuable because of Conway's close association with the press.

Henry Massie Rector

Among the most useful recent works are Michael B. Dougan, *Confederate Arkansas* (University, Ala., 1976); Leo Huff, "The Military Board in Confederate Arkansas," *Arkansas Historical Quarterly* 26 (Spring 1967): 75–95; Jack Benton Scroggs, "Arkansas in the Secession Crisis," *Arkansas Historical Quarterly* 12 (Autumn 1953): 179–224; and *Historical Report of the Secretary of State of Arkansas*, 3 vols. (Little Rock, 1978). For contemporary sources, see the Kie Oldham Collection in the Arkansas History Commission, Little Rock, and the *Arkansas Gazette* and *The War of the Rebellion: A Compilation of the*

Official Records of the Union and Confederate Armies, 70 vols. (Washington, D.C., 1880–1901).

Harris Flanagin

Important sources of information about Flanagin are the Harris Flanagin Papers and the Kie Oldham Collection, both in the Arkansas History Commission, Little Rock. Among the most informative biographical sketches of Flanagin is Farrar Newberry, "Harris Flanagin," *Arkansas Historical Quarterly* 17 (Spring 1958): 3–20. More general studies containing valuable information on Flanagin and his times include Michael B. Dougan, *Confederate Arkansas* (University, Ala., 1976); David Y. Thomas, *Arkansas in War and Reconstruction, 1861–1874* (Little Rock, 1926); George H. Thompson, *Arkansas and Reconstruction: The Influence of Geography, Economics, and Personality* (Port Washington, N.Y., 1976); Robert L. Yerby, *Kirby Smith's Confederacy: The Trans-Mississippi South, 1863–1865* (New York, 1972).

Isaac Murphy

John I. Smith, *The Courage of a Southern Unionist: A Biography of Isaac Murphy, Governor of Arkansas, 1864–68* (Little Rock, 1979), contains much information not easily found elsewhere and is the best place to begin. Thomas S. Staples, *Reconstruction in Arkansas, 1862–1874* (New York, 1923); and David Y. Thomas, *Arkansas in War and Reconstruction, 1861–1874* (Little Rock, 1926), provide essential information about Murphy's troubled administration. Staples's account is the more detailed of the two but presents an extremely negative image of Murphy, one that does not appear to be warranted by the facts. Paige E. Mulhollan, "Arkansas General Assembly of 1866 and Its Effect on Reconstruction," *Arkansas Historical Quarterly* 20 (Winter 1961): 331–43, is an informed, balanced account. No significant collections of Murphy's private papers have survived.

Powell Clayton

The standard work for many years on Arkansas politics during Reconstruction was Thomas S. Staples, *Reconstruction in Arkansas, 1862–1874* (New York, 1923), a scholarly work with a definite anti-Clayton bias. William H. Burnside's *The Honorable Powell Clayton* (Conway, Ark., 1991) is a more objective portrait of Clayton.

Primary materials include Powell Clayton's *The Aftermath of the Civil War in Arkansas* (New York, 1915). The Harmon L. Remmel Papers and the Pratt L. Remmel Papers, both located in Special Collections at the University of Arkansas Library at Fayetteville, contain many documents dealing with Clayton's political career. The Arkansas History Commission in Little Rock has the Clayton Letterbook which contains official gubernatorial correspondence. The U.S. Senate, *Report of the Special Committee to Inquire into*

Certain Allegations against Honorable Powell Clayton (42d Congress, 3d Session, 1872), provides official testimony concerning Clayton's appointment to the Senate by the Arkansas legislature and related events. The Powell Clayton Appointment Papers (National Archives, Diplomatic Branch, Record Group 59) include many laudatory comments on Clayton's political career.

Especially useful newspapers for detailed accounts of important events in Clayton's political career are the *Arkansas Gazette,* the *New York Times,* and, occasionally, the *St. Louis Post-Dispatch.* The *Arkansas State Republican* was the official publication of the Arkansas Republican party.

More recent and more balanced secondary accounts are three doctoral dissertations that, however, deal only tangentially with Clayton's political career: Martha A. Ellenburg, "Reconstruction in Arkansas" (University of Missouri, 1967); George H. Thompson, "Leadership in Arkansas Reconstruction" (Columbia University, 1968), since revised and published as *Arkansas and Reconstruction: The Influence of Geography, Economics, and Personality* (Port Washington, N.Y., 1976); and Garland E. Bayliss, "Public Affairs in Arkansas, 1874–1896" (University of Texas at Austin, 1972). The American Association for State and Local History has recently (1978) published *Arkansas: A Bicentennial History* by Harry S. Ashmore, which includes three chapters with significant portions on Clayton.

Arkansas Historical Quarterly has published many articles dealing with Clayton's political career. Among those dealing with Clayton's governorship are Orval T. Driggs Jr., "The Issues of the Powell Clayton Regime, 1868–1871," 8 (1949): 1–75; Cortez Ewing, "Arkansas Reconstruction Impeachments," 13 (1954): 137–53; William A. Russ Jr., "The Attempt to Create a Republican Party in Arkansas during Reconstruction," 1 (1942): 206–22; and Everette Swinney, "The United States versus Powell Clayton: Use of the Federal Enforcement Acts in Arkansas," 26 (1967): 143–54.

The important issue of Clayton's use of martial law and the state militia to control civil disturbances in the opening months of his administration is particularly dealt with in Otis A. Singletary, "Militia Disturbances in Arkansas during Reconstruction," *Arkansas Historical Quarterly* 15 (1956): 140–50, and in the chapter entitled, "The Arkansas Militia vs. the Ku Klux Klan" in Allen W. Trelease, *White Terror: The Ku Klux Klan Conspiracy and Southern Reconstruction* (New York, 1971). A significant portion of the U.S. Congress investigating committee's 1871 report on *Affairs in the Late Insurrectionary States: The Ku Klux Conspiracy* deals with Arkansas. An unpublished manuscript by Howard C. Westwood, "Arkansas' Powell Clayton: With Knuckles Bared" (Washington, D.C., 1978), also discusses those events in detail.

For information concerning Clayton's ancestry and family, see John W. LeBosquet's unpublished manuscript, "William Henry Harrison Clayton: A Biographical Sketch" (Wichita, n.d.). Portions of *A Fame Not Easily Forgotten* by June Westphal and Catharine Osterhage (Conway, Ark., 1970) outline Clayton's role in building the town of Eureka Springs, Arkansas.

Clayton's army career and pregubernatorial involvement in politics are discussed in the following *Arkansas Historical Quarterly* articles: Edwin Bearss, "Marmaduke Attacks Pine Bluff," 23 (1964): 291–313; Ruth Cowen, "Reorganization of Federal Arkansas, 1862–1865," 28 (1959): 131–57; and Eugene Feistman, "Radical Disfranchisement in Arkansas, 1867–1868," 12 (1953): 126–68. In the *Journal of Southern History*, see Richard Hume, "The Arkansas Constitutional Convention of 1868: A Case Study in the Politics of Reconstruction," 39 (May 1973): 183–206.

Clayton's domination of Republican politics in Arkansas is seen in the following articles in the *Arkansas Historical Quarterly:* James Atkinson, "The Brooks-Baxter Contest," 4 (1945): 124–49; Tom Dillard, "To the Back of the Elephant: Racial Conflict in the Arkansas Republican Party," 33 (1974): 3–15; John W. Graves, "Negro Disfranchisement in Arkansas," 26 (1967): 199–225; Clifton Paisley, "The Political Wheelers and the Arkansas Election of 1888," 25 (1966): 3–21; Earl Woodward, "The Brooks and Baxter War in Arkansas, 1872–1874," 30 (1971): 315–36; and Marvin Russell, "The Rise of a Republican Leader: Harmon L. Remmel," 36 (1977): 234–57. Richard L. Niswonger's "Arkansas Democratic Politics, 1896–1920" (Ph.D. diss., University of Texas, 1973) has a lengthy chapter on nineteenth-century Republican politics in Arkansas.

For Clayton's diplomatic career, see William H. Burnside, "Powell Clayton: Politician and Diplomat, 1897–1905" (Ph.D. diss., University of Arkansas, 1978), or his much briefer article in *Arkansas Historical Quarterly* 38 (1979): 328–44, "Powell Clayton: Ambassador to Mexico, 1897–1905."

Elisha Baxter

For biographical data on Baxter, see Ted R. Worley, ed., "Elisha Baxter's Autobiography," *Arkansas Historical Quarterly* 14 (1955): 172–75. Other works that include information on Baxter's career include Ted R. Worley, ed., "Documents Relating to Elisha Baxter's Imprisonment," *Arkansas Historical Quarterly* 16 (1957): 101–3; John M. Harrell, *The Brooks and Baxter War: A History of the Reconstruction Period in Arkansas* (St. Louis, 1893); Thomas S. Staples, *Reconstruction in Arkansas, 1862–1874* (New York, 1923); George H. Thompson, *Arkansas and Reconstruction: The Influence of Geography, Economics, and Personality* (Port Washington, N.Y., 1976).

Augustus Hill Garland

The Arkansas History Commission in Little Rock has a small collection organized as the Augustus H. Garland Papers, but there is no single large body of his papers. Garland was, however, a copious letter writer, and his letters are scattered in many collections. Collections containing several letters include the A. Howard Stebbins Collection at the Arkansas History Commission; the David Walker Papers, Special Collections, University of Arkansas Library at

Fayetteville; and the Alexander Stephens Papers, Library of Congress, Washington, D.C. Garland's correspondence while in the Confederate Congress was published in *War of the Rebellion: A Compilation of the Official Records of the Union and Confederate Armies*, 70 vols. (Washington, D.C., 1880–1901). Of his official correspondence while governor only one letter-press volume remains: Letters of Governor A. H. Garland, Outgoing Correspondence, Governor's Office, Arkansas History Commission. For Garland's terms as senator and attorney general, the *Congressional Globe* and the *Annual Reports of the Attorney-General, 1885–1888* are most useful. There are also a large number of letters from Garland in the Papers of Grover Cleveland, Library of Congress. Obituaries appeared in many papers including the *New York Times*, 27 January 1899. A master's thesis by Farrar Newberry, *A Life of Mr. Garland of Arkansas* (Little Rock, 1908), is the only biography of Garland.

William Read Miller

Some of Miller's official correspondence as governor is preserved in bound letter books at the Arkansas History Commission, Little Rock. William Read Miller Jr. projected, and may have completed, a biographical sketch of his father. A good sketch of Miller's early career is given in a letter signed "N." to the *Arkansas Gazette*, 7 May 1876. For a more recent view, see Garland E. Bayliss, "Public Affairs in Arkansas, 1874–1896" (Ph.D. diss., University of Texas at Austin, 1972). On repudiation of the state debt, see Dallas T. Herndon in *Arkansas Historical Review*, vol. 1; and Bayless, "Post-Reconstruction Repudiation: Evil Blot or Financial Necessity?" *Arkansas Historical Quarterly* 23 (Autumn 1964): 243–59.

Thomas James Churchill

Among the most valuable sources of information on Churchill are Clement A. Evans, ed., *Confederate Military History*, vol. 10 (New York, 1899); and David Y. Thomas, *Arkansas in War and Reconstruction, 1861–1874* (Little Rock, 1926). Sources of information on Churchill's gubernatorial term include the *Arkansas Gazette*, 1881–1883; *Journal of the House of Representatives of Arkansas, 1881* (Little Rock, 1881); *Journal of the Senate of Arkansas* (Little Rock, 1881). Lengthy obituaries of Churchill appeared in the *Arkansas Gazette*, 16 May 1905, and the *Arkansas Democrat*, 16 May 1905.

James Henderson Berry

The basic source on Berry's life is his own "Autobiography," a brief account written primarily for his family, which appeared in its entirety in the *Arkansas Gazette*, 9 February 1913. A lengthy obituary is also found in the *Gazette*, 31 January 1913. The most complete study is Paige E. Mulhollan, "The Public Career of James H. Berry" (M.A. thesis, University of Arkansas, 1962). A few letters to and from Governor Berry are included in the collection of letter books of Arkansas governors, Arkansas History Commission, Little Rock. In addition, there is a small collection of Berry papers in the University of Arkansas Library at Fayetteville. This collection contains correspondence, speeches, and newspaper clippings relating especially to the closing decade of his life.

Simon P. Hughes

Among the most important sources on Hughes's career are the Simon P. Hughes Gubernatorial Papers at the Arkansas History Commission, Little Rock; Garland E. Bayliss, "Public Affairs in Arkansas, 1874–1896" (Ph.D. diss., University of Texas at Austin, 1972); and *Arkansas Gazette*, 27 June 1884 and 29 June 1906.

James Philip Eagle

The Arkansas History Commission in Little Rock has a small selection of Eagle's correspondence. A detailed account of Eagle's Civil War activities is included in Clement A. Evans, ed., *Confederate Military History*, vol. 10 (New York, 1899). Clifton Paisley analyzes the 1888 political campaign in "The Political Wheelers and the Arkansas Election of 1888," *Arkansas Historical Quarterly* 25 (Spring 1966): 3–21. Eagle's role in the convict-lease system is described by Jane Zimmerman, "The Convict Lease System in Arkansas and the Fight for Abolition," *Arkansas Historical Quarterly* 8 (Autumn 1949): 171–88. Eagle's dispute with Davis is covered in John A. Treon, "Politics and Concrete: The Buildings of the Arkansas State Capitol, 1899–1917," *Arkansas Historical Quarterly* 31 (Summer 1972): 99–149.

For newspaper coverage of Eagle's career, refer to the *Arkansas Democrat*'s centennial edition, 29 May 1938, p. 9B; the *Arkansas Evangel*, 15 June and 23 November 1881; and the *Arkansas Gazette*, 25 December 1904, sec. 1, 5; and 3 January 1937, sec. 2, 12. All contain general biographical information. For more specific reference, see *Arkansas Gazette*, 2 May 1880, p. 4; 18 January 1889, p. 2; 11 August 1889, p. 16; 4 April 1897, p. 1; 18 November 1899, p. 1; 20 April 1902, p. 1; and 10 May 1902, p. 1.

William Meade Fishback

Among the most useful sources on Fishback's life are the Gubernatorial Papers of William Meade Fishback at the Arkansas History Commission in Little Rock; Ralph Wooster, "The Arkansas Secession Convention," *Arkansas Historical Quarterly* 13 (Summer 1954): 172–95; John M. Wheeler, "The People's Party in Arkansas, 1891–1896" (Ph.D. diss., Tulane University, 1975); George H. Thompson, *Arkansas and Reconstruction: The Influence of Geography, Economics, and Personality* (Port Washington, N.Y., 1976); and Waddy W. Moore, ed., *Arkansas in the Gilded Age, 1874–1900* (Little Rock, 1976).

James Paul Clarke

Newspapers provide an important source of information on Clarke's administration as governor. The *Arkansas Gazette* and the *Arkansas Democrat* are the most valuable, and both published obituaries on 2 October 1916. Clarke's hometown newspaper, the *Helena Weekly World*, frequently endorsed his policies. The *Yellville Mountain Echo*, edited by a bitter foe, provides prejudiced but colorful information on Clarke's brawl with the editor in 1895. Also helpful for the gubernatorial years are the inaugural address (1895) and the farewell message (1897) found in "Arkansas: Public Documents" (1897).

A brief summary of Clarke's career appears in *Biographical Directory of the American Congress* (Washington, D.C., 1961). See also *The Goodspeed Biographical and Historical Memoirs of Eastern Arkansas*, vol. 3 (Chicago, 1889). Memorial addresses of his colleagues are contained in *Congressional Record* (64th Congress, 2d Session, 18 February 1917). Arthur Wallace Dunn occasionally reminisces about Clarke in *From Harrison to Harding* (New York, 1922). For a contemporary view, see "Senator Clarke," *Outlook* 114 (11 October 1916): 295–97.

For an account of Clarke's primary election campaign in 1896, see Richard L. Niswonger, "Arkansas and the Election of 1896," *Arkansas Historical Quarterly* 34 (Spring 1975): 41–78. His dealings with Jeff Davis are briefly discussed in Paige E. Mulhollan, "The Issues of the Davis-Berry Senatorial Campaign in 1906," *Arkansas Historical Quarterly* 20 (Summer 1961): 118–26.

Letters and documents relating to Clarke's career can be found in various collections. The papers of Theodore Roosevelt, William Howard Taft, and especially Woodrow Wilson are helpful. The papers of other Arkansas politicians (Thomas Chapman McRae, George Washington Hays, Charles Hillman Brough, and Joseph Taylor Robinson) in the University of Arkansas Library at Fayetteville contain information on Clarke. The David Y. Thomas Papers, in the same location, contain a campaign pamphlet, "How Does Senator Clarke Stand at Washington," which seeks to defend Clarke's career (1914). A more detailed account of Clarke's career and a more complete bibliography is found in Richard L. Niswonger, "Arkansas Democratic Politics, 1896–1920" (Ph.D. diss., University of Texas at Austin, 1974). See also Joe T. Segraves, "Arkansas Politics, 1874–1918" (Ph.D. diss., University of Kentucky, 1973).

Daniel Webster Jones

Obituaries for Jones appear in the *Arkansas Gazette*, 26 December 1918, and the *Arkansas Democrat*, 25 December 1918. *The Goodspeed Biographical and Historical Memoirs of Central Arkansas*, vol. 2 (Chicago, 1889), provides details on Jones's family and early life. Jones recorded his memories of a famous craftsman who lived with his family in *The Story of James Black, Maker for James Bowie of the Famous Bowie Knife* (n.p., n.d.).

Jones's inaugural addresses and farewell message to the general assembly appear in pamphlet form at the University of Arkansas Special Collections, Fayetteville, filed under "Messages to the General Assembly." On the controversial Meiklejohn amendment, see *Debt Settlement, Senate Concurrent Resolution No. 7, The Veto Message of Governor Dan W. Jones* (Little Rock, 1897). The microfilm of material on Jeff Davis in the University of Arkansas Library at Fayetteville, is pertinent to Jones's career as well as to Davis's. Much of Jones's career can only be traced through newspapers. The *Arkansas Gazette*, 8 January 1897, printed a letter from Jones stating his views on industry and agriculture. Helpful books include John Gould Fletcher, *Arkansas* (Chapel Hill, 1947); L. S. Dunaway, *Jeff Davis, Governor and United States Senator: His Life and Speeches* (Little Rock, 1913); and Charles Jacobson, *The Life Story of Jeff Davis: The Stormy Petrel of Arkansas Politics* (Little Rock, 1925). For a detailed account of Jones's battle in the 1896 primaries, see Richard L. Niswonger, "Arkansas and the Election of 1896," *Arkansas Historical Quarterly* 34 (Spring 1975): 41–78. Stephen E. Wood provides some information on the battles with the railroads in "The Development of Arkansas Railroads," *Arkansas Historical Quarterly* 11 (Autumn 1952): 164–75. For political studies of Jones's administration and further bibliographical information, see Richard L. Niswonger, "Arkansas Democratic Politics, 1896–1920" (Ph.D. diss., University of Texas at Austin, 1974); and Joe T. Segraves, "Arkansas Politics, 1874–1918" (Ph.D. diss., University of Kentucky, 1973).

Jeff Davis

The best introduction to Davis's career is Charles Jacobson, *The Life Story of Jeff Davis: The Stormy Petrel of Arkansas Politics* (Little Rock, 1925), an insider's account written by the governor's private secretary. L. S. Dunaway, ed., *Jeff Davis, Governor and United States Senator: His Life and Speeches* (Little Rock, 1913), is a useful collection of speeches and personal reminiscences. The best brief treatment of Davis appears in John Gould Fletcher, *Arkansas* (Chapel Hill, 1947), 287–314. Also useful are Rupert Vance's rollicking folk history, "A Karl Marx for Hill Billies," *Social Forces* 9 (December 1930): 180–90; and L. S. Dunaway, *What a Preacher Saw through a Key-Hole in Arkansas* (Little Rock, 1925). Cal Ledbetter Jr., "Jeff Davis and the Politics of Combat," *Arkansas Historical Quarterly* 33 (Spring 1974): 16–37, is an analysis of Davis's campaign style written by a political scientist. Paige E. Mulhollan, "The Issues of the Davis-Berry Senatorial Campaign in 1906," *Arkansas Historical Quarterly* 20 (Summer 1961): 118–26, provides a narrative of Davis's first senatorial campaign. Raymond Arsenault, "Charles Jacobson of Arkansas: A Jewish Politician in the Land of the Razorbacks, 1891–1915," in *Turn to the South: Essays on Southern Jewry*, Nathan M. Kaganoff and Melvin I. Urofsky, ed. (Charlottesville, 1979), 55–75, is a study of one of Davis's key political operatives.

In addition to these published works, there are several unpublished accounts of Davis's career: Bayless Walker Price, "The Life of Jeff Davis" (M.A. thesis, University of Alabama, 1929); Nevin Neal, "Jeff Davis and the Reform Movement in Arkansas, 1898–1907" (M.A. thesis, Vanderbilt University, 1939); George James Stevenson, "The Political Career of Jeff Davis: An Example of the Southern Protest" (M.A. thesis, University of Arkansas, 1949); and Morton Harrison Fry III, "Jeff Davis of Arkansas: A Study of Neo-Populism and Economic Democracy" (Senior thesis, Princeton University, 1968); and see Raymond Arsenault, *The Wild Ass of the Ozarks: Jeff Davis and the Social Bases of Southern Politics* (Philadelphia, 1984). Richard L. Niswonger, "Arkansas Democratic Politics, 1896–1920" (Ph.D. diss., University of Texas at Austin, 1973); and Joe T. Segraves, "Arkansas Politics, 1874–1918" (Ph.D. diss., University of Kentucky, 1973), are general studies that contain a wealth of information on the Davis era.

John Sebastian Little

Information regarding Little's career is found in the following published sources: *The Goodspeed Histories of Sebastian County, Arkansas* (Columbia, Tenn., 1977), 1337; Dallas T. Herndon, *Outline of the Executive and Legislative History of Arkansas* (Little Rock, 1922), 158–59; *Biographical Directory of the American Congress, 1774–1971* (Washington, D. C., 1971), 1296; *Congressional Record* (53d Congress, 3d Session–59th Congress, 1st Session); *Who Was Who, 1897–1949* (Chicago, 1942), 735–36; *Arkansas Gazette,* 3 March–30 March 1906, 1 January–16 May 1907, 30 October 1916; *Fort Smith Weekly Elevator,* 7 March and 4 April 1890; and *Fort Smith Southwest American,* 31 October and 1 November 1916.

George Washington Donaghey

Of particular value are the Donaghey scrapbook in the Arkansas History Commission, Little Rock, and his own published works: *Autobiography of George W. Donaghey: Governor of Arkansas, 1909–1913* (Benton, Ark., 1939); *Building a State Capitol* (Little Rock, 1937); and *Homespun Philosophy of George W. Donaghey* (Little Rock, c. 1939). Also, see his obituary in the *Arkansas Gazette,* 15 December 1937, and the *New York Times,* 16 December 1937. Among the most useful secondary accounts are Thomas L. Baxley, "Prison Reforms during the Donaghey Administration," *Arkansas Historical Quarterly* 22 (Spring 1963): 76–84; Charles Jacobson, *The Life Story of Jeff Davis: The Stormy Petrel of Arkansas Politics* (Little Rock, 1925); Allen Leon Morton, "The Influence of George Washington Donaghey as Seen in Conway," *Faulkner Facts and Fiddlings* 11 (Winter 1970): 79–85; John A. Treon, "Politics and Concrete: The Building of the Arkansas State Capitol, 1899–1917," *Arkansas Historical Quarterly* 31 (Summer 1972): 99–149; *Who Was Who in America* (Chicago,

1962); Jane Zimmerman, "The Convict Lease System in Arkansas and the Fight for Abolition," *Arkansas Historical Quarterly* 8 (Autumn 1949): 171–881; and Calvin R. Ledbetter Jr., *Carpenter from Conway: George Washington Donaghey as Governor of Arkansas, 1909–1913* (Fayetteville, 1993).

Joseph Taylor Robinson

The most important source for any study of Robinson is the large and rich collection of Joseph Taylor Robinson Papers at the University of Arkansas Library at Fayetteville. The collection includes correspondence, speeches, scrapbooks, photographs, and other materials and is especially rich in materials concerning his senatorial career. Also of value are Gene Newsom and Karl Kastner, *Our Joe* (North Little Rock, 1937); and Nevin E. Neal, "A Biography of Joseph T. Robinson" (Ph.D. diss., University of Oklahoma, 1958). Most scholars, with the exception of Neal, have tended to concentrate on one aspect of Robinson's career. Gilbert Richard Grant, "Joseph Taylor Robinson in Foreign Affairs" (M.A. thesis, University of Arkansas, 1946), provides a brief introduction to that aspect of Robinson's life in politics. John E. Chiles does the same for Robinson's early public career in "The Early Public Career of Joseph Taylor Robinson" (M.A. thesis, Vanderbilt University, 1949). An overview of Robinson as a senator can be found in Beryl Erwin Pettus, "The Senatorial Career of Joseph Taylor Robinson" (M.A. thesis, University of Illinois, 1952). The most significant event of Robinson's long career in politics, FDR's Judicial Reorganization bill, is examined by Betsy Ross in "Joseph T. Robinson and the Court Fight of 1937" (M.A. thesis, University of Maryland, 1950).

The *Arkansas Gazette* is particularly valuable on Robinson's political career in Arkansas, as is Stuart Towns, "Joseph T. Robinson and Arkansas Politics," *Arkansas Historical Quarterly* 24 (Winter 1965): 291–307. Of the many magazine articles written about Robinson, the most perceptive are found in *Time* (15 July 1935): 17–19, and in *Fortune* (January 1937): 88, "The Senator from Arkansas," by Archibald MacLeish.

George Washington Hays

The George Washington Hays Papers cover the period of Hays's administration (1913–1917) but omit more than they reveal. Hays evidently preserved much of this material to justify his ambivalence on the prohibition question. The Charles Hillman Brough Papers contain many references to Hays, primarily from an opposition point of view. The George A. Thornburgh Scrapbooks reveal details about the governor's prohibition stance. The papers of Joseph Taylor Robinson and David Y. Thomas are also pertinent. All these collections are located in the University of Arkansas Library at Fayetteville.

Obituaries appear in the *Arkansas Democrat*, 16 September 1927; the *Arkansas Gazette*, 16 September 1927; and the *Memphis Commercial Appeal*,

16 September 1927. Governor Hays revealed his political and social philoso-
phies in several articles written for national periodicals. See George W. Hays,
"The Necessity for Capital Punishment," *Scribner's Magazine* 81 (June 1927):
577–81; "When Tammany and Dixie Unite," *The Independent* 117 (23 October
1926): 466–68; "The Solid South and Al Smith in 1928," *The Forum* 76
(November 1926): 696–701; "The Solid South Backs 'Al' Smith," *The Nation*
124 (2 February 1917): 117.

The First Biennial Report of the Board of Control for State Charitable
Institutions of Arkansas, 1915–16 (Little Rock, n.d.), contains information relating to one of the controversial agencies of the Hays era. Hays's inaugural
addresses appear in pamphlet form at the University of Arkansas at Fayetteville Special Collections filed under "Messages to the General Assembly." But
most of the information on Hays's political life must be culled from Arkansas
newspapers of the era. Two dissertations with summaries of the Hays administration are Richard L. Niswonger, "Arkansas Democratic Politics, 1896–
1920" (Ph.D. diss., University of Texas at Austin, 1974); and Joe T. Segraves,
"Arkansas Politics, 1874–1918" (Ph.D. diss., University of Kentucky, 1973).

Charles Hillman Brough

An invaluable source of information on Brough is the Charles Hillman
Brough Papers in the University of Arkansas Library at Fayetteville. Also of
significance is Charles W. Crawford, "Charles Hillman Brough: Educator and
Politician" (M.A. thesis, University of Arkansas at Fayetteville, 1957). Among
the published studies of Brough are Charles W. Crawford, "From the
Classroom to the State Capitol: Charles H. Brough and the Campaign of
1916," *Arkansas Historical Quarterly* 21 (Autumn 1962): 213–30; Charles O.
Cook, "'The Glory of the Old South and the Greatness of the New': Reform
and the Divided Mind of Charles Hillman Brough," *Arkansas Historical
Quarterly* 34 (Autumn 1975): 227–41; Ralph W. Widener, "Charles Hillman
Brough," *Arkansas Historical Quarterly* 34 (Summer 1975): 99–121; Foy
Lisenby, "Brough, Baptists and Bombast: The Election of 1928," *Arkansas
Historical Quarterly* 32 (Summer 1973): 120–31; Foy Lisenby, "Charles H.
Brough as Historian," *Arkansas Historical Quarterly* 35 (Summer 1976):
115–26.

Thomas Chipman McRae

No serious study of McRae exists. The only known collection of manuscript
material relating to him is housed in Special Collections, University of
Arkansas Library at Fayetteville. Unfortunately, little within this collection
deals with McRae's years as governor. Written primarily for schoolchildren,
James R. Grant's *The Life of Thomas C. McRae, Arkansas' Educational Governor,
1921–1925* (Russellville, Ark., 1932) is useful as an introduction only. Additional
biographical material can be found in Robert Sobel, ed., *Biographical Directory*

of the Governors of the United States, 1789–1978 (Westport, Conn., 1978), and in *Biographical Directory of the American Congress* (Washington, D.C., 1950). Helpful material relating to McRae's governorship can be found in published editions of his addresses to the different sessions of the general assembly, in a pamphlet entitled *A Tribute to Hon. Thomas Chapman McRae, Democrat* (n.p., 1927), and in the *Arkansas Gazette* (1920–1925). An unpublished senior honors thesis by Larry Cook, "The Good Roads Movement: The Arkansas Experience, 1900–1923" (University of Arkansas, 1977), provides insight into the highway problems of the McRae administration.

Thomas Jefferson Terral

Terral has never been the subject of a full-scale biography or even of a brief monograph. Sketches of his life and career, however, can be found in Robert Sobel, ed., *Biographical Directory of the Governors of the United States, 1789–1978* (Westport, Conn., 1978), 28. Information on his administration as governor is available in copies of his inaugural and retiring addresses and in the *Arkansas Gazette* (1924–1926). No collections of his personal or public papers have been found.

John E. Martineau

Among the most significant primary materials on Martineau are the John E. Martineau Papers, Arkansas History Commission, Little Rock, and the Joseph Taylor Robinson Papers, University of Arkansas Library at Fayetteville. For Martineau's genealogical data, the best source is the Eno Scrapbook 47, p. 60 (b), a collection of newspaper clippings compiled by Clara B. Eno, which also has information on Martineau's life in Concord; it is located in the Arkansas History Commission, Little Rock. Brief sketches of Martineau's early life and career are included in Clio Harper, "Prominent Members of the Arkansas Bar" (typescript, 1940), in the Arkansas History Commission, Little Rock; and H. F. Barnes and L. B. Davis, *Among Arkansas Leaders* (Little Rock, 1934). For a biographical sketch that includes an account of his tenure as governor and federal judge, see *Proceedings of the Bar Association—1941* (n.p., n.d.), 168. Particulars of Martineau's appointment to the chancery bench are in the *Arkansas Gazette*, 22 October 1907; the reputation he earned while chancellor can be determined by an editorial in the *Arkansas Democrat*, 5 August 1916. For the gubernatorial campaign of 1926, see especially the *Gazette*, 15 August 1926. Sketches of Martineau's career as governor and federal judge are also found in the obituaries in the *Democrat*, 6 March 1937, and *Gazette*, 7 March 1937. For specific information on the road program, see the *Acts of Arkansas*, 1927. The *Gazette*, 3 March 1928, also provides data on Martineau's appointment as federal judge. For anecdotal glimpses of Martineau's life and personality, Fay Williams's "John E. Martineau, Arkansas' 29th [*sic*] Governor," *Arkansas Democrat Sunday Magazine* (4 May 1952): 6, is useful.

Harvey Parnell

Parnell's diaries and correspondence are in the Arkansas History Commission at Little Rock; the Harvey Parnell Collection, Speeches and Scrapbooks, 1928–1932, in the University of Arkansas Library at Fayetteville has an assortment of his speeches ranging from inaugural addresses to remarks made before a state convention of barbers; Earl Leroy Higgins, *Source Readings in Arkansas History* (Little Rock, 1964), contains the usual political biography of Parnell with more background on the passage of the income-tax law; Floyd Sharp, *Traveling Recovery Road: The Story of Relief, Work-Relief and Rehabilitation in Arkansas* (Little Rock, 1936), briefly mentions the governor's emergency-relief committees; Floyd W. Hicks and C. Roger Lambert, "Food for the Hungry: Federal Food Programs in Arkansas, 1933–1942," *Arkansas Historical Quarterly* 37 (Spring 1978): 23–43, provides a few more details regarding work relief under Parnell. Gail S. Murray, "Forty Years Ago: The Great Depression Comes to Arkansas," *Arkansas Historical Quarterly* 29 (Winter 1970): 291–312, deals with Parnell as a depression governor who refused to admit that his state was in the throes of economic collapse. Parnell's attempts to downplay the suffering and damage done to Arkansas by the Great Depression may be found in national periodicals such as *The New Republic* 66 (25 February 1931) and *Outlook* 57 (21 January 1931), but the best articles are in *The Literary Digest* 108 (28 March 1931) and the *New York Times*, 6 January 1931. Details on Parnell's administration can be filled in by searching through the pages of the *Arkansas Gazette* and the *Arkansas Democrat*.

Biographical data on Parnell appears in Fay Williams, *Arkansans of the Years* (Little Rock, 1951), which contains a short sketch of Parnell with a few colorful stories that pose problems as to their veracity, and in *Who's Who in America, 1934–1935* (Chicago, 1934), 1845.

Junius Marion Futrell

No definitive study of Futrell's gubernatorial administration has been published. The Arkansas Historical Commission in Little Rock has the best collection of primary sources on his administration. Its collection includes Futrell's indexed personal correspondence as well as his public addresses. The *Arkansas Gazette* (1933–1937) and the *Arkansas Democrat* (1933–1937) are indispensable sources. Various other works treat specific phases of the Futrell administration. A good, but slightly pro-Futrell, study of the highway-refunding controversy is Louie D. Norris's "Years of Crisis: The 'New Deal' Administration of Junius Marion Futrell" (Master's thesis, Arkansas State University, 1971). John P. Broderick, "Arkansas Restores Her Credit," *Barton's Weekly* (4 June 1934), and "Other People's Money: How Much for Arkansas," *New Republic* 77 (January 1934), are also informative accounts of the highway-refunding controversy. For information on the background and adoption of constitutional Amendments Nineteen and Twenty, see Keith

Sharp's "What Were the Issues Surrounding the Adoption of Amendment Nineteen?" (Graduate paper, University of Arkansas at Fayetteville, May 1970). Other materials of value include microfilmed copies of the records and correspondence of the Southern Tenant Farmers Union; David Eugene Conrad, *The Forgotten Farmers, the Story of Sharecroppers in the New Deal* (Chapel Hill, 1971); James D. Holley, *The New Deal and Farm Tenancy: Rural Resettlement in Arkansas, Louisiana, and Mississippi* (Baton Rouge, 1969); David E. Rison, "Arkansas during the Great Depression" (Ph.D. diss., University of California at Los Angeles, 1974); Floyd Sharp's *Traveling Recovery Road: The Story of Relief, Work-Relief and Rehabilitation in Arkansas* (Little Rock, 1936); and C. Calvin Smith, "Arkansas, 1940–1945: Public and Press Reaction to War and Wartime Pressures" (Ph.D. diss., University of Arkansas at Fayetteville, 1978). An interesting personal account of the Futrell administration is Harry L. Williams's *Forty Years behind the Scenes in Arkansas Politics* (Little Rock, 1949). Dallas T. Herndon's *The Arkansas Handbook* (Little Rock, 1936) provides information on Futrell's genealogy and administration.

Carl Edward Bailey

A small collection of Bailey's Papers is located in the Arkansas History Commission in Little Rock. Biographical information on Bailey is found in *Arkansas Gazette*, 10 January and 24 July 1937, 25 October 1948; and *Who Was Who in America* (Chicago, 1950), 2: 37. Fay Williams, "Carl Bailey—A Fighting Heart," in *Arkansans of the Years* (Little Rock, 1951), 1: 19–30, is a popular account. John Wells, Bailey's executive secretary, reminisces in "Arkansas Won't Forget Carl E. Bailey," *Arkansas Gazette*, 31 October 1948, and in *Arkansas Recorder*, 21 September 1956. The Senate race of 1937 is covered in a two-part *Arkansas Gazette* article: Ernest Dumas, "Arkansas 1937: An Old Political Adage Proves True," 27 December 1970, and "Arkansas 1937: John E. Miller Sweeps on to Victory," 3 January 1971. Several doctoral dissertations provide relevant material: Boyce A. Drummond, "Arkansas Politics: A Study of a One-Party System" (University of Chicago, 1957); Nevin E. Neal, "A Biography of Joseph T. Robinson" (University of Oklahoma, 1958); and David E. Rison, "Arkansas during the Great Depression" (University of California at Los Angeles, 1974). Relevant material may also be found in Donald Holley, "Arkansas in the Great Depression," *Historical Report of the Secretary of State of Arkansas* (Little Rock, 1978), 3: 157–74; and in Holley, "Trouble in Paradise: Dyess Colony and Arkansas Politics," *Arkansas Historical Quarterly* 32 (Autumn 1973): 203–16.

Homer Martin Adkins

The Arkansas History Commission in Little Rock has the best collection of primary sources on Adkins's administration. The commission's collection contains the indexed personal correspondence of the governor as well as his public addresses. The Robert A. Leflar Papers and the J. William Fulbright Papers, both in Special Collections, University of Arkansas Library at Fayetteville, are also valuable, while the *Arkansas Democrat* and the *Arkansas Gazette*, for 1940–1945, are indispensable. Other relevant works include Lee Reaves, "Highway Bond Refunding in Arkansas," *Arkansas Historical Quarterly* 2 (1943); Henry M. Alexander, "The Double Primary," *Arkansas Historical Quarterly* 3–4 (1944–1945); *Who Is Who in Arkansas* (Little Rock, 1959); Fay Williams, *Arkansans of the Years* (Little Rock, 1951); Earl Leroy Higgins, ed., *Source Readings in Arkansas History* (Little Rock, 1964); C. Calvin Smith, "Arkansas, 1940–1945: Public and Press Reaction to War and Wartime Pressures" (Ph.D. diss., University of Arkansas at Fayetteville, 1978); John L. Ferguson, *Arkansas Lives, the Opportunity Land Who's Who* (Hopkinsville, Ky., 1965); John Gould Fletcher, *Arkansas* (Chapel Hill, 1947); Congressional Quarterly, Inc., *Guide to U.S. Elections* (Washington, D.C., 1975); and Roy Glashan, *American Governors and Gubernatorial Elections, 1775–1975* (Stillwater, Minn., 1975).

Benjamin Travis Laney Jr.

No biography of Laney has been published nor has his administration been the subject of a comprehensive study. The best source of information is the collection of Laney's Papers at the family residence in Magnolia. This collection includes almost complete records of Dixiecrat proceedings, correspondence between Laney and states' rights leaders, and massive newspaper-clipping scrapbooks on the 1940s. The latter are especially valuable since so many of the dailies and weeklies have ceased publication. Laney genealogy is found in Guy B. Funderbunk, *Laney: Lineage and Legacy* (Monroe, N.C., 1974), and the former governor contributed commentary about his childhood and family experiences that provides insight into his public and political priorities.

Laney's *A Report to the People of Arkansas: Our Stewardship in Public Office, 1945–1949* (n.p., 1949), includes a lengthy statement by the governor as well as reports from his agency and department heads.

V. O. Key Jr., *Southern Politics in State and Nation* (New York, 1949), is the starting point for any study of the region's political activities. Key was unsure of Laney's precise role in the Dixiecrats and describes that relationship as somewhat "mysterious." Also see Emile B. Ader's *The Dixiecrat Movement: Its Role in Third Party Politics* (Washington, D.C., 1955).

Ann Mathison McLaurin's doctoral dissertation at the University of Oklahoma, "The Role of the Dixiecrats in the 1948 election" (1972), is the only study that has utilized the Laney Papers. She also had lengthy personal interviews with the former governor in 1970. McLaurin places Laney in the moderate wing of the states' righters. *A Man for Arkansas: Sid McMath and the Southern Reform Tradition* (Little Rock, 1976) by Jim Lester is an outstanding volume that draws on the author's 1973 personal interviews with Laney and contains information on his 1948 and 1950 activities. Laney's role in the 1948 desegregation of the University of Arkansas law school is discussed in Robert A. Leflar's "Legal Education in Arkansas: A Brief History of the Law School," *Arkansas Historical Quarterly* 21 (1962): 99–131; and Guerdon D. Nichols, "Breaking the Color Barrier at the University of Arkansas," *Arkansas Historical Quarterly* 27 (1968): 3–21. "The Laneys of Camden," Carrie Lee Silliman et al., *The Ouachita County Historical Quarterly* 22 (spring 1991): 20–34, includes numerous rare photographs.

Sidney Sanders McMath

The chief source of primary information on the McMath administration is the Sidney Sanders McMath Collection at the Arkansas History Commission in Little Rock. Also of use are J. A. Morris, "He Wants to Make Something of Arkansas," *Saturday Evening Post* (18 February 1950); and Harry Ashmore, "McMath Enlarges His Beachhead," *The Reporter* (25 April 1950). The most comprehensive study of McMath and his career is Jim Lester, *A Man for Arkansas: Sid McMath and the Southern Reform Tradition* (Little Rock, 1976).

Francis Adams Cherry

There are two collections of Francis Adams Cherry Papers, one in the Arkansas State University Library at Jonesboro, and the other in the Arkansas History Commission in Little Rock. The University of Arkansas Library at Fayetteville holds in its Special Collections Cherry's "Inaugural Address" (1953) and his "Outgoing Address" (1955) as well as the Orval Eugene Faubus Papers. Biographical sketches of Cherry may be found in *Current Biography* (New York, 1954) and in Robert Sobel, ed., *Biographical Directory of the Governors of the United States, 1789–1978* (Westport, Conn., 1978). The media implications of the talkathon are examined by Oliver R. Smith, "Upset in Arkansas Won by Talkathon," *Broadcasting-Telecasting* (11 August 1952): 44–45; and also in "Campaign by Talkathon," *Newsweek* (23 August 1952): 16. An interesting artifact of the 1954 runoff election is the Cherry campaign pamphlet, *Zero Hour for Arkansas: The 1954 Political Campaign* (Little Rock, 1954). One example of national reaction to the Cherry-Faubus contest is "An Arkansas Upset," *New Republic* (23 August 1954): 4–5. Indispensable for Cherry's gubernatorial years are the *Arkansas Gazette* and the *Arkansas Democrat*. The *New York Times* is helpful in understanding Cherry's impact on the national scene. Also useful is Boyce Drummond, "Arkansas, 1950–1954," in *Historical Report of the Secretary of State of Arkansas* (Little Rock, 1978), 3: 175–85.

Orval Eugene Faubus

Coverage of Faubus's life has been uneven, and the bulk of published material to date has emphasized his role in the Little Rock Central crisis of 1957.

With the recent opening of a number of individual manuscript collections, it is probable that a more thorough analysis of all aspects of his career will be forthcoming. The most significant of these collections, the Orval Eugene Faubus Papers at the University of Arkansas Library at Fayetteville, were made available to scholars in mid-August 1980. The University of Arkansas Library at Fayetteville also houses the J. William Fulbright Papers, which treat Faubus's public-service career from 1941 to 1975. This rich collection will be of aid in placing Faubus's career within a national context. Two other collections at Fayetteville are more directly intertwined with the Faubus years: the Arthur Brann Caldwell Papers and the Lawrence Brooks Hays Papers. Other relevant collections include the Sidney Sanders McMath and Francis Adams Cherry Papers, both at the Arkansas History Commission in Little Rock, and the John L. McClellan Papers at Ouachita Baptist University, Arkadelphia, Arkansas.

At this juncture, the best volume on the Southern context of the Faubus phenomenon is William C. Havard, ed., *The Changing Politics of the South* (Baton Rouge, 1972), which updates V. O. Key Jr., *Southern Politics in State and Nation* (New York, 1949), the classical study of political structure in the South in the 1940s. Of particular interest to students of the Faubus era is the essay by Richard E. Yates, "Arkansas: Independent and Unpredictable," in Havard's volume. Other books that provide a general background are Jack Bass and Walter DeVries, *The Transformation of Southern Politics* (New York, 1976); Neal R. Pierce, *The Deep South States* (New York, 1972); and Numan V. Bartley and Hugh D. Graham, *Southern Politics and the Second Reconstruction* (Baltimore, 1975). Transcripts and tapes of Bass and DeVries's interviews with various Arkansas luminaries of the 1960s are housed in the Southern Historical Collection at the University of North Carolina at Chapel Hill. Other oral-history collections on the Faubus era can be found at Columbia University, New York City, and at the Dwight D. Eisenhower Library, Abilene, Kansas. In some instances, the latter two can be used only with the permission of the individuals interviewed.

The best sources for a chronological look at Faubus's entire public career are the three Little Rock newspapers that covered the capital city. The *Arkansas State Press*, now defunct, but previously owned by L. C. Bates, husband of NAACP activist Daisy Bates, provides a record of events as seen from the black perspective. The *Arkansas Gazette*, which won a Pulitzer Prize for its editorial analysis of the Little Rock Central crisis, served as an insightful opponent to Faubus throughout his public life. A selection of the newspaper's prizewinning editorials, *Arkansas Gazette, Crisis in the South: The Little Rock Story* (Little Rock, 1959), has been published. The *Arkansas Democrat* provides a more conservative look at the Faubus regime and serves as a valuable balancing analysis of the governor's career. These and most other Arkansas newspapers of the era are available to the public at the Arkansas History Commission in Little Rock. Also valuable are the *Southern School*

News, published by the Southern Education Reporting Service during the Faubus years; and *Arkansas: A Bicentennial History* (New York, 1978) by Harry Ashmore.

There has been little written about the early Faubus years. The most informative account is provided by Faubus himself in *In This Faraway Land: A Personal Account of Infantry Combat in World War II* (Little Rock, 1976), which deals primarily with the ex-governor's military career but also has an introductory section that gives some description of his childhood. Numerous other sources, some already mentioned, give sketchy descriptions of the Faubus years: C. M. Wilson, "Orval Faubus—How Did He Get That Way?" *Reader's Digest* 74 (February 1959): 82–83; Louis Lomax, "Two Millionaires, Two Senators and a Faubus: The Curious Constellation of Arkansas Politics," *Harper's Magazine* 210 (March 1960): 73–76, 82–84, 86; and Colbert S. Cartwright, "The Improbable Demagogue of Little Rock, Arkansas," *Reporter* 17 (17 October 1957): 23–25.

Faubus's brief stay at Commonwealth College is covered in William H. Cobb's "Commonwealth College: A History" (Master's thesis, University of Arkansas at Fayetteville, 1962). The governor's early political career is virtually untapped with the exception of Faubus's own letters and editorials in the *Madison County Record*. The McMath years are covered in Jim Lester, *A Man for Arkansas: Sid McMath and the Southern Reform Tradition* (Little Rock, 1976); and are also referred to in Harry A. Haines, "The Rural Dimensions of the Faubus Vote" (Master's thesis, Memphis State University, 1971).

Faubus's political career has been dominated by his actions in the Central crisis and there is a spate of literature available on that subject. Besides the pages of the Little Rock newspapers, there are two books that document the day-to-day happenings during the crisis: Corrine Silverman, *The Little Rock Story*, rev. ed. (University, Ala., 1959); Wilson Record and Jane Cassels Record, eds., *Little Rock, USA: Materials for Analysis* (San Francisco, 1960). Numan V. Bartley has provided insight into Faubus's role at Central and its aftermath in *The Rise of Massive Resistance: Race and Politics in the South during the 1950's* (Baton Rouge, 1969) and in a well-written article, "Looking Back at Little Rock," *Arkansas Historical Quarterly* 25 (Summer 1966): 110–16. Another more colorful interpretation can be found in Robert Sherrill, *Gothic Politics in the Deep South: Stars of the New Confederacy* (New York, 1968).

Numerous participants in the Central crisis have published their versions of the events including Daisy Bates, *The Long Shadow of Little Rock* (New York, 1962), which gives the best account from the black perspective; Woodrow Wilson Mann, "The Truth about Little Rock," *New York Herald-Tribune*, 19–31 January 1958, a serialized version of events by the mayor of Little Rock, which severely castigates Faubus as a political opportunist; Brooks Hays, *A Southern Moderate Speaks* (Chapel Hill, 1959), which describes his role as mediator between Faubus and Eisenhower; Little Rock Superintendent Virgil Blossom's version, *It Has Happened Here* (New York, 1959); and a series of articles by the

Arkansas Gazette's executive editor in 1957, Harry S. Ashmore, which include "Southern Challenge and Epitaph for Dixie," *Life* 43 (4 November 1957): 128–30; "Spur to Massive Resistance in the South," *Life* 45 (11 August 1958): 10; and "They Don't Want a Man of Reason," *Reporter* 91 (27 November 1958): 20–21; and a view from segregationist Little Rock School Board member Dale Alford and L'Moore Alford, *The Case of the Sleeping People (Finally Awakened by Little Rock School Frustration)* (Little Rock, 1959). The Faubus version of events at Central has been amply covered in numerous interviews including "Two Choices: Wait for Violence or Prevent It," *U.S. News and World Report* 43 (20 September 1957): 62–66; and "The Story of Little Rock as Governor Faubus Tells It," *U.S. News and World Report* 44 (20 June 1958): 101–6.

Other articles on Faubus and Central worth reading are "Georgia: Rallying Point of Defiance," *Look* 21 (12 November 1957): 34; Thomas F. Pettigrew and Ernest Q. Campbell, "Faubus and Segregation: An Analysis of Arkansas Voting," *Public Opinion Quarterly* 24 (Fall 1960): 436–37; Fletcher Knebel, "The Real Little Rock Story," *Look* 21 (12 November 1957): 31–33; and Cabell Phillips, "Dilemma of the Southern Moderate," *New York Times Magazine* (23 March 1958): 23. More recent works of value include Tony Freyer, *The Little Rock Crisis: A Constitutional Interpretation* (Westport, Conn., 1984); Elizabeth Jacoway, "Taken by Surprise: Little Rock Business Leaders and Desegregation," in *Southern Businessmen and Desegregation*, Elizabeth Jacoway and David R. Colburn, eds. (Baton Rouge, 1982); David L. Chappell, *Inside Agitators: White Southerners in the Civil Rights Movement* (Baltimore, 1994).

The years immediately after the Central crisis, when Faubus closed the schools and there was a school board–based battle to reopen them, have not been covered in as much detail as the crisis itself. One good source is *The Women's Emergency Committee to Open Our Schools, Little Rock Report: The City, Its People, Its Business, 1957–1959* (Little Rock, 1959), which details the struggle begun by Mrs. Adolphine Terry to find a way to combat Faubus's political maneuvering. Samuel Lubell, *White and Black: Test of a Nation* (New York, 1964), describes the STOP/CROSS confrontation; as does Jerry Neill, "Education of Governor Faubus," *Nation* 188 (6 June 1959): 507–9; and "How They Beat Faubus in Little Rock: STOP Committee to Stop This Outrageous Purge," *New Republic* 140 (8 June 1959). Roy Reed, "Another Face of Orval Faubus," *New York Times Magazine* (9 October 1966): 44–45, written the year of Faubus's retirement from the governor's chair, places his political career in perspective.

Faubus's postgubernatorial career has been sketched in the *New York Times* and in more detail in the Little Rock newspapers. Periodical coverage of this period is skimpy. Two articles worth considering are "Orval's Pad," *Time* 90 (4 August 1967): 21, which describes the controversy surrounding the Faubus mansion; and Barlow Herget, "Reports and Comment: Arkansas," *Atlantic Monthly* 227 (February 1971): 14–26, which provides an analysis of the 1970 gubernatorial campaign.

Winthrop Rockefeller

The Winthrop Rockefeller Papers, a vast collection, is housed at the University of Arkansas at Little Rock Archives. Two book-length studies on Rockefeller have been published. *The Arkansas Rockefeller* (Baton Rouge, 1978), by John Ward, a longtime employee of the governor, is highly laudatory. Cathy K. Urwin's *Agenda for Reform: Winthrop Rockefeller as Governor of Arkansas, 1967–71* (Fayetteville, 1991) is a balanced and useful survey. The *Time* cover story on Rockefeller's election is useful (2 December 1966). Rockefeller's role in the GOP is chronicled in Billy B. Hathorn, "The Republican Party in Arkansas, 1920–1982" (Ph.D. diss., Texas A & M University, 1983).

Dale Leon Bumpers

The most complete biographical sketch of Bumpers appears in "Bumpers, Dale (Leon)," *Current Biography* (August 1979): 6–9. The following books provide background information about the state of Arkansas and about the flow of events into which Bumpers's candidacy for governor and his administration fit: Harry Ashmore, *Arkansas: A Bicentennial History* (New York, 1978); Jack Bass and Walter DeVries, *The Transformation of Southern Politics* (New York, 1976); Dan Durning, "Arkansas History: 1954 to Present," in *Historical Report of the Secretary of State of Arkansas* (Little Rock, 1978), 3:186–202; John Ward, *The Arkansas Rockefeller* (Baton Rouge, 1978); and Richard E. Yates, "Arkansas: Independent and Unpredictable," in William C. Havard, ed., *The Changing Politics of the South* (Baton Rouge, 1972), 233–93.

Among the newspaper articles that provide detailed examinations of Bumpers' gubernatorial race and his years in office are Bill Lewis, "Bumpers' Campaign: It Was Nearly Flawless," *Arkansas Gazette*, 13 September 1970, p. 6A; Ginger Shiras, "'We've Been Waiting a Long Time,' Charleston Says," *Arkansas Gazette*, 13 September 1970, p. 16A; Mike Trimble, "Bumpers: Memories of Boswell's Darkest Hour," *Arkansas Gazette*, 16 August 1970, p. 10A; Ernest Dumas, "Dale Bumpers the Governor—Part I," *Arkansas Gazette*, 12 January 1975, p. 1A; Doug Smith, "Dale Bumpers the Governor—Part 2," *Arkansas Gazette*, 13 January 1975, p. 1A; Christopher Lyon, "Fulbright Facing Danger in Tomorrow's Primary," *New York Times*, 27 May 1974, p. 22; Roy Reed, "Arkansas' Giant Killer," *New York Times*, 30 May 1974, p. 26. See also "Primaries: Bumpered," *Newsweek* (10 June 1974): 25–27.

Two excellent discussions of the administrative characteristics of Bumpers as governor are contained in Ernest Dumas, "The Administrative Development of Governor Bumpers," in *Government of Arkansas*, Walter Nunn, ed. (Little Rock, 1973), 168–77; Jo Ann Pryor, "Aides Discuss Obstacles and Pitfalls of Being on Top," *Arkansas Democrat*, 19 April 1979.

Also useful were interviews with Tom McRae, who served on Governor Bumpers' staff, and Charles T. Crow, director of the Department of Planning.

David Hampton Pryor

Pryor has donated his political papers, 1960–1979, to the University of Arkansas Library at Fayetteville, and they will eventually be available for research. At present, however, most information must be gathered from state newspapers of the period, especially the *Arkansas Gazette* and *Arkansas Democrat*. Among the most useful analytical articles in these papers were, in chronological order: Ernest Dumas, "Tight Fiscal Line Sought by Pryor," *Gazette*, 28 November 1974; Doug Smith, "Pryor Fared Well with Assembly Despite Losses," *Gazette*, 30 March 1975; E. Dumas, "Unexciting Race Might Be Pryor's Only Problem in Renomination Bid," *Gazette*, 20 May 1976; E. Dumas, "Governor Heads Long 'Losers' List in 71st Assembly," *Gazette*, 20 March 1977; E. Dumas, "The Legislature Careens in Absence of Leadership," *Gazette*, 10 April 1977; Bill Lewis, "David Pryor: Will It Be No. 3," *Gazette*, 28 May 1978; and Jerry Dean, "Pryor's Accomplishments Open to Debate," *Democrat*, 28 January 1979.

The Arkansas Plan is the most thoroughly analyzed aspect to date of the Pryor administration. See D. Kincaid, "The Arkansas Plan: Coon Dogs or Community Services," *Publius* (January 1979); Doug Smith, "Famed Arkansas Plan: What Went Wrong?" *Arkansas Gazette*, 11 July 1979; and G. Sparrow, C. Ledbetter, and B. Moore, *The Arkansas Plan: A Case Study in Public Policy* (Little Rock, 1979). For commentary on Pryor's appointments, see E. Dumas, "Major Symbolism in Appointments," *Gazette*, 13 November 1977; and D. Kincaid, "Gubernatorial Appointments and Legislative Influence," paper presented to Arkansas Political Science Association, February 1977. This paper is based in part on interviews with Pryor and his staff. Other published interviews with Pryor are "David Pryor: State Employee," *Grapevine*, 6–12 October 1976; and "Pryor's Priorities," *Grapevine*, 22–28 September 1976. A critical treatment of Pryor's style is offered by A. Leveritt and B. Terry, "Play It Again for the 'Guv': David Pryor in Search of an Image," *Arkansas Times* 4 (November 1977). One useful semiofficial document is a "Summary of Accomplishments of the Administration of David H. Pryor, 39th Elected Governor of the State of Arkansas, January, 1975-January, 1979," compiled and distributed by Pryor to all state legislators in January 1979. Excerpts appeared in the *Arkansas Democrat*, 27 January 1979.

Among the sources used for biographical information were *Who's Who in America*, 40th ed.; *Who's Who in American Politics*, 6th ed.; *Congressional Directory* (92nd Congress); and *The Almanac of American Politics*, 1972 and 1974.

William Jefferson Clinton

Clinton's gubernatorial and other papers have not yet been given an official home, and therefore are not yet available for research. However, there is no shortage of information (and pseudo-information) about his life and career.

Researchers may wish to begin with Allan Metz, comp. and ed., *Bill Clinton's Prepresidential Career, An Annotated Bibliography* (Westport, Conn., 1994). While not exhaustive it is extensive, is usefully organized, and has both a subject and author index.

The essay in this volume drew most heavily on the thorough daily coverage of public affairs in the *Arkansas Democrat,* the *Arkansas Gazette* (which was indexed, but which ceased publication on 6 October 1991), and the *Arkansas Democrat-Gazette* (as of 19 October 1991). Especially useful were the lengthy summaries and evaluations of campaigns and of regular and special sessions provided in each newspaper, and the daily political analysis and commentary, often highly contradictory, appearing on each paper's editorial pages.

Biographic information on Clinton was obtained from *Who's Who in America,* and, more cautiously, from some biographies rushed into print for the 1992 presidential campaign: Charles F. Allen and Jonathan Portis, *The Comeback Kid, The Life and Career of Bill Clinton* (New York, 1992); Jim Moore with Rick Ihde, *Clinton, Young Man in a Hurry* (Fort Worth, 1992); and Robert E. Levin, *Bill Clinton: The Inside Story* (New York, 1992). Only the Allen and Portis book is indexed; none were authorized by the campaign. An excellent series of articles by David Maraniss, reviewing Clinton's pre-presidential life and career, appeared in the *Washington Post* on 13, 14, and 15 July 1992. Maraniss's book, *First In His Class,* is forthcoming.

An interesting collection of essays written by Clinton's family and friends is Ernest Dumas, ed., *The Clintons of Arkansas, An Introduction by Those Who Know Him Best* (Fayetteville, 1993). It is unabashedly affectionate. In contrast, Meredith L. Oakley, *On the Make* (Washington, D.C., 1994) is unrelentingly negative. Brief, but balanced, is David Shribman, "Clinton, Arkansas's Best Known Overachiever, Widens His Horizons to Include the White House," *Wall Street Journal,* 8 October 1994. Those consulting Michael Kelly, "The President's Past," *New York Times Magazine,* 31 July 1994, pp. 20–29, 34, 40, 45, should also read the letters taking issue with Kelly's treatment of Clinton in the issues of 21 and 28 August and 4 September 1994.

Additional personal insights can be gained from Clinton's mother's autobiography, published posthumously: Virginia Kelley with James Morgan, *Leading With My Heart* (New York, 1994). Hillary Rodham Clinton also became an object of national interest in 1992. Some brief books about her, which cover Bill Clinton as well, include Rex Nelson with Philip Martin, *The Hillary Factor* (New York, 1993); Donnie Radcliffe, *Hillary Rodham Clinton* (New York, 1993); and Judith Warner, *Hillary Clinton, The Inside Story* (New York, 1993).

The political system and culture within which Clinton campaigned and governed can be explored in Diane D. Blair, *Arkansas Politics and Government: Do the People Rule?* (Lincoln and London, 1988); John Robert Starr, *Yellow Dogs and Dark Horses* (Little Rock, 1987); and Roy Reed, "Clinton Country," *New York Times Magazine,* 6 September 1992, pp. 32–35, 40, 44–45.

In addition to these overviews, other books, essays, and articles provided valuable insight into particular aspects of Clinton's pre-presidential career. Clinton's philosophical tenets and evolution, and his first political race for Congress in 1974, are discussed in Stanley B. Greenberg, *Middle Class Dreams* (New York, 1994). The 1974 race is also treated in Carl Whillock's essay in *The Clintons of Arkansas;* and in Roy Reed, "Inflation Issue Stressed," *New York Times,* 5 September 1974, p. 26. The 1974 race, as well as the 1976 and 1978 races and Clinton's service as attorney general are all discussed in Stephen A. Smith's introduction to Stephen A. Smith, ed., *Bill Clinton on Stump, State, and Stage* (Fayetteville, 1994).

Clinton's first election to and first term as governor are covered and analyzed by Stephen Smith and Rudy Moore in *The Clintons of Arkansas;* but most especially by Phyllis Finton Johnston, *Bill Clinton's Public Policy for Arkansas: 1979–80,* (Little Rock, 1982). Clinton's 1980 defeat was reported and analyzed extensively in the Arkansas press. An interesting outside view is Davis S. Broder, "An Arkansas Parable," *Washington Post,* 26 November 1980, p. 17A. An interesting Arkansas view is in Mike Trimble, "Bill Clinton's Campaign To Become One of Us," *Arkansas Times* 12 (November 1985): 68–71, 90–91.

The changes in both policy and style which accompanied Clinton's return to office are discussed in Diane D. Blair, "Two Transitions in Arkansas, 1978 and 1982," in Thad L. Beyle, ed., *Gubernatorial Transitions* (Durham, N.C., 1985), 96–103. See also Mel White, "A Campaign Journal—Part One," *Arkansas Times* 9 (February 1983): 22–24, 26–28, 30, 32, and "A Campaign Journal—Part Two," *Arkansas Times* 9 (March 1983): 74–79.

The 1983 Special Session on education, its purposes, strategies, and accomplishments, constitute the most written about aspect of Clinton's gubernatorial career. Among the most thorough treatments are Charles Flynn Allen, "Governor William Jefferson Clinton: A Biography with a Special Focus on His Educational Contributions" (Ph.D. diss., University of Mississippi, 1991); Dan Durning, "Education Reform in Arkansas: The Governor's Role in Policymaking," in Eric Herzik and Brent Brown, eds., *Gubernatorial Leadership and State Policy* (New York, 1991); and David Osborne, *Laboratories of Democracy* (Boston, 1988), 83–110. The difficulties faced by Clinton in pursuing his educational agenda are discussed in Goldie Blumenstyk, "Governor of Arkansas Faces Tough Battle with Legislature in Crusade to Raise Taxes for Renewal of Higher Education," *The Chronicle of Higher Education* (25 January 1989): 21–22A; and Diane D. Blair, "When Majorities Matter," *Comparative State Politics Journal* (10 December 1989): 9–13.

Thoughtful attempts to analyze the validity of charges and countercharges in the 1992 presidential campaign regarding Clinton's gubernatorial record include Jerry Dean, "Bush hits Clinton at home, but is he on target?," *Democrat-Gazette,* 27 September 1992; and David Lauter and James Gerstenzang, "Accuracy of Bush, Clinton Accusations," *Los Angeles Times,* 11 October 1992, pp. 36A, 38A. The particulars of the campaign as it was conducted in Arkansas are described in Diane D. Blair, "Arkansas: Ground Zero in the Presidential Race," in Robert P. Steed, Laurence W. Moreland, and Tod A. Bakers, ed., *The 1992 Presidential Election in the South* (Westport, Conn., 1994).

Among the early attempts in the non-Arkansas press to assess the Clinton gubernatorial career and record are Peter Applebome, "Bill Clinton's Uncertain Journey," *New York Times Magazine*, 8 March 1992, pp. 26–29, 36, 60, 63; Sidney Blumenthal, "The Anointed: Bill Clinton, The Nominee-Elect," *New Republic* (3 February 1992): 24–27; Stephen Buel, "The Politics of Agreements: Bill Clinton's Arkansas Reinvented His Politics," *Texas Observer* (8 May 1992): 79, 17; Gary Wills, "Beginning of the Road," *Time* (20 July 1992): 32–34, 55–57, 59; and Joel Brinkley, "Clinton Remakes Home State in Own Image," *New York Times*, 31 March 1992, pp. 1A, 16A. Brinkley's article was the first of a *New York Times* series which explored Clinton's record with respect to education (1 April 1992, p. 22A); economic development (2 April 1992, p. 20A); civil rights (3 April 1992, p. 14A); and the environment (4 April 1992, p.10). An even more detailed overview is Mike Trimble, "Clinton grew up in 12 years in governor's chair," *Arkansas Democrat-Gazette*, 23 November 1992; and a five-part series which appeared in the *Democrat-Gazette* on 25 July, 29 August, 26 September, 31 October and 28 November 1993.

Assessments of the impact of Clinton's education reforms, in addition to the Allen, Durning, and Osborne works cited above, are: Diane D. Blair, Chapter 13, in *Arkansas Politics and Government*, 83–110; Goldie Blumenstyk, "Amid Some Grumbling, Clinton Wins Praise For His Reforms of Arkansas," *Chronicle of Higher Education* (29 April 1992): 23A, 26–27A; Mara Leveritt and Judith M. Gallman, "Grading the Governor: A Special Report," *Arkansas Times* 18 (November 1990): 34–43; and Danny Shameer, "History still grading Clinton's school reforms," *Democrat-Gazette*, 28 November 1993.

Details regarding Clinton's economic development programs can be found in Ernest Dumas, "The Democrat: Bootstrapper or Just Busy?" *Planning* 58, no. 10 (October 1992): 9–11, 13–15; and in a four-part series by Bill Simmons appearing in the *Arkansas Democrat* on 4, 5, 6, and 7 September 1988. Assessments of the impact of these initiatives appear in Allan Murray, "Democrat Frontrunner Backs Industrial Policy With a Populist Twist," *Wall Street Journal*, 23 April 1992, p. 1A; Jeffrey H. Birnbaum, "In Arkansas, Governor Usually Tries to Help Big Local Companies," *Wall Street Journal*, 24 April 1992, p. 1A; Jeffrey H. Birnbaum, "Arkansas Saw Solid Job Growth Under Clinton," *Wall Street Journal*, 1 October 1992, p.18A; Amy Gotlieb, "Down in the Delta," *Democrat-Gazette*, 25 July 1993; and Rachel O'Neal, "Jobs, industry grew on Clinton's watch," *Democrat-Gazette*, 29 August 1993.

Clinton's rhetoric and its meanings are analyzed in Art English, "Bill Clinton: His Promise and His Words," a paper presented at the Annual Meeting of the Arkansas Political Science Association, 27 February 1993; in Stephen A. Smith, ed., *Bill Clinton on Stump, State, and Stage* (Fayetteville, 1994); and in Robert L. Savage and Diane D. Blair, "Constructing and

Reconstructing the Image of Statecraft," in *Political Communication Yearbook 1984* (Carbondale, 1985), 242–261, 313.

Among the more detailed and useful documents produced by the governor's office during Clinton's years are "Moving Arkansas Forward into the 21st Century," 1988, 63 pages; "A Vision of Excellence: A Look at Education in Arkansas," 1988; and "The Arkansas Agenda, New Directions for the '90's," 1991, 18 pages.

Clinton provides his own view of the office he filled in Bill Clinton, "The Changing Role of the Governorship," Second Annual Public Policy Lecture, Vanderbilt Institute for Public Policy Studies, Nashville, 19 January 1988; and in "The Changing View from the Statehouse: An Interview with Governor Bill Clinton," *Change* 22, no. 7 (March, April 1990): 71–73. Other especially interesting interviews with Clinton appeared in the *Arkansas Democrat*, 24 December 1989 and 30 September 1990, as well as in the *Arkansas Times* 16 (July 1990), insert.

Finally, for this essay, the author also drew upon notes taken during Clinton's guest appearances in political science classes, impressions gathered at campaign and other public events, and interviews and conversations with Clinton and his aides over the past twenty-two years.

Frank Durwood White

The Frank White gubernatorial papers are, as of this writing, in storage in Little Rock and not available for research use. He expects to donate them to the archives at the University of Arkansas at Little Rock. The general outline of the White administration can be traced through the daily newspapers, especially the *Arkansas Gazette* and the *Arkansas Democrat*. The administration is placed in its larger historical context in Diane D. Blair's *Arkansas Politics and Government: Do the People Rule?* (Lincoln, Neb., 1988). White's role in the creation science issue is covered in Langdon Gilkey, *Creationism on Trial: Evolution and God at Little Rock* (San Francisco, 1985); and Marcel C. La Follette, ed., *Creationism, Science, and the Law: The Arkansas Case* (Cambridge, Mass., 1983). Also useful were interviews with former Governor White and state representative Carolyn Pollan.

James Guy Tucker Jr.

No biographies of James Guy Tucker Jr. have yet been written. Most of the material for this essay was gleaned from the *Arkansas Gazette* (1991), the *Arkansas Democrat* (1991), and the *Arkansas Democrat-Gazette* (1991–1994). The vertical file at the Special Collections Division, University of Arkansas Libraries at Fayetteville, was also consulted. The governor's office provided a biographical sketch of the governor. Interviews with Ernest Dumas, of the *Arkansas Democrat-Gazette* were of great value. Readers might be interested in Tucker's book: Jim Guy Tucker, *Arkansas Men at War* (Little Rock, 1968).

ACTING GOVERNORS OF ARKANSAS, 1836–1994

Samuel Calhoun Roane

James P. McGaughy, "Judge Samuel C. Roane," *Jefferson County Historical Quarterly* 11 (1978): 24–27; *Biographical and Historical Memoirs of Central Arkansas* (Chicago, 1889), 115; *Territorial Papers of the United States, Territory of Arkansas* (Washington, D.C., 1953), vols. 19–21; *Arkansas Gazette* and *Arkansas Democrat*, 17 December 1852.

Samuel Adams

Ella M. Langford, *Johnson County, Arkansas: The First Hundred Years* (Clarksville, 1921), 143–44; Josiah H. Shinn, *The History of Arkansas* (Little Rock, 1898), 142.

John Williamson

Gladys Powell, "The Political Career of John L. Williamson," *Arkansas Historical Quarterly* 4 (Autumn 1945): 231–33; "Last Will and Testament of John Williamson, 1860," *Pope County Historical Association Quarterly* 4 (December 1969): 30–31; *Little Rock True Democrat*, 4 July 1861.

Richard C. Byrd

Josiah H. Shinn, *The History of Arkansas* (Little Rock, 1898), 107–17, 150; *Little Rock Weekly Gazette*, 16 October 1844; *Little Rock Gazette and Democrat*, 23 June 1854; *Little Rock True Democrat*, 20 June 1854.

John Robinson Hampton

History of Presbyterianism in Arkansas, 1828–1902 (Little Rock, 1902), 127–28; *Arkansas Gazette*, 14 July 1874, 17 February 1880; *Little Rock Gazette and Democrat*, 3 January 1850, 24 December 1852; *Little Rock True Democrat*, 26 August 1856; *Arkansas Democrat*, 17 February 1880; John R. Hampton Materials, Bradley County Historical Society, courtesy of Robert Gatewood.

Thomas Fletcher

Clio Harper, "Prominent Members of the Early Arkansas Bar, 1797–1884," typescript, History Commission, Little Rock, 1940, p. 126; *Arkansas Gazette*, 27 February and 2 March 1880; *Little Rock True Democrat*, 15 December 1858.

Ozro A. Hadley

Arkansas Gazette, 31 July 1915.

Ben T. Embry

Arkansas Gazette, 30 August 1850, 27 January 1892.

John William Stayton

Biographical and Historical Memoirs of Northeast Arkansas (Chicago, 1890), 900–901; John W. Stayton File, Jackson County Historical Society, courtesy of James Morgan.

David Edward Barker

John Wheeler, "The People's Party in Arkansas, 1891–1896" (Ph.D. diss., Tulane University, 1975), 348–50; Barker Family Records in the possession of Rebecca D. Brown; *Arkansas Democrat*, 28 November 1914.

Christopher Columbus Hamby

Arkansas Gazette, 1 February 1921; Ralph P. Hamby, "Christopher Columbus Hamby," in Winnie Hamilton, "Nevada County, Arkansas," 5 vols., typescript, Special Collections, University of Arkansas Library at Fayetteville, vol. 1.

Clay Sloan

Walter E. McLeod, *Centennial Memorial History of Lawrence County* (Russellville, 1936), 145–48; *Biographical and Historical Memoirs of Northeast Arkansas* (Chicago, 1890), 821; *Arkansas Democrat*, 26 March 1891; *Arkansas Gazette*, 18 April 1899, 15 February 1942.

Joseph C. Pinnix

Proceedings of the Bar Association of Arkansas, 1943 (n.p., n.d.), 183; *Arkansas Gazette*, 27 July 1942.

Jerry C. South

Francis Shiras, *History of Baxter County* (n.p., n.d.), 139; *Arkansas Gazette*, 18 April 1899, 25 April 1930; *Who Was Who in America* (Chicago, 1942), 1:1157.

Robert L. Lawrence

Arkansas Gazette, 18 April and 23 September 1899, 25 October 1904.

Michael Pleasant Huddleston

Arkansas Gazette, 4 May 1901, 3 and 4 January 1938; *McGhee Headlight*, 12 January 1915; *Arkansas Democrat*, 3 January 1938; a file of newspaper clippings pertaining to his career is in the possession of his daughter, Wanda Rankin.

Oliver Newton Killough

C. P. J. Mooney, *The Mid-South and Its Builders* (Memphis, 1920), 730; *Biographical and Historical Memoirs of Eastern Arkansas* (Chicago, 1890), 363; *Arkansas Gazette*, 11 December 1904, 24 August 1926.

John P. Lee

Arkansas Gazette, 16 October 1904, 31 March 1941.

John Isaac Moore

C. P. J. Mooney, *The Mid-South and Its Builders* (Memphis, 1920), 440; *Arkansas Gazette*, 15 January, 2 February, and 15 May 1907, 20 March 1937.

Xenophon Overton Pindall

Who Was Who in America (Chicago, 1942), 1: 974–75; *Arkansas Gazette*, 3 January 1935.

Allen H. Hamiter

Arkansas Democrat, 9 May 1908; *Arkansas Gazette*, 17 January 1907, 10, 12, 13, 14, 15, and 16 May 1908.

Jesse M. Martin

Arkansas Gazette, 12 January 1909, 22 and 25 January 1915; *Morrilton Headlight*, 26 January 1915.

James T. Robertson

Arkansas Gazette, 12 May 1909, 30 January 1920.

William Champ Rodgers

Biographical and Historical Memoirs of Southern Arkansas (Chicago, 1890), 289–90; *Arkansas Democrat*, 16 December 1961; *Arkansas Gazette*, 16 December 1961.

William Kavanaugh Oldham

Who Was Who in America (Chicago, 1942), 1:914; *Arkansas Gazette*, 7 and 8 May 1938.

Robert Lee May Bailey

Dallas T. Herndon, *The Arkansas Handbook, 1939–1940* (Little Rock, 1940), 76; *Arkansas Democrat,* 23 December 1957.

William Lee Cazort

Arkansas Gazette, 7 October 1969; H. F. Barnes, *Among Arkansas Leaders* (n.p., n.d.), 10; Charles C. Alexander, "Defeat, Decline, Disintegration: The Ku Klux Klan in Arkansas, 1924 and After," *Arkansas Historical Quarterly* 22 (1963): 311–21.

Lawrence Elery Wilson

Arkansas Gazette, 25 June 1946; D. Y. Thomas, *Arkansas and Its People, A History, 1541–1930, II* (New York, 1930), 193–94.

James Levesque Shaver

Dallas T. Herndon, *Annals of Arkansas, 1947* (Hopkinsville, Ky., n.d.); *Arkansas Gazette,* 2 August 1985.

Nathan Green Gordon

Fay Williams, *Arkansans of the Years* (Little Rock, 1953), 3:104–112; Dallas T. Herndon, *The Arkansas Handbook* (Little Rock, 1948), 19–20; "Home of the Brave," *Arkansas Magazine of the Alumni Association* 43 (spring 1994): 14–15; Nathan Gordon Papers, Special Collections, University of Arkansas Library at Fayetteville.

Maurice L. Britt

Fay Williams, *Arkansans of the Years* (Little Rock, 1951), 2:19–31; Paul Theis, ed., *Who's Who in American Politics, 1969–70* (New York, 1969), 135; *Arkansas Gazette,* 9 July 1944, 13 February 1966; "Maurice 'Footsie' Britt: Biographical Sketch," typescript, 1979, furnished by Britt.

Bob Cowley Riley

Who's Who in the South and Southwest, 1976–77 (Chicago, 1976), 651; *Arkansas Democrat-Gazette,* 17 February 1994.

Joe Edward Purcell

Who's Who in the South and Southwest, 1978–79 (Chicago, 1978), 591; "Biographical Sketch of Joe Purcell, Lt. Governor, State of Arkansas," typescript, 1979, furnished by Purcell.

Winston Bryant

Historical Report of the Secretary of State, Arkansas (Little Rock, 1978), 1:253; *Who's Who in the South and Southwest, 1993–1994* (New Providence, N.J., 1993), 103; Biographical data sheet provided by the Office of the Attorney General.

Nick Wilson

Arkansas Gazette, 10 April 1987, 15, 16, 17, 19, 20, and 21 April, 17 May, 8 July, and 8 October 1988; information furnished by Senator Wilson; *Historical Report of the Secretary of State, 1986* (n.p., n.d.), 84.

Jerry Donal Jewell

Arkansas Times, 19 May 1994; information furnished by Senator Jewell; *Arkansas Democrat-Gazette,* 18, 19, 21, 22, 27, and 30 January 1993.

L. L. "Doc" Bryan

Historical Report of the Secretary of State, 1986 (n.p., n.d.); *Arkansas Democrat-Gazette,* 21 and 22 January 1993.

Mike Huckabee

Annuals of the Arkansas Baptist State Convention, 1989, 1990 (Little Rock, n.d.); *Arkansas Democrat-Gazette,* 30 April, and 26, 27, and 28 July 1993, 3 and 27 February 1994; data furnished by Lt. Gov. Mike Huckabee.

INDEX